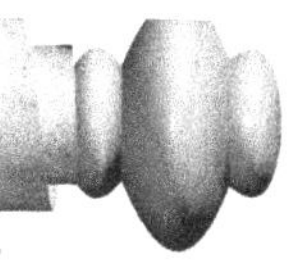

The Ten Commandments of Career Indie Authors

1. Thou shall write!

2. Thou shall read widely

3. Thou shall continue thy self-education

4. Thou shall organize thy paperwork

5. Thou shall not covet thy fellow authors' successes

6. Thou shall resist the temptations of FOMO, Imposter syndrome, Perfection syndrome, and other mental storms

7. Thou shall engage socially with authors

8. Thou shall pay it forward

9. Thou shall chart thy progress

10. Thou shall enjoy thy creativity, whether in a story, an ad or an email

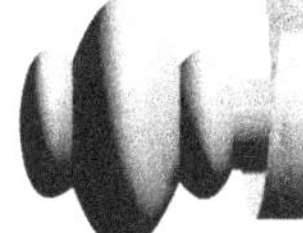

THIS BOOK BELONGS TO

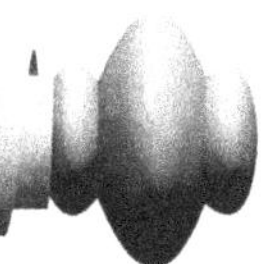

Career Indie Author Quote Book

BOOKS FROM PESCHEL PRESS

Keep up with our appearance schedule and new books,
visit www.peschelpress.com and sign up for our monthly newsletter.

Career Indie Author Series
Career Indie Author by Bill Peschel and Teresa Peschel
Career Indie Author Quote Book by Bill Peschel

The 223B Casebook Series, Notes and Annotations by Bill Peschel
The Best Sherlock Holmes Parodies and Pastiches: 1888-1930
Sherlock Holmes Victorian Parodies and Pastiches: 1888-1899
Sherlock Holmes Edwardian Parodies and Pastiches I: 1900-1904
Sherlock Holmes Edwardian Parodies and Pastiches II: 1905-1909
Sherlock Holmes Great War Parodies and Pastiches I: 1910-1914
Sherlock Holmes Great War Parodies and Pastiches II: 1915-1919
Sherlock Holmes Jazz Age Parodies and Pastiches I: 1920-1924
Sherlock Holmes Jazz Age Parodies and Pastiches II: 1925-1930
The Early Punch Parodies of Sherlock Holmes
The Cases of Blue Ploermell by James Thurber

Annotated Mystery Novels by Bill Peschel
The Complete, Annotated Secret of Chimneys
By Agatha Christie
The Complete, Annotated Murder on the Links
By Agatha Christie
The Complete, Annotated Secret Adversary
By Agatha Christie
The Complete, Annotated Mysterious Affair at Styles
By Agatha Christie
The Complete, Annotated Whose Body?
By Dorothy L. Sayers

The Steppes of Mars Series by Odessa Moon
The Bride from Dairapaska
The White Elephant of Panschin
The Vanished Pearls of Orlov

The Rugeley Poisoner Series, Notes and Annotations by Bill Peschel
The Illustrated Life and Career of William Palmer
The Times Report of the Trial of William Palmer
The Life and Career of Dr. William Palmer of Rugeley

Other Books
Suburban Stockade by Teresa Peschel
Sew Cloth Grocery Bags by Teresa Peschel
A Dictionary of Flowers and Gems by Skye Kingsbury
Hell's Casino by Bill Peschel
Writers Gone Wild by Bill Peschel
The Casebook of Twain and Holmes by Bill Peschel

Career Indie Author Quote Book

Over 2,700 pieces of advice from the eminent and the anonymous on writing and the writing life

"

It could be said of me that in this book
I have only made up a bunch of other men's flowers,
providing of my own only the string
that ties them together.
– Michel de Montaigne

Bill Peschel
Co-author of "Career Indie Author"

PESCHEL PRESS ~ HERSHEY, PA.

Cover and interior design by Bill Peschel.

www.peschelpress.com
www.careerindieauthor.com

ISBN-13: 978-1-950347-27-8

Library of Congress Control Number: 2021902095

First printing: March 2021, version 1.0

Table of Contents

Abuse
Academia
Action
Adventure
Advice, Taking & Giving
African-American Literature
Agents
Aging
Alcohol & Alcoholism
Ambition
American Literature
Anonymous
Argument
Art & Artists
Audience
Authors & Writers
Beginnings
Bestsellers
Biographies & Biographers
Blurbs
Book Awards
Book Awards, Stephen King
Book Covers
Booker Award
Bookkeeping & Record Keeping
Books
Book Signings & Tours
Bookstores
Business
Cats
Celebrity
Censorship
Characters
Children's Books
Clarity
Class
Classics
Columnist
Comedy/Tragedy
Comic Novel
Comics
Commerce
Commercial Fiction
Confidence
Controversy
Courage
Creativity
Crime Fiction
Criticism
Critics
Culture & Popular Culture
Deadlines
Decisions
Dedications
Depression
Dialogue
Diaries
Discipline
Discouragement
Dreaming
Drugs
Early Works
Editing Advice
Editors
Education
Ego
Embarrassment
Emotions
Encouragement
Endings
Envy
Epics
Epigrams
Essays
Evil
Experience
Facts
Failure
Faith
Fame
Family
Fan Fiction
Fans
Fantasy
Fear
Feedback
Fiction, Function of
Fiction, Popular
First Drafts
Forgiveness
Freelance Writing
Genius
Genres
Getting Started
Ghostwriting
Gossip
Grammar
Grants
Great American Novel
Habit
Heroes
Historical Novels
History
Homosexuality
Horror
Humanity
Humor & Humorists
Ideas
Imagination
Immortality
Influences
Inspiration
Intellectuals
Internet
Interpretation
Interruptions
Interviews
Jobs, Outside
Jokes
Journalism
Journals
Landscape
Language
Legacy
Letters
Library
Life & Living
Limitations
Listening
Literature
Logic
Loneliness
Love
Luck
Lying
Magazines & Magazine Writing
Magic
Marketing
Masterpieces
Meaning
Medicine
Mediocrity
Memoir & Autobiography
Memory
Mental Illness
Mentors
Message
Metaphor
MFA Programs

Mind
Mistakes
Money
Morality
Motivation
Movies
Music
Mysteries
Myths & Legends
Names
Negotiating
Networking
Nobel Prize
Nonfiction
Notes, Taking
Novel
Novel, Discouragement
Novel, Finishing a
Novel, Starting a
Novel, What Is a
Novel, Writing a
Novelists
Obscenity
Optimism
Originality
Outline
Paperbacks
Parody
Passion
Pen Names
Perfection
Personality
Photography
Plagiarism
Plays & Playwriting
Plot
Poems
Poems, Learning to Write
Poetry
Poets
Point of View
Polemics
Political Correctness
Political Correctness, Lionel Shriver
Political Correctness, Pen Names
Politics
Posterity
Praise
Prizes
Professionalism
Proofreaders
Psychoanalysis
Public Appearances
Publicity
Publishers & Publishing
Punctuation
Quitting
Quotations
Race & Racism
Racism, *The Autobiography of Nat Turner*
Readers
Reading
Realism
Rejection
Reputation
Research
Revenge
Reviews & Reviewers
Reviews, Bad
Revision
Rituals & Routines
Roman à clef
Romance
Rules
Russian Literature
Sanity
Satire
Schools
Science Fiction
Scottish Literature
Screenwriting
Secrets
Self-Censorship
Self-Confidence
Self-Deception
Self-Doubt
Self-Image
Self-Promotion
Self-Publishing
Self-Revelation
Sentences
Setting
Sex
Sex Scenes
Short Stories
Simile
Simplicity
Slang
Sleep
Solitude
South, The
Speaking
Spouses
Story
Structure
Style
Suburbs, *Revolutionary Road*
Success at Writing
Suffering
Suicide
Surprise
Talent
Talking About Writing
Teaching
Techniques, Writing
Thinking
Thrillers
Time
Titles
Tools, Writing
Transitions
Translations
Truth
Unpublished Works
Usage
Villains
Violence
Voice
Wit
Women
Word Processors
Words
Work
Work Habits
Worldbuilding
Write, How I
Write, How Much To
Write, Learning To
Write, What To
Write, When To
Write, Where To
Write, Why
Writer, Evolution of a
Writer, Image of a
Writer, What Is a
Writer, What Is a Good
Writer's Block
Writers Conferences
Writers, Women
Writing
Writing Advice
Writing Advice, Humorous
Writing, Bad
Writing, Good
Writing, How Often
Writing, Pleasures of
Writing Speed
Writing, Stresses From
Writing, When To Stop
Young Adult
Afterword

Illustration Sources
Index
About the Author

Foreword

> The fake profundities of dead politicians, the treacly outpourings of fifth-rate poets, the moonlit nonsense of minor essayists — this junk makes up the bulk of most quotation books.
>
> **Robertson Davies**

This is a book of quotes unlike any you've seen before. It is for writers of stories, histories, columns, shorts, essays, memories, poetry, chapbooks, memoirs, literature, listicles, quizzes… in short, anyone who writes and wants to get better.

I gathered these snatches of wit, wisdom, and nonsense over far more years than I care to admit. My method of gathering them was haphazard and inconsistent. I would read something – a book of writing advice, a biography, a newspaper interview – and be so struck by the quotation that I'd collect it and file it away.

But what to do with them? In early drafts of *Writers Gone Wild*, when the essays were keyed to certain days, I'd attach a quote to the end of the essay, like a mint at the end of a meal. But in the book's final form, these quotes were dropped.

The idea for a quote book didn't take hold until I launched the Career Indie Author project in 2015. I thought about publishing a line of books and realized I could release two quote books. One is the book in your hand, covering practical information about writing and the writing life, and the other inspired by *Writers Gone Wild*, will cover judgments, favorable and caustic, about notable authors and their opinions on universal concerns.

While organizing the material, I laid down these guidelines:

Only one quote from an author in each category. You could build a quote book around Stephen King's advice alone. To get around this restriction, I'd create a new category for it. If I couldn't create a category and I couldn't decide which quote to drop, then I used both.

Accurate quotes only. I researched the origin of each quote. If I couldn't trace it, I didn't use it. If it was a substantial misquote, I used the original and sometimes appended the inaccurate quote. I broke this rule once for the Tom Robbins quote in "Write, What To." I snagged it long before I started keeping track of the sources. He probably said it in an interview. The quote never made it to the Internet, so I'm trusting Younger Bill's judgment.

Alphabetize quotes by last name. I broke this rule only when one quote was in response to another, such as Susan Cheever's riposte to James Atlas in the "Art and Artists" category.

Use quotes I disagree with. I wanted a wide variety of opinions. Some are amusingly false, such as those railing against novels or female authors. Some espouse opinions I disagree with. Some fell into the category of "I don't understand this, but I hope someone else will."

When especially moved to do so, I added my comment in parentheses.

Expand quotes when necessary. Brevity is the soul of wit, but not necessarily of truth. Some quotes were so condensed that they lost their meaning. Longer quotes fixed that.

In the print version, an author's photo should appear once. In choosing photos for the print version, I wanted as many faces as possible. I also wanted many women and minority faces. I broke this no-duplicates rule two or three times, but overall I'm happy with the result.

Add quotes from Mark Twain in the margin. He is my favorite author, so I decided to not only quote from him extensively, but to place many of them in the margin with a photo taken from throughout his life, from a printer's apprentice to an old man.

No bibliography. Printing the 30,000-word bibliography would have doubled the length of the book, so I moved those to the book's page at the Peschel Press website. It won't always be the original source. Sometimes it's even another quote book.

Finally, this book is dedicated to my son, Mark, who used his programming skills to build the index and check for duplicate quotes, and my wife, Teresa, who edited the manuscript and suggested quotes as well.

Bill Peschel, Hershey, Pa.

”

Action alone is in your control,
Not the results ever.
Let not the fruit of action be your motive.
Nor should you keep company of inaction.

Krishna, Bhagavad Gita

I have weapons in my office and I'll frequently "stage" a fight scene to see if it will work. You can invite some friends over, order pizza and see if what you described is physically possible. Also you can buy a set of mock/toy weapons and experiment. Give the kids rubber knives and see how they spar ;)

Maria V. Snyder

Abuse

Let them kick. It's like I'm a body in the street, and they keep coming by and kicking until they get tired. They wander away and then they come back and kick it some more and then pour a little gasoline on and set it on fire. But, you know, the body is already dead.

Bob Greene

I am firm; *you* are obstinate; *he* is a pig-headed fool.

Bertrand Russell

Academia

(See **Education, MFA Programs**)

The primary object of a student of literature is to be delighted. His duty is to enjoy himself, his efforts should be directed to developing his faculty of appreciation.

David Cecil

Find me one good poet who thinks that the academic concern for literature isn't toxic and depressant.

Geoffrey Grigson

A blonde girl is bent over a poem. With a pencil sharp as a lancet she transfers the words to a blank page and changes them into strokes, accents, caesuras. The lament of a fallen poet now looks like a salamander eaten away by ants.

Zbigniew Herbert

I cannot see that lectures can do so much good as reading the books from which the lectures are taken.

Samuel Johnson

Our American professors like their literature clear and cold and pure and very dead.

Sinclair Lewis

Every place swarms with commentaries; of authors there is great scarcity.

Michel de Montaigne

Fourteen years in the professor dodge has taught me that one can argue ingeniously on behalf of any theory, applied to any piece of literature.

Robert B. Parker

It is bad that English is taught in universities. It's bad over here, where it's sometimes not badly taught, but over there [in the United States], where it's horribly badly taught, it simply stops the thing in its tracks. … It's an absurd error to put modern English literature in the curriculum. You should read contemporary literature for pleasure or not read it at all. You shouldn't be taught to monkey with it.

Rebecca West

Action

Specific action is capable of carrying a heavier emotional load than any other type of narration. This may be a consequence of the fact that Americans (at least those I know) seldom express their more profound emotions in words. They are likely rather to look out the window, to whittle, or to pick up a newspaper. Later on, if at all, comes speech.

John T. Frederick

Things do not happen in this world. They are brought about.

Will Hays

Action carries its own authority. If you move through each scene with clear, physical verbs — taking steps, touching objects — your reader's mind will follow as closely as a dog's eyes track a squirrel.

Chuck Palahniuk

Stories are made of action the way that pigs are made of pork.

Damon Suede

Adventure

In time of peace in the modern world, if one is thoughtful and careful, it is rather more difficult to be killed or maimed in the outland places of the globe than it is in the streets of our great cities, but the atavistic urge toward danger persists and its satisfaction is called adventure. However, your adventurer feels no gratification in crossing Market Street in San Francisco against the traffic. Instead he will go to a good deal of trouble and expense to get himself killed in the South Seas. In reputedly rough water, he will go in a canoe; he will invade deserts without adequate food and he will expose his tolerant and uninoculated blood to strange viruses. This is adventure. It is possible that his ancestor, wearying of the humdrum attacks of the saber-tooth, longed for the good old days of pterodactyl and triceratops.

John Steinbeck

Advice, Taking & Giving

There have been many writerly bromides that have served me well.

Michael Connelly

I think it's awfully dangerous to give general advice. The best one can do for a young poet is to criticize in detail a particular poem of his. Argue it with him if necessary; give him your opinion, and if there are any generalizations to be made, let him do them himself. I've found that different people have different ways of working and things come to them in different ways.

T.S. Eliot

When you write do you take anybody's advice about writing? Don't do it: nothing will so mix you up as advice. If a fellow wants to keep clear about himself he must first of all swear a big oath that he'll never take any advice.

Walt Whitman

African-American Literature

You have Maya Angelou, Alice Walker, James Baldwin — all of these traditional black writers, who wrote about the struggles of racism, injustice, inequality. We're writing about the struggle as it happens now. It's just a different struggle. I'm telling my story. I'm telling the struggle of a black girl from Flint, Michigan, who grew up on welfare.

Ashley Coleman

It is not simply that the white storyteller will not do full justice to the humanity of the black race; he cannot.

William Dickens, educator

The best trashy novels offer something else that their more high-minded counterparts seldom do: an exacting and often irreverent look at quotidian realities, the texture of how we live today. I felt this most keenly while reading a lapful of pop novels from young black writers such as Benilde Little (*Good Hair*) and Yolanda Joe (*He Say, She Say*). Both of these brash, talented novelists are following in Terry McMillan's bestselling footsteps, which is to say that their books steer clear of the depictions of racism, slavery and social pathology that fill the novels of revered black writers like Toni Morrison and Alice Walker. Little's and Joe's breezy,

”

[African-American bookstores are] overrun with novels that . . . appeal exclusively to our most prurient natures — as if these nasty books were pairing off back in the stockrooms like little paperback rabbits and churning out even more graphic offspring that make Ralph Ellison books cringe into a dusty corner.

Nick Chiles

American publishers are not interested in black writers unless they bleed from white torture.

Chester Himes

”

Sometimes I feel like I'd make a lot more money if I charged an hourly rate, like a psychotherapist.

Eric Simonoff, agent

In the beginning, you are full, as they say, of yourself, and when elderly somewhat less so, having dispensed yourself through so many books. Still, each day slightly changes your angle on life, and the blank page remains a site of hopeful possibility.

John Updike

sexy novels don't feel like literature — and that's the point. Their books are aimed squarely at middle-class black readers who are turned off by the relentless high-mindedness of, say, Morrison, and who want to see more of their own experiences and aspirations reflected in the books they read. Morrison may evoke the Song of Solomon, but it takes a different beat to capture the realities of 9-to-5 life in urban America.

Dwight Garner

It is the duty of the younger Negro artist... To change through the force of his art that old whispering "I want to be white," hidden in the aspirations of his people to "why should I want to be white? I am a Negro — and beautiful!"

Langston Hughes

It's part and parcel of black elites' efforts to define not only a literary tradition, but a racial politics. There has always been a sense that because African-Americans' opportunities to represent themselves are so limited in the first place, any hint of criminality or salaciousness would necessarily be a knock on the entire racial politics. One of the pressing debates about African-American literature today is: If we can't include writers like Ashley & JaQuavis [Coleman], to what extent is the foundation of our thinking about black literature faulty? Is it just a literature for elites? Or can it be inclusive, bringing urban fiction under the purview of our umbrella term "African-American literature?"

Kinohi Nishikawa

My major advice to young black artists would be that they shut themselves up somewhere away from all debates about who they are and what color they are and just turn out paintings and poems and stories and novels.

Alice Walker

Agents

The world is a peculiar place, but it has nothing on the world of books. This is largely a fantasy world in which the pecking order goes as follows: if you can't cope with life, write about it; if you can't write, publish; if you can't get a job in publishing, become a literary agent; if you are a failed literary agent — God help you!

Colin Haycraft

This is the age of the middleman. He is generally a parasite. He always flourishes. I have been forced to give him some little attention lately in my particular business. In it, he calls himself a literary agent.

William Heinemann

The reality is there's very few really fine agents, so if you don't learn about the business of publishing and understand the economics of how it works, you become a victim, and you can't protect your art that way.

Dean Koontz

First of all, you must have an agent, and in order to get a good one, you must have sold a considerable amount of material. And in order to sell a considerable amount of material, you must have an agent. Well, you get the idea.

Steve McNeil

Until you've established a track record, it's unlikely you'll attract a skilled agent; and a bad agent — or a shyster masquerading as an agent

— can do one's career far more harm than good.

Robert B. Parker

Let every eye negotiate for itself, and trust no agent.

William Shakespeare

When asked whether I believe in literary agents, I always feel inclined to reply as I should were I asked if I "believed" in spectacles: "Yes, if you need them and can be quite sure of getting the right kind."

Stanley Unwin

Aging

You get older, you feel a certain freedom that you wouldn't feel if you were in your 30s. You'd be far more politic. You'd think, "Well, now, you know, how is my dad going to feel about this? How is my boss at work going to feel about this?" And you get to a certain age, you don't think about that anymore.

Garrison Keillor

The whole process of getting old — it could have been better arranged. But you do learn some things just by doing them over and over and by getting old doing them. And one of them is, you really need less. And I'm not talking minimalism, which is a highly self-conscious mannerist style I can't write and don't want to. I'm perfectly ready to describe a lot and be flowery and emotive, but you can do that briefly and it works better. My model for this is late Beethoven. He moves so strangely and quite suddenly sometimes from place to place in his music, in the late quartets. He knows where he's going and he just doesn't want to waste all that time getting there. But if you listen, if you're with it, he takes you with him. I think sometimes about old painters — they get so simple in their means. Just so plain and simple. Because they know they haven't got time. One is aware of this as one gets older. You can't waste time.

Ursula K. Le Guin

One of the amusements of being old is that I have no illusions about my literary position. I have been taken very seriously, but I have also seen essays by clever young men on contemporary fiction who would never think of considering me. I no longer mind what people think. On the whole, I have done what I set out to do. Now my age makes everyone take me very seriously. If you are a writer, live a long time. I have found that longevity counts more than talent.

W. Somerset Maugham

Without this daily task life would be meaningless ... There is no remedy for the defects of old age — whether they take the form of continuous discomfort or poor quality of output — or both.

Beatrice Webb

Alcohol & Alcoholism

The writer cultivates, extends, raises and inflames his imagination. As he inflates his imagination, he inflates his capacity for anxiety, and inevitably becomes the victim of crushing phobias that can only be allayed by crushing doses of heroin or alcohol.

John Cheever

A man's prose style is very responsive — even a glass of sherry shows in a sentence.

John Cheever

You know what [D.H.] Lawrence

”

In order to write at a high level of competence you need a comprehensive vocabulary, a keen sense of overall structure, and an inner beat or cadence. Your senses must be razor-sharp. Alcohol blunts those senses even as it releases self-restraint. Therefore many writers feel they are getting down to the real story after a belt or two, little realizing they are damaging their ability to tell the real story.

Rita Mae Brown

"

The American novel is a conquest of the frontier; as it describes experience, it creates it.

Ralph Ellison

Oh, it's delightful to have ambitions. I'm so glad I have such a lot. And there never seems to be any end to them — that's the best of it. Just as soon as you attain to one ambition you see another one glittering higher up still. It does make life so interesting.

L.M. Montgomery, Anne of Green Gables

said: "The novel is the highest example of subtle interrelatedness that man has discovered." I agree! And just consider for one second what drinking does to "subtle interrelatedness." Forget "subtle"; "interrelatedness" is what makes novels work – without it, you have no narrative momentum; you have incoherent rambling. Drunks ramble; so do books by drunks.

John Irving

One of the disadvantages of wine is that it makes a man mistake words for thoughts.

Samuel Johnson

Boozing does not necessarily have to go hand-in-hand with being a writer, as seems to be the concept in America. I therefore solemnly declare to all young men trying to become writers that they do not actually have to become drunkards first.

James Jones

If there is an occupational hazard to writing, it's drinking.

Cormac McCarthy

Write first, drink later. To write you must be warm, fed, loved, and sober.

Patrick McGrath

I don't drink a lot. That's perhaps one of the reasons why my characters are always drinking and taking drugs, because I am not.

Robert Stone

Before I start to write, I always treat myself to a nice dry martini. Just one, to give me the courage to get started. After that, I am on my own.

E.B. White

Ambition

Routine, in an intelligent man, is a sign of ambition.

W.H. Auden

My ambition is to always measure myself against these dead [writers]. And that solves all my problems about money and fame, because they're all dead!

Yiyun Li

Winning isn't everything, but wanting to win is.

Vince Lombardi

Learn from me, if not by my precepts, at least by my example, how dangerous is the acquirement of knowledge and how much happier that man is who believes his native town to be the world, than he who aspires to become greater than his nature will allow.

Mary Shelley

American Literature

We don't have any tradition at all that I know of. I don't think the isolation of the American writer is a tradition; it's more that geographically he just is isolated, unless he happens to live in New York City. ...The thing is that here you get to be a writer differently. I mean, a writer like Sartre decides, like any professional man, when he's fifteen, sixteen years old, that instead of being a doctor he's going to be a writer. And he absorbs the French tradition and proceeds from there. Well, here you get to be a writer when there's absolutely nothing else you can do. I mean, I don't know of any writers here who just started out to be writers, and then became writers. They just happen to fall into it.

Nelson Algren

It is one of the paradoxes of American literature that our writers are forever looking back with love and nostalgia at lives they couldn't wait to leave.

Anatole Broyard

First, there ain't no such short stories. Second, if there were, my contracts, which are exclusive, and blanket, would prevent me from permitting any one to publish such stories … I don't mind telling you that had the United States been as kindly toward the short story writer as France has always been kindly, from the beginning of my writing career I would have written many a score of short stories quite different from the ones I have written.

Jack London, to a magazine editor asking for stories he couldn't sell to other magazines

Of the four main characters [in Jonathan Franzen's *Freedom*], only Walter has a real job, about which we learn nothing until it becomes a matter of traveling around with an admiring young assistant. (American novelists never tire of the student-don romance; they just dress it up in different clothes.)

B.R. Myers

I think that the central, most American literary theme is the invention of self. We see it in Henry James's *Bostonians*; we see it in *The Great Gatsby;* we see it in *Breakfast at Tiffany's* ... It's such an American genre, this whole idea of reinventing and creating yourself based on your dream, or how you perceive yourself to be, or not to be.

Chuck Palahniuk

American talent does not survive sophistication. It needs to preserve a certain naiveté, a hayseed element, even a touch of the child, and the primitive, if it is to retain its juice and energy. This is true of *Huckleberry Finn*, of Scott Fitzgerald (always an outsider in Paris and the Cote d'Azur), of Hemingway (with the boyish braggarty of his virility cult), of the out-of-towners who founded and wrote for *The New Yorker*, of Ring Lardner's ingrained and obsessive provincialisms, of Whitman, Sherwood Anderson, Runyon, John Ford ... When urban sophistication lays its hand on the American artist, it is like frost on a bud.

Kenneth Tynan

Anonymous

When he knows the truth he will be uncomfortable. – You are the oddest Creature! … Do not oblige him to read any more. Have mercy on him, tell him the truth and take him an apology. I particularly respect him for wishing to think well of all young ladies; it shows an amiable and a delicate mind. And he deserves better treatment than to be obliged to read any more of my works.

Jane Austen, after a relative's suitor criticized Austin's anonymously published novels

I have seldom felt more satisfaction than when, returning from a pleasure voyage, I found *Waverley* in the zenith of popularity, and public curiosity in full cry after the name of the author.

Walter Scott, who published the Waverley novels anonymously

Argument

Coming away from a violent discussion at Magny's, my heart pounding in my breast, my throat

”

The American novel is always so personal — even when it's not memoir, it's as if it were memoir. I mean, Huck Finn. That's why it's so wrong when I pick up a new edition of "Huckleberry Finn" and I look at the last page and it doesn't say "yours truly" at the end.

Leslie Fiedler

I'm tired of the anonymity of being an unpublished author. I crave the anonymity of being self-published.

Tristan Durie

”

With respect to the requirement of art, the probable impossible is always preferable to the improbable possible.

Aristotle

Anything that is artistic is presumably about some certain thing, but is really always about something else, and it's no good having one without the other, because if you just have the something it is boring, and if you just have the something else it is irritating.

Edward Gorey

and tongue parched, I feel convinced that every political argument boils down to this: "I am better than you are," every literary argument to this: "I have more taste than you," every argument about art to this: "I have better eyes than you," every argument about music to this: "I have a finer ear than you."

Goncourt brothers

Sir, I have found you an argument but I am not obliged to find you an understanding.

Samuel Johnson, to an opponent who said, "I don't understand you sir."

Art & Artists

It is the job of artists (and always has been) to awaken mercy, to help people feel less alone with their deepest, darkest emotions. And, of course, to encourage them to regard their minds as vibrant and expandable.

Steve Almond

Writers and artists wrecked their health, destroyed their marriages, and died young so that the rest of America could enjoy art from a safe distance. The sacrifice had to be made. It was their job. Surely this was the lesson of Hemingway blowing his brains out, of Jackson Pollock wrapping his car around a tree. They died that art might live.

James Atlas, but see Susan Cheever's response below

I was amazed to read James Atlas's romantic evocation of the fun we used to have in the New York Literary World. As someone who was a child at those parties where Literary Greats stumbled around lecherously in an opaque cloud of cigarette smoke, I can testify that for those involved — certainly for many wives and most children — that scene was anything but fun. The tragedy of the generation that came before ours was that many of this country's wonderful writers were also alcoholics. Every drunk — whether or not he can write — leaves a trail of destruction, desolation, confusion, and sadness which goes on for generations.

Susan Cheever

Popular art is the dream of society; it does not examine itself.

Margaret Atwood

To be able to devote one's life to art without forgetting that art is frivolous is a tremendous achievement of personal character. Shakespeare never takes himself too seriously. When art takes itself too seriously, it tries to do more than it can... . In order to continue to exist in any form, art must be giving pleasure.

W.H. Auden

Art is moral passion married to entertainment. Moral passion without entertainment is propaganda, and entertainment without moral passion is television.

Rita Mae Brown

Art, it seems to me, should simplify. That, indeed, is very nearly the whole of the higher artistic process; finding what conventions of form and what detail one can do without and yet preserve the spirit of the whole — so that all that one has suppressed and cut away is there to the reader's consciousness as much as if it were in type on the page.

Willa Cather

Unless the work of art has wholly exhausted its maker's attention, it fails. This is why works of great significance are demanding and why they are infinitely rewarding.

Guy Davenport

Art is the means by which an artist comes to see. It is his peculiar, highly sophisticated and extremely demanding technique of discovery.

Annie Dillard

The conscious utterance of thought, by speech or action, to any end, is art. Art is the spirit's voluntary use and combination of things to serve its end.

Ralph Waldo Emerson

You can depict wine, love, women and great exploits on the condition that you are not a drunkard, a lover, a husband, or a hero. If you are involved in life, you see it badly; your sight is affected either by suffering or by enjoyment. The artist, in my way of thinking, is a monstrosity, something outside nature.

Gustave Flaubert

Art, at those moments when it feels most like art — when we feel most alive, most alert, most triumphant — is less like a cocktail party than a tank full of sharks. Everything's for keeps, nothing's for exercise.

John Gardner

The artist is like Sunday's child: only he sees spirits. But after he has told of their appearing to him, everybody sees them.

Johann Goethe

All men are creative but few are artists.

Paul Goodman

A career in the arts does retard maturity, whoever you are and however old you think you are. ... Strip everything away and you find the equivalent of an over-indulged kid — *Look at me! Listen to me! I'm special! I have something to say! And you have to pay me for it!*

Nick Hornby

Nobody is bored when he is trying to make something that is beautiful, or to discover something that is true.

William Inge

Art proves its value by mattering to people who have been deprived of every other freedom: indeed instead of mattering less, it matters more.

Clive James

We work in the dark — we do what we can — we give what we have. Our doubt is our passion, and our passion is our task. The rest is the madness of art.

Henry James

Real artists ship.

Steve Jobs

His life cannot be otherwise than full of conflicts, for two forces are at war within him: on the one hand the justified longing of the ordinary man for happiness, satisfaction, and security, and on the other a ruthless passion for creation which may go so far as to override every personal desire. If the lives of artists are as a rule so exceedingly unsatisfactory, not to say tragic, it is not because of some sinister dispensation of fate, but because of some inferiority in their personality or an inability to adapt. A person must pay dearly for the divine gift of creative fire.

Carl Jung

The excellence of every Art is its

”

Art is not truth. Art is a lie that makes us realize truth, at least the truth that is given us to understand. The artist must know how to convince others of the truthfulness of his lies. If he only shows in his work that he has searched, and re-searched, for the way to put over lies, he would never accomplish anything.

Pablo Picasso

No one in this world, so far as I know — and I have searched the records for years, and employed agents to help me — has ever lost money by underestimating the intelligence of the great masses of the plain people.

H.L. Mencken

Teachout's First Law of Artistic Dynamics: The best way to make a bad work of art is to try to make a great one.

Terry Teachout

intensity, capable of making all disagreeables evaporate, from their being in close relationship with Beauty & Truth.

John Keats

It is the work of the artist that invents the man who created it. "Great men" as they are venerated are subsequent pieces of minor fiction.

Friedrich Nietzsche

I don't do much more than organize other people's ideas and insights and thoughts and sort of harvest them, and inventory them and present them.

Chuck Palahniuk

It is better to be an artist, and delight in the contemplation of beauty, though this be only represented by nude nymphs, then to be indifferent and incredulous in everything.

Benito Pérez Galdós

The artist seeks out the luminous detail and presents it.

Ezra Pound

It's all in the art, you get no credit for living.

V.S. Pritchett

To succeed thus in gaining recognition, the original painter, the original writer proceeds on the lines adopted by oculists. The course of treatment they give us by their painting or by their prose is not always agreeable to us. When it is at an end the operator says to us: "Now look!" And, lo and behold, the world around us (which was not created once and for all, but is created afresh as often as an original artist is born) appears to us entirely different from the old world, but perfectly clear.

Marcel Proust

The function of art is not to illustrate a truth – or even a question – that is known in advance – but to bring into the world questions (and perhaps also, eventually, answers) that themselves cannot yet be conceived.

Alain Robbe-Grillet

They tried to destroy the memory of Babi Yar, first the Germans and then the Ukrainian government. But after [Yevgeny] Yevtushenko's poems, it became clear that it would never be forgotten. That is the power of art.

Dmitri Shostakovich, Russian composer, about the mass execution of 30,000 Jews in a ravine at Babi Yar, near Kiev, in 1941. Yevgeny Yevtushenko wrote a memorable poem about the event.

This is my dilemma! To be useful, I must be read! To be read I must write "art," but I consider "art" immoral. So: whether to die with a pure soul or carry on with what is for me an immoral activity! Solve that! And then, when I've pondered and fought, along comes that black devil who dwells in my heart, and mocks everything: the epicurean spirit of art awakens in me, and I long for the pleasure that producing works of art affords. And it is a tremendous pleasure, which is precisely what makes it immoral.

August Strindberg

The goal of all art is ... to explain to people the reason for their appearance on this planet; or, if not to explain, at least to pose the question.

Andrei Tarkovsky, movie director

The most important thing in a work

of art is that it should have a kind of focus, i.e., there should be some point where all the rays meet or from which they issue. And this focus must not be able to be completely explained in words. This indeed is one of the significant facts about a true work of art — that its content in its entirety can be expressed only by itself.

Leo Tolstoy

My first thought about art, as a child, was that the artist brings something into the world that didn't exist before, and that he does it without destroying something else. A kind of refutation of the conservation of matter. That still seems to me its central magic, its core of joy.

John Updike

Any authentic work of art must start an argument between the artist and his audience.

Rebecca West

If there is a devil, he's not somebody in a bright red suit with a tail, he's some man in a T-shirt sitting in a room at midday watching daytime television. What's really scary and frightening is boredom and the idea that the world is really winding down through entropy. And what art does is to go in the opposite direction — to inject energy, find pattern, lend meaning and vitality into what seems tepid.

Edmund White

Art is the imposing of a pattern on experience, and our aesthetic enjoyment is recognition of the pattern.

Alfred North Whitehead

Art is useless because its aim is simply to create a mood. It is not meant to instruct, or to influence action in any way. It is superbly sterile, and the note of its pleasure is sterility. If the contemplation of a work of art is followed by activity of any kind, the work is either of a very second-rate order, or the spectator has failed to realise the complete artistic impression.

Oscar Wilde

The intellect of man is forced to choose, perfection of the life or of the work.

W.B. Yeats

Audience

The ideal audience the poet imagines consists of the beautiful who go to bed with him, the powerful who invite him to dinner and tell him secrets of state, and his fellow poets. The actual audience he gets consists of myopic schoolteachers, pimply young men who eat in cafeterias, and his fellow poets. This means, in fact, he writes for his fellow poets.

W.H. Auden

If you say you're making a movie for "them," that automatically puts you on an unsteady footing. The implication is, you're making it for a group that you are not a member of — and there is something very insincere in that. If you're dealing with a storytelling medium, which is a mechanized means of producing and presenting a dream that you're inviting people to share, you'd better believe your dream or else it's going to come off as patronizing.

Brad Bird

Never use the word "audience." The very idea of a public, unless the poet is writing for money, seems wrong to me. Poets don't have an

Never fear [the audience] or despise it. Coax it, charm it, interest it, stimulate it, shock it now and then if you must, make it laugh, make it cry, but above all ... never, never, never bore the hell out of it.

Noël Coward

I'm not writing about the 1 percent of people who have this fairy-tale, amazing life. I'm writing about people like me, who maybe had a rough childhood.

Anna Todd

I study "The New York Times" and "USAToday" lists every single week, and if something is on that list for a long time, I want to know why. What has made this book and this author so popular?

Debbie Macomber

Richard Le Gallienne was lamenting once, that he probably would never be able to write a bestseller like Hall Caine or Marie Corelli. "It's no use," he said. "You can't fake it. Bad writing is a gift."

Heywood Broun

"audience." They're talking to a single person all the time.

Robert Graves

When I'm writing I'm always aware that this friend is going to like this, or that another friend is going to like that paragraph or chapter, always thinking of specific people. In the end all books are written for your friends.

Gabriel Garcia Marquez

A writer doesn't write for his readers, does he? Yet he has to take elementary precautions all the same to keep them comfortable.

Graham Greene

You have come here and paid twenty-five cents to see a fool; I receive seventy-five dollars, and see a whole houseful of fools.

Julia A. Moore, the poetical "Sweet Singer of Michigan" to a jeering audience

Whenever I feel uneasy about my writing, I think: what would be the response of the people in the book if they read the book? That's my way of staying on track. Those are the people for whom I write.

Toni Morrison

I don't know about this business of writing for this audience or that one. ... If I think of my audience at all, I think of a group that includes adults, children, male, female, old, middle-aged, young, everyone who can read. If horses, dogs, cats, or pigeons could read, they'd be welcome to it as well. I don't want to shut anyone out.

Philip Pullman

I've always written for a small audience consisting of people like myself who are well-educated, worldly, skeptical, snobbish (meaning that they rank good taste over bad).

Simon Raven

I don't really write for readers. I think that's the defining characteristic of being serious as a writer. ... And if people like it, great, and if they don't like it, well, that's that — what can you do? You can't go round and hold a gun to their head.

Will Self, who later wrote "The literary novel as an art work and a narrative art form central to our culture is indeed dying before our eyes."

Since we're all capitalist enterprises, we have to capture the lowest possible denominator. What's wrong is that we have to cater to the rancid, infantile, pubescent taste of the public.

Jerry Wexler, record producer

The whole duty of a writer is to please and satisfy himself, and the true writer always plays to an audience of one. Let him start sniffing the air, or glancing, at the Trend Machine, and he is as good as dead, although he may make a nice living.

E.B. White

Authors & Writers

I think of an author as a somebody who goes into the marketplace and puts down his rug and says, "I will tell you a story," and then he passes the hat. And when he's taken up his collection, he tells the story, and just before the denouement he passes the hat again. If it's worth anything, fine. If not, he ceases to be an author. He does not apply for a Canada Council grant.

Robertson Davies

Don't be afraid! We won't make an author of you, while there's an honest trade to be learnt, or brickmaking to turn to.

Charles Dickens, as told to Oliver Twist

The reciprocal civility of authors is one of the most risible scenes in the farce of life.

Samuel Johnson

Authors are easy to get on with — if you're fond of children.

Michael Joseph, British publisher

And yet there is nothing so badly imagined: nature seems to have provided, that the follies of men should be transient, but they by writing books render them permanent. A fool ought to content himself with having wearied those who lived with him: but he is for tormenting future generations; he is desirous that his folly should triumph over oblivion, which he ought to have enjoyed as well as his grave; he is desirous that posterity should be informed that he lived, and that it should be known for ever that he was a fool.

Charles de Montesquieu, paraphrased as "An author is a fool who, not content with having bored those who have lived with him, insists on boring future generations"

There are no writers anymore. Only book-selling louts and big mouths.

J.D. Salinger

The artist is always and specially the creature of the Zeitgeist; however formally antique his tastes, he is in spite of himself in the advanced guard.

Evelyn Waugh, reviewing Graham Greene's The Heart of the Matter

Beginnings

Stories begin when things start to go wrong. You have to visit trouble upon characters one way or another to get some definitive action from them, to get them to engage in the sort of impulsive behavior that I think is often the core of short stories.

Charles Baxter

What comes first is the main character, then scenes. I don't start at the beginning, I write gag-like situations. … I start with the character, plunge her into adventures, and then have faith that all the adventures will add up to something. As the writing progresses, the themes and the plot, the relationships between the characters, start to emerge.

Jennifer Belle

The only safe rule for the student is this: begin the story with action if that is the natural, inevitable way to begin it; but do not begin with action for any other reason.

John T. Frederick

Bestsellers

(See **Success at Writing**)

[A bestselling book needs] a little religion, a little aristocracy, a little sex, a little mystery, as summed up by this sentence, "My God," cried the duchess, "I've been _____! But by whom?"

Anonymous

When you're writing bestsellers, when you reach a large enough audience, you're writing for people who can't tell if your writing's any good or not

Lawrence Block

Only around 1900 did the word [seller] come to mean a book that sold well. This subtle transference of

”

All my direct encounters with the contemporary writers I admire or still admire professionally, ended in bitterness. I mean, I found out that as persons they were not as admirable and respectable as they were as writers. And I am incapable of dividing the judgment between the writer and the private person.

Oriana Fallaci, journalist

A helpful guide to the anxious semi-literate.

Renata Adler, of bestsellers lists

”

No one can write a bestseller by taking thought. The slightest touch of insincerity blurs its appeal. The writer who keeps his tongue in his cheek, who knows that he is writing for fools and that, therefore, he had better write like a fool, may make a respectable living out of serials and novelettes; but he will never make the vast, the blaring, half a million success. That comes of blended sincerity and vitality.

Anne Douglas Sedgwick

ideas was itself interesting, for the very expression "bestseller" or "seller" now implied that a book somehow sold itself: that sales bred more sales. ... A bestseller was a book which somehow sold well simply because it is selling well.

Daniel J. Boorstin

There's no mystique about the writing business, although many people consider me blasphemous when I say that. … To create something you want to sell, you first study and research the market, then you develop the product to the best of your ability.

Clive Cussler

If you can teach people something, you've won half the battle. They want to keep on reading.

Dick Francis

Not many serious novels end up at number one. Some finely executed, entertaining ones do end up there, along with a lot of really terrible ones.

Jonathan Franzen

Once a book has been declared a bestseller, its sales accelerate — like the freshwater polyp, the bestseller breeds from itself — and the book buyer can happily accept the judgment of the great majority.

Frank Muir

I think my stuff succeeds, in part, because of what it's about — a diagnosis by attempting the adventures oneself of universal American daydreams. Now, I'm not saying that any writer who decided to select that device or notion could have written a bestseller; you have to add ingredients that are very special, I agree, but I think I started out with a good pot to make the stew in.

George Plimpton

The most "popular," the most "successful" writers among us ... are ninety-nine times out of a hundred, persons of mere address, perseverance, effrontery — in a word, busybodies, toadies, and quacks.

Edgar Allan Poe

A bestseller is the gilded tomb of the mediocre talent.

Logan Pearsall Smith

Too many writers think that all you need to do is write well — but that's only part of what a good book is. Above all, a good book tells a good story. Focus on the story first. Ask yourself, "Will other people find this story so interesting that they will tell others about it?" Remember: A bestselling book usually follows a simple rule, "It's a wonderful story, wonderfully told;" not, "It's a wonderfully told story."

Nicholas Sparks

One of the easiest ways to become a bestseller writer today is simply to be young. In such an age-discriminative time, the writers who really need some gentleness and care are, in fact, the old ones!

Dubravka Ugresic, Croatian novelist

Biographies & Biographers

Readers of biographies like their meat rare.

Robertson Davies

The secret of biography resides in finding the link between talent and achievement. A biography seems irrelevant if it doesn't discover the overlap between what the individual did and the life that made this possible. Without discovering that, you have shapeless happenings and gossip.

Leon Edel

Autobiography is an unrivaled vehicle for telling the truth about other people.

Philip Guedalla

Writers do not choose their subjects at random — it is often the subconscious that makes that choice for them. So if you want to know about a writer, and about what really makes him or her tick, then simply look at the books. There's a lot to be found out there.

Alexander McCall Smith

Cheever's representation of [Louisa May] Alcott typifies the logic in which biographers credit accomplishments to the individual while blaming setbacks on the society: heads, I win; tails, you lose.

Leah Price,
of Susan Cheever's American Girl

What a wee little part of a person's life are his acts and his words! His real life is led in his head, and is known to none but himself. All day long, and every day, the mill of his brain is grinding, and his *thoughts* (which are but the mute articulation of his *feelings*,) not those other things, are his history. His *acts* and his *words* are merely the visible, thin crust of his world, with its scattered snow summits and its vacant wastes of water — and they are so trifling a part of his bulk! a mere skin enveloping it. The mass of him is hidden — it and its volcanic fires that toss and boil, and never rest, night nor day. *These are his life*, and they are not written, and cannot be written. Every day would make a whole book of eighty thousand words — three hundred and sixty-five books a year. Biographies are but the clothes and buttons of the man — the biography of the man himself cannot be written.

Mark Twain

Authors who write books not of the imagination, who deal with hard fact, have soon to realize that very few facts indeed are hard, and have to use the sceptical process. … Just how difficult it is to write biography can be reckoned by anybody who sits down and considers just how many people know the real truth about his or her love affairs.

Rebecca West

If you start at the beginning of somebody's life and chronologically go to the end, and trace out certain lines of development emotionally, no matter where you go, it all seems to hang together. A person is something like a coat rack; you can keep putting garments on it, but it's still a recognizable object.

Edmund White

Every great man nowadays has his disciples and it is always Judas who writes the biography.

Oscar Wilde

Blurbs

"Do you like *Blankley's*?" she asked.

"Like it? Why, I adore it, and that's no mere figure of speech. Why, people *read* that magazine; they don't leave it on the lower shelf of the library table, or send it to the lighthouse men. They gloat; they devour. *Women* read it, and it's women who make fame and fortune for writers. God! If I could ever take up that magazine, with its picture of a slim, anemic female on the cover, with the blurb underneath: "I consider this number of my

”

A biography has a responsibility which is to present the facts and get all of them straight, so that people can get the basic outlines of a person's life. And then, I think, it has to have a point of view and a shape which has to come out of the biographer as artist. I guess I am arguing for the interpretive biography, you might call it an art biography, as opposed to a compendious … presentation of a lot of facts.

Diane Johnson

I was a Booker judge relatively early in my career. It stopped me thinking that literary prizes are about literary value.

Hilary Mantel

It is almost impossible to persuade someone else of the quality or poverty of a selected novel (a useful lesson in the limits of literary criticism).

James Wood

magazine about the hottest piece of pie that was ever shoved over the counter. It has snap and go and dash and brains in it. Read it, and see if I haven't got Kipling locked into the coal cellar ringing up 'information'" — if I could find a story of mine underneath *that* cover I'd know I'd made good!"

Gelett Burgess, who is credited with creating the word "blurb"

At one point I gave up writing blurbs because you make one friend and 200 enemies.

Leslie Fiedler

On the whole, writers are underpaid, time-strapped and more than a little paranoid. Unbound manuscripts are bulky and hard to read. If they teach fiction, as many writers do, they're already being inundated by former students. Blurbing in itself is a no-win situation. If you read a book and don't like it, you've made an enemy for life. If you like a book and write a flattering blurb, you're giving a leg up to the competition in a world that seems increasingly hostile to books in general and literary fiction in the specific… It's no wonder most writers retreat behind a blanket no-blurb policy.

Rebecca Johnson

I would rather praise it than read it.

Samuel Johnson, of William Congreve's Incognita *(1691)*

Book Awards

Everything is ridiculous, when one thinks of death!

Thomas Bernhard, receiving a book award in Austria

Discussion is futile. No one changes their mind about a book. You might as well have a show of hands right away.

Tibor Fischer

Winning the Hugo Award for "Eurema's Dam" puzzled me completely, and I'm still puzzled by it. It was a pleasant little story, but I had four or five better stories published that year. … I don't believe it had much effect on my career. I think the effect of Hugos is greatly exaggerated. And I've heard four or five different writers express puzzlement over winning Hugos with stories that were pretty ordinary and being passed over on stories which they really believed were earth-shaking.

R.A. Lafferty

A committee is a blunt instrument of literary criticism.

David Lodge

When it comes right down to it, nothing has changed. The English sentence is just as difficult to write as it ever was.

John Steinbeck, after accepting the literature Nobel

It's a feature of prizes that authors often win for their weakest works.

Marina Warner

Book Awards, Stephen King

The publishing industry has stooped terribly low to bestow on King a lifetime award that has previously gone to the novelists Saul Bellow and Philip Roth and to playwright Arthur Miller. By awarding it to King they recognize nothing but the commercial value of his books, which sell in the millions but do little more for humanity than keep the publishing world afloat. If this is going to be the criterion in the future, then perhaps next year the committee should give its award for distinguished contribution to Danielle Steel, and surely the Nobel Prize for literature should go to J.K. Rowling.

Harold Bloom

For those who make a point of pride in saying they have never read anything by John Grisham, Tom Clancy, Mary Higgins Clark or any other popular writer, what do you think? You get social academic brownie points for deliberately staying out of touch with your own culture?

Stephen King

The material is not central to the culture in the way that Dickens' material was. Dickens was writing about the very serious core of British society life in the big city, distinctions of life among the various social classes and King's material is really much more peripheral. He's telling ghost stories, basically.

Alan Cheuse, NPR commentator

To King: It is not for you to gripe about eggheaded and arbitrary distinctions between high and low art. Accept your award with humble aplomb and resume laughing your way to the bank.

To Bloom: Is this really any more detrimental to our culture than the ascendancy of PlayStation II, or those new cellphones you can use to send out pictures of yourself naked?

Lynn Coady, columnist

King's award is not a surprise but a logical consequence of contemporary literary professionalism, which like socialist realism demands that a writer clench his teeth and write within the framework of the given norm or else end up, if not in a prison camp, then in his own personal ghetto of anonymity and poverty. The symbolic meaning of King's award is a Fall of the Literary Wall: a final unification, not of good and bad literature but of literature and trash.

Dubravka Ugresic, Croatian novelist

Book Covers

Aspiring authors, get this through your head. Cover art serves one purpose, and one purpose only, to get potential customers interested long enough to pick up the book to read the back cover blurb. In the internet age that means the thumbnail image needs to be interesting enough to click on. That's what covers are for.

Larry Correia

In the old days, books had awful covers and marvelous content; nowadays, the opposite happens.

Giacomo Leopardi (1837)

I always think that it's wrong to put images of my protagonists on the cover of my novels because readers can identify with characters only if they are given the chance to imagine them independently.

Orhan Pamuk

On the [promotional] postcards my name is still bigger than the book's title. My impression is that I'd asked that this be corrected and that you'd made acquiescence-sounds. Having a 2-book writer's name bigger than the title is absurd. … Shrink my poor old name by 25% starting with

”

One of the lessons I learned in school is that the whole point of a thumbnail drawing, a tiny little sketch, is that if something looks good small, if it's effective small, it's going to look great when it's bigger.

Chip Kidd

Between two products equal in price, function and quality, the better looking will outsell the other.

Raymond Loewy, designer

Books are the carriers of civilization. Without books, history is silent, literature dumb, science crippled, thought and speculation a standstill.

Barbara Tuchman

All books do or should do is encourage people to be able to hold many truths at once, because together they form a greater truth.

Cheryl Strayed

the bound galleys. Please.

David Foster Wallace, letter to his editor, and the resulting cover

Booker Award

Until just now I had thought the Booker Prize a rather trivial, showbizzy caper, but now I consider it a very serious, reliable indication of literary merit.

Kingsley Amis, receiving the Booker for The Old Devils. *See Self-Revelation.*

The prize was founded, in part, to encourage competitiveness. Which of the six novelists will make it to the finishing post? This grisly notion constitutes a perfect recipe for envy, back-biting and self-glorification.

Paul Bailey

The process consists of nothing more rigorous than five people sitting in a room together for a few hours, swapping personal opinions.

Jonathan Coe

The Booker may at times have tended to increase the unhelpful dichotomy between popular storytelling and books which are classified as literary novels, but most of the winners have combined high literary achievement with compelling storytelling.

P.D. James

Some wonderful books win the Booker, of course, just as the flypaper occasionally catches some really large flies.

James Wood

Bookkeeping & Record Keeping

Bookkeeping is a tiresome chore, and nobody enjoys it. Many writers look on it as a distraction from their *real* job of putting words on paper. Actually it's as much a part of the job as typing. A good filing system *saves* you time and energy in the long run because it keeps you from making mistakes or tearing up your office looking for the contract you know was there *somewhere*.

Stephen Goldin

Books

Books, like every other human thing, rarely end by being what they were meant to be. The books we dream of are magnificent, interesting, exhaustive, bulky, but nevertheless not too long. They glow in the imagination like a living coal. The books we write are scrappy, short, not sufficiently interesting, and often appear to be too long in spite of their brevity. So far from glowing, they resemble the ashes of an extinct cigar.

Maurice Baring

Libraries are not made; they grow. Your first two thousand volumes present no difficulty, and cost astonishingly little money. Any ordinary man can ... surround himself with this number of books ... and thenceforward have at least one place in the world in which it is possible to be happy.

Augustine Birrell

The oldest books are still only just out to those who have not read them.

Samuel Butler

A press or a book is not true because it is revolutionary. It has a chance of being revolutionary only if it tries to tell the truth.

Albert Camus

Books are fatal: they are the curse of the human race. Nine-tenths of existing books are nonsense, and the clever books are the refutation of that nonsense. The greatest misfortune that ever befell man was the invention of printing.

Benjamin Disraeli, from Lothair *(1870)*

I am skeptical of progress. My instincts are archaeological. I favor the god Janus, who faces backward and forward at once. Without a vivid link to the past, the present is chaos and the future unreadable. In our culture books form such a link, perhaps the main link.

Joseph Epstein, editor

Books are made not like children but like pyramids, on a premeditated pattern, and by laying great blocks one on top of another, by dint of effort, time and sweat, and it is useless! and it stays in the desert! But dominates it prodigiously … Jackals piss at their foot and the bourgeois climb up on them.

Gustave Flaubert

The world, you must remember, is only just becoming literate. As reading becomes more and more habitual and widespread, an ever-increasing number of people will discover that books will give them all the pleasures of social life and none of its intolerable tedium. At present people in search of pleasure naturally tend to congregate in large herds and to make a noise; in future their natural tendency will be to seek solitude and quiet. The proper study of mankind is books.

Aldous Huxley, from Crome Yellow *(1921), a satire*

I am replacing some of the timber used up by my books. Books are just trees with squiggles on them.

Hammond Innes

Knowledge is praised and desired by multitudes whom her charms could never rouse from the couch of sloth; whom the faintest invitation of pleasure draws away from their studies; to whom any other method of wearing the day is more eligible than the use of books, and who are more easily engaged by any conversation than such as may rectify their notions or enlarge their comprehension.

Samuel Johnson

A book isn't supposed to be a mirror. It's supposed to be a door.

Fran Lebowitz, responding to criticism that books don't reflect progressive politics

A book is a mirror: if an ass peers into it, you can't expect an apostle to look out.

Georg Christoph Lichtenberg

The multitude of books is a great evil. There is no measure or limit to this fever for writing; every one must be an author; some out of vanity, to acquire celebrity and raise up a name; others for the sake of lucre and gain.

Martin Luther

Books ought to be like a man or a woman, with some individual character in it, though eccentric, yet its own; with some blood in its veins and speculation in its eyes and a way and a will of its own.

John Mitchel

To publish a book is to talk at the dinner table in front of the servants.

Henri de Montherlant

A book is the only place in which you can examine a fragile thought without breaking it, or explore an explosive idea without fear it will go off in your face. ... It is one of the few havens

”

Books are like humans. When they're open, they're red.

Clive Barker

A good book is the precious life-blood of a master spirit, embalmed and treasured up on purpose to a life beyond life.

John Milton

”

I have turned my entire attention to Greek. The first thing I shall do, as soon as I receive the money, is to buy Greek authors; after that, I shall buy clothes.

Erasmus, retranslated over time to "When I get a little money, I buy books; and, if any is left, I buy food and clothes."

remaining where a man's mind can get both provocation and privacy.

Edward P. Morgan

Until one has some kind of professional relationship with books, one does not discover how bad the majority of them are. In much more than nine cases out of ten the only objectively truthful criticism would be "This book is worthless," while the truth about the reviewer's own reaction would probably be "This book does not interest me in any way, and I would not write about it unless I were paid to."

George Orwell

A good book is a piece of writing that implies that things don't exist, a kind of absence, or death ... It is futile to look outside the book for a realm that is located beyond the words.

Orhan Pamuk

But even ordinary books are dangerous, and not only the ones like *Make Gelignite the Professional Way*. A man sits in some museum somewhere and writes a harmless book about political economy and suddenly thousands of people who haven't even read it are dying because the ones who did haven't got the joke. Knowledge is dangerous, which is why governments often clamp down on people who can think thoughts above a certain caliber.

Terry Pratchett

No furniture so charming as books, even if you never open them, or read a single word.

Sydney Smith

A book is like a man — clever and dull, brave and cowardly, beautiful and ugly. For every flowering thought there will be a page like a wet and mangy mongrel, and for every looping flight a tap on the wing and a reminder that wax cannot hold the feathers firm too near the sun.

John Steinbeck

Books are good enough in their own way, but they are a mighty bloodless substitute for life.

Robert Louis Stevenson

In all things I sought rest, but I have never found it save in *hoexkens ende boexkens* (in nooks and in books).

Thomas à Kempis

A good book is the best of friends, the same today and forever.

Martin Farquhar Tupper

In a century we have produced two hundred and twenty thousand books; not a bathtub-full of them are still alive and marketable.

Mark Twain

Books came into being, surely, as practical schemes for transmitting or storing information, no more romantic in Gutenberg's time than a computer in ours. It so happens, though — a wholly unforeseen accident — that the feel and appearance of a book when combined with a literate person in a straight chair can create a spiritual condition of priceless depth and meaning. This form of meditation, an accident, as I say, may be the greatest treasure at the core of our civilization. So we should never give up books, surrendering only crass and earthly matters to the printout and the cathode tube.

Kurt Vonnegut

If I had to describe hell, it would be as a place without books. What would life be without their appeal to our fantasy, without their power to change things simply by revealing their hidden message.

Elie Wiesel

There is no such thing as a moral or an immoral book. Books are well written, or badly written. That is all.

Oscar Wilde

Book Signings & Tours

Should you find yourself facing all of America at 8 a.m. remember this: not many people will recall what you say. They will recall how you look and how you act. (Don't wear all white. It glares.)

Rita Mae Brown

No one knew me. I was sitting in a department store and people would ask me where the lingerie sales were.

Mary Higgins Clark

The book tour doesn't always bear fruit right away. It really is about planting seeds, making connections. Even if you had five people at your reading, maybe you had a great conversation with the bookseller who is going to hand-sell your book. The thing is, sales are out of your control. What you focus on is opportunity. People who use the opportunity of having a book as a way to build more opportunities build their own success.

Rebecca Gradinger, agent

Try to enjoy the people in the audience as diverse individuals who you'd otherwise not have a chance to talk to and exchange ideas with — an opportunity for a true human connection … It helped to tone down my nerves in front of big groups — reach out, see faces, try to understand who they are, stop thinking about yourself — as well as placate my ego when only stragglers showed up — here's your chance for a real one-on-one.

Michelle Hoover

Today's writers will be more likely be asked to produce a series of short essays that websites or magazines can use as content. In the United Kingdom that's long been the case. Instead of sleeping, a writer on tour in London will find herself spending the night in the hotel's business center, hammering out a dozen last-minute pieces about her favorite horror story, historical figure, and cure for writer's block. To avoid this pitfall, build your novel with a number of scenes or chapters that can stand alone as short stories. Magazines and websites can excerpt these, and they make a much better advertisement for your book. Plan for the fact that every medium wants free content.

Chuck Palahniuk

There are some lovely moments of meeting people, but 98.9 percent of it takes place in an airport eating Cinnabons.

Ann Patchett

All through dinner, I'm fascinated by the cliques. The literary authors — the folks whose books get long, respectful reviews in *The Times* and go on to sell 10,000 copies — ignore the commercial types. The commercial novelists — those whose books are ignored by *The Times* and get reviewed in *Cosmo* and *People*, and go on to sell 100,000 copies — shun the sci-fi folks, whose books are published in paperback, reviewed nowhere, and sell even more. And everyone seems to ostracize the bubbly, babbling first-time novelist who announces that

”

You want to sound as perky and enthusiastic as possible on a book tour, so your listening audience won't suspect that you really, deep down inside, don't want to talk about your book ever ever ever again. You have come to hate your book. Back at the beginning, you kind of liked it, but now you think of it as a large repulsive insect the cheerful host keep hauling out and sticking in your face and asking you to pet.

Dave Barry

There is always someone else around the corner doing it better, charging less, and cornering the market. One would like to think this law would not apply to writing too, but I'm afraid it does.

Fay Weldon

For a self-published author who is prepared to do extensive marketing and devote at least 40 percent of their time to that activity in the early days, it can be extremely rewarding financially.

Rachel Abbott

she's been working on her book "since college, which was an embarrassingly short time ago." Somebody actually groans out loud. I sit back in satisfaction. There's a nerd at the table, and for once, it isn't me.

Jennifer Weiner

Bookstores

Be nice to booksellers, they are your friends and allies and they work hard! I'm always astonished when I hear of rude or high-handed behavior at readings.

Nicole Aragi, agent

Where is human nature so weak as in the bookstore?

Henry Ward Beecher

Our industry was becoming alienated from its natural diversity by an increasingly homogeneous suburban marketplace, demanding ever more uniform products. Books are written everywhere but they need the complex cultures of great cities in which to reverberate. My publishing years coincided with the great postwar dispersal of city populations and the attrition therefore of city bookstores as suburban malls increasingly became the centers of commerce, so that even the well-stocked chain-bookstore branches located in cities today evoke the undifferentiated culture of shopping malls rather than the cosmopolitanism of the cities in which they happen to have been transplanted.

Joseph Epstein, editor. Critic Patricia Holt objected: "Three lawsuits suggest the demands made by chains of publishers weren't the result of 'morally neutral market conditions' but of greed, with the further result that independents got waylaid by illegal and unfair competitive practices that drove them under, as planned"

The real reason why I should not like to be in the book trade for life is that while I was in it I lost my love of books. A bookseller has to tell lies about books, and that gives him a distaste for them; still worse is the fact that he is constantly dusting them and hauling them to and fro. ... Seen in the mass, five or ten thousand at a time, books were boring and even slightly sickening.

George Orwell

The truth is that even big collections of ordinary books distort space, as can readily be proved by anyone who has been around a really old-fashioned secondhand bookshop, one of those that look as though they were designed by M. Escher on a bad day and has more staircases than storeys and those rows of shelves which end in little doors that are surely too small for a full-sized human to enter. The relevant equation is: Knowledge = power = energy = matter = mass; a good bookshop is just a genteel Black Hole that knows how to read.

Terry Pratchett

Business

Business and marketing are about understanding networks and patterns of influence and behavior. Writers can handle that.

Richard Nash

I remember when I first started freelancing I hated the idea that I was both the manager and the product. I ran the widget factory and I was the widget. And if I ran out of paper clips, I was the one who had to go buy the paper clips.

Susan Orlean

Cats

As an inspiration to the author, I do not think the cat can be overestimated. He suggests so much grace, power, beauty, motion, mysticism. I do not wonder that many writers love cats; I am only surprised that all do not.

Carl Van Vechten

Celebrity

Being a "public person" is like being a deer during hunting season. Everybody wants to take a shot at you.

Tom Clancy

When you have this much happen to you, you have to carve out little areas of the world for yourself where you can feel like an average person. If you don't, you lose your humanity. You become this thing. Everybody acts different because of who you are.

Patricia Cornwell

I have eavesdropped on large groups of people debating the minutiae of my plots. I have received more letters and emails than I can count, saying that I am the best author who has ever lived. I have attended cocktail parties and encountered the response: "I can't believe I'm actually meeting you!" when introduced to a stranger. Five cats have been named after me, and those are just the ones I know about.

Lemony Snicket

You may rely on it you have the best of me in my books, and that I am not worth seeing personally, the stuttering, blundering clod-hopper that I am.

Henry David Thoreau

Censorship

[I]t is a mad world and it will get madder if we allow the minorities, be they dwarf or giant, orangutan or dolphin, nuclear-head or water-conversationalist, pro-computer-ologist or Neo-Luddite, simpleton or sage, to interfere with aesthetics. The real world is the playing ground for each and every group, to make or unmake laws. But the tip of the nose of my book or stories or poems is where their rights end and my territorial imperatives begin, run and rule. If Mormons do not like my plays, let them write their own. If the Irish hate my Dublin stories, let them rent typewriters. If teachers and grammar school editors find my jawbreaker sentences shatter their mush-mild teeth, let them eat stale cake dunked in weak tea of their own ungodly manufacture. If the Chicano intellectuals wish to re-cut my "Wonderful Ice Cream Suit" so it shapes "Zoot," may the belt unravel and the pants fall.

Ray Bradbury

Censorship is the tool of those who have the need to hide actualities from themselves and from others. Their fear is only their inability to face what is real, and I can't vent any anger against them. I only feel this appalling sadness. Somewhere, in their upbringing, they were shielded against the total facts of our existence. They were only taught to look one way when many ways exist.

Charles Bukowski

Obscenity today, in the fevered suspicions of library censors, is the obscurity of racism or sexism located in books like *Huckleberry Finn*, *Dr Dolittle* and *Biggles*.

Editorial, The Times

We are willing enough to praise freedom when she is safely tucked away in the past and cannot be a nuisance. In the present, amidst

"

Surely it is plain to the simplest intelligence that "To Kill a Mockingbird" spells out in words of seldom more than two syllables a code of honor and conduct, Christian in its ethic, that is the heritage of all Southerners. To hear that the novel is "immoral" has made me count the years between now and 1984, for I have yet to come across a better example of doublethink. I feel, however, that the problem is one of illiteracy, not Marxism. Therefore I enclose a small contribution to the Beadle Bumble Fund that I hope will be used to enroll the Hanover County School Board in any first grade of its choice.

Harper Lee

The burning is but a prologue: where books are burned, people in the end are burned too.

Heinrich Heine

If [a sensitivity reader] is a source for a writer who has no other way to get it, then great. But I feel that if it's a risk management tool of some sort, I find that troubling. ... Writing literature is inherently risky. And the further you get from your own experience, the riskier it is. But no one can inoculate you against these risks because they're part of the process.

Hillary Jordan

dangers whose outcome we cannot foresee, we get nervous about her, and admit censorship.

E.M. Forster

Secrecy is the keystone to all tyranny. Not force, but secrecy and censorship. When any government or church for that matter, undertakes to say to its subjects, "This you may not read, this you must not know," the end result is tyranny and oppression, no matter how holy the motives. Mighty little force is needed to control a man who has been hoodwinked in this fashion; contrariwise, no amount of force can control a free man, whose mind is free. No, not the rack nor the atomic bomb, not anything. You can't conquer a free man; the most you can do is kill him.

Robert Heinlein

I take the side of young people, but I am also a realist; it is especially offensive to me when an uptight adult suggests that my stories are "inappropriate" for young readers. I imagine, when I write, that I am writing for young readers — not for uptight adults.

John Irving,
about a school library
banning The Hotel New Hampshire

If the book be false in its facts, disprove them; if false in its reasoning, refute it. But for God's sake, let us hear freely both sides.

Thomas Jefferson

One of the few remaining freedoms we have is the blank page. No one can prescribe how we should fill it.

James Kelman

There are lots of would-be censors out there, and although they may have different agendas, they all want basically the same thing: for you to see the world they see ... or to at least shut up about what you *do* see that's different. They are agents of the status quo. Not necessarily bad guys, but dangerous guys if you happen to believe in intellectual freedom.

Stephen King

There's a wonderful moment when you go from oppression to freedom, there in the middle, when one's still oppressed but one's achieved the first freedoms. By the time you get over to complete freedom you begin to look back almost nostalgically on the days of oppression, because in those days you were ready to become a martyr, you had a sense of importance, you could take yourself seriously, and you were fighting the good fight.

Norman Mailer

I am, in brief, a libertarian of the most extreme variety, and know of no human right that is one-tenth as valuable as the simple right to utter what seems (at the moment) to be the truth.

H.L. Mencken

Who kills a man kills a reasonable creature, God's image; but he who destroys a good book, kills reason itself, kills the image of God, as it were in the eye.

John Milton

Anyone who challenges the prevailing orthodoxy finds himself silenced with surprising effectiveness. … Unpopular ideas can be silenced, and inconvenient facts kept dark, without the need for any official ban. Anyone who has lived long in a foreign country will know of instances of sensational items of news — things which on their own merits would get the big headlines — being kept right out of the British press, not because the Government intervened but because of a general tacit agreement that "it wouldn't do" to mention that particular fact.

George Orwell, from a preface to Animal Farm *that, ironically, was rejected by his publisher*

Destroying intellectual freedom is always evil, but only religion makes doing evil feel quite so good.

Philip Pullman, on banning The Golden Compass

This indictment is a kind of fever that flares up from time to time. It flared up after *Defender of the Faith*, again after *Goodbye Columbus*, and understandably it went way up — to about 107 — after *Portnoy's Complaint*. Now there's just a low-grade fever running, nothing to worry about. I think the generation that got hot and bothered by my work is getting a little tired of the fuss. You know… if you hang around long enough, they begin to get used to you.

Philip Roth

I would rather be banned in Boston than read anywhere else because when you are banned in Boston, you are read everywhere else.

Upton Sinclair

Apparently, the Concord library has condemned Huck as "trash and only suitable for the slums." This will sell us another twenty-five thousand copies for sure!

Mark Twain, about The Adventures of Huckleberry Finn

All these people talk so eloquently about getting back to good old-fashioned values. Well, as an old poop I can remember back to when we had those old-fashioned values, and I say let's get back to the good old-fashioned First Amendment of the good old-fashioned Constitution of the United States — and to hell with the censors! Give me knowledge or give me death!

Kurt Vonnegut

The real fight to be fought is not against writings about sexual intercourse or the use of four-letter words, but against obscenities like calling a black man "nigger" or labeling a person you disagree with "Commie."

Irving Wallace

God forbid that any book should be banned. The practice is as indefensible as infanticide.

Rebecca West

I am beginning to feel a little more like an author now that I have had a book banned. The literary life in this country begins in jail.

E.B. White, after the military banned One Man's Meat, *1942.*

Characters

(See **Heroes**)

The most powerful card in the hand of the novelist interested in character drawing is differentiation by mode of speech.

Kingsley Amis

The first thing is you've got to believe in the characters. You've got to be thinking with the characters and you've got to be within their skins. If you're within their skins then their response to any situation, however bizarre it is, is going to be based upon your sense of them. Any writer's belief in his or her characters — or the situations in

A very famous writer once said, "A book is like a mirror. If a fool looks in, you can't expect a genius to look out." People tend to find in books what they want to find. And I think my books are very moral. I know they have absolutely nothing to do with what this lady is writing about, so I'm afraid I can't give her much help there.

J.K. Rowling, when asked if the Harry Potter series promoted Satanism. The quote in German from G.C. Lichtenberg has also been translated as "A book is a mirror: if an ass peers into it, you can't expect an apostle to look out."

”

I said the hell with Plot. I'm going to write stories about people that interest me, the way I see them. I'm sick of formula. I'm sick of Hero, Heroine, Heavy. ... I'm sick of Characters. I'm going to write about men and women, all classes, types and conditions, within the limits of my own capabilities. People with faults, with nasty tempers, with weaknesses and loves and hates and fears and gripes against each other. People I can believe in because I know and understand them. People who aren't like anybody else's characters because they are themselves, like 'em or don't. ... And all of a sudden I began to sell.

Leigh Brackett

which the characters find themselves — is central to his ability to convince the audience.

As a writer, you have to therefore always try to trip yourself up, look for the places where you've done something which was convenient rather than true. Convenient because sometimes characters can do things which are convenient to plotting, you know? But very often you realize, "This character is not going to do that. This character is going to do X rather than Y." And sometimes that can be a pain in the ass, but it's worth the trouble if it's going to convince the reader of the truth of the situation.

Clive Barker

Motivation is important at those points in a narrative where a reader might wonder why the characters are acting in a certain way when they might act in another, or not act at all. ... I have had particular difficulty supplying my characters with adequate motivation. One time, I recall, I went for several months without writing anything because I couldn't think of a single reason for any character to care strongly enough about anything to take any real action in any direction.

Lawrence Block

Many of the characters are fools and they are always playing tricks on me and treating me badly.

Jorge Luis Borges

Story offers us intense concentrations of character information.

Brian Boyd

A character, to be acceptable as more than a chess piece, has to be ignorant of the future, unsure about the past, and not at all sure of what he's supposed to be doing.

Anthony Burgess

You can't blame a writer for what the characters say.

Truman Capote

When dealing with people, let us remember we are not dealing with creatures of logic. We are dealing with creatures of emotion, creatures bristling with prejudices and motivated by pride and vanity.

Dale Carnegie

The character that lasts is an ordinary guy with some extraordinary qualities.

Raymond Chandler

The legend that characters run away from their authors — taking up drugs, having sex operations, and becoming president — implies that the writer is a fool with no knowledge or mastery of his craft. The idea of authors running around helplessly behind their cretinous inventions is contemptible.

John Cheever

The gem cannot be polished without friction, nor man perfected without trials.

Chinese proverb

The characters in my books are all mainstream and people identify with them. Their trouble comes from the outside, an external force that wreaks havoc in their lives. It's the coincidence of evil that intrigues readers. For example, in *A Stranger is Watching*, a young mother is murdered simply because she had a flat tire. A sad case of being in the wrong place at the wrong time, the slings and arrows of outrageous fortune. I don't say I must do an accident of fate; it's a story. In my books, there is usually a back story — something that happened either two years ago, or in the case of *While My Pretty One Sleeps*, seventeen years ago. And the victim is always the main character in the story. My concern is — Why would someone commit the ultimate crime? What passion drove them to murder, then to concealment? I work on the reactions. I'm fascinated by those moments when something untoward, something shattering, happens to people when they least expect it.

Mary Higgins Clark

Don't you think it would make your tough guys a little more interesting to the reader if once in a while you had one bend down to smell a rose?

Elliott Coleman, writing professor, to a young Russell Baker, who called it "one of the most valuable suggestions I'd ever had about writing"

When I was a Hollywood press agent, I learned how the Hollywood casting system worked. There was a roster of actors who were always perfect as doctors or lawyers or laborers, and the directors just picked the types they needed and stuffed them into film after film. I do the same [with my characters], book after book.

Richard Condon

If you want to know your characters better, ask yourself: "How would they behave in a quarrel?"

Barnaby Conrad

The actual character, Amy Foster, was for many years in our service, and it was her animal-like capacity for sheer uncomplaining endurance that inspired Conrad. That and nothing else.

Jessie Conrad, Joseph Conrad's wife, denying too much that she inspired the dull, plain wife in Victory

If you're going to write about people, you have to write about families. Family is the binding fiber of human experience. I could be reading about a thousand people consumed by a flood, but if my daughter suddenly cried out, all of that would vanish, and the world would be no larger than the space that separated us.

Thomas Cook

Writers shouldn't fall in love with characters so much that they lose sight of what they're trying to accomplish. The idea is to write a whole story, a whole book. A writer has to be able to look at that story and see whether or not a character works, whether or not a character needs further definition.

Stephen Coonts

If I stop seeing, hearing, touching, there will be no story. I will be a writer with nothing to say — a violin with no music to play. The journeys I find myself taking inevitably unfold the story, and the characters who accompany me always reveal more to me with time.

Patricia Cornwell

I always start with a character — character is what motivates me, what interests me. There's some human aspect to the nature of a particular character that has to get its hooks in me. Thereafter I just sort of free-flow scenes with that person or with that person's problem, with general situations that interest me, and I end up with sort of this mass of random scenes, but little by little some of them begin to connect, because I find them the most interesting or the most relevant. … I have to see the beginning, the middle and the ending I want to reach: this is what I'm trying to do

”

If I wrote about the stories of nice people who lived in Hollywood, everyone would be bored to tears by page 2.

Jackie Collins

A man's character may be learned from the adjectives which he habitually uses in conversation.

Olivia Clemens, from her commonplace book and commonly attributed to Mark Twain. Clemens was paraphrasing an essay by Henry Theodore Tuckerman (1813-1871).

”

We don't like change, and we don't like conflict, either. So most of the time we do our best to avoid both. This isn't easy, since the only real constant is change, and change is driven by conflict.

Lisa Cron

People do not spring forth out of the blue, fully formed — they become themselves slowly, day by day, starting from babyhood. They are the result of both environment and heredity, and your fictional characters, in order to be believable, must be also.

Lois Duncan

with this particular story and these characters. When I'm confident in that, I'll begin to write.

Robert Crais

I don't feel sympathetic toward some characters, unsympathetic towards others. I don't love some characters, feel contempt for others. They have attitudes; I don't.

Don DeLillo

He was at a starting-point which makes many a man's career a fine subject for betting, if there were any gentlemen given to that amusement who could appreciate the complicated probabilities of an arduous purpose, with all the possible thwartings and furtherings of circumstance, all the niceties of inward balance, by which a man swims and makes his point or else is carried headlong. The risk would remain even with close knowledge of Lydgate's character; for character too is a process and an unfolding. The man was still in the making, as much as the Middlemarch doctor and immortal discoverer, and there were both virtues and faults capable of shrinking or expanding. The faults will not, I hope, be a reason for the withdrawal of your interest in him.

George Eliot, setting up the character of Tertius Lydgate, the young doctor in Middlemarch

I would never write about someone who is not at the end of his rope.

Stanley Elkin

These are fully rounded characters, and the racism and homophobia are casual attributes, not defining characteristics. When you have characters that the reader empathizes with, who are carrying the story saying "nigger" and "faggot" and "spic," it puts people off. Which is fine. I would like to provoke ambiguous responses in my readers. That's what I want.

James Ellroy

A character is like an acrostic or Alexandrian stanza — read it forward, backward, or across, it still spells the same thing.

Ralph Waldo Emerson

No matter how extraordinary the event described, it will only be ordinary if it's not consolidated within a plight of a character whose action concerns us. What is it that impedes, compromises, jeopardizes the concerns of the character? Locate the actionable conflict. The trick is to impede the character, not the reader.

Hampton Fancher, screenwriter

Give only two or three vivid details when first introducing a character, and to distribute others through conversation and action, as well as to reiterate the details which are most important. The aim should be, not merely to convey to the reader what John Smith says or does, but to make the reader *see* John Smith as he says and does these things.

John T. Frederick

The bad novelist constructs his character; he directs them and makes them speak. The true novelist listens to them and watches them act; he hears their voices even before he knows them.

Andre Gide

[Private detective] Kinsey [Milhone] is my alter ego — the person I might have been had I not married young and had children.

Sue Grafton

When writing a novel a writer should

create living people; people, not characters. A character is a caricature.

Ernest Hemingway

As a novelist, your imagination has got to be free — you can't spend your time worrying about what someone is going to think. As far as I'm concerned you can make a real person anything you like, just as long as people understand that this is not necessarily an accurate version of anything. If you were a historian, it would be different — but you're not.

Philip Hensher

If you want your reader to understand something about a given character, his habits of intellection and control of his emotions, show the reader what the character thinks about, and then the reader will think about it too.

George V. Higgins

"Character is Fate," said Heraclitus in 500 B.C. or thereabouts. But "our characters are the result of our conduct," added Aristotle a hundred years or so later. We will find character and action even more inseparably entwined in fiction than they appear to be in life.

Rust Hills

A genuine creation should have character as well as be one; should have central heating, so to say, as well as exterior lighting.

James Hilton

Character, in any sense in which we can get at it, is action, and action is plot.

Henry James

I have heard people think I am Molly Bloom in *Ulysses*, but I'm not; Molly Bloom was much fatter.

Nora Joyce, James' wife

I do not write from life. I think that my characters came to me because I didn't have any family, and I wanted to have a family, and it was the only way I could get it.

Madeleine L'Engle

I sort of let my characters audition for me. I listen to them and let them do all the talking.

Elmore Leonard

Tolstoy said a great thing [about characterization]: You can tell that a marriage is on the rocks when they speak to each other rationally.

David Mamet

When it comes to people, I try not only to picture them but to imagine what they *sound* like, what they *smell* like, how they act. What they *feel* like too.

G. Masterton

It is a psychological trait in human nature that interest is established in the persons whom the playwright introduces at the beginning of his play so firmly that if the interest is then switched off to other persons who enter upon the scene later, a sense of disappointment ensues.

W. Somerset Maugham

Small objects in life can have great importance in people's lives. For example, Mma Makutsi [in his Botswana series] has a handkerchief that's very important to her, and her shoes are very important to her. She's proud of her shoes, and the fact that someone is proud of their shoes is something that I think is very poignant. And it actually makes a major point about the preciousness of these little things in

”

A character without an internal landscape runs the risk of becoming a stereotype or, worse, a cardboard character. Giving him an internal landscape gives him human dignity. It also adds to the depth of the novel because the character — more fully explored — is now more fully real.

Elizabeth George

You never want to write about a perfect person. Look at Ramona Quimby. She's not perfect but it's the failings that remind us of ourselves. That's what builds character.

Patricia Reilly Giff

Whenever the Godfather opened his mouth, in my own mind I heard the voice of my mother. I heard her wisdom, her ruthlessness, and her unconquerable love for her family and for life itself, qualities not valued in women at the time. The Don's courage and loyalty came from her; his humanity came from her.

Mario Puzo, who admitted he had "never met a real honest-to-god gangster" before starting The Godfather

life and how life is composed of small kindnesses, small ambitions and small episodes of happiness.

Alexander McCall Smith

Faulkner said that he just listens to his own characters and writes down what they say. I *watch* mine, and try, like Conrad, to make the reader see what's going on.

Larry McMurtry

I sometimes lose interest in the characters and get much more interested in the trees and animals.

Toni Morrison

I don't have any control over my characters. At any given time, there are scores of characters yelling at each other, yelling at me, inside my head. Some of them sort of take over, and I become totally intrigued or mesmerized by them.

Bharati Mukherjee

I've used a model for a character only once — he was a bad guy, somebody I didn't like much, and I wanted to write about him, but just that once. All the other characters in my books I have made up from scratch, from zero. Once I make up a character, he or she moves automatically, and all I have to do is watch him or her moving around and talking and doing things.

Haruki Murakami

That trite little whimsy about characters getting out of hand; it's as old as the quills. My characters are galley slaves.

Vladimir Nabokov

There is a technical, literary term for those who mistake the opinions and beliefs of characters in a novel for those of the author. The term is "idiot."

Larry Niven

The character on the page determines the prose — its music, its rhythms, the range and limit of its vocabulary — yet, at the outset at least, I determine the character. It usually happens that the fictitious character, once released, acquires a life and will of his or her own, so the prose, too, acquires its own inexplicable fluidity. This is one of the reasons I write: to "hear" a voice not quite my own, yet summoned forth by way of my own.

Joyce Carol Oates

If there is no possibility for change in a character, we have no interest in him.

Flannery O'Connor

So if you were my student, and if you needed to give a character authority — and build your own as the author — introduce the character as simple-minded, then have her or him let rip with a string of esoteric, complicated facts that shock the audience.

Chuck Palahniuk

All of my characters flow from my life experience, filtered, enlarged, transmorgified and recreated by my imagination. Why wouldn't they; it saves research. ... Every character — murderers, psychopaths, dogs, children — contain bits and pieces of me. I am their mother and their father. They weren't on the page before I started typing.

Robert B. Parker

The writer must always leave room for the characters to grow and change. If you move your characters from plot point to plot point, like painting by the numbers, they often remain stick figures. They will never take on a life of their own. The most exciting thing is when you find a character doing something surprising or unplanned. Like a character saying to me: "Hey, Richard, you may think I work for you, but I don't. I'm my own person."

Richard North Patterson

My novels are based on the fantastic designs made by real human beings earnestly laboring to maladjust themselves to fate. My characters are not slaves to an author's propaganda. I give them their heads. They furnish their own nooses.

Dawn Powell

A great deal of character work lies not in describing the characters, but in describing the shape that they leave in the world. How they react to other people. How they face things. When they keep silent. The manner in which they say things.

Terry Pratchett

I have to have a character worth caring about. In *Nobody's Fool*, I knew when I started that book I'd be able to live happily with Sully for the three or four years that it would take to write the book. I tend not to start writing books about people I don't have a lot of sympathy for because I'm just going to be with them too long. … Once you have that character worth caring about, I have to find a dilemma that the character doesn't know how to resolve and that I don't really have an answer for either.

Richard Russo

The characters have their own lives and their own logic, and you have to act accordingly.

Isaac Bashevis Singer

A character is never a whole person, but just those parts of him that fit the story or the piece of writing. So the act of selection is the writer's first step in delineating character. From what does he select? From a whole mass of what Bernard DeVoto used to call, somewhat clinically, "placental material." He must know an enormous amount more about each of his characters than he will ever use directly – childhood, family background, religion, schooling, health, wealth, sexuality, reading, tastes, hobbies – an endless questionnaire for the writer to fill out. For example, the writer knows that people speak, and therefore his characters will describe themselves indirectly when they talk. Clothing is a means of characterization. In short, each character has a style of his own in everything he does. These need not all be listed, but the writer should have a sure grasp of them. If he has, his characters will, within the book, read like people.

William Sloane

Knowledge must come through action.

Sophocles

Let your characters *do*, so that they can *be*.

Damon Suede

We're past the age of heroes and hero kings. If we can't make up stories about ordinary people, who can we make them up about? … Most of our lives are basically mundane and dull, and it's up to the writer to find ways to make them interesting.

John Updike

"

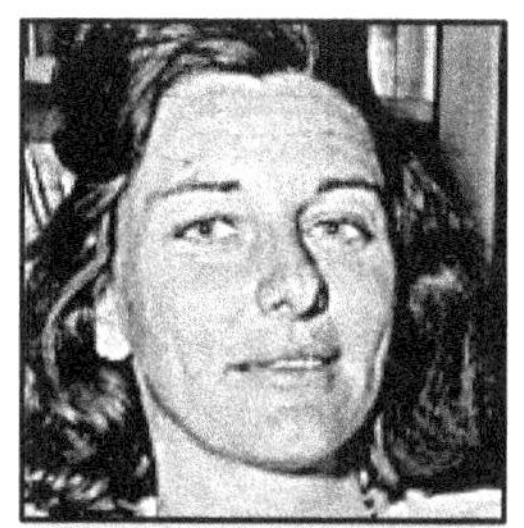

"Fuck structure and grab your characters by the time balls." Each one of us sits in our time; we're born, live and die. She was thinking this and that and I was telling her to get inside her characters' lives.

Anne Sexton, recalling her advice to Maxine Kumin about her novel

I always pulp my acquaintances before serving them up. You would never recognize a pig in a sausage.

Frances Trollope

If you're silent for a long time, people just arrive in your mind.

Alice Walker

It annoys me that there are these books about going to the hospital for young children that say it is really not so bad. If you're a child going to the hospital you're going to have a miserable time; you're probably going to be in pain, you're going to be lonely, it's going to be scary, there are people in masks poking at you. A book that says it is going to be fun is a desperate lie.

Lemony Snicket

When I used to teach creative writing, I would tell the students to make their characters want something right away – even if it's only a glass of water. Characters paralyzed by the meaninglessness of modern life still have to drink water from time to time.

Kurt Vonnegut

Whether we fall by ambition, blood, or lust.
Like diamonds we are cut with our own dust.

John Webster

Nothing can be more trying to the creative writer than to have a clumsy finger point at one of the beings born in that mysterious other-world of invention, with the playful accusation: "Of course we all recognized your aunt Eliza!"

Edith Wharton

As a novelist, I'm concerned solely with what I've discovered about human emotions. I attack not specific things, but only people who are set in one way of thinking.

August Wilson

The principle I always go on in writing a long story is to think of the characters in terms of actors in a play. I say to myself, when I invent a good character for an early scene: "If this were a musical comedy we should have to get somebody like Leslie Henson to play this part, and if he found out that all he had was a short scene in Act I, he would walk out. How, therefore can I twist the story so as to give them more to do and keep them alive till the fall of the curtain?"

P.G. Wodehouse

ONE BIG CHARACTER IS WORTH TWO SMALL ONES. Don't defuse the interest. The absolute cast-iron good rule, I'm sure, in writing a story, is to introduce all your characters as early as possible – especially if they are going to play important parts later.

P.G. Wodehouse

Children's Books

In the case of the great children's writers of the recent past, there was a compensating seriousness. There was – and is – a real sense of mystery, powerful forces, dangerous creatures in dark forests. Susan Cooper's teenage wizard discovers his magic powers and discovers simultaneously that he is in a cosmic battle between good and evil forces. Every bush and cloud glitters with secret significance. Alan Garner peoples real landscapes with malign, inhuman elvish beings that hunt humans. Reading writers like these, we feel we are being put back in touch with earlier parts of our culture, when supernatural and inhuman creatures – from whom we thought we learned our sense of good and evil – inhabited a world we did not feel we controlled. If we regress, we regress to a lost sense of significance we mourn for.

A.S. Byatt

My books are written for adults and always have been ... I *hate* this silly teenager business.

Agatha Christie, when her publisher promoted Thirteen for Luck *to young adults.*

Of 3,200 children's books published in 2013, just 93 were about black people.

Cooperative Children's Book Center, University of Wisconsin

The little bastards'd swallow it.

Roald Dahl, suggesting that Kingsley Amis write children's books for the money

It's hard to write a book. It's harder to write one with living characters, clever scenes, warmth, and wit. And it's harder still when the people you're writing for can't read, or read only a little, when the words you choose must be simple, short and sweet. And if not always sweet, at least short.

Russell Hoban

Everyone said this [*The Phantom Tollbooth*] is not a children's book, the vocabulary is much too difficult, the wordplay and the punning they will never understand, and anyway fantasy is bad for children because it disorients them. I thought, "O.K., it will come out, and end on the remainder table."

Norton Juster

I believe that good questions are more important than answers, and the best children's books ask questions, and make the readers ask questions. And every new question is going to disturb someone's universe.

Madeleine L'Engle

The books one reads in childhood, and perhaps most of all the bad and good-bad books, create in one's mind a sort of false map of the world, a series of fabulous countries into which one can retreat at odd moments throughout the rest of life, and which in some cases can even survive a visit to the real countries which they are supposed to represent.

George Orwell

A large percentage of the people writing children's books are white women in their forties, fifties, and sixties with at least some college education. This probably has been the case for decades. The children's book authors I've met often share a few characteristics: They grew up with books, they've read a lot, they have some sort of connection to children, either through teaching, parenting, or a job that puts them in contact with kids, and they've had the time and money to develop their writing skills and attend conferences. So I think there is definitely a socio-economic factor in becoming a children's book author.

Abigail Samoun, literary agent

Not much, because I think kids enjoy safe scares, like reading about a monster but knowing the book won't go too far or be too disgusting. So, at the same time they know they're safe, just reading in their room, and that there will always be a happy ending.

R.L. Stine, on what it took to scare kids

Clarity

To know how to say what others only know how to think is what makes men poets or sages; and to dare to say what others only dare to think makes men martyrs or reformers – or both.

Elizabeth Charles

Clear writers, like clear fountains, do not seem so deep as they are; the turbid look the most profound.

Walter Savage Landor

How little the all-important art of making pellucid is studied now! Hardly any popular writer except myself thinks of it. Many seem to aim at being obscure. Indeed, they may be right enough in one sense; for many readers give credit for

”

[Children's books represent the] apartheid of literature — in which characters of color are limited to the townships of occasional historical books that concern themselves with the legacies of civil rights and slavery but are never given a pass card to traverse the lands of adventure, curiosity, imagination, or personal growth.

Christopher Myers, illustrator

I see but one rule: to be clear. If I am not clear, my whole world is annihilated.

Stendhal

What is a snob? A snob is anybody who takes a small part of you and uses that to come to a complete vision of who you are.

Alain de Botton

profundity to whatever is obscure and call all that is perspicuous shallow.

Thomas Babington Macaulay

One of the main praises that we give to a writer or a practitioner of any liberal art is that he knows how to explain his ideas clearly, and that even if his subject is lofty and difficult, he knows how to make it plain and intelligible to all by his easy discourse.

Gabriele Paleotti, Cardinal (1524-97) Italian bishop of Bologna

Class

If any writer thinks the world is full of middle-class people of nice sensibilities, then he is out of his mind.

Tom Sharpe

No writer before the middle of the 19th century wrote about the working classes other than as grotesque or as pastoral decoration. Then when they were given the vote certain writers began to suck up to them.

Evelyn Waugh

Classics

The masters of literature were, first, masters of telling a story well, and the writer can learn from them. The writer should do his best for the story, not for the market. His best is to provide entertainment to serve the purpose of the reader. If the writer has a message it must be secondary.

Ray Bradbury

Speak of the moderns without contempt and of the ancients without idolatry; judge them all by their merits, but not by their age.

Lord Chesterfield

Do not suppose, however, that I intend to urge a diet of classics on anybody. I have seen such diets at work. I have known people who have actually read all, or almost all, the guaranteed Hundred Best Books. God save us from reading nothing but the best.

Robertson Davies

When you reread a classic, you do not see more in the book than you did before; you see more in *you* than there was before.

Clifton Fadiman

A young poet should be bound apprentice to Pindar [an ancient Greek lyric poet] for three years, whether his business be the ode or anything else. He will find nothing in the workshop which he expected to find, but quite enough of highly wrought tools and well-seasoned materials.

Walter Savage Landor

The classics are only primitive literature. They belong to the same class as primitive machinery and primitive music and primitive medicine.

Stephen Leacock

Almost all the great writers have as their *motif*, more or less disguised, the "passage from childhood to maturity," the clash between the thrill of expectation, and the disillusioning knowledge of the truth. *Lost Illusion* is the undisclosed title of every novel.

Andre Maurois

The girls today in society go for classical poetry,
So to win their hearts one must quote with ease
Aeschylus and Euripides.
One must know Homer and, b'lieve

me, bo,
Sophocles, also Sappho-ho.

Cole Porter, "Brush Up Your Shakespeare"

For what are the classics but the noblest recorded thoughts of man? They are the only oracles which are not decayed, and there are such answers to the most modern inquiry in them as Delphi and Dodona never gave. We might as well omit to study Nature because she is old. To read well, that is, to read true books in a true spirit, is a noble exercise, and one that will task the reader more than any exercise which the customs of the day esteem. It requires a training such as the athletes underwent, the steady intention almost of the whole life to this object. Books must be read as deliberately and reservedly as they were written.

Henry David Thoreau

Something that everybody wants to have read and nobody wants to read.

Mark Twain

Columnist

Mike Royko: Roeper! Do you use your column to get laid?

Richard Roeper: Excuse me?

Royko: You heard me! Do you use your column to get laid?

Roeper (half jokingly, keep in mind drinks flowing): Of course not. That wouldn't be right!

Royko (pounding the table): Well, what the hell is the point in having a column if you don't use it to get laid!

Bill Zehme

Comedy/Tragedy

Usually in tragedy a good person is made to suffer through a flaw in his goodness. In *Macbeth* this pattern is reversed: it is the streak of goodness that causes pathos and suffering.

W.H. Auden

[Comedy is when] an idea, going in one direction, meets an opposite idea suddenly.

Charlie Chaplin

Almost any industrious dullard can write tragedy — not real tragedy or good tragedy, of course, but the kind of thing that is depressing enough to deceive people who like gloomy reading, and regard misery as a status-mood.

Robertson Davies

Tragedy primes one for humor, and humor primes one for tragedy. They amplify each other.

Jonathan Safran Foer

In tragedy every moment is eternity; in comedy, eternity is a moment.

Christopher Fry

I think it was Esther Friesner who said you have to have tragic relief. If a book is nothing but funny, then it is nothing but funny. There is no contrast and it's hard to take anything seriously. It's hard to worry about the fate of a character. You do need those moments when you bring people down to Earth.

Terry Pratchett

I think it would be harder for me not to write comedy because the comic view of things is the one that comes most naturally to me. People often ask me how I make things funny. I don't make things funny. … Most of the time, with my way of seeing things, as soon as I see something I will see something funny in it.

”

A classic book is a book that survives the circumstances that made it possible yet alone keeps those circumstances alive.

Alfred Kazin

Comedy, I imagine, is harder to do consistently than tragedy, but I like it spiced in the wine of sadness.

Bernard Malamud

Despite it being impressed on me that this over here is literature, and comics are something different, I grew up refusing to distinguish between them. I am getting the same feeling from "Love and Rockets" that I'm getting from "One Hundred Years of Solitude," but I'm supposed to look at one as, "That's comics," and "That's a serious novel?" From a very early age, I thought, "That's bullshit."

Marlon James

Comedy is hard in that it's timing, and you have to get the timing down, which requires a lot of revision, but at the same time you have to be careful not to revise all the humor out of it.

Richard Russo

The fact that we are, I don't know, how many millions of people, yet communication, complete communication, is completely impossible between two of those people, is to me one of the biggest tragic themes in the world.

Georges Simenon

Comic Novel

The real comic novel has to do with man's recognition of his unimportance in the universe.

Anthony Burgess

Comics

In comics at its best, words and pictures are like partners in a dance and each one takes turns leading.

Scott McCloud

Commerce

There are not more useful members in a commonwealth than merchants. They knit mankind together in a mutual intercourse of good offices, distribute the gifts of nature, find work for the poor, add wealth to the rich, and magnificence to the great.

Joseph Addison

Trade, insofar as it aims at making profits, is most reprehensible, since the desire for gain knows no bounds but reaches into the infinite.

Thomas Aquinas

The instinctive sense of the dishonor which money-purchase does to art is so strong that sometimes a man of letters who can pay his way otherwise refuses pay for his work, as Lord Byron did, for a while, from a noble pride.

William Dean Howells

Commercial Fiction

Given a reasonable intelligence and sufficient patience, any man with the smallest gifts may learn to write at least marketable stuff, and may earn an honest livelihood, if he studies the taste of the least exacting portion of the public, and accommodates himself to the whim of the time.

Arlo Bates

There are pleasures in writers like Leonard, King and Grafton that you simply can't get anyplace else — namely, the innate ability to spin out a story so deftly and so quickly that you have no choice but to submit.

Dwight Garner

The classic American bestseller tends to depict three main characters. One character follows orders, is shy and agreeable, a general all-round good girl or boy. The second character is largely the opposite: a rebel who bullies and breaks the rules. And the third is quiet, thoughtful, and acts as the narrator, relating the story to the reader. The passive character commits suicide in some way. The rebel is executed in some way. And the thoughtful witness leaves the circumstances of the story, wiser for having seen the fate of the other two characters, and is ready to relay the cautionary tale to the world.

Chuck Palahniuk, about Gone With the Wind, Valley of the Dolls, One Flew Over the Cuckoo's Nest, Rosemary's Baby, *and his* Fight Club

It seems to me that a novel can withstand nearly every cardinal sin except one — being boring. I've read dozens of books that were "better" written than *Forever Amber* with at least the same enthusiasm I'd bring to a book of carpet swatches. I know that's a shocking state of affairs for writers like Heidi Julavits who, in a much talked about essay on the intellectual poverty of contemporary book reviewers in the premier issue of *The Believer*, writes, "Stephen King and John Gresham. ... Get more favorable treatment for their genre novels, while more ambitious novels are derisively spanked — or, more frequently, flat out ignored. Isn't there something wrong with this picture?" There sure is: the fact that someone would castigate book critics under the mistaken impression that readers pick up books to read intentions instead of results.

Charles Taylor

Confidence

I learned this, at least, by my experiment: that if one advances confidently in the direction of his dreams, and endeavors to live the life which he has imagined, he will meet with a success unexpected in common hours.

Henry David Thoreau

Controversy

Publishers want to take chances on books that will draw a clamor and some legitimate publicity. They want to publish controversial books. That their reasons are mercenary and yours may be lofty should not deter you.

Harlan Ellison

In fashion, you're always creating authority through provocation. The worst thing is to be overlooked because you're not provocative. You have to be on the edge of changing sensibilities.

Milton Glasser, graphic designer and illustrator

Whenever you cause distress, be it deliberately or not deliberately, you also cause delight in others. It balances out, and you get your readers. Folks who don't like what you do aren't going to like you anyway. The more people are hostile to you, the more people rally to you. That always happens: no action without reaction.

Gore Vidal

Courage

I learned that courage was not the absence of fear, but the triumph over it. The brave man is not he who does not feel afraid, but he who conquers that fear.

Nelson Mandela, statesman

Courage is doing what you're afraid to do. There can be no courage unless you're scared.

Eddie Rickenbacker, pilot

As a writer one has to take the chance on being a fool ... yes, to be a fool, that perhaps requires the greatest courage.

Anne Sexton

Courage is resistance to fear, mastery of fear—not absence of fear. … Consider the flea!—incomparably the bravest of all the creatures of God, if ignorance of fear were courage.

Mark Twain

Courage is being scared to death but saddling up anyway.

John Wayne, actor

”

Courage is fear holding on a minute longer.

Gen. George Patton

Creativity is allowing yourself to make mistakes. Art is knowing which ones to keep.

Scott Adams

”

The stupidest possible creative act is still a creative act.

Clay Shirky

Act on your creativity. Allow yourself the gift of time, the gift of play, the gift of practice.

Kristi Tencarre

Creativity

We get our ideas from what I'm going to call for a moment our unconscious — the part of our mind that goes on working, for example, when we're asleep. So what I'm saying is that if you get into the right mood, then your mode of thinking will become much more creative. But if you're racing around all day, ticking things off a list, looking at your watch, making phone calls and generally just keeping all the balls in the air, you are not going to have any creative ideas.

John Cleese

First of all, there's two kinds of thoughts in your mind: there's good thoughts and evil thoughts. Both come through your mind. Some people are more loaded down with one than another. Nevertheless, they come through. And you have to be able to sort them out, if you want to be a songwriter, if you want to be a song singer. You must get rid of all that baggage. You ought to be able to sort out those thoughts, because they don't mean anything, they're just pulling you around, too. It's important to get rid of them thoughts. Then you can do something from some kind of surveillance of the situation. You have some kind of place where you can see it but it can't affect you. Where you can bring something to the matter, besides just take, take, take, take, take.

Bob Dylan

I wrote it one Sunday after matins. I had been thinking about it in church and when I got home, I opened a half-bottle of Booth's Gin, poured myself a drink, and began to write. By lunchtime, the poem, and the half-bottle of gin, were both finished.

T.S. Eliot, on writing "The Journey of the Magi"

Creativeness often consists in turning up what is already there. Did you know that left and right shoes were thought up only little more than a century ago?

Bernice Fitz-Gibbon, advertising executive

No tears in the writer, no tears in the reader. No surprise in the writer, no surprise in the reader. For me the initial delight is in the surprise of remembering something I didn't know I knew. I am in a place, in a situation, as if I had materialized from cloud or risen out of the ground. There is a glad recognition of the long lost and the rest follows.

Robert Frost

Everything is relevant. Making things relevant is the creative process.

William J.J. Gordon

You never really know where the work is coming from, and to be really responsive you just have to follow it like a dowsing rod wherever it will lead you. If you trust the work and give it a daily place in your existence — and by "daily" I mean that even on a book tour, you're writing on a yellow legal pad, even though there's a distinct possibility that none of these sentences will ever see print, just to keep your chops going, just to keep your hand in — you do find that your major ethical and personal concerns come to rest biorhythmically in the fiction.

Allan Gurganus

Find your voice, shout it from the rooftops, and keep doing it until the people that are looking for you find you.

Dan Harmon, TV producer

I have never felt like I was creating anything. For me, writing is like walking through a desert and all at once, poking up through the hardpan, I see the top of a chimney. I know there's a house under there, and I'm pretty sure that I can dig it up if I want. That's how I feel. It's like the stories are already there. What they pay me for is the leap of faith that says: "If I sit down and do this, everything will come out OK."

Stephen King

Do the thing that feeds you, first. Then do the crazy business stuff.

Austin Kleon

Give what you have. To someone, it may be better than you dare to think.

Henry Wadsworth Longfellow

Je ne cherche pas, je trouve.
I do not seek, I find.

Pablo Picasso, on his painting method, meaning he doesn't begin a work with a subject or design in mind. Also expressed as "The search means nothing in painting. To find is the thing." The accuracy of the quote is in dispute, but the idea is not.

"I'll never be 10" [from *Bumble-Ardy*] touches me deeply but I won't pretend that I know exactly what it means. When I thought of it, I was so happy I thought of it. It came to me, which is what the creative act is all about. Things come to you without you necessarily knowing what they mean. ... It comes at a time when I am getting ripe, getting old — and I want to do work that resonates.

Maurice Sendak

You know ... that a blank wall is an appalling thing to look at. The wall of a museum — a canvas — a piece of film — or a guy sitting in front of a typewriter. Then, you start out to do something — that vague thing called creation. The beginning strikes awe within you.

Edward Steichen

I saw the Sex Pistols. They were terrible. … I wanted to get up and be terrible with them.

Bernard Sumner, front man for the band New Order

We mortals can't create, we can only copy.

Mark Twain

[Good nonfiction was a chance to] watch somebody reasonably bright but also reasonably average pay far closer attention and think at far more length about all sorts of different stuff than most of us have a chance to in our daily lives.

David Foster Wallace

That I don't know what I'm doing.

Thom Yorke, front man for the band Radiohead, on his greatest strength

Crime Fiction

(See **Mysteries**)

The appeal of the conventional crime novel is the sense of completion it offers. … No matter how unlikely the cast of suspects or how baffling the strew of clues in an Agatha Christie whodunit or a Robert Ludlum thriller, we know with a certainty not afforded by real life that when the murderer is unmasked or the conspiracy foiled, everything will click into place, like a jigsaw puzzle assembling itself before our eyes.

John Banville

”

To live a creative life, we must lose our fear of being wrong.

Joseph Chilton Pearce

We all think about murdering another person on occasions; what matters is not acting on that impulse. I'm lucky to have fictional characters to do it for me.

Sue Grafton

Criticism can never instruct or benefit you. Its chief effect is that of a telegram with dubious news. Praise leaves no glow behind, for it is a writer's habit to remember nothing good of himself. I have usually forgotten those who have admired my work, and seldom anyone who disliked it. Obviously, this is because praise is never enough and censure always too much.

Ben Hecht

What greater prestige can a man like me have than to have taken a cheap, shoddy, and utterly lost kind of writing, and have made it something that intellectuals claw each other about?

Raymond Chandler

It's not how a cop works a crime, but how a crime works the cop.

Michael Connelly

The detective story begins in the Sherlock Holmes period as an intensification of low mimetic, in the sharpening of attention to details that makes the dullest and most neglected trivia of daily living leap into mysterious and fateful significance.

Northrop Frye

Murder is a kind of making love, a kind of possessing. (Is it not, too, a way of gaining complete and passionate attention, for a moment, from the object of one's attentions?)

Patricia Highsmith

Criticism

I am bound by my own definition of criticism: a disinterested endeavour to learn and propagate the best that is known and thought in the world.

Matthew Arnold

Of all fatiguing, futile, empty trades, the worst, I suppose, is writing about writing.

Hilaire Belloc

Every time you're praised, there's a boot waiting for you. If you've been publishing books for 50 years or so, you're inured to misunderstanding and even abuse.

Saul Bellow

Listen carefully to first criticisms made of your work. Note just what it is about your work that the critics don't like and cultivate it. That's the only part of your work that's individual and worth keeping.

Jean Cocteau

I do in fact believe that all good criticism should be judged the way art is. You shouldn't read it the way you read history or science. Finally, I think [what] I like best is that people who are not experts can not only understand but get engaged by my work.

Leslie Fiedler

I dislike this time intensely. And haven't even bothered to buy the undelivered papers with reviews. A good one in the *New Statesman*, a bad one in the *Times* full of misunderstandings, the voice of the literary establishment. But I know now that, good or bad, they're irrelevant; praise or damnation in this poor sick culture, they alter nothing. Even the harshest reviewer is never the real enemy.

John Fowles, diary entry

I'd worry more if I weren't being hated. Who said it's the writer's job to be liked by everyone?

Jonathan Franzen

Dear Sir (or Madame): You may be right.

Wolcott Gibbs, describing H.L. Mencken's formula for answering controversial letters, "which is final, courteous, and can be used without reading the original letter"

Bob Greene: Think about the things you wake up terrified about in the middle of the night ... that only you know about yourself. ... Are any of them the things that other people have said about you?

Michael Jordan: No. The three-o'clock-in-the-morning things are much worse.

Greene: I know. It's not just you. It's everyone. The worst things that anyone else could ever say about us don't come close to being as bad as the worst things we think about ourselves.

Bob Greene

A man's mind is hidden in his writings; criticism brings it to light.

Solomon ibn Gabirol, c. 1050

The slanderers of the pen pierce to the heart; they rankle longest in the noblest spirit; they dwell ever present in the mind and render it morbidly sensitive to the most trifling collision.

Washington Irving

I would rather be attacked than unnoticed. For the worst you can do to an author is to be silent as to his works.

Samuel Johnson

If critics say your work stinks it's because they want it to stink and they can make it stink by scaring you into conformity with their comfortable little standards. Standards so low that they can no longer be considered "dangerous" but set in place in their compartmental understandings.

Jack Kerouac

This is what you have to remember [about studio notes], and this is the only thing that keeps me sane: is that they're trying to make the movie, too. No one here is your enemy in that room. No one there is giving you notes to fuck with you. They're giving you notes because that is what they need you to do to move the movie to the next level. And as long as you can think of it that way, you will be excited for every rewrite.

Max Landis, screenwriter. The same can be applied to editor's notes.

I'm sensitive enough to criticism that if I pay attention to it, it may make me a worse writer. When I sit down to write, I like to think everybody's going to love me. Or at least I don't think anybody's going to hate me. It's paranoia, right, is that the word? Everybody's out to love me, not everybody's out to hate me? I think basically that way as I move through the world.

Michael Lewis

[The] tendency to degenerate into a mere mouthing of meaningless words seems to be peculiar to so-called art criticism ... Even the most orthodox of the brethren, when he finds himself before a canvas that genuinely moves him, takes refuge in esoteric winks and grimaces and mysterious gurgles and belches.

H.L. Mencken

Criticism hurt me when I had failures. I thought: I'll never write another play: but I am an alligator. Only the alligators remain. The others get out of the water.

Arthur Miller

Here's criticism's trade secret: you can find meaning in anything if you look hard enough. Contemplate a work of art and patterns inevitably emerge, echoes, resonances, allusions which can be brought out and amplified through exegesis, the interpretive conceit by which a critic simultaneously deconstructs and rebuilds, unveils and augments another writer's metaphors, another writer's vision. … Exegesis is only incidentally or latterly concerned with aesthetic quality. Its uncritical methodology can no more tell the difference between *Hollywood Wives* and *The Iliad* than a microscope's lens can, on its own, distinguish between a drop of Jackie Collins'

”

It is long, yet vigorous, like the penis of a jackass.

Sydney Smith, clergyman and essayist, about an article submitted by Lord Brougham to Smith's Edinburgh Review

You should be able to listen to criticism even if the person giving it is a dumb, arrogant bastard. Because maybe, just maybe, the SOB will have a point that will make your work better.

Stirling Silliphant

”

I puff your books, you know, without any regard to their quality.

Rufus Griswold, notorious Poe slanderer, in a letter to publishers Ticknor & Co., 1842

Reviewers are usually people who would've been poets, historians, biographers, etc., if they could; they have tried their talents at one or the other, and have failed; therefore they turn critics.

Samuel Taylor Coleridge

blood and a drop of Homer's.

Dale Peck

One of the commonest but most uncritical faults of criticism — the refusal to consider what it is that the author intended to give us.

George Saintsbury

I quite agree with you, sir, but what can two do against so many?

George Bernard Shaw, after an audience member hissed him at the premiere of Arms and the Man.

Interpretation is the revenge of the intellect upon art.

Susan Sontag

Writing criticism is to writing fiction and poetry as hugging the shore is to sailing the open sea.

John Updike

This egregious commentary did me the immense service. … Every short story, I now saw, like every other work of art, contains within itself the germ of its own particular form and dimensions, and *ab ovo* [from the very beginning] is the artist's only rule. In an instant I was free forever from the bogey of the omnipotent reviewer.

Edith Wharton, after a condescending critic wrote "when Mrs. Wharton has learned the rudiments of her art, she will know that a short story should always begin with dialogue"

The best thing you can do about critics is never say a word. In the end you have the last say, and they know it.

Tennessee Williams

Let others have those things. I have readers.

Walter Winchell, gossip columnist, after being told he lacked "ethics, scruples, decency [and] conscience"

Praise and blame are much the same for the writer. One is better for your vanity, but neither gets you much further with your work.

Jeanette Winterson

Literature is strewn with the wreckage of men who have minded beyond reason the opinion of others.

Virginia Woolf

Critics

(See **Reviewers**)

A true critic ought to dwell rather upon excellencies than imperfections, to discover the concealed beauties of a writer, and communicate to the world such things as are worth their observation.

Joseph Addison

I don't read them. I doubt anyone does, except other critics. It seems like a sealed-off field with its own lieutenants, pretty much preoccupied with its own intrigues. I got a glimpse into the uses of a certain kind of criticism this past summer at a writers' conference, into how the avocation of assessing the failures of better men can be turned into a comfortable livelihood, providing you can back it up with a Ph.D. I saw how it was possible to gain a chair of literature on no qualifications other than persistence in nipping the heels of Hemingway, Faulkner, and Steinbeck.

Nelson Algren

The average pressman, reviewing a book of stories or of poems by an unknown writer, seems not to think "where are the beauties of this work that I may praise them, and by my praise quicken the sense of beauty in others?" He steadily applies himself to the ignoble task of plucking out and gloating over its defects. It is a pity that critics should show so little sympathy with writers, and curious when we consider that most of them tried to be writers themselves, once.

Max Beerbohm

A critic is like a eunuch in a harem — he's in the midst of something exciting but he can take no part in it.

Brendan Behan

We regret that [Kathryn] Olney is offended by some of our books. But we are consoling ourselves with the knowledge that the only thing nobody doesn't like is Sara Lee. Oh, yes, among the many factual errors in the piece is the statement that our series has sold 220 million books. We are happy to report that series sales have reached 245 million.

Stan and Jan Berenstain, responding to criticism of their children's books, particularly for how they portrayed fathers

Never demean yourself by talking back to a critic, never. Write those letters to the editor in your head, but don't put them on paper.

Truman Capote

If I had listened to the critics I'd have died drunk in the gutter.

Anton Chekhov

Literary critics, however, frequently suffer from a curious belief that every author longs to extend the boundaries of literary art, wants to explore new dimensions of the human spirit, and if he doesn't, he should be ashamed of himself.

Robertson Davies

[The critic] must compose his differences with as many of his fellows as possible in the common pursuit of true judgment.

T.S. Eliot

One of the advantages artists have over critics is that they can be nearly complete damn fools and still produce interesting and important, even lasting, art. Critics are not permitted such large margins of stupidity. It matters that they get things right; their opinions, which is all they chiefly have, are crucial. Wisdom, in a critic, is never excess baggage.

Joseph Epstein

Critics? How do they happen? I know how it happened to me. I would send a poem or story to a magazine and they would say this doesn't suit our needs precisely but on the other hand you sound interesting. Would you be interested in doing a review? And then I'd do it and decide that it's easy and you figure you might as well keep your name in front of people and you figure some day they'll run a story.

Leslie Fiedler

I've sold too many books to ever be taken seriously by critics. What I think about is making the best book I've ever written. That's my goal every time.

John Grisham

Asking a working writer what he thinks about critics is like asking a lamp-post how it feels about dogs.

Christopher Hampton, playwright

It is still expected, though perhaps people are ashamed to say it, that a production which is after all only a "make believe" (for what else is a "story"?) shall be in some degree apologetic — shall renounce the pretension of attempting really to represent life. This, of course, any sensible, wide-awake story declines to do, for it quickly perceives that the tolerance granted to it on such a

”

Once you sell a certain number of books, the people who think about "literature" stop thinking about you and assume that any writer who is popular across a wide spectrum has nothing to say. The unspoken postulate is that intelligence is rare.

Betsy Lerner, editor

Being a critic helps you realize that all criticism — good, bad, and indifferent — says more about the writer than it does about the product being reviewed. All criticism is really just veiled autobiography.

Chuck Klosterman

”

Read as little as possible of aesthetic criticism — such things are either partisan views, petrified and grown senseless in their lifeless induration, or they are clever quislings in which today one view wins and tomorrow the opposite. Works of art are of an infinite loneliness and with nothing so little to be reached as with criticism.

Rainer Maria Rilke

condition is only an attempt to stifle it disguised in the form of generosity.

Henry James

Critics are more malicious about poetry than about other books — maybe because so many manqué [inferior] poets write reviews.

Elizabeth Jennings

Every man can exert such judgment as he has upon the works of others; and he whom nature has made weak, and idleness keeps ignorant, may yet support his vanity by the name of a critic.

Samuel Johnson

You *may* abuse a tragedy, though you cannot write one. You may scold a carpenter who has made you a bad table, though you cannot make a table. It is not your trade to make tables.

Samuel Johnson

Never trust the artist. Trust the tale. The proper function of a critic is to save the tale from the artist who created it.

D.H. Lawrence

People whose job it is to generate an instant view … You do that enough, you forget what that person who is creating things did. All you are doing is responding to the things in front of you. Engaging with it is usually a lot more trouble than it's worth.

Michael Lewis, on critics of his work

So you guys are critics, are you? Well, let me tell you something. I'm the best writer in this here gottdamn country and if you, Georgie, and you, Hank, don't know it now, you'll know it gottdamn soon. Say, I've just finished a book that'll be published in a week or two and it's the gottdamn best book of its kind that this here gottdamn country has had and don't you guys forget it! I worked a year on the gottdamn thing and it's the goods, I'm atelling you! Listen, when it comes to writing a novel, I'm so far ahead of most of the men you two think are good that I'll be gottdamned if it doesn't make me sick to think of it! Just wait till you read the gottdamn thing. You've got a treat coming, Georgie and Hank, and don't you boys make no mistake about that!

Sinclair Lewis, meeting H.L. Mencken and George Jean Nathan of The Smart Set. *Mencken would later write Nathan that Lewis' novel,* Main Street, *was "a genuinely excellent piece of work. … I begin to believe that perhaps there isn't a God after all. There is no justice in the world"*

If I am going to go on saying what my anger tells me it is true to say, I must get better at overriding the indifference which comes from the snobs, arbiters, managers and conforming maniacs who manipulate most of the world of letters. ... There may have been too many fights for me ... too much brain-blasting rage at the minuscule frustrations of a most loathsome literary world, necrophilic to the core — they murder their writers, and then decorate their graves.

Norman Mailer

I dislike particularly those critics who preach their aesthetic or ideological doctrines at you. What's important to them is not what the writer has done but how it fits, or doesn't fit, the thesis they want to develop. Nobody can tell a writer what can or ought to be done, or not done, in his fiction. A living death if you fall for it.

Bernard Malamud

[Critics] are poor grammarians, and their vocabularies are tawdry. It is hard enough to interpret one art in terms of another under the best of circumstances, but when the critic has not understood that writing also is an art, his criticism becomes embarrassing self-portraiture.

Samuel Marchbanks

A drama critic is a person who surprises the playwright by informing him what he meant.

Wilson Mizner

A critic should be a conduit, a bridge, but not a law.

Toni Morrison

Either pro or con, past and present, the wearier feeling I get that all they say is something between them and their trade, but, so far as the reality of my play goes, totally irrelevant, except as box office help or hindrance.

Eugene O'Neill

Although I approached my literary debut light-heartedly, *Time* and various critics registered alarm at the idea of books being written by anyone but dyed-in-the-wool, 32-caret, bona fide genius type writers. While I scarcely felt that Sir Cedric Hardwicke, Billy Graham, Barry Goldwater or I were threats to Ernest Hemingway or Somerset Maugham, I did feel that a great many people other than professional writers might have dramatic or amusing stories to tell. … My feelings on the score were born out, I felt, when *I Kid You Not* attained the number two spot among the non-fiction bestsellers, despite the hoots or silence of most of the critics. Even though no New York paper mentioned the book, except for a couple of uncomplimentary lines in one sheet, it sold over 200,000 copies in hardcover and more than one million as a paperback — which gives some indication of the influence critics have on the sale of a book.

Jack Parr

These people who have monumentally unsuccessful lives, and who are talented and bright, and then somehow think that they're smarter than everyone else. I question that a little, honestly. If you're so bright, why is your life so horrifying?

James Patterson

[An] army of reviewers who prefer the perfection of mediocrity to the imperfection of genius.

Max Perkins

Each generation of critics takes the opposite of the truth accepted by their predecessors.

Marcel Proust

To lend freshness to things known, to spread knowledge of things new; an excellent program for a critic.

Charles Augustin Sainte-Beuve

You know Plato's contempt for the image of an image. But as a man's view of things is an image in the first place, and his work is an image of that, and the critic's feelings are an image of that work, and his writings in the image of his feelings, and your idea of what the critic means only an image of his writings, please consider that you are steeping your poor original tea leaves in their fifth wash of hot water, and are drinking slops.

George Santayana

Each story has an author, and each author had an aim in writing it. I

”

Oh! my critics! My critics have almost shredded me to pieces, with all the love or hate in the world! In life, as in art, one can't please everybody, and that's a situation that's always with us. One is always receiving kisses and slaps, caresses and kicks, and that is the life of the poet.

Pablo Neruda

"

We [Maori] like to say that our ancestors are not behind us, they are in front of us. So every time I engage in a book, I am engaging with the ancestor in front of me, the ancestor who interrogates me on who I am, where I come from. The very essence of who Maori are and where we come from is under threat. And I don't like it. I see my writing as drawing a line in the sand.

Witi Ihimaera

believe it to be the critic's function to discover that aim and then, and then only, to pronounce whether the aim has been well or ill achieved.

Dorothy L. Sayers

We should comport ourselves with the masterpieces of art as with exalted personages — stand quietly before them and wait till they speak to us.

Arthur Schopenhauer

Pay no attention to what the critics say. No statue has ever been put up to a critic.

Jean Sibelius

Time is the only critic without ambition.

John Steinbeck

A louse in the locks of literature.

Alfred, Lord Tennyson, of critic Churton Collins

A good drama critic is one who perceives what is happening in the theater of his time. A great drama critic also perceives what is not happening.

Kenneth Tynan

I realize that every writer is necessarily a critic — that is, each sentence is a skeleton accompanied by enormous activity of rejection; and each selection is governed by general principles concerning truth, force, beauty, and so on.

Thornton Wilder

The implied position of the people who know about literature (as is also the case in every other part) is simply that they know what they know, and that they are determined to impose their opinions by main force of eloquence or assertion on the people who do not know.

Edmund Wilson

Culture & Popular Culture

Cultural memory is not bestowed upon us from above. The story of how we live, love, hate and laugh is passed down and across the generations. We have the choice of having our view be as unrestricted as the gaze across the Kansas prairie, or as narrow as the white dot, all that's left when the television set is turned off, before it darkens into oblivion.

Zora Neale Hurston

Anything that aims at engaging the imagination, that aims at decision-making, at the process of self-definition, is adversary to the popular culture. The popular culture says, in fact, the very opposite — Do what you do, your life is predestined, like the installment plan on your house. There's not much you can do about it. Make your payments, live it, get sick, die, don't make any trouble. It is the Master Charge of destiny. Try to get your high credit rating. Life is perceived as an accumulation of objects rather than as an accumulation of experiences or of human reactions. The consumer culture, the life of collectivity, tells us we are already written off in terms of the plot of our lives.

Jerzy Kosinski

Culture is worth a little risk. I am willing to gamble with certain elements in society to save this man's talent.

Norman Mailer, defending paroled killer Jack Henry Abbott after he had murdered a waiter in a dispute

Storytelling is about bringing the context into focus and bringing the thing that context usually brings into focus. I have this sense that human beings spend most of their lives with more or less of a layer of culture between them and the life they are actually living. That there is always something getting in the way. And that a good story points that out. It doesn't shatter that … But it reminds you that you are in essence following some script. Sometimes a very small one, sometimes an overarching predetermining one. And maybe that script is taking you places you don't particularly want to be going. And you want to tweak that. For me, that's the moral heart at the center of storytelling — is to step back a little and point out the ways in which so many assumptions, learned patterns and behaviors just dictate to us and guide us in ways that we don't think about.

Dale Peck

All of writing is a huge lake. There are great rivers that feed the lake, like Tolstoy or Dostoevsky. And then there are mere trickles, like Jean Rhys. All that matters is feeding the lake. I don't matter. The lake matters. You must keep feeding the lake.

Jean Rhys

The book has become a product like any other — that is the price of the marketization of culture. Unwilling or unable to put time and effort into educating ourselves about the options, we end up buying what everybody else buys. Worse, we start enjoying the books we are manipulated into buying — even defending them against pretentious jerks who dare criticize them. In exactly the same way that we slowly become Ikea-people, we also become Booker Prize-people, Harry Potter-people, Stephen King-people.

Dubravka Ugresic, Croatian novelist

Deadlines

I love deadlines. I love the whooshing noise they make as they go by.

Douglas Adams

I always feel that I can do whatever it is I have to do. But looking back I can see that it's a pattern of mind to put off writing that I really care about. It goes back to high school, when I was the salutatorian, and I didn't start writing my speech until after midnight the day before graduation. I always swear that it will never happen again, but on the other hand I've never missed a deadline.

Tom Wolfe

Decisions

Most decisions are seat-of-the-pants judgments. You can create a rationale for anything. In the end, most decisions are based on intuition and faith.

Nathan Myhrvold, business executive

Dedications

To My Wife: / To whom I owe the leaping delight / That quickens my senses in our waking time / And the rhythm that governs the repose of our / sleeping time, the breathing in unison.

T.S. Eliot, to The Elder Statesman

My dear Stella, I have always regarded this as my best book — at any rate as the best book of mine of a pre-war period; and between its writing and the appearance of my next novel nearly 10 years have elapsed, so that whatever I may have since written may be regarded as the work of a different man — as the work of your man. For it is

”

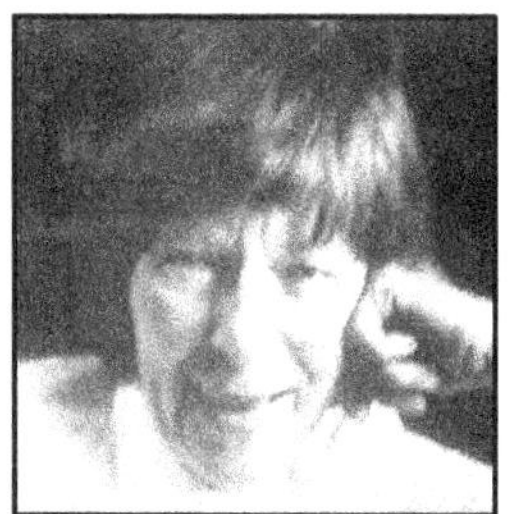

The day I finished the book ["Underfoot in Show Business"], I celebrated by phoning Maxine [Stuart, an actress,] in Hollywood.

"Do you want to hear the dedication?" I asked her.

"Go ahead," said Maxine.

So I read it to her: "To all the stagestruck kids who ever have, or ever will, set out to crash the theatre."

"What do you think of it?" I asked.

"It's much too sentimental," said Maxine. "Why don't you just dedicate it to me?"

So what the hell — This book is for Maxine.

Helene Hanff

”

To my wife: I carry you like a passport everywhere.

Graham Greene, to Journey Without Maps. *Changed after his divorce to: "To my cousin Barbara Strachwitz"*

Remember that you should be able to identify each character by what he or she says. Each one must sound different from the others. And they should not all sound like you.

Anne Lamott

certain that without the incentive to live that you offered me I should scarcely have survived the war-period and it is more certain still that without your spurring me again to write it I should never have written it again. And it happens that, by a queer chance, *The Good Soldier* is almost alone amongst my books in being dedicated to no one: Fate must have elected to let it wait the 10 years that it waited — for this dedication ... And so I subscribe myself in all truth and in the hope that you will accept at once the particular dedication of this book and the general dedication of this edition. Your FMF.

Ford Madox Ford, for a new edition of The Good Soldier

To my daughter Leonora, without whose never-failing sympathy and encouragement this book would have been finished in half the time.

P.G. Wodehouse

To Maxwell Evarts Perkins: A great editor and a brave and honest man, who stuck to the writer of this book through times of bitter hopelessness and doubt and would not let him give in to his own despair, a work to be known as *Of Time and the River* is dedicated with the hope that all of it may be in some way worthy of the loyal devotion and the patient care which a dauntless and unshaken friend has given to each part of it, and without which none of it could have been written.

Thomas Wolfe, Of Time and the River *(1935). The following year, Wolfe left his editor for another publishing house.*

Depression

You spend long hours sitting on your own. Writing can be wonderful therapy, but you are digging into yourself, and if you are writing fiction and creating characters, a certain amount of self-examination and self-doubt is inevitable. Now that there are reviews on Amazon, for example, that happens even more.

Simon Brett

You have to be well. If you're properly clinically depressed, you can't think about rhyme.

Gwyneth Lewis

Dialogue

1. Dialogue should be brief.
2. It should add to the reader's present knowledge.
3. It should eliminate the routine exchanges of ordinary conversation.
4. It should convey a sense of spontaneity but eliminate the repetitiveness of real talk.
5. It should keep the story moving forward.
6. It should be revelatory of the speaker's character, both directly and indirectly.
7. It should show the relationships among people.

Elizabeth Bowen

Explore ways to improve your writing of dialogue by asking what should I have said instead of what I did say. We walk away from situations all the time saying to ourselves, Damn, I wish I would have said this instead of that. That's dialogue. Pay attention to it. Making notes on this stuff is one way you'll learn to write better dialogue. Pay attention to how you say what you say in your head, trust that it's the best way to put something to writing. And make a habit of writing these things down, otherwise you'll be stuck in your head and that might drive you nuts.

Hampton Fancher, screenwriter

A man or woman who does not write good dialogue is not a first-rate writer.

George V. Higgins

The main thing with my dialogue is the rhythm of it — the way people talk, not especially what they say.

Elmore Leonard

Dialogue which does not move the story along, or add to the mood of the story, or have an easily definable reason for being there at all (such as to establish important characterization), should be considered superfluous and therefore cut.

Bill Pronzini

Dialogue has to show not only something about the speaker that is its own revelation, but also maybe something about the speaker that he doesn't know but the other character does know.

Eudora Welty

Diaries

Although I have felt compelled to write things down since I was five years old, I doubt that my daughter ever will, for she is a singularly blessed and accepting child, delighted with life exactly as life presents itself to her, unafraid to go to sleep and unafraid to wake up. Keepers of private notebooks are a different breed altogether, lonely and resistant rearrangers of things, anxious malcontents, children afflicted apparently at birth with some presentiment of loss.

Joan Didion

Each young and ardent person writes a diary, in which, when the hours of prayer and penitence arrive, he inscribes his soul. The pages thus written are, to him, burning and fragrant: he reads them on his knees by midnight and by the morning star; he wets them with his tears; they are sacred; too good for the world, and hardly yet to be shown to the dearest friend. This is the man-child that is born to the soul, and her life still circulates in the babe. The umbilical cord has not yet been cut. After some time has elapsed, he begins to wish to admit his friend to this hallowed experience, and with hesitation, yet with firmness, exposes the pages to his eyes. Will they not burn his eyes? The friend coldly turns them over, and passes from the writing to conversation, with easy transition, which strikes the other party with astonishment and vexation. He cannot suspect the writing itself. Days and nights of fervid life, of communion with angels of darkness and of light, have engraved their shadowy characters on that tear-stained book. He suspects the intelligence or the heart of his friend. Is there then no friend?

Ralph Waldo Emerson

I had started keeping a journal, and I was discovering that I didn't need school in order to experience the misery of appearances. I could manufacture excruciating embarrassment in the privacy of my bedroom, simply by reading what I'd written in the journal the day before. Its pages faithfully mirrored my fraudulence and pomposity and immaturity. Reading it made me desperate to change myself, to sound less idiotic.

Jonathan Franzen

In the diary you find proof that in situations which today would seem

”

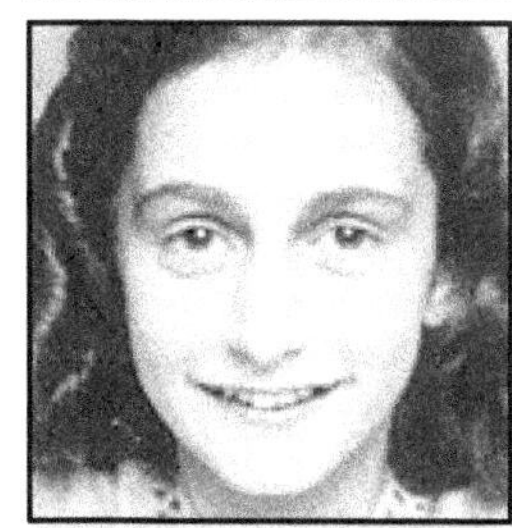

It's an odd idea for someone like me to keep a diary; not only because I have never done so before, but because it seems to me that neither I — nor for that matter anyone else — will be interested in the unbosomings of a thirteen-year-old school girl.

Anne Frank

I've been keeping a diary for thirty-three years and write in it every morning. Most of it's just whining, but every so often there'll be something I can use later: a joke, a description, a quote. It's an invaluable aid when it comes to winning arguments. "That's not what you said on February 3, 1996," I'll say to someone.

David Sedaris

unbearable, you lived, looked around and wrote down observations, that this right hand moved then as it does today, when we may be wiser because we are able to look back upon our former condition, and for that very reason have got to admit the courage of our earlier striving in which we persisted even in sheer ignorance.

Franz Kafka

This diary is my kief, hashish, and opium pipe. This is my drug and my vice. Instead of writing a novel, I lie back with this book and a pen, and dream, and indulge in refractions and defractions … I must relive my life in the dream. The dream is my only life. I see in the echoes and reverberations, the transfigurations which alone keep wonder pure. Otherwise all magic is lost.

Anaïs Nin

I am thinking now of what I read today (when I went up to 122 Bd. St-G to check for her mail) in H's journal about me — that curt, unfair, uncharitable assessment of me which concludes by her saying that she really doesn't like me but my passion for her is acceptable and opportune. God knows it hurts, and I feel indignant and humiliated. … Do I feel guilty about reading what was not intended for my eyes? No. One of the main (social) functions of a journal or diary is precisely to be read furtively by other people, the people (like parents + lovers) about whom one has been cruelly honest only in the journal.

Susan Sontag

What is a diary as a rule? A document useful to the person who keeps it, dull to the contemporary who reads it, invaluable to the student, centuries afterward, who treasures it!

Ellen Terry, actress

Discipline

I like a certain amount of distraction. It keeps me from being anxious. It keeps things at a little bit more of an arm's length.

Chuck Close

All this advice from senior writers to establish a discipline — always to get down a thousand words a day whatever one's mood — I find an absurdly Puritanical and impractical approach. Write, if you must, because you feel like writing, never because you ought to write.

John Fowles

Recollect that only when habits of order are formed can we advance to really interesting fields of action — and consequently accumulate grain on grain of wilful choice like a very miser — never forgetting how one link dropped undoes an indefinite number.

William James, who according to biographer Robert D. Richardson lived a "buzzing blooming confusion" life of few habits

Discipline is never a restraint. It's an aid. The first commandment of the romantic school is: "Don't worry about grammar, spelling, pronunciation, vocabulary, plot or structure — just let it come." That's not writing; that's vomiting, and it leads to uncontrolled, unreadable prose. Remember: easy writing makes hard reading, but hard writing makes it easy reading.

Florence King

I know that to sustain these true

moments of insight one has to be highly disciplined, lead a disciplined life.

Henry Miller

I am disciplined — that's my wiring. I have a fast writing pace — also just wiring. I was educated (nine years of Catholic school) by the nuns. Nobody lays a foundation of discipline like the Sisters. Trust me on this. I was raised by parents who instilled, and demonstrated by example, the responsibility of doing your work, doing it well, meeting your responsibilities. I don't miss deadlines.

Nora Roberts

I had no discipline. I didn't know that you needed some kind of schedule. No one ever said to me, it's not about inspiration; you have to sit down. You have to write. I spent a long time just walking around thinking, Well! I'm uninspired.

Saïd Sayrafiezadeh

Flaubert's "Faire et se taire." This translates as "Do your work and keep quiet about it" — though interviews like this one would soon fizzle out if we all took that advice. I like to (mis)translate it as "Shut up and get on with it."

Helen Simpson, describing a note she keeps over her desk

Discouragement

A writer's life is only ever acceptance or rejection, surfeit or famine, and nothing in between. That's an emotionally draining way to live. As a result, it isn't necessary to discourage young writers. Life will do that soon enough. There are yards of writers under the age of 30, but not many who stay the course. The ones who do aren't necessarily the most gifted but those who can focus well, discipline themselves, persevere through hard times, and spring back after rejections that would cripple others.

Diane Ackerman

I feel generally resentful of younger writers. You're not thrilled to see some blazing talent coming up on your flank. Dislike and resentment of younger writers is something fairly universal among writers.

Martin Amis

If you want to write badly enough, then you're going to be doing it, you're not going to be talking about it. And nothing I can say is going to take you the first step.

Clive Barker

The most difficult thing about this work, by far, is being convinced that one's writing is no good. And this has been increasingly a problem in the past several years. Early on, I sailed blissfully along — a lot of what I wrote then wasn't very good, but I never doubted it at all. Now, when the work is generally pretty good, or certainly as good as it's ever been for me, while I'm writing, I'm consumed with doubt and anxiety about it. I think one reason, maybe, is that the stakes are higher; people expect more; I get paid more.

Lawrence Block

There are moments when I positively lose heart. For whom and for what do I write? ... Does the public need me or not? I cannot make it out. Write for money? But I never have money, and from the habit of it I am almost indifferent to it. For the sake of money I work poorly.

Anton Chekhov

Practice means to perform, over and over again in the face of all obstacles, some act of vision, of faith, of desire. Practice is a means of inviting the perfection desired.

Martha Graham, dancer

Literature will neither yield the bread, nor a stomach to digest bread with; quit it in God's name.

Thomas Carlyle, to Ralph Waldo Emerson

I sometimes think that I'm just one of the people who comes here every day and does it, even though I don't feel like it, even though it's difficult and I feel stupid and brain-dead and unequal to the task. ... I think a certain fearlessness in the face of your own ineptitude is a useful tool.

Michael Cunningham

Your life story would not make a good book. Don't even try.

Fran Lebowitz

Q: What do you do when you feel like giving up?

There is no such goddamn thing. There is only getting up and doing it all over again, smarter and harder, until something ups and fucking kills you, because that's the only thing big enough to stop you. This is The Great Work, and all you have to do is choose it, not look back and never fucking stop until you're in your box, under the dirt and flowers are growing between your teeth. And that is why I'll never be asked to do motivational speaking. G'night.

Warren Ellis

In the burning core of what I believe to be true about the art and craft of writing, I know that one *cannot* discourage a *real* writer. Like von Kleist, "I write only because I cannot stop." And that is the way of it for a *real* writer, not for the fuzzyheaded dreamer or parvenu who thinks it's an easy way to make fame and fortune. You can break a real writer's hands, and s/he will tap out the words with noses and toes. Anyone who can be discouraged, *should* be. They will be happier and more useful to the commonweal as great ballerinas, fine sculptors, sensitive jurists, accomplished historians, imaginative scientists.

Harlan Ellison

Most people who seek attention and regard by announcing that they're writing a novel are actually so devoid of narrative talent that they can't hold the attention of a dinner table for 30 seconds, even with a dirty joke.

Paul Fussell

As for giving up, well, sure, if you want to. Being a writer is a very peculiar sort of a job: it's always you versus a blank sheet of paper (or a blank screen) and quite often the blank piece of paper wins. It has no job security of any kind, and depends mostly on whether or not you can, like Scheherazade, tell the stories each night that'll keep you alive until tomorrow. There are undoubtedly hundreds of easier, less stressful, more straightforward jobs in the world. Personally, I can't think of anything else I'd rather do, but that's me.

Neil Gaiman

I'd get sick of it. I'd want to sleep later some mornings, or go to bed early some nights. I had a lot of self-doubt. I'd walk in a bookstore and see all those books and think, "Who wants to read this story I'm writing?" I'd see all those books and think, "There's no room for me up there." I'd see articles about how Americans don't read much anymore. There are always thousands of reasons not to do something. You can always think of more reasons not to do it than to do it.

John Grisham

Everyone has a book inside them, which is exactly where I think it should, in most cases, remain.

Christopher Hitchens

You tell me never to despair — I wish it was as easy for me to observe the saying — truth is I have a horrid Morbidity of Temperament which has shown itself at intervals — it is I have no doubt the greatest Enemy and stumbling block I have to fear — I may even say that it is likely to be the cause of my disappointment.

John Keats

If a man has no constant lover who shares his soul as well as his body, he must have a diary — a poor substitute, but better than nothing. That is all there is to it in my case.

James Lees-Milne, English diarist

The pen has become to me what the oar is to a galley slave.

C.S. Lewis, on his daily habit of responding to all his fan mail

But I hate my book. Read, edit, wince, print, scowl, rewrite, print, stock printer with paper, change ink, despair, doubt self-worth, consider Amway career, repeat. This is why I hate the final stages of book preparation — by the time you've finished prepping it for the publisher, you just hate it. There's nothing new or original. Oh, now and then a bit of mild japery prods a glimmer of a grin, but that's rare. Of course, I thought this about the *Gallery [of Regrettable Food]*, and it went over well, so let's hope [*Interior Desecrations*] isn't the career-ending wadocrap it looks like now.

James Lileks

I would quit while you're ahead. Really, it's an awful field. Just torture. Awful. You write and write, and you have to throw almost all of it away because it's not any good. I would say just stop now. You don't want to do this to yourself. That's my advice to you.

Philip Roth

My mother said as I graduated from high school that I had plagiarized Sara Teasdale. Something about a statement of hers ... I had been writing a poem a day for three months, but when she said that, I stopped. ... My mother was top billing in our house.

Anne Sexton

[The world] does not ask people to write poems and novels and histories; it does not need them. It does not care whether Flaubert finds the right word or whether Carlyle scrupulously verifies this or that fact. Naturally, it will not pay for what it does not want.

Virginia Woolf

I have a distinct feeling about people who think of writing. It is this. If anything can stop them it is probably no great loss.

Alexander Woollcott

Dreaming

Many characters have come to me … in a dream, and then I'll elaborate from there. I always write down all my dreams.

William S. Burroughs

Don't let anybody tell you you're wasting your time when you're gazing into space. There is no other way to conceive an imaginary world... I daydream about my characters... Take pen and paper and try to report what I've witnessed.

Stephen Vizinczey

Drugs

I've tried it long ago, with hashish and peyote. Fascinating, yes, but no good, no. This, as we find in alcohol, is an *escape* from awareness, a cheat, a momentary substitution, and in the end a destruction of it. With luck, someone might have a fragmentary *Kubla Khan* vision. But with no meaning. And with the steady destruction of the observing and remembering mind.

Conrad Aiken

”

We write to be able to transcend our life, to reach beyond it. We write to teach ourselves to speak with others, to record our journey into the labyrinth, we write to expand our world, when we feel strangled, constricted, lonely. We write as the birds sing. As the primitive dance their rituals. If you do not breathe through writing, if you do not cry out in writing, or sing in writing, then don't write, because our culture has no use for it.

Anaïs Nin

I keep going on gin and Dexedrine.

Georgette Heyer

My first reaction, rereading these stories, was oh my God, accompanied by physical symptoms we shouldn't dwell upon.

Thomas Pynchon

The chemical life.

W.H. Auden, referring to his daily dose of Benzedrine, which, with alcohol, coffee, and tobacco he considered "labor-saving devices"

I have absolutely *no* pleasure in the stimulants in which I sometimes so madly indulge. It has not been in the pursuit of pleasure that I have periled life and reputation and reason. It has been the desperate attempt to escape from torturing memories, from a sense of insupportable loneliness and a dread of some strange impending doom.

Edgar Allan Poe

Early Works

Ah, yes, I wrote the "Purple Cow,"
I'm Sorry, now, I wrote it;
But I can tell you, Anyhow
I'll Kill you if you Quote it!

Gelett Burgess

Think of it as something written by an earnest young graduate student rather than anything I did.

Orson Scott Card, of his early short story "Happy Head," which he refuses to have reprinted

Aargh. If I stick my fingers in my ears, I can't hear you reading this.

Terry Pratchett, on reprinting his first published short story in his collection A Blink of the Screen *(2012)*

I wish the unhappy little thing, representing all that I came (so soon after) to fervently dislike, could be buried for ever.

J.R.R. Tolkien, of his poem "Goblin Feet" with its twee lines ("O! I hear the tiny horns / Of enchanted leprechauns / And the padded feet of many gnomes a-coming!")

Editing Advice

All bones look much the same. The hair and skin are what make us recognizable.

Margaret Atwood, when an editor defended his edits of her essay with "[I'd] left the bones where they were, and just moved around some of the skin and hair"

Irrelevance, in any part, is a cloud and a drag on, a weakener of, the novel. It dilutes meaning. Relevance crystallizes meaning.

Elizabeth Bowen

If rewriting is necessary, I always rewrite from emotion. If a scene needs to be redone, I throw out the old one, refuse to look at it and do an entire new scene boldly and in high fever. If one tried to rewrite as coldly as one analyzed the problem, again one would wind up with two kinds of fish, one dead and one alive. So rewriting must be an identical process to the original one that got the story off in the first place.

Ray Bradbury

Dumbest, deafest, shittest [sic] of all, you have removed the unstressed "a" so that the stress that should have fallen on "nosh" is lost, and my piece ends on an unstressed syllable. When you're winding up a piece of prose, metre is crucial. Can't you hear? Can't you hear that it is wrong? It's not fucking rocket science. It's fucking pre-[General Certificate of Secondary Education] scansion. I have written 350 restaurant reviews for *The Times* and I have never ended on an unstressed syllable. Fuck. fuck, fuck, fuck.

Giles Coren, email to the editor who changed his restaurant review so it ended with "boys and girls in the street outside smiling gaily to each other, and wondering where to go for nosh"

It has been my opinion for years — not simply as a hastening critic, anxious to finish a book, but as an ordinary reader — that most books suffer from being too long; there is a *right* length for every book, whether it is 900 pages or 90, but most writers overshoot the mark because they will not tighten their work.

Robertson Davies

You have no idea of the labour inseparable from the editing of such a Journal as *All The Year Round*, when you suppose it within the bounds of possibility that those who discharge such duties can give critical reasons for the rejection of papers. To read professed contributions honestly, and communicate a perfectly unprejudiced decision respecting every one of them to its author or authoress, is a task, of the magnitude of which you evidently have no conception.

Charles Dickens, to a complaining contributor

In all the proof that has reached me, windrow has been spelled window. If, in the bound book, windrow still appears as window, then neither rain nor hail nor gloom of night nor fleets of riot squads will prevent me from assassinating the man who is responsible. If the coward hides behind my finding, I shall step into Scribner's and merely shoot up the place Southern style.

Gordon Dorrance

Try to preserve an author's style if he is an author and has a style.

Wolcott Gibbs

Read over your compositions, and where ever you meet with a passage which you think is particularly fine, strike it out.

Samuel Johnson

I would write a book, or a short story, at least three times — once to understand it, the second time to improve the prose, and a third to compel it to say what it still must say.

Bernard Malamud

As I begin the work of editing, coarse and fine, I begin to understand the cliché "God is in the details." It's also the case that failed intentions are in the details, and confusion is in the details, and the unconscious is in the details, and camouflaged freight is in the details, and deception is in the details, and self-deception is in the details, and provocation is in the details, and surreptitious editorializing is in the details, and so on. God — if by God the agnostic means precision, clarity, genuine feeling, accuracy — is in the details only when the writer (or speaker, for that matter) knows himself and exactly what he is doing: rare.

Daniel Menaker

Rely on the sudden erection of your small dorsal hairs.

Vladimir Nabokov

Part of being a writer is being able to read what you've written and see what's missing, see what needs development, see what's suggested by what you wrote. It's like a trampoline. You know, you're jumping up and down on this draft, and each jump is an idea.

Philip Roth

In composing, as a general rule, run your pen over every other word you have written; you have no idea what vigor it will give to your style.

Sydney Smith

"

What lasts in the reader's mind is not the phrase but the effect the phrase created: laughter, tears, pain, joy. If the phrase is not affecting the reader, what's it doing there? Make it do its job or cut it without mercy or remorse.

Isaac Asimov

The most important lesson in the writing trade is that any manuscript is improved if you cut away the fat.

Robert Heinlein

An editor should have a pimp for a brother, so he'd have somebody to look up to.

Gene Fowler

Stay grounded to the people you love. Watch out for ego exploitation, as it will turn your success into a wall behind which you will be very lonely.

Ottessa Moshfegh

Write freely and as rapidly as possible and throw the whole thing on paper. Never correct or rewrite until the whole thing is down. Rewrite in process is usually found to be an excuse for not going on.

John Steinbeck

Blot out, correct, insert, refine,
Enlarge, diminish, interline;
Be mindful, when invention fails,
To scratch your head, and bite your nails.

Jonathan Swift

A successful book is not made of what is *in* it, but what is left *out* of it.

Mark Twain

Editors

My definition of a good editor is a man who I think charming, who sends me large checks, praises my work, my physical beauty, and my sexual prowess, and who has a stranglehold on the publisher and the bank.

John Cheever

Perhaps, but so are most writers.

T.S. Eliot, when asked if most editors were failed writers

Some editors will "get" what you write; others won't. The key is to have patience to learn from the criticisms of the former, the strength to ignore the indifference of the latter, and the wisdom (and good luck) to know the difference between the two.

Bruce Feirstein

Everyone needs an editor.

Tim Foote, commenting on Adolf Hitler's original title for Mein Kampf: Four-and-a-Half Years of Struggle Against Lies, Stupidity, and Cowardice.

An editor has to be selfless and yet also has to be strong-minded. If you don't know what you think, or if you're nervous about expressing your opinion, what good is that to a writer?

Robert Gottlieb

Editor: A person employed by a newspaper whose business it is to separate the wheat from the chaff and to see that the chaff is printed.

Elbert Hubbard

Take joy in the fact that someone read your book carefully enough to notice that a character's January birthday actually equates to a different sign in the Chinese zodiac than you thought, because Chinese New Year is in February. Or that that department store didn't exist yet in Chicago in 1985. Or that Blue Öyster Cult is spelled with an umlaut.

Kelly Luce

He and I share a belief that if you take care of all the tiny problems in a piece, all the small attention will somehow make a big difference. Sometimes I think that's just a touching faith of ours, and that, in fact, nobody ever notices whether, say, you use the same word twice in a paragraph. At other times I'm convinced that the details are all that matter.

Charles McGrath, of editor Robert Gottlieb

I never write with Bob [Gottlieb, editor] in mind; that would be very bad for me. He isn't the ideal reader for the product, but he is the ideal editor for it.

Toni Morrison

By "editor," I suppose you mean proofreader. Among these I have known limpid creatures of limitless tact and tenderness who would discuss with me a semicolon as if it were a point of honor — which, indeed a point of art often is. But I have also come across a few pompous avuncular brutes who would attempt to make a "suggestion" which I countered with a thunderous "stet."

Vladimir Nabokov

An editor is often a father figure, a mother figure, a kind of ministerial figure. … Someone who stands in authority over you and has something to tell you.

Cynthia Ozick

An editor does not add to a book. At best he serves as a handmaiden to an author. Don't ever get to feeling important about yourself, because an editor at most releases energy. He creates nothing.

Max Perkins

I found him authoritative, but he also had that nice quality of saying, "all right, if that's what you feel." I think a good editor does that, unless you're obviously headed for the cliffs.

James Salter

Education

(See **Academia, MFA Programs**)

The last thing in the world I would do was waste my time going to college, because I knew what I wanted to do. … If you want to be a writer, and you are a writer already, and you can spell, there's no reason to go to college.

Truman Capote

You don't have to go to college to get an education — all you have to do is open up a damn book. You can learn anything in a book. Anything.

Terry McMillan

There is no true expertise in the humanities without knowing all of the humanities. Art is a vast, ancient interconnected webwork, a fabricated tradition. Over-concentration on any one point is a distortion.

Camille Paglia

Most people won't realize that writing is a craft. You have to take your apprenticeship in it like anything else.

Katherine Anne Porter

There's nothing worse than the writer who learns to do something and then goes on doing it because it's comfortable and safe. It is a gift of wings, and you learn to trust yourself, that you will not fall — or if you do, that you will just sweep up again.

Jeanette Winterson

Ego

The trick is not caring about what everybody thinks of you and just caring about what the right people think of you.

Brian Michael Bendis

I've known all my life I could take a bunch of words and throw them up in the air and they would come down just right. I'm a semantic Paganini.

Truman Capote

Writers are too self-centered to be lonely.

Richard Condon

I am an enormously talented man, after all, it's no use pretending that I am not, and I was bound to succeed.

Noël Coward

When you're all alone out there, on

”

I am to my generation what Charles Dickens was to his.

Harold Robbins

What is the worst is a fashion designer who talks all the time of his or her creativity, what they are, how they evolve it. Just do it and shut up.

Karl Lagerfeld

Follow your curiosity and passion. What fascinates you will probably fascinate others. But, even if it doesn't, you will have devoted your life to what you love.

Diane Ackerman

Take out another notebook, pick up another pen, and just write, just write, just write. In the middle of the world, make one positive step. In the center of chaos, make one definitive act. Just write. Say yes, stay alive, be awake. Just write. Just write. Just write.

Natalie Goldberg

the end of the typewriter, with each new story a new appraisal by the world of whether you can still get it up or not, arrogance and self-esteem and deep breathing are all you have. It often looks like egomania. I assure you it's the bold cover-up of the absolutely terrified.

Harlan Ellison

Writing a novel, especially a long novel, is an immense act of ego. You're not only asking people to pursue your vision, you are also asking them to pay to do so — and to applaud.

William Gaddis

I don't care what is written about me so long as it isn't true.

Katharine Hepburn

Don't they know I'm Amy Lowell? And it was this month that my book of poems was coming out here! What attention will it get with this going on? What has happened to England? Why doesn't she simply stop the war?

Amy Lowell, referring to the outbreak of World War I during her visit to London

Every author, however modest, keeps a most outrageous vanity chained like a madman in the padded cell of his breast.

Logan Pearsall Smith

I'm one of the five most translated writers in the world. There's Tolstoy, Gorky, Jules Verne, somebody else, and me.

Mickey Spillane

I am foolish over my own book. I have a copy which I constantly read and find very illuminating. Swift confesses to something of the sort with his own compositions.

W.B. Yeats

Embarrassment

Compulsive avoidance of embarrassment is a form of suicide.

Colin Marshall

Emotions

Differences ... simplify character distinctions [and] maximize emotional legibility.

Brian Boyd

We romantic writers are there to make people feel and not think.

Barbara Cartland

The less one feels a thing, the better one is able to express it.

Gustave Flaubert

The job of the writer is to present emotionally significant events at an aesthetic distance that enables us to recognize them, experience them, and assimilate them to ourselves.

Keith Oatley

Your reader reads first and foremost for emotional stimulation

Dwight Swain

Encouragement

Every human being has exactly the same amount of time, and yet consider the output of Robert Louis Stevenson, John Peabody Harrington, Isaac Asimov, Ray Bradbury, William Goldman, Neil Simon, Joyce Carol Oates, Agatha Christie, and John Gardner. How did they accomplish what they have? They weren't deflected from their priorities by activities of lesser importance. The work continues, even though everything else may have to give. They know that their greatest resource is themselves. Wasting time is wasting themselves. When people ask them, "Where'd you find the time?" They wonder, "Where do you lose it?"

Kenneth Atuchity

Whom the gods wish to destroy they first call promising.

Cyril Connolly

Nothing great was ever achieved without enthusiasm.

Ralph Waldo Emerson, borrowing from Samuel Taylor Coleridge

I have never understood why "hard work" is supposed to be pitiable. True, some work is soul-destroying when it is done against the grain, but when it is part of "making," how can you grudge it? You get tired, of course, but the struggle, the challenge, the feeling of being extended as you never thought you could be is fulfilling and deeply, deeply satisfying.

Rumer Godden

Many people die with their music still in them. Why is this so? Too often it is because they are always getting ready to live. Before they know it, time runs out.

Oliver Wendell Holmes

Writing a novel is a very hard thing to do because it covers so long a space of time, and if you get discouraged it is not a bad sign, but a good one. If you think you are not doing it well, you are thinking the way real novelists do. I never knew one who did not feel greatly discouraged at times, and some get desperate, and I have always found that to be a good symptom.

Max Perkins

Beware of *cleverness*; think of nothing but greatness. Make up your mind to write the greatest short stories in the world, and do not permit yourself even to dream that you cannot write them. You may not do it; but the attempt will be there, and the attempt will count.

Edwin Arlington Robinson

Leave the dishes unwashed and the demands on your time unanswered. Be ruthless and refuse to do what people ask of you.

Lynne Sharon Schwartz

Try stuff. Make your best stab and keep stabbing. If it's there in your heart, it will eventually find its way out. Or you will give up and have a prudent, contented life doing something else.

Teller, of Penn and Teller

A note: despair at the badness of the book; can't think how I ever could write such stuff — and with such excitement: that's yesterday: today I think it good again. A note, by way of advising other Virginias with other books that this is the way of the thing: up down up down — and Lord knows the truth.

Virginia Woolf

Believe in your own identity and your own opinions. Proceed with confidence, generating it, if necessary, by pure willpower. Writing is an act of ego and you might as well admit it. Use its energy to keep yourself going.

William Zinsser

Endings

I have no idea what the word "epiphany" means. It's been explained to me many times, and there's something about the idea of it that I simply reject. It seems like a word you'd use to describe something that is only real in the most vague way possible. As such,

They have to come to a bad end, see, because that way the people who read me can get off the subway and go home feeling better about their own crappy lives and luckier than the people they've been reading about.

Jacqueline Susann, about why she made her rich and beautiful characters suffer

”

The writer's vanity holds that everything that happens to him is material ... As he submerges himself in the bilge of everyday life, in all its disorder and tedium, he holds his thumb out at arm's length and squints, as if to get a take on this patch of swarming nonsense. Each new occurrence offers a new end to the story, in the light of which everything that proceeds must be revised.

Edmund White

it's something that can't really happen in a piece of writing. Of course it does occur marvelously and beautifully in many pieces of writing, but it really is so complex and subtle that I can never quite identify it as a thing you'd call "epiphany."

Deborah Eisenberg

Good endings ought to be satisfying and both surprising and inevitable. I couldn't have plotted, say, the last chapter in *The Graveyard Book* without having written the book that came before it, because now I knew what my book was about and how it had to end.

Neil Gaiman

Why worry about the ending anyway? Why be such a control freak? Sooner or later every story comes out *somewhere.*

Stephen King

People love to see others suffer and lose. Perhaps this trend toward losers explains the horror vogue in the same period [late 1960s, early '70s]. From *Rosemary's Baby* to *The Omen, The Sentinel, Burnt Offerings,* and *The Stepford Wives,* we watched innocent people abused and destroyed by sinister forces beyond their awareness. The formula varies in small ways, but it remains a pornography of someone else's suffering.

Chuck Palahniuk

If one does not know to which port one is sailing, no wind is favorable.

Seneca the Younger

If you start out to write a poem about two dogs fucking, and you write a poem about two dogs fucking – then you wrote a poem about two dogs fucking.

Gerald Stern

Envy

The antidote to envy is one's own work. Always one's own work. Not the thinking about it. Not the assessing of it. But the doing of it. The answers you want can come only from the work itself. It drives the spooks away.

Jiddu Krishnamurti

On location in Wales, we slept in the same bedroom and I remember seeing him one morning staring into the mirror.

"Which is more horrible," he asked. "With a mustache or without one?"

"What do you want to look horrible for?" I asked.

"The only way to succeed," he said, "is to make people hate you. That way, they remember you."

Josef von Sternberg, actor and director

Epics

Long books, when read, are usually overpraised, because the reader wishes to convince others and himself that he has not wasted his time.

E.M. Forster

All bad writers are in love with the epic.

Ernest Hemingway

A long poem is a test of invention which I take to be the Polar star of poetry, as fancy is the sails, and imagination the rudder.

John Keats

Epigrams

What is an Epigram? A dwarfish

whole,
Its body brevity, and wit its soul.

Samuel Taylor Coleridge

Essays

The essay is a literary device for saying almost everything about almost anything.

Aldous Huxley

The essayist is a self-liberated man, sustained by the childish belief that everything he thinks about, everything that happens to him, is of general interest.

E.B. White

Evil

If Shakespeare returned to the earth to-morrow, and if it were found that his favourite recreation was raping little girls in railway carriages, we should not tell him to go ahead with it on the ground that he might write another *King Lear*.

George Orwell

To do evil a human being must first of all believe that what he's doing is good, or else that it's a well-considered act in conformity with natural law. ... it is in the nature of a human being to seek a justification for his actions.

Aleksandr Solzhenitsyn

Experience

A writer shouldn't be engaged with other writers, or with people who make books, or even with people who read them. The farther away you get from the literary traffic, the closer you are to sources. I mean, a writer doesn't really live, he observes.

Nelson Algren

You develop an extra sense that partly excludes you from experience. When writers experience things, they're not really experiencing them anything like 100 percent. They're always holding back and wondering what the significance is, or wondering how they'd do it on the page.

Martin Amis

You've got to get drunk and be in danger once in a while. You've got to fall in love, you've got to be hurt – this is an old story but it's exactly true. It's not just about prisons and it's not just about autopsies. It's about experiencing stuff. It's about writing out of your own pain, writing out of your own doubt, writing out of your own anger.

Clive Barker

Writing teachers invariably tell students, write about what you know. That's, of course, what you have to do, but on the other hand, how do you know what you know until you've written it? … I've had very little experience in my life. In fact, I try to avoid experience if I can. Most experience is bad.

E.L. Doctorow

Mostly, we authors must repeat ourselves – that's the truth. We have two or three great moving experiences in our lives – experiences so great and moving that it doesn't seem at the time that anyone else has been caught up and pounded and dazzled and astonished and beaten and broken and rescued and illuminated and rewarded and humbled in just that way ever before.

F. Scott Fitzgerald

Writers don't write from experience, though many are resistant to admit

”

It should surprise no one that the life of the writer — such as it is — is colorless to the point of sensory deprivation. Many writers do little else but sit in small rooms recalling the real world. This explains why so many books describe the author's childhood. A writer's childhood may well have been the occasion of his only firsthand experience.

Annie Dillard

”

All the things we experience in life can be separated into two realms, the realm of the concept and the realm of the senses.

Scott McCloud

How can you know that something is worth writing about if you haven't seen anything else?

Paul Theroux

that they don't. I want to be clear about that. If you wrote from experience, you'd get maybe one book, maybe three poems. Writers write from empathy.

Nikki Giovanni

Don't put down too many roots in terms of a domicile. I have lived in four countries and I think my life as a writer and our family's life have been enriched by this. I think a writer has to experience new environments. There is that adage: No man can really succeed if he doesn't move away from where he was born. I believe it is particularly true for the writer.

Arthur Hailey

(I wonder what Eudora Welty and Jane Austen would say to that?)

I think that if you're writing about the world, you should get out and deal with the world. I do that as much as I can. It's as important as reading. If you do nothing but read, and don't get into the world, you're inevitably going to replicate what you read. And that may be beautiful, but it could quite possibly be dead.

Colin Harrison

Experience is not a matter of having actually swum the Hellespont, or danced with the dervishes, or slept in a doss-house. It is a matter of sensibility and intuition, of seeing and hearing the significant things, of paying attention at the right moments, of understanding and coordinating. Experience is not what happens to a man; it is what a man does with what happens to him.

Aldous Huxley

Of course, you bank on your experience, but as a sounding board. It isn't that you write down what happens to you every day — you wouldn't be a writer if you did that. But it gives you a sense of, you know, from your experience what life is like, and you weigh what you invent against your sense of actuality.

Philip Roth

Go for broke. Always try and do too much. Dispense with safety nets. Take a deep breath before you begin talking. Aim for the stars. Keep grinning. Be bloody-minded. Argue with the world. And never forget that writing is as close as we get to keeping a hold on the thousand and one things … that go on slipping, like sand, through our fingers.

Salman Rushdie

In all my writing I tell the story of my life, over and over again. … Only the dilettantes try to be universal; a real writer knows that he's connected with a certain people, a certain time, a certain environment, and there he stays. There he stays put, I would say, and he doesn't mind it because there is enough to investigate and to learn even from a small world.

Isaac Bashevis Singer

How vain it is to sit down to write when you have not stood up to live!

Henry David Thoreau

Literature is an art, not an inspiration. It is a trade, so to speak, and must be learned. And its capital is experience. I wish to impress upon you this truth: that at the moment you venture outside your own experience, you are in peril. Whatever you have lived you can write & by your hard work and genuine apprenticeship you can learn to write well; but what you have not lived you cannot write, you can only pretend to write it.

Mark Twain

Facts

What is fictitious in a novel is not so much the story but the method by which thought develops into action, a method which never occurs in daily life.

Alain (a.k.a. E.A. Chartier)

What I often do nowadays when I have to, say, describe a room, is to take a page of a dictionary, any page at all, and see if with the words suggested by that one page in the dictionary I can build up a room, build up a scene. … I even did it in a novel I wrote called *MF*. There's a description of a hotel vestibule whose properties are derived from Page 167 in R.J. Wilkinson's *Malay-English Dictionary*. Nobody has noticed. … As most things in life are arbitrary anyway, you're not doing anything naughty, you're really normally doing what nature does, you're just making an entity out of the elements. I do recommend it to young writers.

Anthony Burgess

The author makes a tacit deal with the reader. You hand them a back-pack. You ask them to place certain things in it – to remember, to keep in mind – as they make their way up the hill. If you hand them a yellow Volkswagen and they have to haul this to the top of the mountain — to the end of the story – and they find that this Volkswagen has nothing whatsoever to do with your story, you're going to have a very irritated reader on your hands.

Frank Conroy

In journalism just one fact that is false prejudices the entire work. In contrast, in fiction one single fact that is true gives legitimacy to the entire work.

Gabriel Garcia Marquez

You cannot write well without data.

George V. Higgins

A writer need not devour a whole sheep in order to know what mutton tastes like, but he must at least eat a chop. Unless he gets his facts right, his imagination will lead him into all kinds of nonsense, and the facts he is most likely to get right are the facts of his own experience.

W. Somerset Maugham

On occasions when the facts have particularly infuriated me, fuck the facts!

Farley Mowat

Get your facts first, and then you can distort 'em as much as you please.

Mark Twain

Failure

It started as a lark, but it ended as an ostrich.

Saul Bellow, about a failed Broadway play he wrote

And then there's the most chastening thing of all. You know what that is? It's to see books gathering dust on the shelves of some summer cottage. You rent a cabin in the woods, on a lake, and you look at the books moldering on the shelves and you see the names of authors you've long forgotten and authors you never knew existed. My god, what a fate, to end up on the shelves of a summer rental cottage. If that's one of the possibilities, you would just rather not think at all

”

Good writing is remembering detail. Most people want to forget. Don't forget things that were painful or embarrassing or silly. Turn them into a story that tells the truth.

Paula Danziger

It is not in the least likely that any life has ever been lived which was not a failure in the secret judgment of the person who lived it.

Mark Twain

"

To live a life full of joy, you'll need to embrace whatever you enjoy regardless of your skill level. Don't be afraid of failure. If something is worth doing, it's worth doing badly.

Cami Ostman, psychotherapist

Teach a highly educated person that it is not a disgrace to fail and he must analyze every failure to find its cause. He must learn how to fail intelligently, for failing is one of the greatest arts of the world.

Charles Kettering, business executive

about the future of your books.

E.L. Doctorow

Anything worth doing is worth doing poorly at first.

Robert Downey Jr.

Failure is quite interesting, and it's something I have a certain amount of experience with. I wasn't a failure in the way lots of people are failures – I could always get published, that was pretty straightforward. Literary failure is funny because it's not like you get this massive slap in the face and become a figure of ridicule. It's more that you do this thing, you write this book, and then this big thing is poised to happen on publication. And nothing happens. It's just a weird non-event. The literary Richter scale doesn't register any kind of tremor. That was happening to me for a very long while, and then I managed to persuade myself that these serial failures were perhaps a kind of liberation in that it meant I was free from any kind of pressure from publishers. The stakes were so low that it didn't really make any kind of difference to anybody that I went from writing a novel to writing a book about the First World War. So I've certainly known what it's like for a book to simply, well, disappear.

Geoff Dyer

Your shortcomings and incapacities are your friends in fiction. They teach you both what you can't do and what you can do. If you can't do such-and-such a thing you're trying to do, you find yourself pushed into doing something you can do which you didn't even recognize as a possibility.

Deborah Eisenberg

More people fail at becoming successful businessmen than fail at becoming artists

John Gardner

The contrast between the terrible threat of his swing and the futility of the result is a banquet for the malicious, which includes us all. There is no more completely satisfactory drama in literature than the fall of Humpty Dumpty.

William DeWolf Hopper, on his success at performing "Casey at the Bat."

Writing is a failure. Writing is not only useless, it's spoiled paper. It's perfectly good white paper that you mess up with and you spoil it and you fail. I learned to write predicating everything on failure.

Padgett Powell

Most books come into the world with the fanfare of a stillborn.

James Purdy

Failure is not our only punishment for laziness: there is also the success of others.

Jules Renard

We often discover what *will* do, by finding out what will not do; and probably he who never made a mistake never made a discovery.

Samuel Smiles

Who does nothing, makes no mistakes; and who makes no mistakes, never makes any progress.

Paul Winkler

She knows that there's no success like failure / And that failure's no success at all.

Robert Zimmerman, Nobel Prize winner

Faith

Despair is no good for the writer,

for anyone. Only hope can carry us aloft, can keep us afloat. Only hope, and a certain faith that the incredible structure that has been fashioned by this most strange and ingenious of all the mammals cannot end in ruin and disaster. This faith is a writer's faith, for writing itself is an act of faith, nothing else.

E.B. White

Fame

Between the reputation of the author living and the reputation of the same author dead there is ever a wide discrepancy.

Thomas Bailey Aldrich

In America only the successful writer is important, in France all writers are important, in England no writer is important, and in Australia you have to explain what a writer is.

Geoffrey Cotterell

Fame is a powerful aphrodisiac.

Graham Greene

It is advantageous to an author that his book should be attacked as well as praised. Fame is a shuttlecock. If it be struck at only one end of the room, it will soon fall to the ground. To keep it up, it must be struck at both ends.

Samuel Johnson

Fame gets in the way of creativity.

Ken Kesey

Just as we are suspicious of the gold digger's love for her ninety-year-old husband, we view the writer who courts fame with suspicion, as if being serious about your work and being determined to see it disseminated were at cross-purposes.

Betsy Lerner

Fame and tranquility can never be bedfellows.

Michel de Montaigne

The more you are talked about, the more you will wish to be talked about. The condemned murderer who is allowed to see the account of his trial in the press is indignant if he finds a newspaper which has reported it inadequately. ... Politicians and literary men are in the same case.

Bertrand Russell

Literary fame is the only fame of which a wise man ought to be ambitious, because it is the only lasting and living fame. … Pour out your mind in a great poem, and you will exercise authority over the feelings and opinions of mankind as long as the language lasts in which you write.

Robert Southey

I hear on all sides of the extent of my reputation — which some even call "fame." It is the thing I have most wanted from childhood — although of course in much greater degree — and now that I seem to have it I have no understanding whatever of its basis — of what it is that makes people respond to what I say, for I think of it as of a simplicity and of a naivety almost extreme.

Lionel Trilling

Family

The title, *The Children of Lovers*, is part of a proverb; the children of lovers are orphans, and that's really I suppose meant to be a clue that our parents were very wrapped up in each other and themselves, and that comes out in the book. Am I being fair? I don't know. Are children ever fair about their

”

I love the autobiographical stuff. There were moments as a kid when I didn't — if you were about to do something bad the threat was never "you'll be grounded" or "there'll be no telly for a week," it was "if you do that I'll put it in a comic."

Hayley Campbell, daughter of cartoonist Eddie Campbell

There's Louisa Alcott. I wonder where she's going, what she has got on, how she does, what she is thinking about, and why she does not make me her bosom friend.

Louisa May Alcott, on her delight at leaving Concord for the anonymity of Boston

A woman came up to me the other day and said, "You're the kiddie-book man!" I wanted to kill her.

Maurice Sendak

parents? God knows I hope mine never write a memoir of me.

Judy Carver, daughter of William Golding

The writing came first, but isn't it the same with anyone creative? People always suffer in the background. If you'd asked mother, she would have said that she couldn't have achieved what she did if she had been more relaxed about things.

Jane Murray Flutter, Rumer Goddard's daughter

When it's all added up, papa it will be: he wrote a few good stories, had a novel and fresh approach to reality and he destroyed five persons – Hadley, Pauline, Marty [Gellhorn], Patrick, and possibly myself. Which do you think is the most important, you self-centered shit, the stories or the people?

Gregory Hemingway, at 21, writing to his father, Ernest

If you have reason to believe that you're another Dostoevsky, there is no reason to be concerned about the effect what you write might have on the life of some member of your family. Your art is considerably more important than any such consideration. ... If you have reason to believe that you're another Dostoevsky, you can say anything you need to say. If you don't have reason to believe that you're another Dostoevsky, you can't.

Calvin Trillin

Fan Fiction

I know there's a certain appeal for creators to work on the classic characters like Batman, Superman and Spider-Man, but I've said this before: I asked creators who have worked on those books who the people were doing the books ten years ago, and they don't know! But I can say, "Who worked on *Sin City?*" and they'll go "Frank Miller." "Who worked on *Hellboy?*" "Mike Mignola." "Who worked on *The Goon?*" "Eric Powell." They know it instantly. So to me, the lure of creating your own character and owning it – owning your own universe and being associated with that – in the long run for talented writers and artists makes me question why someone would toil away on a company-owned character for years and years of their lives.

Mike Richardson, comic book publisher

Fans

If I poured out my heart to you, you would feel sorry for me and become my friend ... . I have written lots of pages and would like to send them to you.

Anonymous reader, to Balzac

Wanting to meet an author because you like his work is like wanting to meet a duck because you like pâté.

Margaret Atwood, who added "In order for the pâté to be made and eaten, the duck must first be killed. And who is it that does the killing?"

There is no denying the fact that writers should be read but not seen. Rarely are they a winsome sight.

Edna Ferber

I know I have a reputation as a cantankerous man of letters and I don't try and play it down. A writer, more or less living on his own, will be persecuted by his readers. They want to see you and talk to you. And they don't realize that very often that gets on one's nerves.

John Fowles

(Fowles' journals, published after his death, confirmed his reputation)

This passion for wanting to meet the latest poet, shake hands with the latest novelist, get hold of the latest painter, devour … what is it, what is it they want from a man total that they didn't get from his work? What do they expect? What is there left of him when he's done his work? What's any artist but the dregs of his work? The human shambles that follows it around.

William Gaddis

The worst letters come from retired high school English teachers. They will literally take a book and pick it to pieces and send me 14 pages of notes.

John Grisham

Dearest madam, you had better let it alone; the best part of every author is in general to be found in his book, I assure you.

Samuel Johnson, when asked for an introduction to a celebrated writer

Readers have a loyalty that cannot be matched anywhere else in the creative arts, which explains why so many writers who have run out of gas can keep coasting anyway, propelled on to the bestseller lists by the magic words AUTHOR OF on the covers of their books.

Stephen King

Zamira Drakasha, leaping across the gap between burning ships with twin sabers in hand to kick in some fucking heads and sail off into the sunset with her toddlers in her arms and a hold full of plundered goods, is a wish-fulfillment fantasy from hell. I offer her up on a silver platter with a fucking bow on top; I hope she amuses and delights. In my fictional world, opportunities for butt-kicking do not cease merely because one isn't a beautiful teenager or a muscle-wrapped font of testosterone. In my fictional universe, the main characters are a fat ugly guy and a skinny forgettable guy, with a supporting cast that includes "SBF, 41, nonsmoker, 2 children, buccaneer of no fixed abode, seeks unescorted merchant for light boarding, heavy plunder."

Scott Lynch, answering objections to making a middle-aged mother a pirate

When I walk down the street and somebody says, "Excuse me, Mr. Murakami, very nice to meet you," I feel strange, you know. I'm nothing special. Why is he happy to meet me? But I think that when I'm writing I am kind of special — or strange, at least.

Haruki Murakami

In a way, it's that whole light-in-a-bushel-basket thing too. You get your thing out into the world, and it starts to attract like-minded people, and the whole synchronicity thing starts, and that's really exciting, and also a little frightening too, because then it's so beyond you and it can really grow beyond yourself.

Chuck Palahniuk, quoting the New Testament: "Hide not your light in a bushel basket, and it shall shineth unto all that are in the house"

People are always imagining that if they get hold of the writer himself and, so to speak, shake him long enough and hard enough, something exciting and illuminating will drop out of him. But it doesn't. What's due to come out has come out, in the only form in which it ever can come out. All one gets by shaking is the odd paper clip and crumpled carbons of his wastepaper basket. ... What we

”

No, it did a lot of other things, too.

James Joyce, response to a man's request to "kiss the hand that wrote Ulysses"

I have no fans. You know what I got? Customers. And customers are your friends.

Mickey Spillane

I have learned to live each day as it comes, and not to borrow trouble by dreading tomorrow. It is the dark menace of the future that makes cowards of us.

Dorothy Dix

Everything is will and the great obstacle is fear. It comes down in every instance to the dualism between what one wants and what one may be afraid to have.

Gordon Lish

make is more important than what we are, particularly if making is our profession.

Dorothy L. Sayers

I have both of your letters — the good one which was written that night at three a.m. and then the contrite one, the next day. One's best things are always followed by apoplectic, apologetic seizure.

Anne Sexton, quoting Saul Bellow's response to her exuberant fan letter after reading Henderson the Rain King, *and her mortified apology. He enclosed a manuscript page from* Henderson *with this circled: "With one long breath caught and held in his chest, he fought his sadness over his solitary life. Don't cry you idiot, live or die, but don't poison everything." Sexton would title a poetry collection* Live or Die.

Writing is my trade, and I exercise it only when I am obliged to. You might make your request of a doctor, or a builder, or a sculptor, and there would be no impropriety in it, but if you asked either of those for a specimen of his trade, his handiwork, he would be justified in rising to a point of order. It would never be fair to ask a doctor for one of his corpses to remember him by.

Mark Twain, to autograph hunters

Fantasy

Fantasy is literature for teenagers.

Brian Aldiss

Most of my books have been written in the form of fantasy. Using the device of an imaginary world allows me in some strange way to go to the central issues — it's one of many ways to express feelings about real people, about real human relationships. My concern is how we learn to be genuine human beings.

Lloyd Alexander

All the fantasy writers I know have a way of dwelling on their own fears and phobias. A writer spends his life being his own psychiatrist.

Charles Beaumont

The secret to writing good fantasy is to make certain it relates to what we know about our own world. Readers must be able to identify with the material in such a way that they recognize and believe the core truths of the storytelling.

Terry Brooks

All fantasy fiction is essentially about the concept of power; great fantasy fiction is about people who find it at great cost or lose it tragically; mediocre fantasy fiction is about people who have it and never lose it but simply wield it.

Stephen King

Fear

I'm very cynical. I don't believe in Extra Sensory Perception or poltergeists or flying saucers. I don't believe in ghosts, either. What I do believe in is the capacity of the human mind to create objects of fear. What is more frightening, for instance, than Frankenstein's monster? What we fantasy writers do is create substitutes for belief.

Charles Beaumont

My biggest battle has always been about fear. I think that's why I write what I do. I grew up with a lot of fear. Things were uncertain after my parents divorced. I was molested by a neighborhood security guard when I was five and had to go to a grand jury hearing.

Patricia Cornwell, who added, "My way of dealing with fear is to walk right into it"

Consider, Sir, how insignificant this will appear a twelvemonth hence.

Were this consideration to be applied to most of the little vexatious incidents of life, by which our quiet is too often disturbed, it would prevent many painful sensations.

Samuel Johnson

Imagine the anxiety level of a job that requires you start from square one every day. This is the writer's predicament.

Betsy Lerner

When I dare to be powerful — to use my strength in the service of my vision, then it becomes less and less important whether I am afraid.

Audre Lorde

When I was younger, I was afraid of [writing] something that didn't make a lot of sense. But now I'm not. I have nothing to worry about. It doesn't matter.

Maurice Sendak

Writing, particularly fiction writing, is an act of quiet terror. You are alone all at once with your genius and your ineptitude, and your errors are as public as possible. To be a writer of fiction requires extreme self-discipline and extreme self-confidence, and many of the people drawn to writing have neither. It can be a recipe for dismal failure.

Gene Weingarten

Feedback

I had feedback every day, all day. I always just felt like a puppet master playing with everybody's emotions and doing this with the characters.

Anna Todd, on using Wattpad readers' comments while writing After

Fiction, Function of

Fiction has nothing to say to probability; the capable writer gives it not a moment's attention, except to make what is related *seem* probable in the reading — *seem true*. Suppose he relates the impossible; what then? Why, he has but passed over the line into the realm of romance, the kingdom of Scott, Defoe, Hawthorne, Beckford and the authors of *Arabian Nights* — the land of the poets, the home of all that is lasting and good in the literature of the imagination.

Ambrose Bierce

I am bored with the world I inhabit. I appreciate its technology and general wealth, but don't feel inspired to love it. For me, whether reading it or writing it, fiction is an escape.

Richard Blake

It was one of Woolf's contributions to insist, in her fiction, that the world is too huge and mysterious, to impenetrably itself, for fiction as fiction is so often written; that any writer's attempt to clear the field of its vines and creepers, to frighten off the hostile animals so as to set up a table for tea and begin to demonstrate a proper sense of right and wrong, is unlikely to come to a good or useful end.

Michael Cunningham

Fiction's essential activity is to imagine how others feel, what a Saturday afternoon in an Italian town in the 2nd Century looked like. My ambition is solely to get some effect, as of light on stone in a forest on a September day.

Guy Davenport

Fiction keeps its audience by retaining the world as its subject matter. People like the world. Many people actually prefer it to art and spend their days by choice in the

”

Good fiction is not preaching. If the writer is trying hard to convince you of something, then he or she should stick to nonfiction.

Terry McMillan

A wondrous dream, a fantasy incarnate, fiction completes us, mutilated beings burdened with the awful dichotomy of having only one life and the ability to desire a thousand. This gap between real life and the desires and fantasies demanding that it be richer and more varied is the realm of fiction.

Mario Vargas Llosa

The purpose of a fiction story is to create passionate curiosity and then to gratify it unexpectedly, orgasmically. Isn't that what we expect from all contacts?

F. Scott Fitzgerald

If anybody looked at the book ["Omensetter's Luck"] carefully, I think they would see that it really says nothing at all about the 1890s, nothing about the Ohio river towns, of which I have no knowledge whatever. Fiction, god damn it, is fiction. When will that simple truth be acknowledged?

William Gass

thick of it. When the arts abandon the world as their subject matter, people abandon the arts.

Annie Dillard

All the fiction I write is in some way tendentious [e.g., promote a particular cause or point of view, esp. controversial], but I think all great fiction is tendentious. Even Jane Austen.

Howard Fast, communist

Fiction creates a vivid and continuous dream in the reader's mind. Any reader knows at a glance that this is true, and that if a given work does not bring a vivid and continuous dream to the reader — almost instantly, after five or six words — the fiction is either bad or, what may be the same thing, a so-called metafiction.

John Gardner

We understand that fiction is a lie to begin with. To ignore the truth inside the lie is to sin against the craft, in general, and one's own work in particular.

Stephen King

Fiction does not teach, it is not didactic. Fiction dramatizes you from within, the visual culture pacifies you from without. The principle of reading is the closest to the principle of having one's imagination revitalized. And that is life.

Jerzy Kosinski

The hope in fiction, as Aristotle says, is to discover not the history of what happened, but principles of what is possible.

Keith Oatley

Fiction is an extension of criticism by other means.

Wilfrid Sheed, critic

Truth is stranger than fiction, but it is because Fiction is obliged to stick to possibilities; Truth isn't.

Mark Twain

The good ended happily, and the bad unhappily. That is what fiction means.

Oscar Wilde, to which Tom Stoppard, in Rosencrantz and Guildenstern Are Dead, *added "The bad ended unhappily, the good unluckily. That is what tragedy means"*

All fiction for me is a kind of magic and trickery — a confidence trick, trying to make people believe something is true that isn't. And the novelist, in particular, is trying to convince the reader that he is seeing society as a whole.

Angus Wilson

Fiction, Popular

The tawdry novels which flare in the bookshelves of our railway stations, and which seem designed ... for people with a low standard of life.

Matthew Arnold

[A species of] romance where the incidents defy the probabilities, and march just inside the borders of the possible.

John Buchan

This is commercial fiction. It's a little different from really serious literature. There, the publishers or editors will wait until the whole manuscript comes in. With my work, I get pages early and if the story has gone the wrong way, or if it's losing steam, then I say, "hold it — let's talk. We're off track in terms of what should be driving this story ahead," or "I'm losing interest in the narrator." Sometimes there's not enough tension. I'll do any number of outlines or re-writes on the pages. I've done as much as nine drafts of a book after the original comes in.

James Patterson

First Drafts

Be willing to write really badly. It won't hurt you to do that. I think there is this fear of writing badly, something primal about it, like: "This bad stuff is coming out of me…" Forget it! Let it float away and the good stuff follows. For me, the bad beginning is just something to build on. It's no big deal. You have to give yourself permission to do that because you can't expect to give yourself permission to do that because you can't expect to write regularly and always write well. That's when people get into the habit of waiting for the good moments, and that is where I think writer's block comes from.

Jennifer Egan

I just give myself permission to suck. I delete about 90 percent of my first drafts, so it doesn't really matter much if on a particular day I write beautiful and brilliant prose that will stick in the minds of my readers forever, because there's a 90 percent chance I'm just going to delete whatever I write anyway. I find this hugely liberating.

John Green

The first draft of anything is shit. When you first start to write you get all the kick and the reader gets none, but after you learn to work it's your object to convey everything to the reader so that he remembers it not as a story he had read but something that happened to himself.

Ernest Hemingway

The only true creative aspect of writing is the first draft. That's when it's coming straight from your head and your heart, a direct tapping of the unconscious. The rest is donkey work. It is, however, donkey work that must be done.

Evan Hunter

It is completely raw, the sort of thing I feel free to do with the door shut — it's the story undressed, standing up in nothing but its socks and undershorts.

Stephen King

Put your notes away before you begin a draft. What you remember is probably what should be remembered; what you forget is probably what should be forgotten. No matter; you'll have a chance to go back to your notes after the draft is completed. What is important is to achieve a draft which allows the writing to flow.

Donald M. Murray

The first draft is just you telling yourself the story.

Terry Pratchett

Get through a draft as quickly as possible. Hard to know the shape of the thing until you have a draft. Literally, when I wrote the last page of my first draft of *Lincoln's Melancholy* I thought, Oh, shit, now I get the shape of this. But I had wasted years, literally years, writing and rewriting the first third to first half. The old writer's rule applies: Have the courage to write badly.

Joshua Wolf Shenk

Forgiveness

What I learned to do many years ago was to forgive myself. It is very important for every human being to forgive herself or himself because if you live, you will make mistakes — it is inevitable. But once you do and you see the mistake, then you

”

Getting the first draft finished is like pushing a peanut with your nose across a very dirty floor.

Joyce Carol Oates

I would advise any beginning writer to write the first drafts as if no one else will ever read them — without a thought about publication — and only in the last draft to consider how the work will look from the outside.

Anne Tyler

If you describe things as better than they are, you are considered to be a romantic; if you describe things as worse than they are, you will be called a realist; and if you describe things exactly as they are, you will be thought of as a satirist.

Quentin Crisp

Satire is people as they are; romanticism, people as they would be; realism, people as they seem with their insides left out.

Dawn Powell

forgive yourself and say, "Well, if I'd known better I'd have done better," that's all. So you say to people you think you may have injured, "I'm sorry," and then you say to yourself, "I'm sorry." If we hold on to the mistake, we can't see our own glory in the mirror because we have the mistake between our faces and the mirror; we can't see what we're capable of being. You can ask forgiveness of others, but in the end the real forgiveness is in one's own self.

Maya Angelou

Freelance Writing

There's really a shortage of good freelance writers. … There are a lot of talented people who are very erratic, so either they don't turn it in or they turn it in and it's rotten; it's amazing. Somebody who's even maybe not all that terrific but who is dependable, who will turn in a publishable piece more or less on time, can really do very well.

Gloria Steinem

Genius

Genius does what it must, and talent does what it can.

Edward Bulwer-Lytton

A great writer creates a world of his own and his readers are proud to live in it. A lesser writer may entice them in for a moment, but soon he will watch them filing out.

Cyril Connolly

True genius walks along a line, and, perhaps, our greatest pleasure is in seeing it so often near falling, without being ever actually down.

Oliver Goldsmith

Talent hits a target no one else can hit; genius hits a target no one else can see.

Arthur Schopenhauer

Many a true Genius appears in the world — you may know him by this infallible Sign; that the Dunces are all in Confederacy against him.

Jonathan Swift

Genius and disease, like strength and mutilation, may be inextricably bound up together.

Edmund Wilson

Genres

Did no one, any more, no one in all this wide world, change their record now and then? Was everyone nowadays thirled [enslaved] to a formula? Authors today wrote so much to a pattern that their public expected it. The public talked about "a new Silas Weekley" or "a new Lavinia Fitch" exactly as they talked about "a new brick" or "a new hairbrush." They never said "a new book by" whoever it might be. Their interest was not in the book but in its newness. They knew quite well what the book would be like.

D.I. Alan Grant, in Josephine Tey's The Daughter of Time, *lamenting formulaic genre fiction*

Sentence for sentence, there is more going on in a page of George Higgins or Thomas Harris than in a whole chapter of, say, Margaret Drabble. They have a better ear for what we say, or try to say, or don't notice we're saying — for the small ways in which the mind works and stumbles. They have fun with the truth. There is no excuse for a boring pulp novelist, but a good one somehow plugs into the grid of our speech, into the power surge of ordinary fantasies, with a jolt that would knock more delicate writers across the room. This is why we should turn to the *Times* list every Sunday morning. If the language is still alive down at this end of the market — if there is juice running through the art of basic narrative — then we have no cause to be downhearted. Conversely, if the list is crammed with John Grisham, then we can all go out to brunch and rue the decline of the West.

Anthony Lane

One of the things that's been a revelation for me is the welcoming nature of those genre communities — horror, sci-fi, spec fiction. There are people who just want books to be good and who aren't coming in with their arms crossed, like, "You better wow me." They're just like, "I want to be wowed." It's so huge, that tiny difference.

Victor LaValle

What you want to put your stuff over is ACTION. … The more I write, the more I am convinced that the only way to write a popular story is to split it up into scenes, and have as little stuff between the scenes as possible. See what I mean? Well, look here. I wrote a story the other day — "The Return of Battling Billson" — and the only thing that was arrived at in the first 1,500 words was that I met Battling Billson down in the East End and gave him Ukridge's address, which he had lost. But by having me go into a pub and get a drink and have lost my money and be chucked out by the barman and picked up by Billson, who happened to be passing, and then having Billson go in and clean up the pub and manhandle the barman I got some darned good stuff which, I think, absolutely concealed the fact that nothing had really happened except my giving him the address.

P.G. Wodehouse

Getting Started

With the first two books, I got up at 5 in the morning. I'd tell myself I had to be at my desk with my first cup of coffee by 5:30. Those little games you play with yourself work. I told myself that in the first 30 minutes, I had to get my first page out of the way.

John Grisham

I wrote my first novel because I wanted to read it.

Toni Morrison

I always have at this very start a curiously clear preview of the entire novel before me or above me.

Vladimir Nabokov

You're looking, as you begin, for what's going to resist you. You're looking for trouble. Sometimes in the beginning uncertainty arises not because the writing is difficult, but because it isn't difficult enough. Fluency can be a sign that nothing is happening; fluency can actually be my signal to stop, while being in the dark from sentence to sentence is what convinces me to go on.

Philip Roth

I rarely have a very clear idea of where I'm going when I start. Just people and a situation. Then I fool around — writing and rewriting until the stuff jells.

James Thurber

I never had any thought behind anything I did in the beginning, to be honest.

Anna Todd

I believe a writer can weave in and out of genres — do it all. It is a gluttonous point of view, to be sure. Then again, when it comes to writing, that is what I truly am and nothing less: a glutton.

Cynthia Ozick

I suspect that all writers have some didactic intention. That starts the motor. Or let us say: many of the things we eat are cooked over a gas stove, but there is no taste of gas in the food.

Thornton Wilder

”

Would you convey my compliments to the purist who reads your proofs and tell him or her that I write in a sort of broken-down patois which is something like the way a Swiss waiter talks, and that when I split an infinitive, God damn it, I split it so it will stay split, and when I interrupt the velvety smoothness of my more or less literate syntax with a few sudden words of bar-room vernacular that is done with the eyes wide open and the mind relaxed.

Raymond Chandler

Ghostwriting

It seems perfectly incomprehensible to me that anyone should want to sign a book that someone else had written. I think it a kind of insanity. I hated to be alone with people like that.

Katherine Anne Porter

I don't use ghosts, co-authors, I don't have collaborators. Why is that so hard for some to accept? I don't brainstorm with other writers, with my editor or my agent on storylines. It's not my wiring. I love my agent, my editor, and respect them just as much as I love them. If either or both of them insisted we brainstorm, I will be forced to kill them until they were dead.

Nora Roberts

Gossip

What did they expect? I'm a writer, I use everything. Did all those people think I was just there to entertain them?

Truman Capote, on being dropped by his wealthy friends over excerpts from his roman à clef Answered Prayers

A man or woman without any interest in gossip may be impressive in his or her restraint, but also wanting in curiosity, uninterested in the variousness of human nature, dead to the wildly abundant oddity of life, and thereby, in some central way, deficient.

Joseph Epstein

Most people delight in censure, when they themselves are not the objects of it, if any are offended by my publicly exposing their private vices, I promise they shall have the satisfaction, in a very little time, of seeing their friends and neighbors in the same circumstances

Benjamin Franklin

In general I'd rather talk about other people. Gossip, or as we gossips like to say, is character analysis.

Elizabeth Hardwick

That alchemy of quiet malice, by which women can concoct a subtle poison from ordinary trifles.

Nathaniel Hawthorne

Blood sport is brought to its ultimate refinement in the gossip columns.

Bernard Ingham

It is one thing to tell the nastiest story to all your fifty best friends; it's another to set it down in cold Century Expanded type.

Liz Smith, about Truman Capote's Answered Prayers, *which Betsy Lerner called "the literary equivalent of premeditated murder: in cold type"*

Pray send me some treasonable news about the Queen ... and don't leave me in this odious state of innocence, and make me as wickedly instructed as yourself.

Sydney Smith

Grammar

Avoid the passive voice whenever possible. University term papers bleed with the passive voice. It seems to be the accepted style of Academia. Dump it.

Rita Mae Brown

There are three classes of people who always say "we" instead of "I." They are emperors, editors, and men with a tape-worm.

Roscoe Conkling

All fine prose is based on the verbs

carrying the sentences. They make the sentences move.

F. Scott Fitzgerald

The verbs are most important. Let the student analyze an especially vigorous, vivid, and condensed place description, and he will find, in all probability, that verbs are responsible for most of its effectiveness. He should try to work out for himself the possibility of letting a single verb do the work of half a dozen other words.

John T. Frederick

You can be a little ungrammatical if you come from the right part of the country.

Robert Frost

The fact is I think I am a verb instead of a personal pronoun. A verb is anything that signifies to be; to do; or to suffer. I signify all three.

Ulysses S. Grant

The art of verbs isn't an art of invention. It's the art of observation — learning to see dynamism in everyday events.

Constance Hale

The road to hell is paved with adverbs.

Stephen King

It is indeed acceptable practice to sometimes split an infinitive. If infinitive splitting makes available just the shade of meaning you desire or if avoiding the separation creates a confusing ambiguity or patent artificiality, you are entitled to happily go ahead and split!

Richard Lederer

If it sounds like writing, I rewrite it. Or, if proper usage gets in the way, it may have to go. I can't allow what we learned in English composition to disrupt the sound and rhythm of the narrative.

Elmore Leonard

Don't say it was "delightful;" make us say "delightful" when we've read the description. You see, all those words (horrifying, wonderful, hideous, exquisite) are only like saying to your readers "Please will you do my job for me?"

C. S. Lewis

The editorial "we" has often been fatal to rising genius; though all the world knows that it is only a form of speech, very often employed by a single needy blockhead.

Thomas Babington Macaulay

Nothing makes it clearer how intimately and deeply pronouns are embedded in our lives than having to alter them to refer to someone you've known all your life.

Mary Norris, New Yorker *copy editor, referring to the time her younger brother was surgically turned into her younger sister*

Truly knowing about grammar in the way that is relevant for a writer is not a matter of book learning. It is not a matter of knowing the names for the parts of speech. It's not a matter of remembering rules you were given in high school. It is, quite simply, a matter of music. You know when someone has made a grammatical mistake the same way you know when someone is singing "White Christmas" off-key. You know because you have heard it on-key so many times, and even if you can't tell whether the singer is sharp or flat, you know that "it just doesn't sound right." … To know

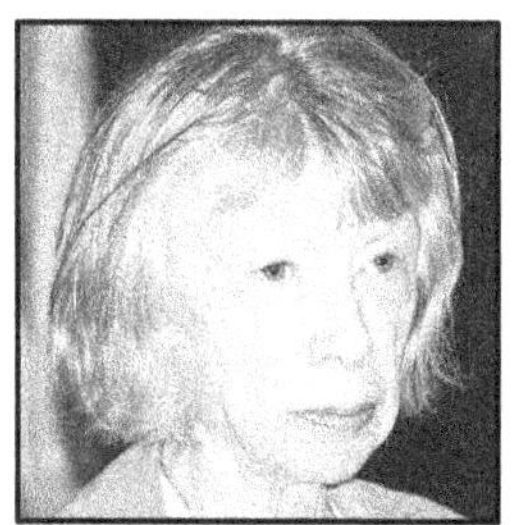

Grammar is a piano I play by ear. … All I know about grammar is its infinite power. To shift the structure of a sentence alters the meaning of that sentence, as definitely and inflexibly as the position of a camera alters the meaning of the object photographed.

Joan Didion

If the noun is good and the verb is strong, you almost never need an adjective.

J. Anthony Lukas

”

I have a book at home called "Modern English Literature: Its Blemishes and Defects." In it I find examples of bad grammar and slovenly English from the pens of Carlyle, Disraeli, Macaulay, Shakespeare, Milton. ... If you should climb the mighty Matterhorn to look out over the kingdoms of the earth, it might be a pleasant incident to find strawberries up there. But Great Scott! You don't climb the Matterhorn for strawberries!

Mark Twain, responding to criticism of the grammar Ulysses S. Grant used in his memoirs, which Twain published

good grammar is to be able to hear when something just doesn't sound right.

Gary Provost

Remember to never split an infinitive.

William Safire

Forward motion in any piece of writing is carried by verbs. Verbs are the action words of the language and the most important. Turn to any passage on any page of a successful novel and notice the high percentage of verbs. Beginning writers always use too many adjectives and adverbs and generally use too many dependent clauses. Count your words and words of verbal force (like that word "force" I just used).

William Sloane

[Adjectives are] the leeches that infest the pond of prose, sucking the blood of words.

William Strunk Jr.

When I read some of the rules for speaking and writing the English language correctly, as that a sentence must never end with a participle, and perceive how implicitly even the learned obey it, I think

Any fool can make a rule
And every fool will mind it.

Henry David Thoreau

Word has somehow got around that the split infinitive is always wrong. That is of a piece with the outworn notion that it is always wrong to strike a lady.

James Thurber

Most sentences in English open with the subject, and they move from the known to the unknown.

Virginia Tufte

I notice that you use plain, simple language, short words and brief sentences. That is the way to write English — it is the modern way and the best way. Stick to it; don't let fluff and flowers and verbosity creep in. When you catch an adjective, kill it. No, I don't mean utterly, but kill most of them — then the rest will be valuable. They weaken when they are close together. They give strength when they are wide apart. An adjective habit, or a wordy, diffuse, flowery habit, once fastened upon a person, is as hard to get rid of as any other vice.

Mark Twain

Subjunctive to the last, he preferred to ask, "And that, sir, would be the Hippodrome?"

Alexander Woollcott, of newspaper editor William Allen White

Grants

I do think that if the government supports its artists, they need have no feeling of gratitude — the meanest and most sniveling attribute in the world — or baskets being brought to them, or apple-polishing. Working for the state — for Christ's sake, are you grateful to your employers? ... The artists are a part of their country and their country should recognize this, so both it and the artists can take pride in their efforts.

Dorothy Parker

Great American Novel

All modern American literature comes from one book by Mark Twain called *Huckleberry Finn*. If you read it you must stop where the Nigger Jim is stolen from the boys.

That is the real end. The rest is just cheating. But it's the best book we've had. All American writing comes from that. There was nothing before. There has been nothing as good since.

Ernest Hemingway

The whole idea of a Great American Novel is bullshit. But if you twist my arm, I'm probably gonna say *American Tabloid* and *Love and Rockets* [are two.]

Marlon James

Habit

It is by sitting down to write every morning that one becomes a writer. Those who do not do this remain amateurs.

Gerald Brenan

Results have very little to do with the goals you set and nearly everything to do with the systems you follow. You do not rise to the level of your goals. You fall to the level of your systems.

James Clear

I never could have done what I have done without the habits of punctuality, order, and diligence, without the determination to concentrate myself on one subject at a time.

Charles Dickens

They had this peculiarity in their condition, that they were always in sight of the Road of Reason, always wishing for her presence, and always resolving to return tomorrow. In these was most eminently conspicuous the subtlety of Habit, who hung imperceptible shackles upon them, and was every moment leading them farther from the road. … They wandered on … with the chains of Habit hanging secretly upon them. … Discontent lowered in their looks, and Sadness hovered round their shades; yet they crawled on reluctant and gloomy, till they arrived at the depth of the recess ... where the dominion of Indolence terminates, and the hopeless wanderer is delivered up to Melancholy; the chains of Habit are rivetted for ever; and Melancholy, having tortured her prisoner for a time, consigns him at last to the cruelty of Despair.

Samuel Johnson, which posterity whittled down to "The chains of habit are too weak to be felt until they are too strong to be broken"

An often overlooked factor in one's writing success is discovering the conditions you need in order to write, and then managing to create those conditions.

Robert B. Parker

Heroes

(See **Characters**)

The real hero is always a hero by mistake; he dreams of being an honest coward like everybody else. If it had been possible he would have settled the matter otherwise, and without bloodshed. He doesn't boast of his own death or of others'. But he does not repent. He suffers and keeps his mouth shut; if anything, others then exploit him, making him a myth, while he, the man worthy of esteem, was only a poor creature who reacted with dignity and courage in an event bigger than he was.

Umberto Eco

It's my contention that the difference between a hero and an anti-hero is where you stop the story, and if you're true to life, given these ingredients, then the story goes on, because human beings go on. Now, you can confine

”

Ill-fitting grammar are like ill-fitting shoes. You can get used to it for a bit, but then one day your toes fall off and you can't walk to the bathroom.

Jasper Fforde

When you are dealing with the blackest side of the human soul, you have to have someone who has performed heroically to balance that out. You have to have a hero.

Ann Rule

Writing history ... is similar to accounting: you enter facts into the accounting system you've devised and support each entry with a document delivered into the system from the real world. I was going to say writing history is more creative than that, but then we've all heard about how creative accounting can be.

Richard Rhodes

your story to one individual, and therefore as far as he's concerned the story begins with birth and ends with death. But if you're dealing with larger movements, as they are [in *Dune*], there is no real ending. It's just the place where you stop the story.

Frank Herbert

Historical Novels

Let me begin by showing how [language] shouldn't be done. Take this: The King rose up upon his couch. "Thou shalt, before this night is out," he quoth, "mount upon thy trusty charger and bring me the head of the false Bobindrell."

Whether people may once have spoken like this in England is beside the point. What matters is that it sounds ridiculous now, and it distances a reader from the characters in a novel. Whether your novel is set in England c. 1550, or some other time and place, here is how I suggest it should be done:

Still smiling, the King leaned closer. "I want the fuck dead," he breathed. "I don't care how you do it. Just make sure none of the blame ever drifts my way." He took another swig from his cup and went back to watching the jugglers.

Richard Blake

I don't think I write historical novels. All novels are set in the past, if you think about it. I'll define a novel as historical if it makes literary history.

E.L. Doctorow

The historical novel, as I learnt with some concern after I had written two or three, belongs in a despised genre. But the tale of narrative set in the past may have its particular, time-free value; and the candid reader will not misunderstand me, will not suppose I intend any preposterous comparison, when I observe that Homer was further removed in time from Troy than I am from the Napoleonic wars; yet he spoke to the Greeks for two thousand years.

Patrick O'Brian

I don't usually turn to the [history] books until I've got a first draft of my story. I don't want to be caged in by reality, as it were. I want my imagination to go wherever it wants to go. If it's outlandish then of course I'll get rid of it. Then, two or three drafts in, I begin to read books.

Philip Roth

The dynamic use of setting is a weapon that no historical novelist can afford to ignore. To describe scenes, dresses, ways of life of a different age, may make the story move like a pageant in front of us; but to take us alive into another period of time, the senses must be invoked.

Mary Stewart

History

As for things like sexual morality and the taste for recreational substances you'll find in my [historical] novels, these are fully evidenced in the sources. Life is usually awful when it isn't boring. The answer has always been to find the right mix of chemicals to make things seem better than they are.

Richard Blake, on his historical novels

Good history is the ability to walk to the top of a tall hill. From there we can see not only what existed in the past, but the power of what is to come.

G.K. Chesterton

There is properly no history; only biography.

Ralph Waldo Emerson

History offers no comfort. It hands out hard lessons. It makes absurd reading, mostly. Admittedly, it moves on, but progress is not the result of history. History is never-ending. We are always inside history, never outside it.

Günter Grass

History repeats itself. Historians repeat each other.

Philip Guedalla

The past lies upon the Present like a giant's dead body.

Nathaniel Hawthorne

For what is history, but ... [a] huge libel on human nature, to which we industriously add page after page, volume after volume, as if we were holding up a monument to the honor, rather than the infamy of our species.

Washington Irving

Homosexuality

If I went around hiding, maybe life would be easier, or my book sales would be better. But I think for every straight person I've lost, I've probably gotten a gay [reader]. In the early days when this all started coming out, it was, "Ooh, this could really turn off your male readers." And you know what I want to say: "Do you not know what straight men's favorite form of pornography is? It's women with women, honey!" I should have more of it in my books, and if I didn't embarrass myself, I would!

Patricia Cornwell

Somehow this is always a question in the gay community. A lot of gay men have been made to feel that no one could possibly understand them because they have been so marginalized and so misunderstood. But I do what every writer does. I use my imagination and my power to empathize and to see things through others' points of view. I feel that it's important to continue to write about men from a woman's point of view. I wish there were gay men out there writing about lesbians.

Patricia Nell Warren

Horror

Perhaps the real reason for the present lack of interest in ghost stories rises from the fact that they are extremely hard to write; because, to be successful, a ghost story has to be terrifying, and it is much easier to be ingenious than it is to be terrifying. The writer of detective stories must present his readers with a crime and an ingenious solution for it. But the writer of ghost stories must freeze his reader's marrow, and that is anything but easy.

Robertson Davies

There's terror on top, the finest emotion any writer can induce; then horror; and, on the very lowest level of all, the gag instinct of revulsion. Naturally, I'll try to terrify you first, and if that doesn't work, I'll try to horrify you, and if I can't make it there, I'll try to gross you out. I'm not proud.

Stephen King

Humanity

Psychoanalysts in France, structuralists in the United States and France, conservative, liberal,

The very ink with which all history is written is merely fluid prejudice.

Mark Twain

The first condition of human goodness is something to love; the second something to reverence.

George Eliot

”

Humor is laughing at what you haven't got when you want to have it.

Langston Hughes

Truth is funnier than most things you can make up.

Margo Kaufman

and left-wing thinkers and contemporary schools of linguistic philosophy agree about one thing: man became man not by the tool but by the Word. It is not walking upright and using a stick to dig for food or strike a blow that makes a human being, it is speech. And neither intelligent apes nor dolphins whispering marvels in the ocean share with us the ability to transform this direct communication into the written word, which sets up an endless chain of communication and commune between peoples and generations who will never meet.

Nadine Gordimer

I have this philosophy, which has proved true for me: if you're observant, any square mile on the face of the Earth will tell you all you need to know about life and people.

Dean Koontz

The human comedy is always tragic, but since its ingredients are always the same — dupe, fox, straight, like burlesque skits — the repetition through the ages is comedy. The basis of tragedy is man's helplessness against disease, war and death; the basis of comedy is man's helplessness against vanity (the vanity of love, greed, lust, power).

Dawn Powell

The ancient commission of the writer has not changed. He is charged with exposing our many grievous faults and failures, with dredging up to the light our dark and dangerous dreams for the purpose of improvement.

Furthermore, the writer is delegated to declare and to celebrate man's proven capacity for greatness of heart and spirit — for gallantry in defeat — for courage, compassion and love. In the endless war against weakness and despair, these are the bright rally-flags of hope and of emulation. I hold that a writer who does not passionately believe in the perfectibility of man, has no dedication nor any membership in literature.

John Steinbeck
(History teaches us that achieving "the perfectibility of man" involves breaking a few million lives)

Humor & Humorists

Clever. Cute. Bizarre. Cruel. Naughty. Recognizable.

Scott Adams, at least three of these makes a comic strip funny

Men will let you abuse them if only you will make them laugh.

Henry Ward Beecher

Of course, nobody who has ever tried it thinks that being funny is play; whether in the circus, on the stage, or in writing, being funny is highly skilled work, which demands an individual technique, a fine sense of timing, and a sense of form in addition to the indispensable requisite of a sense of humor.

Robertson Davies

The difference between a satirist and a humorist is that the satirist shoots to kill while the humorist brings his prey back alive.

Peter De Vries

The best playwrights — Tennessee Williams, for instance — will punctuate the most serious moment with an outrageous laugh. The audience delights in it. They need the relief. They need laughter. … The more an audience laughs, the more it feels. Shakespeare knew this — there's comedy in his most serious plays.

Jerome Lawrence

I suspect [humor] is an attribute of everything, and the substance of nothing, so if I had to define a sense of humor I would say it lay in the perception of shadows.

Samuel Marchbanks

Make him [the reader] laugh and he will think you a trivial fellow, but bore him in the right way and your reputation is assured.

W. Somerset Maugham

Study Andy Rooney. Watch everything he does. And don't do it. Be funny about things that matter. Your opinion of Velcro doesn't.

P.J. O'Rourke

A lot of the humor (and possibly a lot of the power in the Discworld series) comes from thinking logically about those things which we don't normally think logically about, that we just accept. For example, in a horror story we just sort of accept the idea of werewolves and vampires without actually going a little deeper into it. It seemed to me that a thinking creature that spends part of its time as a wolf and part of its time as a human is going to be a very interesting creature, with a very interesting psychology.

Terry Pratchett

Well, of course, winning is great, but it's not funny. And there are no happy endings in my stories because happiness, too, isn't funny.

Charles M. Schulz, cartoonist, on why Charlie Brown never won

Mark Twain is in much the same position as myself: he has to put matters in such a way as to make people who would otherwise hang him believe that he is joking.

George Bernard Shaw

The humorous writer professes to awaken and direct your love, your pity, your kindness — your scorn for untruth, pretension, imposture. ... He takes upon himself to be the week-day preacher.

William Makepeace Thackary

Authors of light pieces have, nobody knows why, a genius for getting into minor difficulties: they walk into the wrong apartments, they drink furniture polish for stomach bitters, they drive their cars into the prize tulip beds of haughty neighbors, they playfully slap gangsters, mistaking them for old school friends. To call such persons "humorists," a loose-fitting and ugly word, is to miss the nature of their dilemma and the dilemma of their nature. The little wheels of their invention are set in motion by the damp hand of melancholy.

James Thurber

Ideas

I do keep files of ideas and stories that didn't quite work a year ago, five years ago, ten years ago. I come back to them later and I look through the titles. It's like a father bird coming with a worm. You look down at all these hungry little beaks — all these stories waiting to be finished — and you say to them, Which of you needs to be fed? … And the story that yells the loudest, the idea that stands up and opens its mouth, is the one that gets fed.

Ray Bradbury

Just as I'm wrapping up one, the

"

Every idea is my last. I feel sure of it. So, I try to do the best with each as it comes and that's where my responsibility ends. But I just don't wait for ideas. I look for them. Constantly. And if I don't use the ideas that I find, they're going to quit showing up.

Peg Bracken

Ideas are cheap. I have more ideas now than I could ever write up. To my mind, it's the execution that is all-important.

George R.R. Martin

You have to do what your imagination wants, not what your fastidious literary taste is inclined towards, not what your finely honed judgment feels comfortable with, not what your desire for the esteem of critics advises you to. Good intentions never wrote a story worth reading: only the imagination can do that.

Philip Pullman

Everyone thinks you have a great imagination, but the truth is, you just have a lot of problems.

Markus Zusak

other story is there. It's crazy; it's as though your new houseguests are sitting outside impatiently waiting for you to say goodbye to the ones leaving. I've never had a situation where I've finished a book and said, "Good God, I've no ideas."

Mary Higgins Clark

A writer of fiction lives in fear. Each new day demands new ideas and he can never be sure whether he is going to come up with them or not.

Roald Dahl

Old ideas give way slowly; for they are more than abstract logical forms and categories. They are habits, predispositions, deeply ingrained attitudes of aversion and preference.

John Dewey

An invasion of armies can be resisted, but not an idea whose time has come.

Victor Hugo

Every book is the wreck of a perfect idea.

Iris Murdoch

The ideas for stories (for me) nearly always come from the geography, but an occasional overheard phrase can start the machinery as well. You can make a story out of almost nothing if you have a mind that is inclined toward stories.

Annie Proulx

My advice is not to wait to be struck by an idea. If you're a writer, you sit down and damn well decide to have an idea. That's the way to get an idea.

Andy Rooney

Sometimes the ideas just come to me. Other times I have to sweat and almost bleed to make ideas come. It's a mysterious process, but I hope I never find out exactly how it works. I like a mystery, as you may have noticed.

J.K. Rowling

An idea that is not dangerous is unworthy of being called an idea at all.

Oscar Wilde

You need dynamite to dislodge an idea that has got itself firmly rooted in the public mind. … It is embedded in the world's folklore, and nothing will ever get it out.

P.G. Wodehouse, about accusations that he collaborated with the Nazis

Imagination

It's very important to root your material, your fiction, in some kind of reality. ... Solid research gives you a great place to move off from. It allows you a springboard, if you like, out into the fantastical. And also sometimes it throws up extraordinary things that you could never have guessed.

Clive Barker

The imagination is not an escape, but a return to the richness of our true selves; a return to reality.

George Mackay Brown

The Fancy is indeed no other than a mode of memory emancipated from the order of time and space.

Samuel Taylor Coleridge

To write a story one must first live the story, imaginatively if not actually. He must be able to enter into this fragment of the great sum of human experience, and make it authentic in his own life. … The capacity to see, to feel, to understand — and the thirst to make others see, feel, and understand — these are the first essentials.

John T. Frederick

Why be yourself if you can be somebody interesting? Imagine a life. Imagine yourself being something other than what you are.

Philip Levine

People tend to underestimate the power of my imagination and my capacity of evolving serial selves in my writings.

Vladimir Nabokov, on people trying to find traces of him in his work

The key to writing believable fiction is a powerful, yet controlled imagination. Before you begin to write about any fictional happening, be it a gun battle, the meeting of two lovers, or something as innocuous as a stroll through a park, you — the author — must be certain that you have imagined it fully. If you can't manage to part the curtain that veils what is essentially your daydream, if you can't see the event unfolding in its entirety with your mind's eye, when you translate that vision into words, it will surely be shrouded in a thick, oily gray mist. Then, to make the action more vivid, you'll be tempted to litter the landscape with mangled corpses and buckets of gore.

Robert B. Parker

The essential condition to become a creator in the artistic domain, particularly in the novel, is to be able to enter into the skin of people.

Georges Simenon

Imagination is the power that enables us to perceive the normal in the abnormal, the opposite of chaos in chaos.

Wallace Stevens

Imagination! Imagination! I put it first years ago, when I was asked what qualities I thought necessary for success upon the stage.

Ellen Terry, actress

Immortality

From bloated celebrity advances to rejected masterpieces, the market is more than just a poor arbiter of lasting quality; it tends to obscure that quality behind purely economic motivations.

Colin Dickey

My constant preoccupation is to save the name of Goncourt from oblivion in the future by every sort of survival: survival through works of literature, survival through foundations, survival through the application of my monogram to all the *objets d'art* which have belonged to my brother and myself.

Edmond Goncourt

If I gave it all up immediately, I'd lose my immortality. I've put in so many enigmas and puzzles that it will keep the professors busy for centuries arguing over what I meant, and that's the only way of insuring one's immortality.

James Joyce, when asked by his wife, "Why don't you write books people can read?"

Influences

It's quite curious how perceptive people — reviewers, critics, knowledgeable students — will point out things to you about your books and the connection between them and other works that you simply didn't know about, and yet which, once you've seen them, you know that you're not ever going to make anybody believe you didn't have it in mind when you wrote

”

Horatio Alger's books conveyed a powerful message to me and many of my young friends: that if you worked hard at your trade, the big chance would eventually come. As a child I didn't regard it as a myth, and as an old man I think of it as the story of my life.

Groucho Marx

your book.

John Barth

There are two primary influences in a writer's life: those influences that come so early in childhood, they seem to soak into the marrow of our bones and to condition our interpretation of the universe thereafter; and those that come a little later, when we are old enough to exercise some control of our environment and our response to it, and have begun to be aware not only of the emotional power but the strategies of art.

Joyce Carol Oates

Love something besides magic in the arts. Get inspired by a particular poet, film-maker, sculptor, composer. You will never be the first Brian Allen Brushwood of magic if you want to be Penn & Teller. But if you want to be, say, the Salvador Dali of magic, well, THERE'S an opening.

Teller, of Penn and Teller, advising future magician Brushwood

”

I felt like poisoning a monk.

Umberto Eco, about why he wrote The Name of the Rose

I've always disliked words like inspiration. Writing is probably like a scientist thinking about some scientific problem, or an engineer about an engineering problem.

Doris Lessing

Inspiration

I shall always be depressed, but what comforts me is the realization that I can now accept this dark side as the commanding side of my personality. In accepting it, I will make it work for me.

Samuel Beckett

(In other words, Beckett couldn't go on, but went on anyway.)

It's all got to be instinctive, joyful and fun. You've got to play at it, don't take anything too seriously. You must never imagine that you're Norman Mailer — that's dangerous.

Ray Bradbury

I don't wait for moods. You accomplish nothing if you do that. Your mind must know it has got to get down to work.

Pearl S. Buck

I am forced to the appalling conclusion that I would never have become a writer but for Joan's death, and to the realization of the extent to which this event has motivated and formulated my writing. I live with the constant threat of possession, and a constant need to escape from possession, from control. So the death of Joan brought me in contact with the invader, the ugly spirit, and maneuvered me into a lifelong struggle in which I have had no choice except to write my way out.

William S. Burroughs, who accidentally killed his wife in Mexico playing William Tell with a revolver

Inspiration is for amateurs. The rest of us just show up and get to work.

Chuck Close

You know what's fucking scary? The fact that I could literally change my life at any moment. I could stop talking to everyone that makes me unhappy. I could kiss whoever I want. I could shave my head or get on a plane or take my own life. Nothing is stopping me. The world is in my hands, and I have no idea what to do with it.

Sarah Coghlan

[Ashley] just wasn't talking [recovering from an ectopic pregnancy]. She was laying in bed. I said, "You know what? I bet you I could write a better book than you." My wife is real competitive. So I said, "Yo, all right, $500 bet." And I saw her eyes spark, like, "What?! You can't write no better book than me!'"So I wrote about three chapters. She wrote about three chapters. Two days later, we switched.

JaQuavis Coleman, on how they started collaborating on their best-selling urban thrillers

The literary world is not conducted according to Marquis of Queensberry rules; if you find somebody's private papers, you immediately rootle through them, looking for raw material. This is something non-literary people never understand. They are apt to confuse it with a vulgar, prying nature.

Robertson Davies

One day I sat down right there in the office and wrote a western story, because I thought I could lie about the west better than the people I was reading. It was a parody, a western to end all westerns. And then the man I was working for, the story editor, read it and said, This is good; you ought to turn it into a novel. Of course, "parody" as a term covers a wide range of possibilities, and somewhere along the line I saw the book developing not as a satire but as something done in counterpoint. What intrigued me finally was the idea of taking a disreputable genre and making something out of it, writing quite seriously in counterpoint to the reader's expectations. And, of course, this book was teaching me something about myself: I was not the kind of writer who could walk into a party and listen to the talk and see how the people were dressed and what they were up to and who was sleeping with whom and then go home and write a story about it. I was not given to literary realism; I was not a reporter, I needed distance, I needed a dramatized voice to work in. Whatever light came to me would have to shine through a prism of invention.

E.L. Doctorow, using his lessons from reading screenplays for Columbia Pictures to write his first novel, Welcome to Hard Times

I know so many writers who get freaked out about distractions, but when I was young I read about some of the Russian writers who were incredibly poor and lived with nine relatives and three screaming babies. They had to turn out 1,500 words every day and rush it in to be serialized in the newspaper. I thought if those guys could work like that, then it's really just a matter of concentration.

Katherine Dunn

What stimulates me to write a poem is that I have something inside me that I want to get rid of. I have to get it out. It is almost a kind of defecation.

T.S. Eliot

Everything is copy.

Nora Ephron, quoting her mother's favorite saying. She explained: "When you slip on a banana peel, people laugh at you; but when you tell people you slipped on a banana peel, it's your laugh. So you become the hero rather than the victim of the joke. I think that's what she meant"

Unprovided with original learning, unformed in the habits of thinking, unskilled in the arts of composition, I resolved to write a book.

Edward Gibbon

I was sitting one day and thinking about cannibalism, because that's what guys like me do, and I thought, suppose a guy was washed up on a rocky island, how much of himself could he eat?

Stephen King

”

When I sit at my table to write, I never know what it's going to be till I'm under way. I trust in inspiration, which sometimes comes and sometimes doesn't. But I don't sit back waiting for it. I work every day.

Alberto Moravia

When I want to get going I read Faulkner. It's good because you can't write like him.

Ken Kesey

”

This is the American fantasy of getting into a big-ass muscle car, getting completely fucked up on drugs, having great sex, killing a bunch of people, and driving west into the night as fast as you can. We've seen that story so many times that we almost buy into the idea that it might be a fun thing to do. It's just a desire, an appetite, running unchecked, which is what the culture asks us to do. We know it's the worst thing in the world for us... but it's fun, too!

Stewart O'Nan

It's like a gift. You know how hard you work. But you also know it takes a confluence of things over which you have no control. I don't want to sound like Shirley MacLaine or anything, but it's like [the book] is being channeled to me. But you can't take the credit. You can't say, "Boy, am I a genius." There's this component to the creative process when the work is really flowing, and you really feel you're in touch with some higher power.

Dean Koontz

Don't loaf and invite inspiration; light out after it with a club, and if you don't get it you will nonetheless get something that looks remarkably like it.

Jack London, rendered afterward as "You can't wait for inspiration. You have to go after it with a club"

When I walk up the stairs [to my office], my whole wall is covered — there are probably 40 author signatures on my wall … These are the authors I admired and loved, and this is my wall of mentors. … And every time I walk up the stairs I'm reminded of the power of story.

Debbie Macomber

I don't wait to be struck by lightning and don't need certain slants of light in order to write.

Toni Morrison

Whenever I'm stuck, I know that if I'm stuck on a plot element, I've gotten somebody to the point where I don't know where to go, it's time to take a shower. … But when I'm taking a shower, I will be sitting there in the water and I will get the most extraordinary ideas. I don't know what it is between taking a shower or something like lifting weights — something mindless and physical — or washing dishes even, with my hands in the water, or even drinking a glass of water. It's just really evocative of good ideas. And it's stupid, but that's my ritual.

Chuck Palahniuk

I'll give you an example from *The Humbling*. I began with a line, which is the first line of the book: "He lost his magic." I was thinking of an actor — not a particular actor, but an actor, who couldn't act. The idea just intrigued me.

Philip Roth

I decided it would be fun to write a story, but I couldn't get an idea. I took long walks, I sat at the typewriter, but I couldn't seem to come up with an idea. Then one day I got a call from my accountant. He said the money was starting to run short. And you know what? All of a sudden, I started getting one idea after another.

Mickey Spillane

There are those who...think that the man who works with his imagination should allow himself to wait till — inspiration moves him. When I have heard such doctrine preached, I have hardly been able to repress my scorn. To me it would not be more absurd if the shoemaker were to wait for inspiration, or the tallow-chandler for the divine moment of melting. If the man whose business it is to write has eaten too many good things, or has drunk too much, or smoked too many cigars — as men who write sometimes will do — then his condition may be unfavourable for work; but so will be the condition of a shoemaker who has been similarly imprudent....I was once told that the surest aid to the writing of a book was a piece of cobbler's wax on my chair. I certainly believe in the cobbler's wax much more than the inspiration.

Anthony Trollope

When writers meditate, they don't pick bland, meaningless mantras to say over and over to themselves. They pick mantras that are hot and prickly, full of the sizzle and jingle-jangle of life. They jazz the heck out of their inner beings with the mantras they pick. I will give you some examples: *War and Peace, The Origin of Species, The Iliad, Decline and Fall of the Roman Empire, Critique of Pure Reason, Madame Bovary, Life on the Mississippi, Romeo and Juliet, The Red Badge of Courage.*

Kurt Vonnegut

I got dumped in 1998. I'd been going out with this guy for a long time. I thought he was the one and he wasn't. It ended up being one of those passive-aggressive things where he was so awful to me that I ended up being the one to say, "OK, let's take a break here," and he found another girlfriend ten minutes later, demonstrating a speed and alacrity I rarely glimpsed during our years together. So there I was, totally miserable and brokenhearted; I wanted him back, and he wanted no part of me. I wanted to write something in the voice that I had in my head, the voice of this girl who'd been so hurt and brokenhearted. That voice became the bones of *Good in Bed*.

Jennifer Weiner

Intellectuals

I still think that it belongs to the essence of being an intellectual that one fabricates ideas about everything. No one ever blamed someone if he "coordinated" because he had to take care of his wife or child. The worst thing was that some people really believed in Nazism! For a short time, many for a very short time. But that means that they made up ideas about Hitler, in part terrifically interesting things! Completely fantastic and interesting and complicated things!

Hannah Arendt

[Thomas] Carlyle said that men were mostly fools. Christianity, with a surer and more reverent realism, says that they are all fools. This doctrine is sometimes called the doctrine of original sin. It may also be described as the doctrine of the equality of men. But the essential point of it is merely this, that whatever primary and far-reaching moral dangers affect any man, affect all men. All men can be criminals, if tempted; all men can be heroes, if inspired. And this doctrine does away altogether with Carlyle's pathetic belief (or any one else's pathetic belief) in "the wise few." There are no wise few. Every aristocracy that has ever existed has behaved, in all essential points, exactly like a small mob.

G.K. Chesterton. When asked the population of England, Carlyle replied, "Thirty million, mostly fools."

The most fluent talkers or most plausible reasoners are not always the justest thinkers.

William Hazlitt

Only those capable of silliness can be called truly intelligent.

Christopher Isherwood

When I was a kid I thought there were a lot of brilliant people who wrote dull stuff because they were corrupt. And it took me a long time

There is nothing so absurd that it has not been said by some philosopher.

Cicero

I think if you're a fiction writer and you're too intelligent, you cannot write. But if you're stupid, you cannot write. You have to find a position in between. That is very difficult.

Haruki Murakami

Don't expose yourself to the idiocy of other people, don't read the comments section in places where you've placed essays, don't read your Amazon or Goodreads reviews. Have a trusted friend send the good ones to you. Reading the comments section is like being in high school and sitting in a stall with your feet on the toilet seat so nobody knows you're there, and listening to what the girls are saying.

Masie Cochran, editor

to realize that most of them just couldn't write that much better.

Pauline Kael

[Saul] Bellow and I spent half the night talking about Mary McCarthy's alleged story. Perhaps there is something of an outraged masculine reaction involved (as I believe there was in much of the critical reaction to her first book) but we believe this thing is so vile, so perfect an example of everything that is nasty in New York and everything that is sterile in recent American writing, that we came to the conclusion that something should be done about it.

Harold Kaplan, about The Oasis, *which satirized New York intellectuals*

In countries like Britain or the United States, the literary intelligentsia has grown large enough to constitute a world in itself. One important result of this is that the opinions which a writer feels frightened of expressing are not those which are disapproved of by society as a whole. To a great extent, what is still loosely thought of as heterodoxy has become orthodoxy. It is nonsense to pretend, for instance, that at this date there is something daring and original in proclaiming yourself an anarchist, an atheist, a pacifist, etc. The daring thing, or at any rate the unfashionable thing, is to believe in God or to approve of the capitalist system.

George Orwell

This phenomenon of new elites, which... rise up from the lower strata of society, mount up to the higher strata, flourish there, and then fall into decadence, are annihilated or disappear — this is one of the motive forces of history.

Vilfredo Pareto, (1848-1923) Italian economist and sociologist

Being intelligent isn't, for me, like doing something "better." It's the only way I exist. If I'm not [being] intelligent, I hover near being catatonic.

Susan Sontag

[New York intellectuals of the mid-century] were overbearing and arrogant, excessively competitive; they lacked magnanimity and often they lacked common courtesy.

Diana Trilling

I would add that novelists are not only unusually depressed, by and large, but have, on the average, about the same IQs as the cosmetics consultants at Bloomingdale's department store. Our power is patience. We have discovered that writing allows even a stupid person to seem halfway intelligent, if only that person will write the same thought over and over again, improving it just a little bit each time. It is a lot like inflating a blimp with a bicycle pump. Anybody can do it. All it takes is time.

Kurt Vonnegut

What is a highbrow? It is a man who has found something more interesting than women.

Edgar Wallace

Internet

The cardinal rule to leading a happy life is that you must never, under any circumstances, Google yourself.

Caitlin Flanagan

Buy your domain name: yourname.com. I didn't think *Jean Kwok* was a common name but there are twelve of us on Facebook. It's a pain if someone else owns your domain name and has put up a website selling vacuum cleaners on it.

Jean Kwok

I've been suggesting to people that almost every publication now has a big online presence. I think that there's a lot more openness to new writers on websites. I mean, I can see this with *The New Yorker* — the chance of getting something on the website is infinitely greater than getting in the print magazine.

Susan Orlean

Interpretation

There are things you do that you don't understand until you're told. It was a critic who described *World's Fair* as a portrait of the artist as a young boy. I had never thought of it that way, but it's a fair way to look at it.

E.L. Doctorow

Interruptions

Any day's routine interruptions and distractions don't much hurt a work in progress and may actually help it in some ways. It is, after all, the dab of grit that seeps into an oyster's shell that makes the pearl, not pearl-making seminars with other oysters.

Stephen King

Interviews

I have, you know, spent time being interviewed by people, and then when I see what they've written, I've often been dismayed. I think every writer can take the same subject, and every writer will make a different story out of it, putting the emphases in different places, highlighting this, deciding to leave out that. If you're the subject what you will see when you read that work is something often quite different than the reality you remember. It's a somewhat disturbing process.

Joyce Johnson, Jack Kerouac's lover and biographer

Never mind the work, let's review the author. Someone who sits alone for hours at a time, typing, must be really fascinating and it beats having to think about anything, doesn't it?

A.L. Kennedy

In your interview you have certainly been most accurate … But you have not a word of explanation; why my manner was at several points is not indicated. Therefore, no reader can possibly know where I was in earnest and where I was joking; or whether I was joking altogether or in earnest altogether. Such a report of a conversation has no value. It can convey many meanings to the reader, but never the right one. To add interpretations which would convey the right meaning is a something which would require — what? An art so high and fine and difficult that no possessor of it would ever be allowed to waste it on interviews. … Leave the whole interview out; it is rubbish. I wouldn't talk in my sleep if I couldn't talk better than that.

Mark Twain

It rots a writer's brain, it cretinizes you. You say the same thing again and again, and when you do that happily you're well on the way to becoming a cretin. Or a politician.

John Updike

People who can't talk interviewed by people who can't write for

”

This business of writing about writers is more ambivalent than the end product normally admits. As a fan and reader, you want your hero to be genuinely inspirational. As a journalist, you hope for lunacy, spite, deplorable indiscretions, a full-scale nervous breakdown in mid-interview...

Martin Amis

My plan was to get the easiest, most boring job possible so that I would have the mental energy for writing.

Sophie Hannah

people who can't read.

Frank Zappa, on music journalism

Jobs, Outside

The best job that was ever offered to me was to become a landlord in a brothel. In my opinion it's the perfect milieu for an artist to work in. It gives him perfect economic freedom; he's free of fear and hunger; he has a roof over his head and nothing whatever to do except a few simple accounts and to go once every month and pay off the local police. The place is quiet during the morning hours, which is the best time of the day to work. There's enough social life in the evening, if he wishes to participate, to keep him from getting bored; it gives him a certain standing in his society; he has nothing to do because the madam keeps his books; all the inmates of the house are females and would defer to him and call him "sir." All the bootleggers in the neighborhood would call him "sir." And he could call the police by their first names. So the only environment the artist needs is whatever peace, whatever solitude, and whatever pleasure he can get at not too high a cost.

William Faulkner

We made a solemn vow not to take any job outside of show business. We borrowed money from parents and friends, rather than take that lethal job waiting tables. This forced us to take any job offered to us. Anything. We once did a show in the middle of the Benjamin Franklin Parkway in Philadelphia as part of a fashion show on a hot July night while all around our stage, a race-riot was fully under way. That's how serious we were about our vow.

Teller, of Penn and Teller

Jokes

I'm writing a book. I've got the page numbers done.

Steven Wright, comedian

Journalism

The newspaper functions the same way in most of our communities today as the artist who does not know how to create, doesn't know what he's creating, or how to go about relaxing tensions. The newspaper is the hairball of our time. And it creates these tensions. It thrusts them into our mind, and it winds up delivering us into the hands of a feeling which says, "Life is no damned good. We might as well blow our brains out. We might as well destroy Russia and ourselves on the same magnificent day." Well, any time you're playing around with a death wish in this way, any time you're playing around with the dark side of mankind, with the destructive side of mankind, it behooves you to know what you're playing with. … You cannot in your art duplicate the "half function" that is going on in your society, in the newspapers and other places in your society, where a certain tension is not being relieved. It is up to the artist to look to that tension and see if he can relieve it, not by playing the Pollyanna, not by giving happy endings, but by making sure that the sickness is a whole, and that the sickness finally results in a cleansing by being really sick.

Ray Bradbury

A journalist is stimulated by a deadline. He writes worse when he has time.

Karl Kraus

It is amazing how much contempt

People who are drawn to journalism are usually people who, because of their cynicism or emotional detachment or reserve or whatever, are incapable of being anything but witnesses to events. Something prevents them from becoming involved, committed, and allows them to remain separate.

Nora Ephron

Through the absence of all wholesome restraint the newspaper has become in a large degree a national curse, and will probably damn the Republic yet.

Mark Twain

there is for the professional media that surrounds any given enterprise. I find it all the time. Silicon Valley entrepreneurs think the tech journalists are all stupid. The sports people think that about the sports journalists. They don't say that to the sports journalists, because they want the sports journalists to be nice to them. But the level of contempt is very high. You need to kind of cut through that. You've got to be willing to not be a member of the tribe.

Michael Lewis

Most of us novelists who are any good are invariably half-educated; inaccurate, albeit brilliant on occasion; insufferably vain of course; and — the indispensable requirement for a good newspaper — as eager to tell a lie as the truth.

Norman Mailer

The difference between journalism and literature is that journalism is unreadable and literature is not read.

Oscar Wilde

Journals

I will keep no further journal ... to prevent me returning, like a dog, to the vomit of memory.

Lord Byron, journal entry, April 19, 1814.
He did not stop, however

Superficial to understand the journal as just a receptacle for one's private, secret thoughts like a confidante who is deaf, dumb and illiterate. In the journal I do not just express myself more openly than I could to any person; I create myself.

Susan Sontag, journal entry

I have long kept a journal to which I consign meditations about "the omniscience of the novelist" and thought about how time can be expressed in narration, and so on. But I never reread those entries. They are like the brief canters that a man would take on his horse during the days preceding a race. They inform the buried critic that I know he's there, and I hope he's constantly at work clarifying his system of principles, helping me when I'm not aware of it, and that I also hope he will not intrude on the day of the race.

Thornton Wilder

Landscape

A true description of Nature should be very brief and have a character of relevance. … One ought to seize upon the little particulars, grouping them in such a way that, in reading, when you shut your eyes, you get a picture. For instance, you will get the full effect of a moonlit night if you write that on the mill-dam a little glowing star-point flashed from the neck of a broken bottle, and the round, black shadow of a dog, or a wolf, emerged and ran, etc. Nature becomes animated if you are not squeamish about employing comparisons of her phenomena with ordinary human activities.

Anton Chekhov

To write about a place you have to hate it, like you hate your own wife.

William Faulkner

Vegetation has a most important influence on the quality of places. Vegetation is life, and its degree of density indicates the amount of life a place harbors. Places devoid of plant life are associated with deprivation and death, places of abundant vegetation are pleasant and erotic. Deserts and mountain tops present the terrifying aspects of lifeless matter whereas the forest is

”

What usually comes first is the setting. I can have what I think is a strong response to the spirit of a place. I can be perhaps in an old house or a community of a people, a lonely stretch of beach and say this is where it happened.

P.D. James

It is the deepest desire of every writer, the one we never admit or even dare to speak of: to write a book we can leave as a legacy. And although it is sometimes easy to forget, wanting to be a writer is not about reviews or advances or how many copies are printed or sold. It is much simpler than that and much more passionate. If you do it right, and if they publish it, you may actually leave something behind that can last forever.

Alice Hoffman

life in an active, wild state.

Leonard Lutwack

If you get the landscape right, the characters will step out of it, and they'll be in the right place.

Annie Proulx

Too many writers ignore landscape to their peril. Perhaps the problem is their lack of visual acuity. We are unpracticed in the art of looking . Many authors know this about landscape: that it is the setting or background for their characters. But the better authors realize much more. Place can be shorthand (or longhand) to explain a hero or villain: Think of the difference between the living green forest of Ents and the Orc-made desert of Modor in *The Lord of the Rings*. Better writers also know that landscape can be metaphor, can be a parallel to their characters' lives, can become central to the action, can even be a character in itself. Think of R.L. Stevenson's Davie Balfour, striding across the harsh, Highland countryside, becoming a man. The territory he treads helps to shape him. Think of the uncompromising sea through which Captain Ahab plows and how it defines him, creates him just as the whale Moby Dick "tasks" and "heaps" him. Or how the rough island on which Robinson Crusoe is marooned is the making of his soul.

Jane Yolen

Language

Language is a skin: I rub my language against the other. It is as if I had words instead of fingers, or fingers at the tip of my words. My language trembles with desire.

Roland Barthes

Language: the one tool that enables us to grasp hold of our lives and transcend our fate by understanding it.

Molly Haskell

Never has a human language, (I mean a grammatical one) achieved half the animation, wit, elegance, and spirit that a cat reveals in the waving of her tail or a bird of paradise in the silvery plumage of its wedding attire.

Herman Hesse

The vitality of language lies in its ability to limn the actual, imagined and possible lives of its speakers, readers, writers. Although its poise is sometimes in displacing experience, it is not a substitute for it. It arcs toward the place where meaning may lie.

Toni Morrison

Language is the autobiography of the human mind.

Max Müller

The problem with defending the purity of the English language is that English is about as pure as a cribhouse whore. We don't just borrow words; on occasion, English has pursued other languages down alleyways to beat them unconscious and rifle their pockets for new vocabulary.

James Nicoll

Words are the most powerful shaping tool. Writing, speech, language don't just communicate fact, they create fact.

David Treuer

The future author is one who discovers that language, the exploration and manipulation of the resources of language, will serve him in winning through to his way. This does not necessarily mean that he is highly articulate in persuading or cajoling or outsmarting his parents and companions, for this type of child is not usually of the "community" type — he is at one remove from the persons around him. (The future scientist is at eight removes.) Language for him is the instrument for digesting experience, for explaining himself to himself.

Thornton Wilder

Legacy

Some books are undeservedly forgotten; none are undeservedly remembered.

W.H. Auden

Everyone must leave something behind when he dies, my grandfather said. A child or a book or a painting or a house or a wall built or a pair of shoes made. Or a garden planted. Something your hand touched some way so your soul has somewhere to go when you die, and when people look at that tree or that flower you planted, you're there.

Ray Bradbury

You have to judge them by their work. Their lives are a mess but so is everyone's.

Liz Calder, publisher

Poetry will steal death from me.

Rene Char

It matters not how a man dies, but how he lives. The act of dying is not of importance, it lasts so short a time.

Samuel Johnson

If I should die, I have left no immortal work behind me — nothing to make my friends proud of my memory — but I have lov'd the principle of beauty in all things, and if I had had time I would have made myself remember'd.

John Keats

I don't really have a style so much as a sensibility. I'm working on mostly hardcover books that are supposed to be by definition archival. So I try to imagine what X will look like in five years. What will it look like in 10 years? What will it look like in 20 years? And there are certain basic formal considerations that won't change. Big and small, dark and light, certain conceptual things; that's kind of it. Will this look good a long time from now or will it look dated?

Chip Kidd

I am reasonably happy with what I have written and with the reception it has had. But I can't think of any work or event that makes it to the "greatest thrill" category. It's a little bit like asking a man who has loved his breakfast eggs for 60 years to name the most thrilling egg he ever ate. … They were all so good!

R.A. Lafferty

It's such an odd notion, particularly in this technological society, of whether your life is justified by being a novelist. And the nice thing about getting older is that I no longer worry about that. I've come to the simple recognition that would have saved me much woe 30 or 40 or 50 years ago — that one's eventual reputation has very little to do with one's talent. History determines it, not the order of your words.

Norman Mailer

Looking back, I imagine I was

The marble tomb of Messala is split by the wild fig, and the audacious muleteer laughs at the mutilated horses of the statue of Crispus. But as for writings, they are indestructible either by thieves or the ravages of time; such monuments alone are proof against death.

Marcus Valerius Martial, 1st century A.D.

”

One thing alone I charge you. As you live, believe in life! Always human beings will live and progress to greater, broader and fuller life. The only possible death is to lose belief in this truth simply because the great end comes slowly, because time is long.

W.E.B. Du Bois, sociologist, civil rights activist

Life is a kiln in which one bakes one's experiences: some are taken out half done, some underdone and some undone.

Nuruddin Farah

always writing. Twaddle it was, too. But better far write twaddle or anything, anything, than nothing at all.

Katherine Mansfield

The elect sneer at popularity; they are inclined even to assert that it is a proof of mediocrity; but they forget that posterity makes its choice not from among the unknown writers of a period, but from among the known. It may be that some great masterpiece which deserves immortality has fallen still-born from the press, but posterity will never hear of it; it may be that posterity will scrap all the bestsellers of our day, but it is among them that it must choose.

W. Somerset Maugham

All the modern greats — Lawrence, Yeats, Pound — in one way or another, or on the subject of women or Jews, had views that are unacceptable by today's standards. But you have to see them in their historical context. And you must also remember that many of the right-on thinkers of their day were lesser talents as imaginative writers.

Blake Morrison, critic and poet

There are thousands of people who don't like what I do. Fortunately, there are millions who do.

James Patterson

We live as nouns, but we'll be remembered as verbs.

Bill Peschel

If you live long enough, the venerability factor creeps in; you get accused of things you never did and praised for virtues you never had.

I.F. Stone, journalist and publisher

Perhaps the critics are right: this generation may not produce literature equal to that of any past generation — who cares? The writer will be dead before anyone can judge him — but he *must* go on writing, reflecting disorder, defeat, despair, should that be all that he sees at the moment, but ever searching for the elusive love, joy, and hope.

William Styron

In the end, you're measured not by how much you undertake but by what you finally accomplish.

Donald Trump

No really great song can ever attain full purport till long after the death of its singer — till it has accrued and incorporated the many passions, many joys and sorrows, it has aroused.

Walt Whitman

I don't care if I'm known or remembered, respected or get famous. The reason I write music is because I like to listen to it. And if there are other people who like to listen to it, then that's fine.

Frank Zappa

Letters

The great secret in life ... [is] not to open letters for a fortnight. At the expiration of that period you will find that nearly all of them have answered themselves.

Arthur Binstead

I have made this letter longer only because I have not had time to make it shorter.

Blaise Pascal

Library

I have always imagined that Paradise will be a kind of library.

Jorge Luis Borges

The closest you will ever come in this life to an orderly universe is a good library.

Ashleigh Brilliant

If humanity were to lose its libraries, not only would it be deprived of certain treasures of art, certain spiritual riches, but, more important still, it would lose its recipes for living.

Georges Duhamel

(With librarians dumping classics in favor of the fashionable, the rot is coming from inside the building.)

A man's library is a sort of harem, and tender readers have a great prudency in showing their books to a stranger.

Ralph Waldo Emerson

No place affords a more striking conviction of the vanity of human hopes than a public library.

Samuel Johnson

Life & Living

I didn't invent this buzzing confusion. It's all around us ... the only chance of renewal is to open our eyes and see the mess.

Samuel Beckett

Writing is not apart from living. Writing is a kind of double living. The writer experiences everything twice. Once in reality and once in that mirror which waits always before or behind him.

Catherine Drinker Bowen

A writer's life is not designed to reassure your mother.

Rita Mae Brown

The true life is not reducible to words spoken or written, not by anyone, ever.

Don DeLillo

Be regular and orderly in your life like a bourgeois, so that you may be violent and original in your work.

Gustave Flaubert

(No connection to the contemporary phrase "A lady in the streets and a freak in the sheets," inspired by noted artist Ludacris.)

If you would not be forgotten,
As soon as you are dead & rotten
Either write things worth reading
Or do the things worth writing.

Benjamin Franklin

Art is long, life short; judgment difficult, opportunity transient.

Johann Goethe

Life is made up of sobs, sniffles, and smiles, with sniffles predominating.

O. Henry

There is no real life except in working, that is to say in the imagination.

Patricia Highsmith

Your time is limited, so don't waste it living someone else's life. Don't be trapped by dogma — which is living with the results of other people's thinking. Don't let the noise of others' opinions drown out your own inner voice. And most important, have the courage to follow your heart and intuition.

Steve Jobs

It is not difficult to conceive, however, that for many reasons a man writes much better than he lives. For without entering into refined speculations, it may be shewn much easier to design than to perform.

Samuel Johnson

The world keeps ending but new people too dumb to know it keep showing up as if the fun's just started.

John Updike, **Rabbit is Rich**

Truly the beauty of life is its uncertainty.

Yoshida Kenko

”

Literature duplicates the experience of living in a way that nothing else can, drawing you so fully into another life that you temporarily forget you have one of your own. That is why you read it, and might even sit up in bed till dawn, throwing your whole tomorrow out of whack, simply to find out what happens to some people who — you know perfectly well — are made up.

Barbara Kingsolver

No culture has yet solved the dilemma each has faced with the growth of a conscious mind: How to live a moral and compassionate existence when one is fully aware of the blood, the horror inherent in life, when one finds darkness not only in one's culture but within oneself. If there is a stage at which an individual life becomes truly adult, it must be when one grasps the irony in its unfolding and accepts responsibility for a life lived in the midst of such paradox. One must live in the middle of contradiction because if all contradiction were eliminated at once life would collapse. There are simply no answers to some of the great pressing questions. You continue to live them out, making your life a worthy expression of leaning into the light.

Barry Lopez

A struggle of existence is not life; life is the life of the spirit, surely; of feeling, of sensibility, of expansion.

Vita Sackville-West

The secret of life is paying attention.

Damon Suede

People are boxed in by whatever their circumstances are. We would all like to try different lives and one of the really sad things is that so many people cannot and they are truly enslaved in the lives they have even if it is a comfortable life. This is how many women feel and this is why feminism is such a major force in the world. Women, even very comfortable women, who are chained to a role, their husbands often are just as chained.

Alice Walker

I feel profoundly in the depths of my being that in the last resort nothing matters.

Leonard Woolf. Paul Theorux comments: "The title of his last volume [of memoirs], The Journey Not the Arrival Matters, *suggests that he might have changed his mind"*

Limitations

There was an art-school truism, saying "less is more" or something. I remember thinking that I didn't have to be Eric Clapton or whatever. If I could play the right three notes, or an interesting set of three notes, that I could be more effective than playing a hundred notes. So I found a way out of that problem. If I realized what my limitations are, if I worked within that, then I could make something ... just as powerful as music by somebody who has real chops.

David Byrne

The only way of finding the limits of the possible is by going beyond them into the impossible.

Arthur C. Clarke

In a lot of ways book cover design is really quite limited. Which is good. There's a saying one of my teachers used to have, which is that limits are possibilities and, if your choices are limited, you're forced to think more.

Chip Kidd

Listening

When people realize they're being listened to, they tell you things.

Richard Ford

It's all about paying attention. Attention is vitality. It connects you with others. It makes you eager. Be eager.

Susan Sontag

An essential element for good writing is a good ear: One must listen to the sound of one's prose.

Barbara Tuchman

Literature

Literature is nothing less, after all, than an ongoing discussion about what it means to be human. It is intended to awaken compassion within the reader and, when necessary, distress.

Steve Almond

Books say, "She did this because." Life says, "She did this." Books are where things are explained to you; life is where things aren't. I'm not surprised that some people prefer books. Books make sense. The only problem is that the lives they make sense of are other people's lives, never your own.

Julian Barnes

Literature is recognizable through its capacity to evoke more than it says, is based on artful selection, throws up symbols, suggests a theology or metaphysic of which the story itself is a kind of allegory.

Anthony Burgess

If we want to be sincere, we must admit that there is a well-nourished love and an ill-nourished love. And the rest is literature.

Colette

The best literary work is that which leaves the reader better for having read it.

Arthur Conan Doyle

Literature is the art of writing something that will be read twice; journalism is what will be grasped at once.

Cyril Connolly

(And much genre fiction is grasped and rarely retained at all.)

Proust was right: life is represented better by bad music than by a *Missa solemnis* [Latin: "solemn mass"]. Great art makes fun of us as it comforts us, because it shows us the world as the artists would like the world to be. The dime novel, however, pretends to joke, but then it shows us the world as it actually is — or at least the world as it will become. ... What has taken place in the real world was predicted in penny dreadfuls.

Umberto Eco

The experience of each new age requires a new confession, and the world seems always waiting for its poet.

Ralph Waldo Emerson

The student who undertakes to write for literary rather than commercial ends enjoys a freedom which would be impossible were he aiming at a market: of necessity the editors of commercial magazines reject, in deference to the sensibilities and prejudices of their readers, most stories with tragic endings and all stories dealing honestly with certain phases of undeniably significant experience.

John T. Frederick

Ultimately, literature is nothing but carpentry. With both you are working with a reality, a material just as hard as wood.

Gabriel Garcia Marquez

[People who read for lifelike characters or plots] are really not interested in literature. They are interested in folks.

William Gass

It's a curious bargain that we make as writers to assume that our emotional lives are synchronous in

”

Once you allow yourself to identify with the people in a story, then you might begin to see yourself in that story even if on the surface it's far removed from your situation. This is what I try to tell my students: this is one great thing that literature can do — it can make us identify with situations and people far away. If it does that, it's a miracle.

Chinua Achebe

”

Literature could be said to be a sort of disciplined technique for arousing certain emotions.

Iris Murdoch

A story is a formula for extracting meaning from chaos, a handful of water we scoop up to recall an ocean.

John Edgar Wideman

large part with those of every other member of the species. That's the great lesson of literature, that it's predicated on the notion that we are not just similar but unanimous. It's the only form that I can think of right now that makes that basic assumption. It's thrilling to think that I can sit down and read a passage from Montaigne and weep real tears, or be moved by Dante's vision or Chaucer's vision. These people have been fog on a coffin lid for four or five hundred years, yet they've left their emotional traces with such precision that those traces become my own.

Allan Gurganus

The only sensible ends of literature are, first, the pleasurable toil of writing; second, the gratification of one's family and friends; and, lastly, the solid cash.

Nathaniel Hawthorne

The primary duty of literature – to tell us the truth about ourselves by telling us lies about people who never existed.

Stephen King

In the beginning was the review copy, and a man received it from the publisher. Then he wrote a review. Then he wrote a book which the publisher accepted and sent on to someone else as a review copy. The man who received it did likewise. This is how modern literature came into being.

Karl Kraus

Literature is mostly about having sex and not much about having children. Life is the other way around.

David Lodge

We have to acknowledge that the thing we call "literature" is more pluralistic now, just as society ought to be. The melting pot never worked. We ought to be able to accept on equal terms everybody from the Hasidim to Walter Lippmann, from the Rastafarians to Ralph Bunche.

Toni Morrison

I think literature should be read privately. Literature is not for the young. Literature is for the old, the experienced, the wounded, the damaged, who read literature to find echoes of their own experience and balm of a certain sort. Contented tribal societies don't need literature. They pound their yams and they're quite happy.

V.S. Naipaul

Fiction is no longer the dominant storytelling device of our time. In the 19th century it worked great and fiction was the king, but it's not the king any more. And the audience for fiction now is the smartest audience that's ever existed.

Chuck Palahniuk

One of the fascinating things about literature is that it's an absolutely unnecessary product that people for whatever reasons seem to think is vital. And that in and of itself makes it incredibly precious to me.

Dale Peck

Literature is news that stays news.

Ezra Pound

Literature is an occupation in which you have to keep proving your talent to people who have none.

Jules Renard

The literature of the future will, I clearly see, be amazing. At last it'll tell the truth, and be indecent and amusing, and romantic, and even (after about 100 years) be written well. ... To live in those days, when books will pour out from the press reeking with all the filth of Petronius, all the frenzy of Dostoevsky, all the romance of the Arabian Nights, and all the exquisiteness of Voltaire! But it won't be only the books that will be charming then. The people! The young men! … even the young women … but the vistas are too exacerbating.

Lytton Strachey

Literature is well enough, as a time-passer, and for the improvement and general elevation and purification of mankind, but it has no practical value.

Mark Twain

Odd how nineteenth-century literature is sealed off at both ends by an anal scandal: Wilde up Bosie's bum, Byron up Annabella's.

Kenneth Tynan

If you make people laugh or cry about little black marks on sheets of white paper, what is that but a practical joke? All the great story lines are great practical jokes that people fall for over and over again.

Kurt Vonnegut

Literature is the orchestration of platitudes.

Thornton Wilder

My contention is that Sherlock Holmes is literature on a humble but not ignoble level, whereas the mystery writers most invoke now are not. The old stories are literature... by virtue of imagination and style.

Edmund Wilson

Every great and original writer, in proportion as he is great or original, must himself create the taste by which he is to be relished; he must teach the art by which he is to be seen.

William Wordsworth, quoting Coleridge

Logic

I have a favorite little saying to myself: "Logic is dull."

Alfred Hitchcock

Loneliness

We are lonesome animals. We spend all our life trying to be less lonesome. One of our ancient methods is to tell a story begging the listener to say – and to feel – "Yes, that's the way it is, or at least that's the way I feel it. You're not as alone as you thought."

John Steinbeck

In 1996, with movies and TV doing such good jobs of holding the attention of literates and illiterates alike, I have to question the value of my very strange, when you think about it, charm school. There *is* this: Attempted seductions with nothing but words on paper are so cheap for would-be ink-stained Don Juans or Cleopatras! They don't have to get a bankable actor or actress to commit to the project, and then a bankable director, and so on, and then raise millions and millions of buckareenies from manic-depressive experts on what most people want.

Still and all, why bother? Here's *my* answer: Many people need desperately to receive this message: "I feel and think much as you do, care about many of the things you care about, although most people don't care about them. You are not alone."

Kurt Vonnegut

”

The world opens itself up to those who are willing to be lonely. No one was paying any attention to me when I was a teenager. I didn't go to the junior prom. I didn't have peers who shared my interests. Neglect gave me the sense that the world was mine, because no one knew who I was or what I was doing. I felt the freedom to take risks.

Richard Rodriguez

Luck is a fine thing for a writer, but take note: Good writing creates luck.

Bill Roorbach

”

The cruelest lies are often told in silence.

Robert Louis Stevenson

Any sufficiently advanced technology is indistinguishable from magic.

Arthur C. Clarke

Love

I still believe in love. Especially when it helps sustain the plot structure.

Kinky Friedman

Before I am able to write anything, I must first of all experience the fever of love.

Leo Tolstoy

Luck

I am a great believer in luck, and I find the harder I work the more I have of it.

Stephen Leacock

My humiliation before the Yeshiva belligerents — indeed, the angry Jewish resistance that I aroused virtually from the start — was the luckiest break I could have had. I was branded.

Philip Roth

Lying

There are two ways for a writer to be dishonest in this world. One is to write for the dollar, for the fast buck. That will insure him against ever knowing or discovering himself in any way. The second way is to slant one's stories toward an intellectual bias. For instance to cynically observe, this is the Color Year, so I will write a story about the Negro problem, or this is the year that Kafka is A-OK, so I will write a Kafka-kind story. Or this is the year of Ionesco or Baldwin or Albee, so I will write me an Ionesco or Baldwin or Albee type play. This, too, is the work of liars and cheats, of frauds and mountebanks, to carve one's work in the likeness of others, to follow literary or intellectual tastes, to cross your political t's as others tell you. When you look to the taste of your time to tell your direction, you are already dead. You might as well quit then, for you will never be individual, never different, never exciting. Worst of all, you will come to the end of your life, with your well undug, your secret bones unrattled and your hidden tongue unspoken. What a shame, what a damned shame that would be.

Ray Bradbury

The most common human act that writing a novel resembles is lying. The working novelist lies daily, very complexly, and at great length. If not for our excessive vanity and our over-active imaginations, novelists might be unusually difficult to deceive.

William Gibson

When I was a little boy they called me a liar but now that I am a grown-up they call me a writer.

Isaac Bashevis Singer

Magazines & Magazine Writing

I'd write about spastic colons, foot fungus, you name it. It was really good training, and great discipline. You have to write to a prescribed word length, and make whatever you're writing interesting, to keep the reader turning the page.

Candace Bushnell, on writing for women's magazines

I note what you say about your aspiration to edit a magazine. I am sending you by this mail a six-chambered revolver. Load it and fire every one into your head. You will thank me after you get to hell and learn from other editors there how dreadful their job was on earth.

H.L. Mencken, to a young William Saroyan asking for advice about editing a magazine

It seems to me that if you are to go on writing for popular magazines you will deliberately have to make your stuff cheaper. At present you are working from character to plot, and what they want, I'm convinced, is the story that contains only obvious characters who exist simply for the sake of the plot.

P.G. Wodehouse

Magic

The bridge between the words glamour and grammar is magic. According to the OED, glamour evolved through an ancient association between learning and enchantment.

Roy Peter Clark

We, and I think I'm speaking for many writers, don't know what it is that sometimes comes to make our books alive. All we can do is to write dutifully and day after day, every day, giving our work the very best of what we are capable. I don't think that we can consciously put the magic in; it doesn't work that way. When the magic comes, it's a gift.

Madeleine L'Engle

Wisdom begins in wonder.

Socrates

There's magic in the world. There is. People will tell you there isn't – they just want you to get back to work and be quiet and not ask questions. These are people who don't know where to look or who were not blessed with eyes that could see magic. Magical eyes. If you have them, develop them.

Tennessee Williams

Marketing

Jurassic Park would absolutely have sold a similar amount, whether it had my cover on or not. I'm very much against the idea that the cover will sell the book. Marketing departments of publishing houses tend to latch onto this concept and they can't let go. But it's about whether the book itself really connects with the public, and the cover is only a small part of that.

Chip Kidd

If you look at most of the great artists of the twentieth century, they were also amazing marketers. Andy Warhol was a marketing *genius*. ... Paul McCartney is a self-promotion whiz; he knows what he's doing. So to color all previous artists as not having anything to do with self-promotion is really a disservice that people pay to themselves.

Austin Kleon

As soon as my book is out, I'm on Facebook and Twitter several times a day talking about it. I'll go on to forums and post them under my name and various other names.

Stephen Leather, who was criticized for his use of fake accounts to promote his books

Nobody reads a mystery to get to the middle. They read it to get to the end. If it's a letdown, they won't buy anymore. The first page sells that book. The last page sells your next book.

Mickey Spillane

Without promotion something terrible happens … Nothing!

WDVA Radio Ad, misattributed to P.T. Barnum

"

About WT [Weird Tales] covers — they really are too trivial to get angry about. If they weren't totally irrelevant and unrepresentative nudes, they'd probably be something equally awkward and trivial, even though less irrelevant ... I have no objection to the nude in art — in fact the human figure is as worthy a type of subject-matter as any other object of beauty in the visible world. But I don't see what the hell Mrs. Brundage's undressed ladies have to do with weird fiction.

H.P. Lovecraft

I wish I'd never written it. It was too big of an opening into my life. I've never said this to anyone, but as soon as it came out, I realized, "You know, the reason you've never done this before is because you should not do it." When it went out of print, I never let them reprint it. It just always seemed to me that there's a reason I go through my whole life without opening it up. I'm not sure what it is, but there's a reason.

Bob Greene, about Good Morning, Merry Sunshine: A Father's Journal of His Child's First Year

Masterpieces

The future only has time for masterpieces.

Michael Dirda, book critic

Masterpieces are no more than the shipwrecked flotsam of great minds.

Marcel Proust

A great book should leave you with many experiences, and slightly exhausted at the end.

William Styron

Meaning

Storytelling reveals meaning without committing the error of defining it.

Hannah Arendt

[Criticism of my writing style] makes me think that some readers read a book as if it were an instruction manual, expecting to understand everything first time, but of course when you write, you put into every sentence an overflow of meaning, and you create in every sentence as many resonances and double meanings and ambiguities as you can possibly pack in there, so that people can read it again and get something new each time.

Hilary Mantel

The author wraps his meaning in mystery so that the vulgar shall not participate in it. His soul is a secret garden into which the elect may penetrate only after overcoming a number of perilous obstacles.

W. Somerset Maugham

Be sure that you go to the author to get at his meaning, not to find yours.

John Ruskin

They have to be given some meaning, the facts. What do they mean? The meaning's going to be influenced by a lot of things in you and your own culture. And some of these things you may be unaware of. But every historian has some kind of philosophy of life and society. … All kinds of strands and currents and factors are involved. You have to separate and put together and from that we should deduce that there's no situation in the present that's simple, either. No simple answers. And the historian, when he looks over one of these situations, is going to try and consider all these things and try to be objective and fair and balanced, but what he picks out as the meaning will, of course, be what he himself believes.

T. Harry Williams

Medicine

Alleviating suffering is very good, but it comes at the cost of what I would call a narrative understanding of one's life. You don't need to have a story anymore. Your story becomes: the chemicals in my brain were bad; I fixed those chemicals. From a humanitarian standpoint, that's great, but it makes for a less interesting world.

Jonathan Franzen

[A]s a writer I have never felt that medicine interfered with me but rather that it was my very food and drink, the very thing which made it possible for me to write. Was I not interested in man? There the thing was, right in front of me. I could touch it, smell it. It was myself, naked, just as it was, without a lie telling itself to me in its own terms.

William Carlos Williams, who trained as a doctor

Mediocrity

Among the public there are always people who prefer mediocrity, and when they get it, say, "What a relief! Here's some real poetry again." And there are also people who like poetry to be modern but for whom the really creative stuff is too strong — they need something diluted.

T.S. Eliot

Memoir & Autobiography

I feel that what I remember often is not completely true. It's always simplified by my own beliefs, by my experiences, and I am a storyteller so I like to tell the stories in ways that certain things are highlighted. My husband would say: "That's a lie." It's not a lie, exactly. It's a literary lie.

Isabel Allende

If the dullest person in the world would only put down sincerely what he or she thought about his or her life, about work and love, religion and emotion, it would be a fascinating document.

A.C. Benson

At autobiography is an obituary in serial form with the last installment missing.

Quentin Crisp

The first requisite of a good autobiography is not that the author should of had an interesting life, but that he should be able to write. Any life is interesting in the hands of a writer of genius; no life, however packed with incident, is interesting if recounted by a writer whose abilities are mediocre, or worse.

Robertson Davies

My advice to memoir writers is to embark upon a memoir for the same reason that you would embark on any other book: to fashion a text. Don't hope in a memoir to preserve your memories. If you prize your memories as they are, by all means avoid — eschew — writing a memoir. Because it is a certain way to lose them. You can't put together a memoir without cannibalizing your own life for parts. The work battens on your memories. And it replaces them.

Annie Dillard

Life is not what one has lived, but what one remembers and how one chooses to tell it.

Gabriel Garcia Marquez

Monsieur Renan calls me an "indiscreet individual." I accept the reproach and I am not ashamed of it... For ever since the world began, the only memoirs of any interest have been written by "indiscreet individuals."

Edmond Goncourt

Memoirs belong to the category of literature, not of journalism. It is a misunderstanding to read a memoir as though the writer owes the reader the same record of literal accuracy that is owed in newspaper reporting or literary journalism. What the memoirist owes the reader is the ability to persuade that the narrator is trying, as honesty as possible, to get to the bottom of the experience at hand.

Vivian Gornick, defending using composite characters and events in her memoirs

(There's already a category for writers who do this: novels.)

For 70-odd years I have been writing about myself, which has led

”

An autobiography is the truest of all books; for while it inevitably consists mainly of extinctions of the truth, shirkings of the truth, partial revealments of the truth, with hardly an instance of plain straight truth, the remorseless truth is there, between the lines, where the author-cat is raking dust upon it which hides from the disinterested spectator neither it nor its smell (though I didn't use that figure) — the result being that the reader knows the author in spite of his wily diligences.

Mark Twain

”

Biographies of writers were then much in fashion, confessional books by or about Jewish authors all shook up with angst. I was not one of those, and might that not be a piquant novelty?

Herman Wouk, answering his wife's objection to writing a memoir: "Dear, you're not that interesting a person"

to a familiar scene: I meet someone, we chat, something stirs my memory, I begin to tell an anecdote — and the head in front of me nods up and down and smiles. She knows this story because I have put it in print, possibly three times.

Donald Hall

Next to the writer of real estate advertisements, the autobiographer is the most suspect of prose artists.

Donal Henahan

Yes, I should have left all of the interesting people and stories out of the book.

Christopher Hitchens, accused of name-dropping in his memoir

I get the rewards, the people I wrote about get the hurt.

Karl Ove Knausgaard, of My Struggle, *his 3,500-page epic memoir*

Because I knew that this book would never be read as autobiography. I was much freer to raid the darkest parts of my mind to write it.

Laura Lippman, of Every Secret Thing, *a standalone separate from her Tess Monaghan mystery series*

No one can tell the whole truth about himself.

W. Somerset Maugham

I was an 18-year-old girl. I was a forming person. It was not the wisest thing, while in the act of growing, to be in the public eye. It makes for a kind of dishonesty. It requires you to present to the world a finished product when you're not a finished product.

Joyce Maynard, whose essay "An Eighteen Year Old Looks Back on Life" in The New York Times *launched her literary career and her subsequent affair with J.D. Salinger*

The author that interested me most was naturally Sirin ... Across the dark sky of exile, Sirin passed... like a meteor, and disappeared, leaving nothing much else behind him than a vague sense of uneasiness.

Vladimir Nabokov. As a Russian exile in Berlin, he wrote his early novels under the pen name "Sirin"

Twenty-five seems to be the latest age at which anybody should write an autobiography. It has an air of finality about it, as though one had clambered to the summit of the great Hill, and were waving goodbye to some distant country which can never be revisited.

Beverly Nichols, whose first memoir was Twenty-Five *(1926)*

I would think that it was not terrifically important to me when you choose not to indulge in or claim that particular weightiness that attaches to the claim of truth. Which is part of the reason I considered publishing this book [*What We Lost*] as a novel. I didn't want to make too great a claim to the truth here. These are things that actually happened to my father. His reaction to them is something I can only base on my own observations of what he said.

And to some degree, as in any act of writing like this, part of what I am trying to do is give voice to feelings that I feel like he has never been able to fully express. Or else the story would not be as resonant as it is in our family history.

Dale Peck

History is written by the winners. Memoirs are written by the whiners.

Bill Peschel

To write one's memoirs is to speak

ill of everybody except oneself.

Henri Philippe Pétain, French political and military leader

The professional writer who spends his time becoming other people and places, real or imaginary, finds he has written his life away and has become almost nothing. The true autobiography of this egotist is exposed in all its intimate foliage in his work.

V.S. Pritchett

My goal when I sit down to write out of my own circumstances is not to make myself transparent. In fact, I am building an edifice. Stone by stone, I am constructing a story. Brick by brick, I am learning what image, what memory belongs to what. I am arranging the pieces that come my way, as Virginia Woolf suggests in her diary. I am attempting to make a piece of music as clear, as emotionally resonant and orderly, as a sonata. I am striving to make order out of chaos, which is the sweetest pleasure I know. When I succeed, I have a thing, this story, to offer. It isn't me. It isn't even a facsimile.

Dani Shapiro

A writer must rearrange reality so it will seem reasonably real to the reader.

John Steinbeck, note in Travels with Charley

I would say hooray for Steinbeck. If you want to get at the spirit of something, sometimes it's important to use the techniques of a fiction writer.

Jay Parini, Steinbeck biographer, excusing the fictions discovered in Travels with Charley

(Betraying the reader, like betraying a lover, is not a good way to maintain a relationship.)

What is more autobiographical than the sort of travel book, a dozen tomes, that I have been writing for the past 40 years? In every sense it goes with the territory. All you would ever want to know about Rebecca West is contained in the half-million words of *Black Lamb and Gray Falcon*, her book about Yugoslavia.

Paul Theroux

Memory

We are bombarded today by such a quantity of images that we can no longer distinguish direct experience from what we have seen for a few seconds on television. The memory is littered with bits and pieces of images, like a rubbish dump.

Italo Calvino

(These days, we don't know if it is live or is it a meme.)

No memory is ever alone; it's at the end of a trail of memories, a dozen trails that each have their own associations.

Louis L'Amour

Sit and quiet yourself. Luxuriate in a certain memory and the details will come. Let the images flow. You'll be amazed at what will come out on paper. I'm still learning what it is about the past that I want to write. I don't worry about it. It will emerge. It will insist on being told.

Frank McCourt

Near-total recall would be a cruel handicap. You cannot write imaginatively about past moments if you remember them too clearly. Their details become too burdensome, and hence their essences escape.

Peter Stillman

”

I was nobody; he [Gene Kelly] was a living legend. I was always around him like a terrier around his ankles. He taught me you have to have the enthusiasm of a child and be able to tell a story. He taught me to believe in myself. He taught me to have courage. So now I can stand on stage and fill a space I have to fill. You can't do that unless you have someone who inspires you. They can't teach you, they have to inspire you. All good things come from people who inspire you.

Michael Crawford, future Phantom of the Opera, on working with Gene Kelly on Hello, Dolly!

”

You almost feel that any idiot with a nickel's worth of talent can emerge from writing class able to write a competent story. In fact, so many people can now write competent stories that the short story as a medium is in danger of dying of competence. We want competence, but competence by itself is deadly. What is needed is the vision to go with it, and you do not get this from a writing class.

Flannery O'Connor

Composition, in crystallizing memory, displaces it.

John Updike

Writers often forget what they have written, since the act of writing is a letting go of a piece of one's mind.

Gore Vidal

Mental Illness

No one is creative when paralytically depressed, psychotic, institutionalized, in restraints, or dead because of suicide

Kay Redfield Jamison

It's terrible, Bob, to think that all I've suffered, and all the suffering I've caused, might have arisen from the lack of a little salt in my brain.

Robert Lowell, to his publisher Robert Giroux, about his lithium treatments

Mentors

My experience with trying to help people to write has been limited but extremely intensive. I have done everything from giving would-be writers money to live on to plotting and rewriting their stories for them, and so far I have found it all to be a waste. The people whom God or nature intended to be writers find their own answers, and those who have to ask are impossible to help. They are merely people who want to be writers.

Raymond Chandler

Authors are sometimes like tomcats. They distrust all the other toms but they are kind to kittens.

Malcolm Cowley, literary critic

Meek young men grow up in libraries, believing it their duty to accept the views, which Cicero, which Locke, which Bacon, have given, forgetful that Cicero, Locke, and Bacon were only young men in libraries, when they wrote these books.

Ralph Waldo Emerson

You're finding your way, going through the first of the four stages – imitate, emulate, equal, and surpass.

Pete Hamill, reassuring a young writer copying his style

The absence of true sages – men and women of deep sensibility – leads us to make false gods of rock poets and B-grade philosophers, injecting comic strips and children's books with significance their authors never knew they had.

Joyce Maynard

Found heaps of letters, some of them from poets and authors, who are the pest of my life. … Another begging to know whether I was acquainted with "any man or woman to whom money was for a time useless," who would venture £100 upon a literary speculation he had in hand.

Thomas Moore

Those who are around you will either be your greatest encouragers, pushing you toward that extra page or chapter, or be the reason why you abandon those stories in that unnamed desktop folder. Choose them wisely and choose them well.

Wayétu Moore

His friendship was different from anyone else's. ... He knew more about my writing ambition than I had dared to tell my own family.

Paul Theroux, about V.S. Naipaul

Such a friend I found in Walter Berry. … He alone not only encouraged me to write, as others had already done, but had the patience and the intelligence to teach me how. Others praised, some flattered — he alone took the trouble to analyze and criticize. … Once I found my footing and had my material in hand, his criticisms became increasingly searching. With each book he exacted a higher standard in economy of expression, in purity of language, in the avoidance of the hackneyed and the precious.

Edith Wharton

Message

The book [*The Women in His Life*] has no message. It's a book people can read quite easily. I work very hard to make it easy to read, without descending into an infantile prose style.

Barbara Taylor Bradford

Metaphor

Metaphor is supposed to state the unknown in terms of the known. It is supposed to say X equals Y. Yet when we say "John is a lion," we do not think of John with a mane, with four clawed paws, nor with a pompom-tipped tail. We extract from "lion" the emotional equivalent we need and let the rest go. The real metaphoric formula is X does-and-does-not-equal Y.

John Ciardi

MFA Programs

(See **Academia, Education**)

Even during my MFA program, I tried to do as much as I could to gain professional skills in a range of areas. I was thinking of my career more holistically: How could I be part of the creative and intellectual community without necessarily teaching? I edited the literary magazine, I ran a reading series, I started a professional development series.

Cara Blue Adams

So much of the material read on such occasions is so bland, so competently but un-excitingly written, so interchangeable in style and substance that it very seldom stimulates a distinct response.

John W. Aldridge, critic

The MFA life can be very lonely. I'm not talking about the solitude most writers need in order to work. Rather, it's that MFA students tend to be competitive and guarded, angling for the right publishing connections. The cliquishness is so bad that you might think you're back in high school. And the careerism is so bad that you might think you're in B-school. It's like living in 17th century New England, wondering if you are among the Puritan elect. It can get so bad, you can't even write a postcard anymore.

"Chris Altacruise," pseudonym of a former MFA student

To a large extent, contemporary literature is shaped by writing programs in universities. It's not that the writing programs harm people. But an awful lot of people influence people who shouldn't be influencing people … Today the kids are standing on the shoulders of midgets.

Stanley Elkin

This department has gone the way — not that all colleges have gone, but they talk not any human language. They talk Derrida-style, Lacan or Foucault.

Leslie Fiedler

I've never been involved in a creative writing program. In my

”

The most interesting part of the MFA vs. NYC model ... was never the question of literary culture (Brooklyn brownstones vs. Midwestern dive bars; obscure short stories vs. high-profile debut novels) so much as the question of money. The binary points to the two major means by which American writing is funded: the publishing industry and the university system.

Leslie Jamison

I am a creature of impulse; but I have to cash the checks that my mouth has written. I have some big extravagant idea of what I am going to do and I tell everyone about it; then I have to do it so I don't look like a twat.

Alan Moore

case, that was mostly because I knew I wanted to be a writer, and had enough hubris to know that I'd rather make my mistakes on the job. It was also because I had a vague suspicion that people in authority might suggest that I should write respectable but dull fiction, and then I'd be forced to kill them, and it would all end in tears or in prison.

Neil Gaiman

Mind

I've taken a lot from cognitive psychology about the way children develop theories of other minds. It's a part of the emerging into full consciousness. People who are psychotic or autistic can't read other minds. They might be frighteningly logical but they have no emotional commitment. We are all on a scale between an icy pursuit of self-interest and being overwhelmed by an awareness of what other people think.

Ian McEwan

The mind is like the stomach. It is not how much you put into it that counts, but how much it digests.

Albert Jay Nock

Mistakes

Punk still informs everything I do. You have to be willing to make mistakes and you have to be willing to make mistakes in public. Sometimes the best way to learn something is by doing it wrong and looking at what you did.

Neil Gaiman

Money

The publisher thought it [*Little Women*] FLAT, and so did I and neither hoped much for or from it. We found out our mistake, and since then, though I do not enjoy writing "moral tales" for the young, I do it because it pays well.

Louisa May Alcott

[*A Clockwork Orange* was] knocked off for money in three weeks, it became known as the raw material for a film which seemed to glorify sex and violence. The film made it easy for readers of the book to misunderstand what it was about, and the misunderstanding will pursue me till I die.

Anthony Burgess

I never write — indeed, I am physically incapable of writing — anything that I don't think I will be paid for.

Truman Capote

Instead of hitting the block like we used to, we hit the laptops. I know what every word is worth. So while I'm writing, I'm like: "Okay, there's a hundred dollars. There's a thousand dollars. There's five thousand dollars."

Ashley Coleman

An enormous number of writers write as though people live very superficial lives and that all they think about is money and sex. Well, money and sex are splendid subjects. They're wonderful. They couldn't be better. But if you mix money and sex up with philosophy and psychology, you've got a better mixture, because philosophy and psychology are what people think about when they're lying in bed before they go to sleep.

Robertson Davies

I think the literary novelist who makes money is like a fish in a tweed suit.

Jonathan Franzen

No writer is entitled to earn a living

from his writing, or even to be paid for his writing; once you seek payment, you have to consider the market for what you're producing, especially during a time when supply outpaces demand.

Jane Friedman

Time is money — says the vulgarest saw known to any age or people. Turn it around about, and you get a precious truth — money is time.

George Gissing

A good deal of advice is given to authors. They are told their work ought to be written with a view to elevating the public taste — write literature, have style, no matter whether it pays or not; money is a matter that should never be considered in connection with writing. All I can say in reply is that I write to please my public, and I write to make a living. A dead man does not get much satisfaction because his work happens to have caught on with posterity, mainly because what he has written is sold in a cheap, attractive form. Some publishers appear to exist on dead men's brains; I prefer a publisher who pays cash down to living authors.

Nat Gould

My work is important to me, and I have never written for the money. But I do understand I'm working in a marketplace, and I have to produce stuff that people actually want to read or watch. That's not the same thing as writing commercially.

Nick Hornby

Money's a horrid thing to follow, but a charming thing to meet.

Henry James

Royalties are nice and all that, but shaking the beads brings in money quicker.

Gypsy Rose Lee, who wrote two mystery novels

As a culture we are interested only in success, and by that measure the successful artist's suffering is negated when he wins either monetary or critical acclaim. While the writer whose work fails to find any currency is utterly dismissed. It's a no-win situation.

Betsy Lerner, editor

Financial necessity can be extremely clarifying. When your goal is to make enough money to pay the rent, writing loses a lot of its artistic mystique and becomes something much more mundane: a job.

Malinda Lo

Anyone who sees in his own occupation merely a means of earning money degrades it; but he that sees in it a service to mankind ennobles both his labor and himself.

A. Lawrence Lowell, educator

There is no downside. Money allows you to whine to your heart's content, and to be as happy or miserable as you choose. If your friends don't want to listen to your complaints, cast them aside! There are plenty of people who, for a large fee, will listen to the whines of the wealthy.

Frank McCourt

Almost anyone can be an author; the business is to collect money and fame from this state of being.

A.A. Milne

In the writing world, [money] is a very loaded subject. We're not talking about a profession that has any sort of systemized pay scale. In almost every

”

I must write one about a college girl suicide ... There is an increasing market for mental health stuff.

Sylvia Plath, journal entry that inspired The Bell Jar

If you want to see something sad, ask a room full of freelance writers about their tax strategies. It's like asking a pack of baby kittens about space travel.

Choire Sicha

”

To be a novelist is not a calling to be a good or honest man.

Michael Dirda, book critic

The best regimen is to get up early, insult yourself a bit in the shaving mirror, and then pretend you're cutting wood.

Lawrence Durrell

other profession, people have a pretty good idea of what others are making, and I think, in writing, among the people I know, people have no idea. And the difference between people who do very well and people who are just getting along is a big range.

Susan Orlean

Need of money, dear.

Dorothy Parker, when asked why she wrote

Spenser was a cash cow. And we felt that Bob would want to see Spenser live on.

Joan Parker, widow, on hiring a ghostwriter to continue the series

If you're not writing for money, you're just jacking off on paper.

Teresa Peschel

Money is good for bribing yourself through the inconveniences of life.

Gottfried Reinhardt, German-born U.S. film producer

Writing is the only profession where no one considers you ridiculous if you earn no money.

Jules Renard

The trouble, Mr. Goldwyn, is that you are only interested in art and I am only interested in money.

George Bernard Shaw, to producer Sam Goldwyn during negotiations to the movie rights to his plays

Commerce and literature are still meant to be separate in England. If you're writing mass-market fiction, it doesn't matter your price: you can be as vulgar as you want in terms of money. But somehow that isn't the same for literary fiction.

Peter Straus, literary editor, about the uproar over Martin Amis seeking a six-figure advance for The Information

We're only hurting ourselves as writers by being so secretive about money. There's no other job in the world where you get your master's degree in that field and you're like, Well, I might make zero or I might make $5 million.

Cheryl Strayed

Morality

You simply couldn't stand by with your arms folded.

Samuel Beckett, on why he joined the Resistance after seeing his Jewish friends mistreated by the Nazis

Who was the moral man? Still more pertinently, who was the moral woman? The beauty or ugliness of a character lay not only in its achievements, but in its aims and impulses; its true history lay, not among things done, but among things willed.

Thomas Hardy, from Tess of the D'Urbervilles

Books are by-products of our lives. Deliver me from writers who say the way they live doesn't matter. I'm not sure a bad person can write a good book. If art doesn't make us better, then what on earth is it for?

Alice Walker

Motivation

A certain ruthlessness and a sense of alienation from society is as essential to creative writing as it is to armed robbery. The strong-armer isn't out merely to turn a fast buck any more than the poet is out solely to see his name on the cover of a book, whatever satisfaction that event may afford him. What both need most deeply is to get even.

Nelson Algren

I have a self-starter — published 20 million words — and have never received, needed or wanted a kick in the pants.

Isaac Asimov

What the writer needs is an empty day ahead.

Catherine Drinker Bowen

Twice I have written forty-thousand-word pamphlets in a week, but in each case I was sustained by a burning indignation, which is the best driving power.

Arthur Conan Doyle

Every principal character has an enterprise. Question it. If it's not there the character won't move. There's got to be more than what just meets the ear.

Hampton Fancher

[An artist is] a creature driven by demons — he usually doesn't know why they chose him and he's usually too busy to wonder why.

William Faulkner

I was mad. I was mad. I got motivated by anger at him. "Well, goddamn it, Dave! I've got one advantage over you, and that's that I'm still alive, and I'm going to show what I can do." … I was finally flying through the chapters. I would come home at two o'clock in the afternoon after five or six hours of solid concentration, and would just sit in a chair for half an hour and feel, "I don't owe anybody anything and I don't have to feel bad today because I just wrote 1,200 words." And that's a great feeling.

Jonathan Franzen, on writing Freedom *after David Foster Wallace's suicide*

Rage is to writers what water is to fish.

Nikki Giovanni

The world owes all its outward impulse to men ill at ease. The happy man inevitably confines himself within ancient limits.

Nathaniel Hawthorne

I don't think a writer, or any artist for that matter, should need a whip other than the one inside that drives him to create. The more you indulge in any neurotic notions about a set of necessary conditions that will enable you to write, the colder the trail will get. The problem is, none of this is writing. It's stalling.

Betsy Lerner

Being goal-oriented instead of self-oriented is crucial. I know so many people who want to be writers. But let me tell you, they really don't want to be writers. They want to have been writers. They wish they had a book in print. They don't want to go through the work of getting the damn book out. There is a huge difference.

James A. Michener

A man always has two reasons for what he does — a good one and the real one.

J.P. Morgan

My starting point is always a feeling of partisanship, a sense of injustice. When I sit down to write a book, I do not say to myself, "I am going to produce a work of art." I write it because there is some lie that I want to expose, some fact to which I want to draw attention, and my initial concern is to get a hearing. But I could not do the work of writing a book, or even a long magazine article, if it were not also an aesthetic experience.

George Orwell

[Samuel] Johnson's guilt takes that

”

My life isn't very long and I must get one good book written before it ends. The others have been make-shifts, experiments, practices. For the first time I am working on a real book that is not limited and that will take every bit of experience and thought and feeling that I have. And so to work.

John Steinbeck, from his writing diary for The Grapes of Wrath

If there's anything you want to do, do it now. We shall all be in little boxes soon enough.

Josephine Tey

”

Crime writers tend to be a very benign and generous bunch. I can only think it's the obvious psychology: they put all the evil into their books and, as it were, siphon it off.

Simon Brett

All work dealing with criminal matters is a cheap way of rousing the interest of the reader.

Arthur Conan Doyle

form: less a regret for actions taken than a deeply religious sense of failing to do what he should have done – fears of squandering what he truly believed were his gifts from God. His journals abound with acknowledgments of failings and resolutions to do better: laments that "this day I have trifled away," repeated resolutions "to rise early," reminders to "to do good as occasion offers itself," even, late in life, "to review former resolutions."

Levi Stahl

In order to paint you need equipment and a room and somebody to pay for the room. For a woman being a painter can be difficult. But all a writer needs is a pencil and a piece of paper and a corner and nobody noticing and the desire to do it; that's all it takes.

Fay Weldon

Movies

No writer wants to see his ox turned into a bouillon cube

John le Carré

About 15 minutes or so into it, the woman sitting in front of me turned to her husband and said, "This is the worst picture I ever saw." And I agreed with her wholeheartedly and all three of us got up and left.

Elmore Leonard, on seeing The Big Bounce *(1970) based on his first crime novel*

The dream is to package something really well with a great showrunner and actor and producer and send it out to the world like that so people fight over it. We are in the business of sales. Selling projects and actors and writers. I'd rather call a producer and say, "I have a project and Danny Boyle wants to direct it," than, "I have a Word document coming your way!" If they know someone else is already interested, they'll put it at the top of their pile. Otherwise, it's a recipe for getting ignored.

Priyanka Mattoo, producer / director

Music

I have learned so many things from music about writing. I think there are three important elements: rhythm, harmony, and free improvisation. I learned these things from music, not from literature.

Haruki Murakami

I can't write at the same moment that good music is playing; the sounds are too interesting to concentrate on anything else! What I do is alternate, all day long: an hour or two of writing, then half an hour to an hour of intense listening, for refreshment and inspiration.

Richard Powers

I might, if I felt the poem come on, put on a certain record, sometimes the *Bachianas Brasileiras* by Villa-Lobos. I wrote to that for about three or four years. It's my magic tune.

Anne Sexton

So when I go to a Patti Smith concert, I enjoy, participate, appreciate, and am tuned in better because I've read Nietzsche. The main reason I read is that I enjoy it. There's no incompatibility between observing the world and being tuned into an electronic, multimedia, multi-tracked, McLuhanite world and enjoying what can be enjoyed about rock 'n' roll.

Susan Sontag

Mysteries

(See **Crime Fiction**)

I suspect that the typical reader of detective stories is, like myself, a person who suffers from a sense of sin. From the point of view of ethics, desires and acts are good or bad, and I must choose the good and reject the bad, but the I which makes this choice is ethically neutral; it only becomes good or bad in its choice. To have a sense of sin means to feel guilty at there being an ethical choice to make, a guilt which, however "good" I may become, remains unchanged. As St. Paul says: "Except I had known the law, I had not known sin."

W.H. Auden

Love interest nearly always weakens a mystery because it introduces a type of suspense that is antagonistic to the detective's struggle to solve the problem. It stacks the cards, and, in nine cases out of ten, it eliminates at least two useful suspects. The only effective kind of love interest is that which creates a personal hazard for the detective — but which, at the same time, you instinctively feel to be a mere episode. A really good detective never gets married.

Raymond Chandler

I am of the same belief as Dorothy Sayers that the detective story is the direct successor of the old Morality Play. It is the triumph of good over evil — the deliverance of the innocent from the aggressor — that is what makes it exciting.

Agatha Christie

The point is justice usually triumphs in the end. The rightful balance is restored, the villain is bound and justice is administered.

Mary Higgins Clark

It was astonishing to me how frequently in detective novels nothing happens but a kind of catechism between the detective and his suspects — it's nothing but questions. "Where were you on the night of?" "On that night I wasn't anywhere — I was out of it, I was out of town that night." … It's the seesaw rhythm that the genre falls into that finally is not very engaging. … Another thing about the detective novel is that it has no protagonist. The detective really has nothing at stake, except that he's looking to solve a puzzle, looking to solve a problem. It's like writing a novel about a mathematician, who's worrying about, you know, whatever mathematicians worry about, and you read the process of his solution to the problem. That makes a mathematician, but it does not make for a protagonist. Nothing happens to the guy. The detective is going to come out on top — you know that he's not going to die in the end. So he's in control, and it seems to me fiction is about people who are not in control.

Stanley Elkin

The English [mystery] tradition offers the great tapestry novel, where you have the emotional aspects of a detective's personal life, the circumstances of the crime and, most important, the atmosphere of the English countryside that functions as another character.

Elizabeth George

There is no finer form of fiction than the mystery. It has structure, a story line and a sense of place and pace. It is the one genre where the reader and the writer are pitted against each other. Readers don't want to guess the ending, but they don't want to be so baffled that it annoys them. … The

Almost every novel is a mystery novel.

Susanna Moore

I like my detective stories pretty plain — a mystery, its solution, and its development; and lean rather toward Mr. [T.S.] Eliot's strict canonical ban on mystery stories which depend on other elements. But I am convinced that a writer who knew how could involve anything from sexual passion to a passion for higher mathematics in the folds of the story itself — and so long as the story held its own way, there would be no room for protest

Gilbert Seldes

The detective novel is the art-for-art's-sake of our yawning Philistinism, the classic example of a specialized form of art removed from contact with the life it pretends to build on.

V.S. Pritchett

The mystery story is really two stories in one: the story of what happened in the story of what appeared to happen.

Mary Roberts Rinehart

research you do is crucial. In mystery fiction, you have to tell the truth. You can't fool the reader and expect to get away with it.

Sue Grafton

Do you abominate detective stories? I read two a week in bed at night; can't concentrate on much else then. To me they are a great solace, a sort of mental knitting where it doesn't matter much if you drop a stitch.

Rupert Hart-Davis

I've tried to use the well-worn conventions of the mystery and subvert them, stretch them, use them to say something true about my characters, about men and women and the society in which they live. The mystery is an artificial form, but then all fiction is an artificial form. All fiction is the rearrangement of the author's compulsions, visions, ideas in what the writer hopes is a compelling and logical form. I've often said it's just as absurd to say you can't write a good novel within the form of a mystery as it is to say, how could you possibly write great poetry in the sonnet form? After all, you've only got 14 lines and you've got to have a strict rhyming sequence. I think many writers find that the discipline and conventions of the detective novel are in fact liberating.

P.D. James

Most of my published novels are of the folk dancing category, the steps, the patterns traditionally imperative, the retributions obligatory.

John D. Macdonald

Great works of literature, perhaps the greatest – the *Oresteia*, *Hamlet*, even the Bible – have been stories of mystery and crime.

John Mortimer

Almost all of the North American novelists of this school – the detective novel – are perhaps the most severe critics of the crumbling North American capitalist society.

Pablo Neruda

The reading of detective stories is simply a kind of vice that, for silliness and minor harmfulness, ranks somewhere between smoking and crossword puzzles.

Edmund Wilson

Myths & Legends

A people needs legends, heroes, myths. Deny them these and you have won half the battle against them.

John Oliver Killens

Names

[Joseph Heller's *Something Happened* is] a deeply disturbing book about a very conflicted man – a man who is consumed with anxiety and all kinds of serious moral problems – and his name was Bill Slocum. Well, we went through the whole book, and divided it up into chapters and all the rest of it, and at the end of the process I said, Joe, this is going to sound crazy to you but this guy is not a Bill. He said, Oh really, what do you think he is? I said, He's a Bob. And Joe looked at me and said, He was a Bob, and I changed his name to Bill because I thought you would be offended if I made him a Bob. I said, Oh no, I don't think he's anything like me, it's just that this character is a Bob. So we changed it back.

Robert Gottlieb

The non-norm names began because, as a reader, I disliked names that all sounded alike. I was constantly losing track of whether

Joe was the lawyer or the murderer, and Jim the magician or the tennis pro, or John the archery instructor or the bartender. So, in the beginning I chose unusual names for characters as a mnemonic device to aid the reader.

Annie Proulx, on why she gave her characters odd names such as Queeda, Clatter, Verl, Bonita and Mizpah

Negotiating

The No. 1 rule in any negotiation is don't take yourself hostage. People do this to themselves all the time by being desperate for "yes" or afraid of "no," so they don't ask for what they really want. Instead, they ask for what they can realistically get. I've heard many people say, "Well, that's a non-starter, so we won't even bring it up."

Christopher Voss

Networking

The writing community is full of lame-o people who want to be published in journals even though they don't read the magazines that they want to be published in. These people deserve the rejections that they will undoubtedly receive, and no one should feel sorry for them when they cry about how they can't get anyone to accept their stories. … It has surprised me, over the years, how few of my creative writing students have made any effort to engage with the community that they supposedly want to be a part of.

Dan Chaon

Writers are always selling somebody out.

Joan Didion

I think the best advice to writers attending a conference or beginning a writing class is to ascertain where you stand in relation to the other participants and learn from those who are a step or two ahead.

Betsy Lerner

If you're going to become a writer, you have to start introducing yourself to people. You have to know how to talk. People need to like you in this business, to remember you well.

Richard Rodriguez

Nobel Prize

After I won the Nobel Prize. I found myself thrust in the position of a public servant in the world of culture. I was supposed to seem benevolent and to pontificate and bless with my presence — elder statesman whether I liked it or not. The price you have to pay.

Saul Bellow

If you really want to know what Nobel Prize winners are like, you should have been in the breakfast line seeing all these brilliant people wandering around randomly trying to find the scrambled eggs. It was like anything but a group of brilliant folks.

Dr. Michael S. Brown

It is nice money to pay taxes with, but otherwise it only furnishes people with some sort of a license to intrude on your privacy.

Ernest Hemingway

You don't say! Listen, Ferd, I can say that better than you. Your Swedish accent's no good. I'll repeat it to you. "You haf de Nobel Brize."

Sinclair Lewis, not taking seriously the phone call from the Swedish Academy informing him that he won the Nobel. His wife's first response when he told her was, "Well, I have the Order of the Garter!"

I think early on I had a knack for being strategic about choices I made. Either something was going to be really fun — the reporting or the experience — or it paid really well, or it would be useful in some other incarnation down the road. Like, this assignment maybe isn't so valuable in and of itself, but this is a good editor to know.

Susan Orlean

”

The first book is the book you have to write to get back at your parents; the book you always had in you. Once you get that out of your way, you can start writing books.

Shirley Jackson

There is no more beautiful mission than to create the free novel, then to fabricate a world that we will never reach, regardless of how long we live!

Ramón Gómez de la Serna

A gesture of courtesy toward the [retiring] dean of the Academy, who at that time was nearly 90 years old.

Nobel Prize judge, about why Hemingway was given the award. Senior judge Per Hallstrom loved Hemingway's work

[This] reactionary bourgeois award [was given to a] lampooner who had blackened the socialist revolution.

Pravda, *criticizing Boris Pasternak for winning the prize for* Dr. Zhivago

It is not the same thing if I sign Jean-Paul Sartre or if I sign Jean-Paul Sartre, Nobel Prize winner. A writer must refuse to allow himself to be transformed into an institution, even if it takes place in the most honorable form.

Jean-Paul Sartre, rejecting his award

It saved me from the painful necessity of dealing in some way with money – generally regarded as very necessary and useful, but which I regard as the source of every kind of evil.

Leo Tolstoy, on why he didn't mind not winning the Nobel Prize

Stop babbling, man! How much?

W.B. Yeats, on being told over the phone that he had won the prize

Nonfiction

You can write the most wonderful piece in the world about someone and the only word they'll see is "plump" … You learn very early that you're not in the business to be friends with the people you write about. If you are, you start pulling punches.

Nora Ephron

I'd go see the people I wrote about. I'd go see the main characters, the people whose lives I kind of entered. I would go through them. I might not even talk to me. You don't write about the person; you write about the person's effect.

Michael Lewis, on how to write about Michael Lewis

Begin your article with conflict that produces tension, often revealed by including a brief example or anecdote and problem that will be resolved at the end. It's a good rule to start as near the end as possible and then plunge your reader into the central tension. When you've involved your reader in this way, weave in background facts or information as you think the reader needs it to understand the purpose and point of your piece.

Donald M. Murray

A nonfiction form will allow you to make even the most fantastic, the most maudlin, the most silly story seem completely plausible.

Chuck Palahniuk

Write in the form of a Q. Begin with an anecdote or revealing detail; write all around the subject; come back to the beginning – and give it a twist.

James Reston, reporter

Real historical writers probe factual uncertainties, but they do not invent convenient facts and they do not ignore inconvenient facts. People are entitled to their own opinions, but not to their own facts.

William Kelleher Storey

Whether in biography or straight history, the writer's object is – or should be – to hold the reader's attention. … I want the reader to turn the page and keep turning to the end. This is accomplished only when the narrative moves steadily ahead, not when it comes to a weary standstill, overloaded with every item uncovered in the research whether significant or not.

Barbara Tuchman

The time to begin writing an article is when you have finished it to your satisfaction. By that time you begin to clearly and logically perceive what it is that you really want to say.

Mark Twain

Every successful piece of nonfiction should leave the reader with one provocative thought that he or she didn't have before. Not two thoughts, or five — just one.

William Zinsser

Notes, Taking

All the time my father was dying, I was at the bedside making copious notes. You can't just slap these things down. You have to take trouble.

Arnold Bennett

The gestatory period before I start to write is very important to me. That's when I'm persuading myself of the truth of what I want to say, and I don't think I could persuade my readers unless I'd persuaded myself first.

August Wilson

Novel

I never tire of reading the master novelists. Can anything as vivid as the characters in their books be dead?

Saul Bellow

There was a time when the novel was subject to a scathing critique as a bourgeois invention of selfhood, which was politically incompatible with the mass state that Communism wanted to build. But in straightforward historical terms, the novel is a middle-class genre. And the middle-class, in part, is all about individuality. … I don't see how you can have a novel fulfilling that function of preserving individuality if you're not demonstrating true character, that individuals can still exist. The tension for any novelist working today who's attuned to the real world is the tension between that — the exigencies of creating of a character who is a real individual — and the sort of leveling and crowd-forming impulses of the culture at large that [Don] DeLillo is always pointing to.

Jonathan Franzen

It can do simply everything, and that is its strength and its life. Its plasticity, its elasticity is infinite.

Henry James

A great obstacle to good education is the inordinate passion prevalent for novels, and the time lost in that reading which should be instructively employed. When this poison infects the mind, it destroys its tone and revolts it against wholesome reading. Reason and fact, plain and unadorned, are rejected. Nothing can engage attention unless dressed in all the figments of fancy, and nothing so bedecked comes amiss. The result is a bloated imagination, sickly judgment, and disgust towards all the real businesses of life.

Thomas Jefferson

The real seduction of [writing a novel] is that you get to tell the truth better. Many of the stories in the book are based on things that really happened, but I'm allowed to make

”

I like looking at a novel and you don't know what you're gonna type next.

Charles Bukowski

What is a novel but a universe in which action is endowed with form, where final words are pronounced, where people possess one another completely and where life assumes the aspect of destiny?

Albert Camus

My ambitions seem far beyond my talents, and light-years beyond the vicissitudes of my character, and I think of this enormous novel I'm now starting, which could well take ten years, and if done properly, it must be unpublishable except in green-backed French "dirty" editions, and I'll be middle-aged when it's done, and somehow I just don't believe in myself the way I used to, and indeed, worst of all, it doesn't even seem terribly important.

Norman Mailer

it go the way I want it to. I just found that so amazing. It's such an obvious thing, that in fiction you can make shit up. Most of my friends who've read it say that it's more about me and more honest than the stuff that I've written that really is about me.

Penn Jillette, of Penn and Teller

If I were going to write a novel, I'd be sure to know the history of the genre before I attempted to add to it.

Alan McKillop, Larry McMurtry's teacher at Rice University

Secrets. Need to disguise. The novel was born of this.

Anaïs Nin

Life — the inner life — is not in the production of story lines alone, or movies would suffice. The microuniverse of the modem? Never mind. The secret voices in the marrow elude these multiplying high-tech implements that facilitate the spread of information. (High tech! Facilitate the spread of information! The jargon of the wooden leg, of the wooden tongue.) The din in the head, that relentless inward hum of fragility and hope and transcendence and dread where, in an age of machines addressing crowds, and crowds mad for machines, can it be found? In the art of the novel ... and nowhere else.

Cynthia Ozick

A novel worth reading is an education of the heart. It enlarges your sense of human possibility, of what human nature is, of what happens in the world. It's a creator of inwardness.

Susan Sontag

A novel is a mirror which passes over a highway. Sometimes it reflects to your eyes the blue of the skies, at others the churned-up mud of the road.

Stendhal

Certainly one knows more at 40 than one did at 20. And contrary to all American mythology, the novel is the rightful province not of the young but of the middle-aged.

Gore Vidal

Novel, Discouragement

By now you're probably ready to give up. You're past that first fine furious rapture when every character and idea is new and entertaining. You're not yet at the momentous downhill slide to the end, when words and images tumble out of your head sometimes faster than you can get them down on paper. You're in the middle, a little past the half-way point. The glamour has faded, the magic has gone, your back hurts from all the typing, your family, friends and random email acquaintances have gone from being encouraging or at least accepting to now complaining that they never see you any more — and that even when they do you're preoccupied and no fun. You don't know why you started your novel, you no longer remember why you imagined that anyone would want to read it, and you're pretty sure that even if you finish it, it won't have been worth the time or energy and every time you stop long enough to compare it to the thing that you had in your head when you began — a glittering, brilliant, wonderful novel, in which every word spits fire and burns, a book as good or better than the best book you ever read — it falls so painfully short that you're pretty sure that it would be a mercy simply to delete the whole thing. Welcome to the club. That's how novels get written.

Neil Gaiman

I wish that I had known back then that a mastery of process would lead to a product. Then I probably wouldn't have found it so frightening to write.

Elizabeth George

What is writing a novel like? The beginning: a ride through a spring wood. The middle: the Gobi desert. The end: going down the cresta run [a toboggan track in Switzerland]... I am now (p. 166 of *The Buccaneers*) in the middle of the Gobi desert.

Edith Wharton

Novel, Finishing a

Almost every writer I know goes through the same reaction after a novel is finished — there are 24 hours of euphoria and then all the negative thoughts you have shut out while finishing it come out, and either you get drunk or depressed or get the flu. The other point is two-thirds or three-quarters of the way through a novel, when almost all writers get what I call the "three-quarters sag," when the only thing you like less about what you've written so far is the ideas you have for finishing the book.

Simon Brett

Neil, you never learn how to write novels. You just learn how to write the novel you're on.

Gene Wolfe, responding to Neil Gaiman's announcement that "I think I learned how to write novels"

Novel, Starting a

I don't see how anybody starts a novel without knowing how it's going to end. I usually make detailed outlines: how many chapters it will be and so forth.

John Barth

I found myself writing [*Ragtime*] after staring at the wall for several days in desperation, writing about the wall, and then the house it was attached to. This was our home, we were living in New Rochelle, then, in this house that was built in 1906. Soon enough I was thinking what things must have looked like in New Rochelle in 1906, in fact what the whole country was like in 1906, and so there I was off the wall and into the book.

E.L. Doctorow

With me, a story usually begins with a single idea or memory or mental picture. The writing of the story is simply a matter of working up to that moment, to explain why it happened or what caused it to follow.

William Faulkner

One of the most difficult things is the first paragraph. I have spent many months on a first paragraph, and once I get it, the rest just comes out very easily. In the first paragraph you solve most of the problems with your book. The theme is defined, the style, the tone.

Gabriel Garcia Marquez

On November 18th of alternate years Mr. Earbrass begins writing "his new novel." Weeks ago he chose a title at random from a list of them he keeps in a little green note-book. It being tea-time of the 17th, he is alarmed not to have thought of a plot to which *The Unstrung Harp* might apply, but his mind will keep reverting to the last biscuit on the plate.

Edward Gorey

I always begin with a character, or

”

No one ever, ever gets to see draft zero. This is the draft that you write to tell yourself what the story is. ... I sit there and I bash the stuff out. I don't edit — I let it flow. The important thing is that the next day I sit down and edit like crazy. But for the first month or so of writing a book I try to get the creative side of the mind to get it down there on the page. Later on I get the analytical side to come along and chop the work into decent lengths, edit it and knock it into the right kind of shape.

Terry Pratchett

”

I'm sick to death of novels with an earnest purpose. I'm sick to death of outbursts of eloquence, and large-minded philanthropy, and graphic descriptions, and unsparing anatomy of the human heart, and all that sort of thing ... Why, so far as telling a story is concerned, the greater part of them might as well be sermons as novels. Oh, dear me! What I want is something that seizes hold of my interest, and makes me forget when it is time to dress for dinner; something that keeps me reading, reading, reading, in a breathless state, to find out the end.

Wilkie Collins, from The Queen of Hearts

characters, and then try to think up as much action for them as possible.

John Irving

I never start until the whole of the story is very clear in my mind, and indeed down in the notebook. I know the suspects. I know what their motives are. Despite the careful preparation, I never get exactly the book I thought I was writing.

P.D. James

I already know the ending; that's where I start.

Toni Morrison

The beginning of the novel is a time of awful torment, when you're dealing with a lot of dead pieces and you have to wait and wait for some kind of animation.

Iris Murdoch

For a long time before I start to write a novel, anywhere from one year to two, I make it up ... The novel in my imagination travels with me like a small lavender moth making loopy circles around my head. … As soon as I put it on the page I kill it.

Ann Patchett

If I didn't know the ending of the story, I wouldn't begin. I always write my last line, my last paragraph, my last page first.

Katherine Anne Porter

Among the many problems which beset the novelist, not the least weighty is the choice of the moment at which to begin his novel.

Vita Sackville-West

Sometimes you get a line, a phrase, sometimes you're crying, or it's the curve of a chair that hurts you and you don't know why, or sometimes you just want to write a poem, and you don't know what it's about. I will fool around on the typewriter. It might take me 10 pages of nothing, of terrible writing, and then I'll get a line, and I'll think, "that's what I mean!" What you're doing is hunting for what you mean, what you're trying to say. You don't know when you start.

Anne Sexton

Novel, What Is a

A novel is balanced between a few true impressions and the multitude of false ones that make up most of what we call life.

Saul Bellow

Novel, *n.* A short story padded. A species of composition bearing the same relation to literature that the panorama bears to art. As it is too long to be read at a sitting the impressions made by its successive parts are successively effaced, as in the panorama. Unity, totality of effect, is impossible; for besides the few pages last read all that is carried in mind is the mere plot of what has gone before.

Ambrose Bierce

To me, everything in a novel comes down to people making choices. You must figure out in advance what those choices are going to be.

Marion Zimmer Bradley

The novel is always pop art, and the novel is always dying. That's the only way it stays alive. It does really die. … The novel is the first art form that is an honest-to-god commodity. I guess that's what I mean by "pop." That's what makes it different from both high art and folk art.

Leslie Fiedler

One of the things a really good novel can do is give you a sense of recognition about the strange private life you are leading. Our life is not just our parents' dying or being angry about what we read in the paper. It's about questions: Should I take Prozac or not? What is my personality then? What is my self then? In our technologically changed world, it seems to me that a book not only has to do justice to those private stories, which are really old-fashioned stories of loss or love or longing or anxiety, but also take into account that those stories are now unfolding in a regime that seems to be resisting the narrative account and replacing it with material accounts: you can buy or drug your way out of unhappiness. For people who are struggling with "What does my life mean?" and "How should I live it?" the best novel you can write is the one that's going to take into account both.

Jonathan Franzen

All novels are really letters aimed at one person.

Stephen King

The ugly fact is books are made out of books. The novel depends for its life on the novels that have been written.

Cormac McCarthy

For me the moral core of the novel is inhabiting other minds. That seems to be what novels do very well and also what morality is about: understanding that people are as real to themselves as you are to yourself, doing unto others as you would have done to yourself.

Ian McEwan

It seemed to me that the essence of a novel was that it should deal with human relations, and the best way of dealing with human relations — given what talents I possessed and what talents I lacked — was to put my people into a wooden box, to set them at sea at a time of war, with the danger of the enemy, the perils of the elements, extreme heat, extreme cold, the likelihood of shortage of water, shortage of food, the almost certain ... the near certainty of scurvy, and the total inability of anybody to walk away. They had to be there, they had to react one upon the other like it or leave it and that, just as heat intensifies chemical reactions, so those circumstances would accelerate human relations.

Patrick O'Brian

The novel is an art form and when you use it for anything other than art, you pervert it... If you manage to use it successfully for social, religious, or other purposes, it is because you must make it art first.

Flannery O'Connor

A novel is a river, but a short story is a glass of water. A novel is a forest, but the short story is a seed. It is more atomic. The atom may contain the secret structures of the universe.

Ben Okri

A novel is nothing more than a strongly expressed opinion and that you need to respond strongly and with vitality.

Dale Peck

No one says a novel has to be one thing. It can be anything it wants to be, a vaudeville show, the six o'clock news, the mumblings of wild men saddled by demons.

Ishmael Reed

"

In any work that is truly creative, I believe, the writer cannot be omniscient in advance about the effects that he proposes to produce. The suspense of a novel is not only in the reader, but in the novelist, who is intensely curious about what will happen to the hero.

Mary McCarthy

”

Novels are for showing people what other people are like. It's the only way I can write. I wouldn't be any good at deconstruction. I didn't have much education. So I've had to do it myself really, to educate myself by reading. My family wouldn't have thought of sending me to university. In my generation, most girls didn't.

Elizabeth Jane Howard

The lies of novels are never gratuitous: they compensate for the inadequacies of life.

Mario Vargas Llosa

The writing of a novel is taking life as it already exists, not to report it but to make an object, toward the end that the finished work might contain this life inside it and offer it to the reader. The essence will not be, of course, the same thing as the raw material; it is not even of the same family of things. The novel is something that never was before and will not be again.

Eudora Welty

Novel, Writing a

The day-to-day business of writing a novel often seems to consist of nothing but decisions — decisions, decisions, decisions. Should this paragraph go here? Or should it go there? Can that chunk of exposition be diversified by dialogue? At what point does this information need to be revealed? Ought I use a different adjective and a different adverb in that sentence? Or no adverb and no adjective? Comma or semicolon? Colon or dash? And so on.

These decisions are minor, clearly enough, and they are processed more or less rationally by the conscious mind. All the major decisions, by contrast, have been reached before you sit down at your desk; and they involve not a moment's thought. The major decisions are inherent in the original frisson — in the enabling throb or whisper (a whisper that says, Here is a novel you may be able to write).

Very mysteriously, it is the unconscious mind that does the heavy lifting. No one knows how it happens.

Martin Amis

It is important that a novel be approached with some urgency. Spend too long on it, or have great gaps between writing sessions, and the unity of the work tends to be lost.

Anthony Burgess

Two questions form the foundation of all novels: "What if?" and "What next?" (A third question, "What now?", is one the author asks himself every 10 minutes or so; but it's more a cry than a question.) Every novel begins with the speculative question, what if "X" happened? That's how you start.

Tom Clancy

When I start on a book, I have been thinking about it and making occasional notes for some time — 20 years in the case of *Imperial Earth*, and 10 years in the case of the novel I'm presently working on. So I have lots of theme, locale, subjects, and technical ideas. It's amazing how the subconscious self works on these things. I don't worry about long periods of not doing anything. I know my subconscious is busy.

Arthur C. Clarke

Beginning a novel is always hard. It feels like going nowhere. I always have to write at least 100 pages that go into the trash can before it finally begins to work. It's discouraging, but necessary to write those pages. I try to consider them pages 100 to zero of the novel.

Barbara Kingsolver

One is improvising when one writes, and you pick up in the same way a musician starts to improvise and detect the inner structure of what he's playing — that's the way I think it works in the writing of a novel. You pick up the beat.

Robert Stone

Novelists

A novelist is a cannibal and may eat his friends for his professional purposes.

Brooks Baekeland, about his friend James Jones, who used the family murder case for a novel

[N]ovelists who take the bitterest view of our modern condition make the most of the art of the novel. … The writer's art appears to seek a compensation for the hopelessness or meanness of existence.

Saul Bellow

I am a fiction writer only to the extent that my characters are invented. In every other sense, I'm still a reporter.

Patricia Cornwell

I hold that the novelist is the historian of the present, just as the historian is the novelist of the past.

Georges Duhamel

I am a man, and alive … For this reason I am a novelist. And being a novelist, I consider myself superior to the saint, the scientist, the philosopher, and the poet, who are all great masters of different bits of man alive, but never get the whole hog. The novel is the one bright book of life.

D.H. Lawrence

The novelist says in words what cannot be said in words.

Ursula K. Le Guin

The complete novelist would come into the world with a catalog of qualities something like this. He would own the concentration of a Trappist monk, the organizational ability of a Prussian Field Marshal, the insight into human relations of a Viennese psychiatrist, the discipline of a man who prints the Lord's Prayer on the head of a pin, the exquisite sense of timing of an Olympic gymnast, and, by the way, a natural instinct and flair for exceptional use of language.

Leon Uris

Obscenity

If the word *arse* is read in a sentence, no matter how beautiful the sentence, the reader will react only to that word.

Jules Renard

Optimism

Let us think the unthinkable, let us do the undoable. Let us prepare to grapple with the ineffable itself, and see if we may not eff it after all.

Douglas Adams

I believe in some blending of hope and sunshine sweetening the worst lots. I believe that this life is not all; neither the beginning nor the end. I believe while I tremble; I trust while I weep.

Charlotte Brontë

It is just as stupid to be a narrow pessimist as an idiot optimist.

Robertson Davies

Men love to wonder, and that is the seat of our science, and such is the mechanical determination of our age, and so recent are our best contrivances, that use has not dulled our joy and pride in them. ... These arts open great gates of the future, promising to make the world plastic and to lift human life out of its beggary to a godlike ease and power.

Ralph Waldo Emerson

Optimism: A kind of heart stimulant

”

An original writer is not one who imitates nobody, but one whom nobody can imitate.

François-René de Chateaubriand

Originality does not consist in saying what no one has ever said before, but in saying exactly what you think yourself.

J.F. Stephens

For the first dozen or so books I worked from an outline. Then, when I did the first [Raymond] Chandler book, I tried to be as Chandleresque as possible. He never outlined, so I didn't. I just got the idea and let the characters lead the way. Since then I have done so in each book.

Robert B. Parker

[I]f a man will only stick to the thing he loves most he will do it right, and end right.

Max Perkins

— the digitalis of failure.

Elbert Hubbard

The commitment to optimism in today's literary world can also be traced to Stalinism, which didn't permit what was called defeatism. If there had been camps for literary characters back then, Eeyore the melancholy donkey — with whom I closely identify — would have been among the first inmates. The contemporary literary marketplace is almost as repressive. It rewards only the artistically obedient, the adaptable, the diligent, the optimistic. Optimists, after all, are the only reliable consumers.

Dubravka Ugresic, Croatian novelist

Originality

Don't worry about people stealing an idea. If it's original, you will have to ram it down their throats.

Howard Aiken, computing pioneer, to a student worried about theft of his thesis

Some writers confuse authenticity, which they ought always to aim at, with originality, which they should never bother about.

W.H. Auden

It is not easy to find words which have never been pronounced

Bacchylides, Greek lyric poet

The writer who slants his material is striving to copy something. He should develop his own product, should know what it is, and should have some idea of where to sell. But he shouldn't be writing the typical X Magazine story. The editor can get that from his regular writers.

Ray Bradbury

The most original thing a writer can do is write like himself. It is also his most difficult task.

Robertson Davies

It is perfectly easy to be original by violating the laws of decency and the canons of good taste.

Oliver Wendell Holmes

O that I might find unknown phrases, strange expressions, new speech not yet uttered, free of repetitions, not sayings such as the ancestors used.

Khakheperreseneb, Egyptian priest, about 1,800 B.C.E.

A sequel is an admission that you been reduced to imitating yourself.

Don Marquis

Who is original? Everything that we are doing, everything that we think, exists already, and we are only intermediaries, that's all, who make use of what is in the air.

Henry Miller

There's nothing said nowadays that hasn't been said before.

Terence (c.195/185-c.159 BCE)

What a good thing Adam had — when he said a good thing he knew that nobody had said it before.

Mark Twain

The most original writers borrowed from one another. The instruction we find in books is like fire. We fetch it from our neighbor's, kindle it at home, communicate it to others, and it becomes the property of all.

Voltaire

Outline

(See **Plot, Structure**)

What difference does it make to anybody whether I outline my novel before writing?

John Barth

An outline is crucial. It saves so

much time. When you write suspense, you have to know where you're going because you have to drop little hints along the way. With the outline, I always know where the story is going. So before I ever write, I prepare an outline of 40 or 50 pages.

John Grisham

If you have a plan — if you know the end when you start — it's no fun to write that novel. You know, a painter may draw sketches before he starts painting, but I don't. There is a white canvas, I have this paintbrush, and I just paint the picture.

Haruki Murakami

I make a very tight outline of everything I write before I write it. … By writing an outline you really are writing in a way, because you're creating the structure of what you're going to do. Once I really know what I'm going to write, I don't find the actual writing takes all that long.

Tom Wolfe

Paperbacks

To write a chapter of a book without having to worry about character, action or plot would call for little more than the ability to hit the keys of a typewriter. ... They were straightforward, cheap paperbacks for a public that would neither read nor relish anything better. ... And besides, I would be under no obligation to read the stuff. I would merely have to write it.

Leslie McFarlane, about the Hardy Boys *series*

Parody

You only parody the things you love. We rarely went as far as admitting the next step — and the truth — that you only parody what you once loved and now loathe. ... Parody is also a way of owning and containing what you were once in awe of.

Tony Hendra

Passion

A modern stoic knows that the surest way to discipline passion is to discipline time: decide what you want or ought to do during the day, then always do it at exactly the same moment every day, and passion will give you no trouble.

W.H. Auden

If you're not passionate about what you're writing, you're writing about the wrong thing.

Robert Crais

There's a selfishness to it. *Do what you love* implies that the only person you're responsible for is yourself, but if you have children or a sick spouse or people to take care off. ... The other side of that kind of thinking is that it makes people with good day jobs feel like shit, too. And then there's the idea that you *could* make a living doing anything you love. Like, if you love avant-garde poetry ... I mean, c'mon, man.

Austin Kleon

If you speak with passion, many of us will listen. We need stories to live, all of us. We live by story. Yours enlarges the circle.

Richard Rhodes

Pen Names

It's the worst name in publishing. The worst mistake of my career was not taking my mother's name after my first couple of books. I'd be John Gregory and I'd be selling, no kidding, 10 times as many books.

Only the mediocre are always at their best.

Jean Giraudoux, French playwright

None of us like mediocrity, but we all reverence perfection. The girl's music was perfection in its way; it was the worst music that had ever been achieved on our planet by a mere human being.

Mark Twain

Plagiarism has many advantages over the labor of creation. It is much easier to carry out and less hard work. You can finish twenty works of plagiarism in the time it takes to produce one creative work.

Bernardo Atxaga

Next o'er his books his eyes began to roll,
In pleasing memory of all he stole.

Alexander Pope

When people like my books they don't know how to tell anybody else. They say, "I just read this book by this guy, John somebody, Le-somebody." And the person goes, "Oh, John le Carré?" and they say, "Oh yeah, probably."

John Lescroart

I have thought all the time of publishing things under different names. I don't because for me the association of a text with a consciousness that created it is probably paramount in my understanding of literature. I absolutely refuse to accept any notion of universal truth, of things delivered from on high, for which a writer is merely a channel. I find that sort of thing to be complete and utter bullshit.

Dale Peck

Perfection

Perfection is the enemy of finished.

Anonymous

Perfectionism is the voice of the oppressor, the enemy of the people.

Anne Lamott

Personality

Personality is the glitter that sends your little gleam across the footlights and the orchestra pit into that big black space where the audience is.

Mae West

Photography

The camera cannot lie. But it can be an accessory to untruth.

Harold Evans

Plagiarism

Great literature must spring from an upheaval in the author's soul. If that upheaval is not present, then it must come from the works of any other author which happened to be handy and easily adapted.

Robert Benchley

The difference between a bad artist and a good one is: the bad artist seems to copy a great deal; the good one really does.

William Blake

They lard their lean books with the fat of others' work.

Robert Burton

Plagiarists are always suspicious of being stolen from, — as pickpockets are observed commonly to walk with their hands in their breeches' pockets.

Samuel Taylor Coleridge

One of the surest of tests is the way in which a poet borrows. Immature poets imitate; mature poets steal; bad poets deface what they take, and good poets make it into something better, or at least something different. The good poet welds his theft into a whole of feeling which is unique, utterly different from that from which it was torn; the bad poet throws it into something which has no cohesion.

T.S. Eliot

When a thing has been said and well said, have no scruple; take it and copy it. Give references? Why should you? Either your readers know where you have taken the passage and the precaution is needless, or they do not know and you humiliate them.

Anatole France

There is nothing so foolish as this

reproach of plagiarism; there is in art no Sixth Commandment; the poet may grasp and grab boldly wherever he finds material for his works … Goethe understood this very well, as did Shakespeare long before him.

Heinrich Heine

When 'Omer said 'is bloomin' lyre,
He'd 'eard men sing by land an' sea;
An' what 'e thought 'e might require,
'E went an' took — the same as me!

Rudyard Kipling

Though old the thought and oft exprest,
'Tis his at last who says it best.

James Russell Lowell

For such a kind of borrowing as this, if it be not bettered by the borrower, among good authors is accounted Plagiarè.

John Milton

When you steal from one author, it's plagiarism; if you steal from many, it's research.

Wilson Mizner

If a man's talk is commonplace and his writings distinguished, it means that his talent lies in the place from which he borrows, and not in himself.

Michel de Montaigne

I can tell you it is not always so safe to leave a play in the hands of those who write themselves. … Steal! — to be sure they may; and, egad, serve your best thoughts as gypsies do stolen children, disfigure them to make 'em pass for their own.

Richard Brinsley Sheridan, from his play The Critic

All of us who deal with real characters in history transcribe and adopt original sources in the original domain. I've used these sources and I've completely transformed them. … There's a larger argument to be made that all of literature is a series of references and allusions.

Susan Sontag, defending copying passages from history books for her novel In America

Shall we forever make new books, as apothecaries make new mixtures, by pouring only out of one vessel into another? Are we forever to be twisting and un-twisting the same rope?

Laurence Sterne, ironically, he stole the line from Robert Burton's The Anatomy of Melancholy

Oh, dear me, how unspeakably funny and owlishly idiotic and grotesque was that "plagiarism" farce! As if there was much of anything in any human utterance, oral or written, except plagiarism! The kernel, the soul — let us go further and say the substance, the bulk, the actual and valuable material of all human utterances — is plagiarism. For substantially all ideas are second-hand, consciously and unconsciously drawn from a million outside sources, and daily use by the garnerer with a pride and satisfaction born of the superstition that he originated them; whereas there is not a rag of originality about them anywhere except the little discoloration they get from his mental and moral calibre and his temperament, and which is revealed in characteristics of phrasing. …To think of those solemn donkeys breaking a little child's heart with their ignorant rubbish about plagiarism! … Why, their whole lives, their whole histories, all their learning, all their thoughts, all their opinions were one solid rock of plagiarism, and they didn't know it and never suspected it. A gang of dull and hoary pirates piously setting themselves the task of disciplining and purifying a kitten

”

I believe that one of the most sound ideas in dramatic writing is that in order to create the universal, you must pay very great attention to the specific. Universality, I think, emerges from truthful identity of what is.

Lorraine Hansberry

Plays are much easier to write than books, because you can see them in your mind's eye, you are not hampered by all the description that clogs you so terribly in a book and stops you getting on with what's happening.

Agatha Christie

Plot is fate. Fate is inevitable. There can be no fate without characters whose fate concerns us. So for now forget plot except how it grows from character — the plight of your characters.

Hampton Fancher, screenwriter

Cynics have claimed there are only six basic plots. "Frankenstein" and "My Fair Lady" are really the same story.

Leslie Halliwell

that they think they've caught filching a chop! Oh, dam —

Mark Twain, letter to his friend, Helen Keller. At age 12, she had been accused, and later cleared, of plagiarizing Margaret Canby's "Frost Fairies" for her short story, "The Frost King."

I do borrow from other writers, *shamelessly!* I can only say in my defense, like the woman brought before the judge on a charge of kleptomania, "I do steal; but, Your Honor, only from the very best stores."

Thornton Wilder

Plays & Playwriting

I wanted to get to learn the technique of the theater so well that I could then forget about it. I always feel it's not wise to violate rules until you know how to observe them.

T.S. Eliot

In a good play everyone is in the right.

Friedrich Hebbel

Produce a play and you will know better than I can tell you, how such an ordeal — odious in its essence! — is made tolerable and palatable by great success; and in how many ways, accordingly, non-success may be tormenting and tragic, a bitterness of every hour, ramifying into every throb of one's consciousness.

Henry James, who failed as a playwright

The structure of a play is always the story of how the birds came home to roost.

Arthur Miller

Stage plays are sinful, heathenish, lewde, ungodly Spectacles, and most pernicious Corruptions, condemned in all ages, as intolerable Mischiefs to Churches, to Republickes, to the manners, mindes and soules of men.

William Prynne, English pamphleteer

No one has written worse plays than me. Maybe Henry James. I couldn't figure it out. Maybe there is no way to figure it out. Maybe that's why there are very few good plays. But I couldn't figure it out. I couldn't get anything that resembled my mind into the plays.

Philip Roth

You write a hit play the same way you write a flop.

William Saroyan

Rehearsing a play is making the word flesh. Publishing a play is reversing the process.

Peter Shaffer

A novel is a static thing that one moves through; a play is a dynamic thing that moves past one.

Kenneth Tynan, theater critic

A dramatist is one who believes that the pure event, an action involving human beings, is more arresting than any comment that can be made upon it. On the stage it is always now ... a novel is what took place.

Thornton Wilder

Plays and short stories are similar in that both start when all but the action has finished.

August Wilson

Plot

(See **Outline, Structure**)

I've always figured the only way I could finish a book and get a plot was just to keep making it longer and longer until something happens — you know, until it finds its own plot — because you can't outline and then fit the thing into it. I suppose it's a slow way of working.

Nelson Algren

Find out what your hero or heroine wants, and when he or she wakes up in the morning, just follow him or her all day.

Ray Bradbury

I usually center on my main character and think and decide about what I want them to go through and learn in the story. I then build the crime and plot around that. This is often something that is going on at the same time. I have a plot idea that matches up well with the character idea and it all comes together. I focus on the killer/motive last simply because it is least interesting to me.

Michael Connelly

I plot as I go. Many novelists write an outline that has almost as many pages as their ultimate book. Others knock out a brief synopsis. … Do what is comfortable. If you have to plot out every move your characters make, so be it. Just make sure there is a plausible purpose behind their machinations. A good reader can smell a phony plot a block away.

Clive Cussler

I suspect over the next decade people are going to go for plot first and foremost, because we've had so many decades of talking about motivation. You read a long book and have enormous insight into a criminal's mind but nothing much happens. I think if Homer were alive today he'd be an extraordinarily highly paid TV executive. He would take over all the soaps. He had a hugely creative mind for imaginative development of a story. Ovid would be even better, if he were alive.

Colin Dexter

In nearly all good fiction, the basic — all but inescapable — plot form is: a central character wants something, goes after it despite opposition (perhaps including his own doubts), and so arrives at a win, lose, or draw.

John Gardner

Sequential causality is generally considered to be very important in plotting. It is often thought to be the difference between a simple story, which just presents events as arranged in their time sequence, and a true plot, in which one scene prepares for and leads into and *causes* the scene that comes after it.

Rust Hills

"The cat sat on a mat" is not a story. "The cat sat on the dog's mat" is a story.

John le Carré

The problem for me is finding my own plots. They take a long time. … I like to have it happen, just like in our own lives. We don't always know where they're going, and if we make formal decisions on a given night, if we sit down and put a list of things we're going to do on a piece of paper, they almost never work out right.

Norman Mailer

I like to think of what happens to characters in good novels and stories as knots — things keep knotting up. And by the end of the story — readers see an "unknotting" of sorts. Not what they expect, not the easy answers you get on TV, not

"

We call it the "MacGuffin." It is the mechanical element that usually crops up in any story. In crook stories it is always the necklace and in spy stories it is always the papers. We just try to be a little more original.

Alfred Hitchcock

There are two situations that make interesting stories: when an extraordinary person is plunged into the commonplace, and when an ordinary person gets involved in extraordinary events.

Helen Prejean

”

Since I started to deal with information theory I have often meditated upon the conciseness of poems; how can a single line of verse contain far more "information" than a highly concise telegram of the same length. The surprising richness of meaning of literary works seems to be in contradiction with the laws of information theory. The key to this paradox is, I think, the notion of "resonance." The writer does not merely give us information, but also plays on the strings of the language with such virtuosity, that our mind, and even the subconscious self resonate. A poet can recall chains of ideas, emotions and memories with a well-turned word. In this sense, writing is magic.

Gabor J. Szekely, statistician

wash-and-wear philosophies, but a reproduction of believable emotional experiences.

Terry McMillan

A guy comes home from college to find his mother sleeping with his uncle, and there's a ghost running around. Write it good, it's *Hamlet;* write it bad, it's *Gilligan's Island.*

Lorne Michaels

There's a phrase I use called "The Valley Full of Clouds." Writing a novel is as if you are going off on a journey across a valley. The valley is full of mist, but you can see the top of a tree here and the top of another tree over there. And with any luck you can see the other side of the valley. But you cannot see down into the mist. Nevertheless, you head for the first tree. At this stage in the book, I know a little about how I want to start. I know some of the things that I want to do on the way. I think I know how I want it to end. This is enough.

Terry Pratchett

I'll get into a novel knowing something about the beginning, knowing less about the middle and knowing nothing about the end. I don't want to know anything about the end until I get there, and I hope I'll be able to recognize the end when I get there.

Theodore Taylor

There is only one plot — things are not what they seem.

Jim Thompson

Now it is a strange thing, but things that are good to have and days that are good to spend are soon told about, and not much to listen to; while things that are uncomfortable, palpitating, and even gruesome, may make a good tale, and take a deal of telling anyway.

J.R.R. Tolkien, The Hobbit

I am going on a new system this time, making the scenario very full, putting in atmosphere and dialogue etc., so that when I come actually to write it the work will be easy. So far I have scenarioed it out to about the 40,000-word mark; and it has taken me 13,000 words to do it! … By this means you avoid those ghastly moments when you suddenly come on a hole in the plot and are tied up for three days while you invent a situation. I found that the knowledge that I had a clear path ahead of me helped my grip on the thing. Also, writing a scenario of this length gives you ideas for dialogue scenes and you can jam them down in skeleton and there they are, ready for use later.

P.G. Wodehouse

Poems

You don't have to suffer to be a poet; adolescence is enough suffering for anyone.

John Ciardi

I take pride in never being rude to anyone on this earth, which contains a great number of unbearable villains who set upon you to recount their sufferings and even recite their poems.

Heinrich Heine

One way of ending the poem is to turn it back on itself, like a serpent with its tail in its mouth.

Maxine Kumin

Writing a book of poetry is like dropping a rose petal down the Grand Canyon and waiting for the echo.

Don Marquis

A poem is never finished; it's always an accident that puts a stop to it — that is to say, gives it to the public.

Paul Valéry

Poems, Learning to Write

His voice was soft and slow as he read the students' poems. At first I felt the impatient desire to interrupt his slow, line-by-line readings. He would read the first line, stop, and then discuss it at length. I wanted to go through the whole poem quickly and then go back. I couldn't see any merit in dragging through it until you almost hated the damned thing, even your own poems, especially your own. At that point, I wrote to [poet and mentor W.D.] Snodgrass about my impatience, and his reply went this way, "Frankly, I used to nod my head at his every statement, and he taught me more than a whole gang of scholars could. " So I kept my mouth shut and Snodgrass was right. Robert Lowell's method of teaching is intuitive and open.

Anne Sexton

Poetry

It is a sad fact about our culture that a poet can earn much more money writing or talking about his art than he can by practicing it.

W.H. Auden

It's silly to suggest the writing of poetry is something ethereal, a sort of soul crashing, devastating emotional experience that wrings you. I have no fancy idea about poetry. It's not like embroidery or painting on silk. It doesn't come to you on the wings of a dove. It's something you have to work hard at.

Louise Bogan

Free verse is like free love; it is a contradiction in terms.

G.K. Chesterton

I wish our clever young poets would remember my homely definitions of prose and poetry; that is, prose = words in their best order; poetry = the *best* words in their best order.

Samuel Taylor Coleridge

Form is never more than an extension of content.

Robert Creeley

Poetry and every other art was and is and forever will be strictly and distinctly a question of individuality... . Nobody else can be alive for you; nor can you be alive for anybody else.

E.E. Cummings

Lying of an inspired, habitual, inventive kind, given a personality, a form, and rhythm, is mainly what poetry is.

James Dickey

Superstition is the poetry of life.

Johann Goethe

I should define a good poem as one that makes complete sense; and says all it has to say memorably and economically, and has been written for no other than poetic reasons.

Robert Graves

I can no more define poetry than a terrier can define a rat when he comes across one; and I recognise poetry by definite physical sensations, either down the spine, or at the back of the throat, or in the pit of the stomach

A.E. Housman

The reader doesn't come into the poem at all. ... Poetry is nobody's business except the poet's, and

Poetry is what makes the invisible appear.

Nathalie Sarraute

I like to think of poetry as statements made on the way to the grave.

Dylan Thomas

If you're ashamed of being human — weak, stupid, as well as God's greatest creation — you'll never be a good poet. Novelists have to love humanity to write anything worthwhile. Poets have to love themselves.

Marita Golden

everybody else can fuck off.

Philip Larkin

It is the monster hiding in a child's dark room, it is the scar on a beautiful person's face. It is the last blade of grass being picked from the city park.

Brian Patten

Poetry, I feel, is a tyrannical discipline. You've got to go so far, so fast, in such a small space, that you've got to burn away all the peripherals.

Sylvia Plath

Poetry is the revelation of a feeling that the poet believes to be interior and personal but which the reader recognizes as his own.

Salvatore Quasimodo

I've had it with these cheap sons of bitches who claim they love poetry but never buy a book.

Kenneth Rexroth

Be careful who your critics are. Be specific. Tell almost the whole story. Put your ear close down to your soul and listen hard.

Anne Sexton

All things exist as they are perceived: at least in relation to the percipient. "The mind is its own place, and of itself can make a heaven of hell, a hell of heaven." But poetry defeats the curse which binds us to be subjected to the accident of surrounding impressions. ... It reproduces the common universe of which we are portions and percipients, and it purges from our inward sight the film of familiarity which obscures from us the wonder of our being.

Percy Bysshe Shelley

Poetry proves again and again that any single overall theory of anything doesn't work. Poetry is always the concert under the window of the room in which the official version of reality is being written.

Charles Simic

All poetry is experimental poetry.

Wallace Stevens

I drank up women's tears and spat them out as 10-point Janson, Roman and ital.

John Updike

If [Bob] Dylan had just been a poet with no guitar saying those same things, it wouldn't have worked; but you can't ignore poetry when it shoots into the Top 10.

Andy Warhol

Meters are used for gas, not the outpourings of the human heart.

H.G. Wells, responding to criticism that his poetry lacks meter

I think writing verse is a great training for a writer. It teaches you to make your points and get your stuff clear, which is the great thing.

P.G. Wodehouse

Poetry is the spontaneous overflow of powerful feelings; it takes its origin from the motion recalled in tranquility.

William Wordsworth

Poets

The poet married the language, and out of this marriage the poem is born.

W.H. Auden

True poets should be chaste, I know,

But wherefore should their lines be so?

Catullus

Modesty is a virtue not found among poets, for almost every one of them thinks himself the greatest in the world.

Cervantes

Turn pimp, flatterer, quack, lawyer, parson, be chaplain to an atheist, or stallion to an old woman, anything but a poet. A modern poet is worse, more servile, timorous, and fawning than any I have named.

William Congreve

If a poet is anybody, he is somebody to whom things made matter very little — somebody who is obsessed by Making. Like all obsessions, the Making obsession has disadvantages; for instance, my only interest in making money would be to make it. Fortunately, however, I should prefer to make almost anything else, including locomotives and roses. It is with roses and locomotives (not to mention acrobats Spring electricity Coney Island the 4th of July the eyes of mice and Niagara Falls) that my "poems" are competing.

E.E. Cummings

[Poets] tend to fall in love with a woman (sometimes consciously even) in order to beget a poem upon her; and when that's done, gradually withdraw.

Cecil Day-Lewis

Poets don't drive cars. [Laughs] Poets don't go to the supermarket. Poets don't empty the garbage. Poets aren't on the PTA. Poets, you know, they don't go picket the Better Housing Bureau, or whatever. Poets don't… poets don't even speak on the telephone. Poets don't even *talk* to anybody. Poets do a lot of listening and … and *usually they know why they're poets!* [Laughs]

Bob Dylan

The writers of free verse got their idea from incorrect proof pages.

Robert Frost

To be a poet is a condition rather than a profession.

Robert Graves

I mistook [Oliver St. James] Gogarty's white-robed maid for his wife — or his mistress. I expected every poet to have a spare wife.

Patrick Kavanagh

Poets are born, not paid.

Wilson Mizner

There is no advice to give young poets.

Pablo Neruda

Poets are ... the trumpets which sing to battle and feel not what they inspire ... Poets are the unacknowledged legislators of the world.

Percy Bysshe Shelley

A poet, starving in a garret,
Conning old topics like a parrot,
Invokes his mistress and his muse,
And stays at home for want of shoes.

Jonathan Swift

Point of View

The advantage of a single viewpoint are fairly clear-cut, in detective stories or any other sort of fiction. Reader and writer identification is facilitated considerably. Similarly, the disadvantages are also quite clear, and I suspect the chief one is tedium.

Lawrence Block

"

It seems that God took away the minds of poets that they might better express his.

Socrates

The little girl had the making of a poet in her who, being told to be sure of her meaning before she spoke said: "How can I know what I think till I see what I say?"

Graham Wallas

"

I'm all for young writers but I'm also for writers who don't have to be young. What should be judged is the merit of the work, not whether it's by a black, white, old, young, gay, androgynous or whatever writer. The rigidity by which things are judged in our cultural world irks me very much. I would write a political play, I would write about Darfur if I knew Darfur, but I don't.

Edna O'Brien

There are tremendous built-in advantages to writing from a child's point of view. You are allowed to express wonder and amazement for all the ordinary things in the world that most adults don't see or feel anymore. You have a texture to your prose that you might not have otherwise. Of course, you find yourself steering a vehicle that almost drives itself, the *bildungs-roman*, the sentimental education. It's an unbeatable form of literary transportation.

E.L. Doctorow

Many stories can better be told from the point of view of a minor character than from that of a major character. In this way the reader may come to know equally two or more people in the story without shift in point of view.

John T. Frederick

Instead of writing about a character, write from within a character. This means that every way the character describes the world must describe the character's experience. … That means you can't use abstract measurements. No more six-foot-tall men. Instead you must describe a man's size based on how your character or narrator perceives a man whose height is seventy-two inches. A character might say "a man too tall to kiss" or "a man her dad's size when he's kneeling in church."

Chuck Palahniuk

How does it feel looking through a microscope, when you adjust the focus? Everything depends upon how close you want to bring the naked object to the naked eye. And vice versa. Depends on what you want to magnify, and to what power.

Philip Roth

Most novels usually have an omniscient narrator with such a strong, stylized voice that you wonder who it is, or a first person narrator who's absolutely infallible, able to trace every single step of his or her internal processes. You probably have five sudden realizations in your life that actually stick, but for these narrators they're all contained within a two hundred-page novel that takes place over three weeks ... I'm frustrated by the ineptitude of narration.

Lemony Snicket

Polemics

We are not philosophers, though our philosophy will be implicit in what we write. We are not preachers, though occasionally our work may have more impact than a sermon. We are only storytellers. If we tell our stories honestly and courageously, we can safely trust that they will carry the right messages.

Lawrence Block

Political Correctness

Everyone has a few good stories about a workshop group trying to beat a renegade into conformity. Like the night a story about Washington, D.C., was being discussed in the professor's living room. The writer placed the scene at the Metro stop and describe a newspaper boy, hawking papers, as "black." For 45 minutes the group tore into the writer as a racist, a closet Klansman, based on that one word. The professor wound up lecturing the other writers on their responsibility to write about America's class society as it is rather than present a delusional utopia. Afterward the group reconvened in the darkness outside and agreed that the big man himself was another racist.

"Chris Altacruise," pseudonym of former MFA student

Each of us, helplessly and forever, contains the other—male in female, female in male, white in black, and black in white. We are part of each other.

James Baldwin

I am a male animal, and there's nothing I can do about that. I can't stop writing and disappear just because someone chooses to project onto me her grievance with a million years of sexist human history. I can only do what I've always done, which is try to be gender-balanced in the books I recommend, the authors I write criticism about, the characters I put into my novels. ... The point where I draw the line is when politics starts dictating literary judgments. I don't think we should call pedestrian writing great, or vice versa, just because it makes someone feel better.

Jonathan Franzen

The function of fiction is not to render verdicts or effect social justice but to give evidence, and the truthful impressions of a male chauvinist better serve both noble ends than a squirmy political correctness.

John Updike

Political Correctness, Lionel Shriver

(See **Racism, The Autobiography of Nat Turner**)

(At the Brisbane Writers' Festival in 2016, Lionel Shriver gave the keynote speech and responded to critics who objected to her use of Latino and black characters in The Mandibles*).*

Membership of a larger group is not an identity. Being Asian is not an identity. Being gay is not an identity. Being deaf, blind, or wheelchair-bound is not an identity, nor is being economically deprived.

Lionel Shriver

Nothing less than a *celebration* of the *unfettered exploitation* of the experiences of others, under the guise of fiction. ... [Shriver's dismissal of cultural appropriation is] the kind of attitude that lays the foundation for prejudice, for hate, for genocide.

Yassmin Abdel-Magied, Sudanese-Australian author and activist

By their logic, black actors should not be allowed to play Lear, Macbeth, Julius Caesar, or other "white" roles in Shakespeare, and nonwhite performers should be completely excluded from taking part in any opera or classical ballet given that both are "white" European art forms, in the same way that jazz or blues music could be said to belong exclusively to black people.

Jonathan Foreman

The most upsetting aspects of the speech won't be found in the transcript. It was the sight of a white woman who has had great literary success playing the victim.

Suki Kim, Korean-American novelist

Unexamined, entitled, and just plain ignorant.

Nesrine Malik, The Guardian

I can think of only a few situations in which humor is entirely out of line, but a white woman (even one who describes herself as a "renowned iconoclast") speaking to an ethnically diverse audience might have considered the ramifications of

"

If you have had much to do with liberal intelligentsia in the U.S., they like to think they are above their own country, and they often have contempt for their compatriots, and they think they're better. They think that being super-critical of the United States exempts them. When they talk about Americans, they don't think they're talking about themselves. They're the same people who are always vowing if Bush wins the election, they're moving to Italy. They never move to Italy.

Lionel Shriver

[I'm proud] that I do not think any political motivation can be detected in my long books. My idol is Emile Zola. He was a man of the left, so people expected of him a kind of "Les Miserables," in which the underdogs are always noble people. But he went out, and found a lot of ambitious, drunk, slothful, and mean people out there. Zola simply could not — and was not interested in — telling a lie. You can call it honesty, or you can call it ego, but there it is. There is no motivation higher than being a good writer.

Tom Wolfe

playing the touchy subjects of race and identity for easy laughs.

Francine Prose

There are all sorts of ways to borrow another person's position: respectfully and transformatively, in ignorance, or with disdain . . . One of the worst ways to wear a sombrero, I think, is to be a white keynote speaker at a literary festival, saying, "I am hopeful that the concept of 'cultural appropriation' is a passing fad."

Jia Tolentino

I can live with offending people. In fact, it's become politically important to offend people, because we have to fight back against this notion that being offensive should be against the law or something, and that everyone supposedly deserves "respect" for their often dopey views.

Lionel Shriver

Political Correctness, Pen Names

Academics and intellectuals found the affair painful to elucidate. If it was true that the Balkanization of literature was justified by the supposition that only people who belongs to a certain category of people could truly understand, write about, interpret, and sympathize with the experiences of people in that same category, so that, for example, only women could write about women for women, and only blacks about blacks for blacks (the very careers of many academics now depending upon such a supposition), how is it possible that a Church of England vicar had been able, actually without much difficulty, to persuade a feminist publishing house that he wrote as a woman, and as a Muslim woman of Indian subcontinental origin at that? Was he not in fact telling us, as presumably a good Christian should, that mankind is essentially one, and that if we make a sufficient effort we too can enter into the worlds of others who are in many ways different from ourselves? Was he not implying that the traditional view of literature, that it expresses the universal in the particular, was not only morally and religiously superior, but empirically a more accurate description of it as an enterprise than the view of literature as a series of stockades, from which groups of the embittered and enraged endlessly fired arrows at one another without ever quite achieving victory?

Theodore Dalrymple, about "Rahila Khan," whose stories about British Asian teens led to a publishing contract with feminist Virago Press, until it was discovered that Khan was really Rev. Toby Forward, a Church of England vicar who ministered in London's Asian neighborhoods.

Politics

I seldom read a book when I find out the writer has an axe to grind. I want a story, not a potpourri of egotistical opinions, expressed with a disregard for the feelings of others.

Nat Gould

I don't believe any real artists have ever been nonpolitical. They may have been insensitive to this particular plight or insensitive to that, but they were political because that's what an artist is – a politician.

Toni Morrison

Posterity

I just don't think about it [affecting

history]. It's not an idea I want to apply to my own work. It's dangerous for a writer to think of such things. It's far healthier to feel about a book that you've done the best you can, and whatever happens is not in your hands.

E.L. Doctorow

It's not to anybody's best interest to think about how they will be perceived tomorrow. It hurts you in the long run.

Bob Dylan

Q: [You said 17 years ago] No honest poet can ever feel quite sure of the permanent value of what he has written. He may have wasted his time and messed up his life for nothing. [Do you feel the same now, at 70?]

Eliot: There may be honest poets who do feel sure. I don't.

T.S. Eliot

(Eliot died in 1965, long before his book of light poetry, Old Possum's Book of Practical Cats*, became the basis for the hit musical* Cats)

His literary reputation was dead long before his natural death. I consider an author's literary reputation to be alive only while his name will insure a good price for his copy from the booksellers.

Oliver Goldsmith

Praise

At this point I'd worry more if I weren't being hated. Who said it's the writer's job to be liked by everybody?

Jonathan Franzen, who said he avoids all mentions of himself on the internet

I believe that nothing completely satisfies an imaginative writer but copious and continuous draughts of unmitigated praise, always provided it is accompanied by a large and increasing sale of his works.

Frederick Locker-Lampson

Prizes

I was inspired by the recognition that the Pulitzer gave me, even though I was aware that it didn't mean all that much. After all, they have to give a Pulitzer Prize every year, and I was just one in a long line.

Anne Sexton

I have been very ambitious from the start on this prize. I wanted it badly.

Lionel Shriver, on winning the Orange Prize for We Need to Talk About Kevin.

Professionalism

A professional writer is an amateur who didn't quit.

Richard Bach

A professional can write even when he doesn't feel like it. An amateur can't — even when he *does*.

Arthur C. Clarke

Only those who risk going too far can possibly find out how far one can go.

T.S. Eliot

I take a certain amount of pride in not being a professional novelist, in apparently being a lifelong amateur. I don't want to be slick.

Jonathan Franzen

Traveler, there is no road. The road is made by walking.

Antonio Machado

No professional writer can afford only to write when he feels like it. If

”

Real pros really know what it is they do and they know how to do what they do and they know when you know what you're doing or not. ... It's not automatic. You really have to learn it, to feel it, and you have to understand it, and that's when the artistry really comes. When you're stuck, something really isn't working, what do you do? Where do you go? How do you fix it? If you're a pro, you'll find a way.

Ron Friedman, TV producer professionalism

James Patterson has mastered the art (if you can call it that) of writing mindless, page-turning bestsellers that sell millions of copies, then disappear as quickly as last night's fast-food meal.

Chicago Sun-Times *critic, which a Little, Brown publicist changed in its promotional material to: "Patterson has mastered the art of writing page-turning bestsellers."*

The public is a thick-skinned beast and you have to keep whacking away at its hide to let it know you're there.

Walt Whitman

he waits till he is in the mood, till he has the inspiration, he waits indefinitely and ends by producing little or nothing. The professional writer creates the mood. He has his inspiration too, but he controls and subdues it to his bidding by setting himself regular hours of work. But in time writing becomes a habit, and like the old actor in retirement, who gets restless when the hour arrives at which he has been accustomed to go down to the theatre and make up for the evening performance, the writer itches to get to his pens and paper at the hours at which he has been used to write. Then he writes automatically.

W. Somerset Maugham

On every level of life, from housework to heights of prayer, in all judgment and efforts to get things done, hurry and impatience are sure marks of the amateur.

Evelyn Underhill

Proofreaders

In the first place God made idiots. This was for practice. Then he made proofreaders.

Mark Twain

Psychoanalysis

If I hadn't been analyzed I wouldn't have written *Portnoy's Complaint* as I wrote it, or *My Life as a Man* as I wrote it, nor would *The Breast* resemble itself. Nor would I resemble myself. The experience of psychoanalysis was probably more useful to me as a writer than as a neurotic, although there may be a false distinction there. It's an experience that I shared with tens of thousands of baffled people, and anything that powerful in the private domain that joins a writer to his generation, to his class, to his moment, is tremendously important for him, providing that afterwards he can separate himself enough to examine the experience objectively, imaginatively, in the writing clinic.

Philip Roth

Public Appearances

What *can* you say about how you write books? What I mean is, first you've got to think of something, and when you've thought of it you've got to force yourself to sit down and write it. That's all. It would have taken me just three minutes to explain that, and then the Talk would have been ended and everyone would have been very fed up. I can't imagine why everybody is always so keen to *talk* about writing. I should have thought it was an author's business to *write,* not *talk.*

Ariadne Oliver (a.k.a. Agatha Christie)

Publicity

For artists, the great problem to solve is how to get oneself noticed.

Honoré de Balzac

There's no such thing as bad publicity except your own obituary.

Brendan Behan

[George Bernard] Shaw relished every opportunity to have himself painted, sketched, photographed or carved, because each likeness provided him with a new extension of himself.

Peter Conrad

My father was a very wise man. He was a newspaper publisher and one of the things he used to say was, "You should never believe your own publicity." You begin to pay too much attention to that and you get vain and silly and you think that everything you write is golden. It isn't. You've just got to keep going as hard as if you were eighteen and you were trying your first novel.

Robertson Davies

Giving the public details about oneself is a bourgeois temptation I have always resisted.

Gustave Flaubert

When you survive a thing like that, you realize, you know, that it's all just words and it's not going to hurt me. So if anything, I hold back less now. Earlier in my life I might have been afraid to say some of these things, because I didn't want to be disliked. But it's like, boy, is that horse already out of the barn for me.

Jonathan Franzen, after he criticized Oprah Winfrey and her book fans

The most important thing to remember: nobody cares that you wrote a book. So don't lead your pitch with the book. Lead with the hook or the story, and what your book will do for people.

Jane Friedman

My life isn't of interest — my books (I hope) are. I'm sick to death of chatty bits about authors, & LOATHE this form of advertisement.

Georgette Heyer

It is dangerous to let the public behind the scenes. They are easily disillusioned and then they are angry with you, for it was the illusion they loved; they do not understand that what interests you is the way in which you have created the illusion. Anthony Trollope ceased to be read for 30 years because he confessed that he wrote at regular hours and took care to get the best price he could for his work.

W. Somerset Maugham

As for the Daguerreotype (I spell the word right from your sheet) that's what I can not send you, because I have none. And if I had, I would not send it for such a purpose, even to you. — Pshaw! you cry — and so cry I. — "This is intensified vanity, and not true modesty or anything of that sort!" — Again, I say so too. But if it be so, how can I help it. The fact is, almost everybody is having his "mug" engraved nowadays; so that this test of distinction is getting reversed; and therefore, to see one's "mug" in a magazine is presumptive evidence that he's a nobody. So being as vain a man as ever lived; and believing that my illustrious name is famous throughout the world — I respectfully decline being oblivionated by a Daguerreotype (what a devil of an unspellable word!)

Herman Melville, refusing to provide an author photo for his friend's magazine.

If a young man tells his date how handsome, smart and successful he is - that's advertising. If the young man tells his date she's intelligent, looks lovely, and is a great conversationalist, he's saying the right things to the right person and that's marketing. If someone else tells the young woman how handsome, smart and successful her date is - that's PR.

S.H. Simmons

A new book is like a new brand of detergent. You have to let the public know about it. What's wrong with that?

Jacqueline Susann

You can create excitement, you can do wonderful promotion and get all kinds of press... But if you don't deliver the goods, people will eventually catch on.

Donald Trump

”

Name-brand best-selling authors as Tom Clancy, Michael Crichton, Stephen King, Dean Koontz, and John Grisham, whose faithful readers are addicted to their formulaic melodramas, no more need publishers to edit and publicize their books than Nabisco needs Julia Child to improve and publicize Oreos.

Joseph Epstein, editor

”

I think the change is going to have to come from within those who are affected just like any under-represented group in any profession. But since the return on investment for the author is so low, I don't know how many people of color are going to have the desire to climb the mountain to publication that every new author faces, or have the luxury of dedicating the time it takes to master the craft.

Abigail Samoun, literary agent

Publishers & Publishing

I would advise the author never, from any considerations of vanity or self-confidence, to pay money to a publisher for bringing out his book. … Remember that to be asked for money to pay for the expense of publication is to be told that your work is not good enough to be published.

Walter Besant, 1885

Publication is the Auction of the Mind of Man.

Emily Dickinson

One of the obstacles is that the world of publishing has not quite caught up with [the Latino] market's potential. Part of this is due to a lack of diversity in publishing itself.

Adriana Dominguez, literary agent

The most important difference between poetry and any other department of publishing is, that whereas with most categories of books you are aiming to make as much money as possible, with poetry you are aiming to lose as little as possible.

T.S. Eliot

Publishing four books in one year is an index of the emptiness of your life.

Kinky Friedman

EASIER CHANGE PUBLISHER THAN TITLE

Graham Greene, cablegram response to publisher's objection to Travels With My Aunt *as a title*

Be exceedingly careful in choosing your agent or your publisher. Don't send the book to anyone who charges a fee for reading it or publishing it. In the real world of publishing, people pay you for your work.

Evan Hunter

Publishers don't nurse you; they buy and sell you.

P.D. James

Curse the blasted, jelly-boned swines, the slimy, the belly-wriggling invertebrates, the miserable sodding rutters, the flaming sods, the sniveling, dribbling, dithering, palsied, pulse-less lot that make up England today. They've got the white of egg in their veins and their spunk is that watery it's a marvel they can breed.

D.H. Lawrence, after Heinemann rejected Sons and Lovers

Having been unpopular in high school is not just cause for book publications.

Fran Lebowitz

Books, nowadays, are printed by people who do not understand them, sold by people who do not understand them, read and reviewed by people who do not understand them, and even written by people who do not understand them.

Georg Christoph Lichtenberg, 1799

If you would be thrilled by watching the galloping advance of a major glacier, you'd be ecstatic watching changes in publishing.

John D. MacDonald

The Market is so comfortably intangible that no one is worried I will go knocking down any doors. The Market, I am told, just doesn't demand this kind of book ... because white kids won't buy a book with a black kid on the cover — or so The Market says, despite millions of music albums that are sold in just that way.

Walter Dean Myers

The skill that is commonly associated with the pinnacle of editorial talent — picking the right book — is, frankly, nonsense. Success, in terms of picking things, is a hybrid of luck with the non-self-evident and money with the self-evident, and even the self-evident often requires luck. ... Publishing has no particular ability to discern what is good or not, what is successful or not. ... This is not a knock on publishing. There's no evidence that stockbrokers can pick good stocks, or touts good horses.

Richard Nash

Navigating the complexities of an industry that still hasn't dealt with its own institutional racism is a struggle I wouldn't wish on anyone.

Daniel Jose Older

The sales department always wants a novel. They want to turn everything into a novel. They would have turned the New Testament into one if it had come to us for publication.

Max Perkins

Publication is a messy business. You'll see what I mean one day. All those loutish cocktail party-going opinion-givers, so ready to pass judgment. Bad enough when they do that to a writer. But when they start in on your characters — and they do — it's murder.

J.D. Salinger

No, Virginia, there is not and never has been a Santa Claus in the publishing world, nor a time when editors were all like Max Perkins and the patriarchs were benign lovers of good books. The noses were as hard as they are today, though the manners were better. If writers are treated like cans of beans now, they were all too often treated like Bob Cratchit then.

Mary Lee Settle

Publishing is not ordinary trade. It is gambling. The publisher bets the cost of manufacturing, advertising and circulating a book, plus the overhead of his establishment, against every book he publishes exactly as a turn bookmaker bets against every horse in the race. The author, with his one book, is an owner backing his favorite at the best odds he can get from the competing publishers. Both are gamblers.

George Bernard Shaw

The profession of book writing makes horse racing seem like a solid, stable business.

John Steinbeck

The shelf life of an average trade book is somewhere between milk and yogurt.

Calvin Trillin

If ever a publisher gets a non-terminable contract with an author, that author can never buy his freedom from that slavery on any terms. A publisher is by nature so low and vile that he — that he — well from the bottom of my heart I wish all publishers were in hell.

Mark Twain

The difference between being in print and out of print is the same as the difference between being alive and being dead.

Donald E. Westlake

”

When speaking aloud, you punctuate constantly — with body language. Your listener hears commas, dashes, question marks, exclamation points, quotation marks as you shout, whisper, pause, wave your arms, roll your eyes, wrinkle your brow. In writing, punctuation plays the role of body language. ... [Punctuation] exists to serve you. Don't be bullied into serving it.

Russell Baker

”

Sometimes it seems my only accomplishment my education ever bestowed on me was the ability to think in quotations.

Margaret Drabble

Few things are more tempting to a writer than to repeat, admiringly, what he has said before.

John Kenneth Galbraith

Punctuation

No iron can stab the heart with such force as a period put just at the right place.

Isaac Babel

I use punctuation for effect, not in obedience to some rule book or style sheet. I want a sentence to fall upon a reader's inner ear in a particular way, and that's why I punctuate a sentence as I do. My approach is intuitive rather than logical, and I'm satisfied that I punctuate correctly.

Lawrence Block

You must make the reader read in your cycle, and you can only do that with punctuation. Always punctuate that way instead of grammatically, and don't let anybody change that. You'll trap your reader into your own breathing, and then the reader is trapped.

Truman Capote

Here is a lesson in creative writing. First rule: Do not use semicolons. They are transvestite hermaphrodites representing absolutely nothing. All they do is show you've been to college.

Kurt Vonnegut

Dots, dashes, exclamation points were dropped out of prose because they "reeked of sentiment." But an ! is someone getting carried away. Why not? The writer carefully not using this punctuation doesn't bother to convey what's exciting to the reader. Sure, dots and dashes slow down the eye. That's good. That's the best thing that can happen. It's reproducing the abruptness that occurs in your mind when you're thinking.

Tom Wolfe

Short paragraphs put air around what you write and make it look inviting, whereas one long chunk of type can discourage the reader from even starting to read.

William Zinsser

Quitting

Don't quit. It's very easy to quit during the first 10 years. Nobody cares whether you write or not, and it's very hard to write when nobody cares one way or the other. You can't get fired if you don't write, and most of the time you don't get rewarded if you do. But don't quit.

Andre Dubus

Most people quit. If you don't quit, if you rewrite, if you keep publishing in fancier places, you will understand that "What's the secret?" is not the question, which is, "Are you having fun?"

Robert Lipsyte

Quotations

The surest way to make a monkey of a man is to quote him.

Robert Benchley

Surely no one buys a book of quotations when sober.

Marcus Berkmann, book reviewer

There is always the option of being emotionally lazy, that is, of quoting.

Alain de Botton

Most anthologists of poetry or quotations are like those who eat cherries or oysters, first picking the best and winding up by eating everything.

Nicolas-Sebastien Chamfort

To be apt in quotation is a splendid and dangerous gift. Splendid, because it ornaments a man's speech with other men's jewels; dangerous, for the same result. A man who quotes too easily risks the loss of any capacity he may have had for personal expression. … Furthermore, many people are so impressed by his ability to quote that they overvalue the sense of what he has so elegantly said.

Robertson Davies

Immortality. I notice that as soon as writers broach this question they begin to quote. I hate quotation. Tell me what you *know*.

Ralph Waldo Emerson

A writer expresses himself in words that have been used before because they give his meaning better than he can give it himself, or because they are beautiful or witty, or because he expects them to touch a cord of association in his reader, or because he wishes to show that he is learned and well read. Quotations due to the last motive are invariably ill-advised; the discerning reader detects it and is contemptuous; the undiscerning is perhaps impressed, but even then is at the same time repelled, pretentious quotations being the surest road to tedium.

Henry W. Fowler

He wrapped himself in quotations — as a beggar would enfold himself in the purple of emperors.

Rudyard Kipling

There is no reason why a book of quotations should be dull; it has its uses in idleness as well as in study.

H.L. Mencken, about his own quote book

If, with the literate, I am
Impelled to try an epigram,
I never seek to take the credit;
We all assume that Oscar said it.

Dorothy Parker

A book that furnishes no quotations is, *me judice* (Latin: "with me as a judge"), no book — it is a plaything.

Thomas Love Peacock

Misquotation is ... the pride and privilege of the learned. A widely-read man never quotes accurately for the rather obvious reason that he has read too widely. ... Misquotations are the only quotations that are never misquoted.

Hesketh Pearson

It [is] gentlemanly to get one's quotations very slightly wrong. In that way one unprigs oneself and allows the company to correct one.

Lord Ribblesdale

I always have a quotation for everything — it saves original thinking.

Dorothy L. Sayers

I often quote myself; it adds spice to my conversation.

George Bernard Shaw

In the dying world I come from quotation is a national vice. It used to be the classics, now it's lyric verse.

Evelyn Waugh

Race & Racism

I'm an unregenerate white Anglo-Saxon Protestant heterosexual. So are my men. Their racism and homophobia is appalling, but it's germane to their characters, and people will either get that or not get it. That's that. You can't really respond to the press and say, "I'm not a racist or a homophobe." Nobody's going to believe you.

James Ellroy

If you're an indigenous professor, why should you be teaching your students Shakespeare? He is a

”

As I discovered who I was, a black teenager in a white-dominated world, I saw that these characters, these lives, were not mine. I didn't want to become the "black" representative, or some shining example of diversity. What I wanted, needed really, was to become an integral and valued part of the mosaic that I saw around me.

Walter Dean Myers

”

You're not in control of how people read a book. They're doing their own interpretation.

Margaret Atwood

Always remember the reader. Always level with him and never talk down to him. You may think you're some kind of smart guy because you're the great writer. Well, if you're such a smart guy, how come the reader is paying you? Remember the reader's the boss. He's hired you to do a job. So do it.

Jay Anson

colonizing influence and we should not be privileging the continuation of the European text. We should be privileging our own. But where are they? We don't have them at the moment, so we have to create them.

Witi Ihimaera

To sell an extra hundred thousand books, depict a white person teaching a black person how to read. White people who love to read think everyone should love to read. Plus it flatters readers to show them a character who can't read. It's the ultimate way to make your reader feel superior and thus to sympathize with a character. … Whether it's the movie *Fame* or *Driving Miss Daisy* or *The Color Purple*, teaching a black person to read is a plot device that never, ever gets old.

Chuck Palahniuk

There are white writers who can write as if they're in America and there aren't Native American or black people. I can never assume I live in a world that is all black or all Native American or all white. It's really hard to read those books, because when I open one up it seems so unreal to me.

Alice Walker

Racism, The Autobiography of Nat Turner

(See **Political Correctness, Lionel Shriver**)

[H]onkies such as William Styron do not have the right or authority from black people to speak for us or interpret our heroes.

Black Anti-Defamation Association

Looking back over thirty years and trying to remember how I felt, I think the real reason I condemned the book was my eagerness to placate my increasingly distant black colleagues and my increasingly volatile black students. I placated no one, of course, and as imitations of angry Black Power rhetoric erupted in sudden, irrelevant bursts, I made the retreat many white teachers and many older black teachers did — into silence.

Dorothy Bryant, literary critic

What makes Styron a better historian than any of his critics is that he will not bury unpleasant evidence or minimize the complexities of past experience in order to serve some presumed contemporary need.

Martin Duberman, historian

It is clear that the black intelligentsia faces a serious crisis. Its political affinities lie with the Black Power movement, which increasingly demands conformity, mythmaking, and historical fabrication.

Eugene D. Genovese

An unreconstructed Southern racist.

Ernest Kaiser, New York Public Library librarian

Styron's novel ignited a much-deserved criticism as he annihilated Turner's character. ... Reimagining [Turner] played directly into white America's fear and anxieties surrounding the intention and potential of the contemporary Black male.

Nate Parker

When I was young I was in a constant rage ... and often let it out ... I was saved by the class system and some education. Had I not been brought up in nice Virginia bourgeois surroundings, my renegade impulses might have led me to prison.

William Styron

In regard to *Nat Turner*, I will say that the Negroes' reaction was racist: a writer, black or white, must be able to write about any human being of whatever color.

William Styron

I am certain that it was his encouragement — so strong that it was as if he were daring me not to — that caused me finally to impersonate a black man.

William Styron, of James Baldwin

Is it possible for a white Southern gentleman to tune in on the impulses, beliefs, emotions, and thought-patterns of a black slave?

Mike Thelwell, Jamaican novelist and professor

Readers

It's the difference between writing by yourself and writing on a stage. I mean, if the book were your own, you'd be satisfied just to have the guy walk down the sidewalk and fall on his head. In a reader's book, you'd have him turn a double somersault. You're more inclined to clown, I think, in a reader's book. You've got one ear to the audience for yaks. It's just an obligation you have to fulfill.

Nelson Algren, describing the difference between writing for yourself versus a "reader's book."

You have to love the reader. It's not about toadying to the reader but loving and respecting them. A book is nothing without a reader. The relationship between writer and reader is very mysterious and fascinating and not terribly well explained. There is an intimacy to reading a novel because you feel you know the writer embarrassingly well. The great excuse for a public event is that it's great to meet a reader.

Martin Amis

There is a great deal of difference between the eager man who wants to read a book, and the tired man who wants to read a book. A man reading a Le Queux mystery wants to get to the end of it. A man reading the Dickens novel wishes that it might never end. Men read a Dickens story six times because they know it so well. If a man can read a Le Queux story six times it is only because he can forget it six times.

G.K. Chesterton

He began [his lecture on Shakespeare] by observing that Readers might be divided into four classes.
1. Sponges: persons absorbed what they read and returned it nearly in the same state, only a little dirtied.
2. Sandglasses, who permitted everything to pass away and were contented to doze away their time in actual idleness.
3. Strainbags, who retained only the dregs of what they received.
4. Great Mogul Diamonds who are equally rare and valuable.

Samuel Taylor Coleridge, from John Payne Collier's diary, Nov. 21, 1811

Some read to think, these are rare; some to write, these are common; and some read to talk, and these form the great majority. The first page of an author not unfrequently suffices all the purposes of this latter class, of whom it has been said, that they treat books as some do lords; they inform themselves of their titles, and then boast of an intimate acquaintance.

Charles Caleb Colton

Readers, after all, are making the world with you. You give them the materials, but it's the readers who build that world in their own minds.

Ursula K. Le Guin

If a book and a head knock against each other and there is a hollow sound, is it always the book?

Georg Christoph Lichtenberg

If you hate people, maybe you should not be a writer. You are in an audience-based profession. Without readers, there is no writing. Readers matter more than writers. Hopefully all writers are also readers, but readers don't have to be writers. They win.

Porochista Khakpour

Knowing the passion of chambermaids for novels, I often bear them in mind when I write my own.

George Sand

Better to write for yourself and have no public, then write for the public and have no self.

Cyril Connolly

People read fiction for emotion — not information.

Barnaby Conrad, quoting Sinclair Lewis's advice

I don't care if a reader hates one of my stories, just as long as he finishes the book.

Roald Dahl

A lot of writers underestimate their readers. They think that they're dumb. I've heard them using the expression, "Dumb it down," you know, for some public. Well, I have a lot of readers who don't want things dumbed down, but they'd like them cleared up as much as possible. I feel that's part of my job as a writer.

Robertson Davies

There's no room for the reader in your mind; you don't think of anything but the language you're in.

E.L. Doctorow

You better make them care about what you think. It had better be quirky or perverse or thoughtful enough so that you hit some chord in them. Otherwise it doesn't work. I mean we've all read pieces where we thought, "Oh, who gives a damn."

Nora Ephron

Only write for those who can read between the lines.

Kinky Friedman

Everyone, in fact, merely reads himself out of a book; and, if he is a forceful personality, he reads himself into it.

Johann Goethe

If you despise your readers, they will probably despise you.

Andrew Greeley

A writer is like a beggar with a bowl. No one has to read fiction. A man can always spend his spare cash on beer. The reader I have in mind is someone who bought my book instead of a six-pack of beer. My purpose is to be entertaining enough to get him to do it again.

Robert Heinlein. More commonly seen as the untraced "We write for Joe's beer money, and Joe likes his beer. It's our obligation to give him at least as much fun from our books as he'd get from a six-pack"

Never tell your reader what your story is about. Reading is a participatory sport. People do it because they are intelligent and enjoy figuring things out for themselves.

George V. Higgins

They could see that there were things wrong with it — a novel is a prose narrative of some length that has something wrong with it — but they felt that, somehow, the things didn't matter.

Randall Jarrell, talking about Christiana Stead's The Man Who Loved Women

A book is a friend whose face is constantly changing. If you read it when you are recovering from an illness, and return to it years after, it is changed surely, with the change in yourself.

Andrew Lang

[My relationship with readers] scares me shitless! Because it's a responsibility. Over time, someone reads your book, and something happens. People want intimacy, and I have a terrible time saying no.

Madeleine L'Engle

An author who assures you that he writes for himself alone and that he does not care whether he is heard or not is a boaster and is deceiving either himself or you.

Francois Mauriac

The amount of people that seriously read books is only about 5 percent of the human population. So if you think about it that way, if we only have 5 percent, that's plenty. That's all we need to keep the world turning. Does that put your worries at ease a little?

Haruki Murakami, advising a teacher wondering if she should promote reading to her students

A few readers go a long way when they're the right kind. There are so many of the other kind. The writer is only free when he can tell the reader to go jump in the lake. You want, of course, to get what you have to show across to him, but whether he likes it or not is no concern of the writer.

Flannery O'Connor

I have a saying. If you want to write for yourself, get a diary. If you want to write for a few friends, get a blog. But if you want to write for a lot of people, think about them a little bit. What do they like? What are their needs? A lot of people in this country go through their days numb. They need to be entertained. They need to feel something.

James Patterson

Fuck 'em. Let the readers do some work for a change.

Harold Robbins, when told the characters' names in the second half of his latest manuscript were not the same as the first

A writer is first of all a reader. It is from reading that I derive the standards by which I measure my own work and according to which I fall lamentably short. It is from reading, even before writing, that I became part of a community — the community of literature — which includes more dead than living writers.

Susan Sontag

When I write I try not to think of the reader. I think of my reader as a very intimate part of me and my mother and my editor and not really a stranger or a critic.

Amy Tan

The reader of the novel will doubt, even for a brief moment, his own physical reality and will believe himself to be, like us, no more than a character from a novel.

Miguel de Unamuno

Fiction for me is a conversation for me between me and something that May Not Be Named — God, the Cosmos, the Unified Field, my own psychoanalitic cathexes, Roqoq'oqu, whomever. I do not feel even the hint of an obligation to an entity called READER — do not regard it as his favor, rather as his choice, that, duly warned, he has expended capital/time/retinal energy on what I've done.

David Foster Wallace

No one can write decently who is distrustful of the reader's intelligence, or whose attitude is patronizing.

E.B. White

Let the audience add up two plus two. They'll love you forever.

Billy Wilder, movie director
(See the next quotation for examples.)

”

Reading is supposed to be an educational tool of independence, and most people use it like sleeping pills; it is supposed to make us free and mature, and how many does it serve merely as a way of passing time and as a way of remaining in a condition of eternal immaturity.

Johann Adam Bergk, 1799

”

This American in the cast [of "South Pacific" in London, Connery's first acting job] ... gave me a list of books to read: all of George Bernard Shaw, "An Actor Prepares" and "My Life in Art" by Stanislavsky, all of Thomas Wolfe, all of Oscar Wilde, all of Ibsen, "Remembrance of Things Past" by Proust, Joyce's "Finnegan's Wake," and "Ulysses." It was tough going! But the power of those works does seep through... . On the nights we were dark, I'd see every play I could, meet the actors and learn. But it's the books, the reading, that can change one's life. I'm the living evidence.

Sean Connery

I've become accustomed to readers' taking widely different views of the intentions in my books and plays. Many thank me for the "comfort" they found in the last act of *Our Town;* others tell me it is a desolating picture of our limitation to "realize" life almost too sad to endure. Many assured me that *The Bridge of San Luis Rey* was a satisfying demonstration that all the accidents of life were overseen and harmonized in providence; and a society of atheists in New York wrote that it was the most artful exposure of shallow optimisms since *Candide* and asked me to address them.

Thornton Wilder

The natural habit of any good and critical reader is to disbelieve what you are telling him and try to escape out of the world you are picturing. Some novelists try to make the magic work by taking you deep down inside one person. I try to multiply the worlds I put into the books — so that, like the ripples of the stone thrown into the brook, you feel the repercussions going farther and farther out, and at the same time bringing more in. ... I've always thought this had something to do with the endings of Shakespeare's tragedies. An entirely new lot of people come in — Fortinbras in *Hamlet*, for example, and it's the same with *Macbeth* and *Lear*. You believe in the tragedies more because these others from outside confirm them.

August Wilson

Readers have the power that professors pretend they wield. Millions of words of professorial contempt have failed to kill Kipling. Praising Shaw to the skies has been in vain.

Gene Wolfe

Reading

Young people are turning away from the great books that might save them. ... It's NOT because Americans are dumb or lazy, but because they fear the chaos of their feelings. Our masters of commerce are quite happy with this arrangement. They want us in this state of terror, as it makes us more likely to obey their constant buy messages. The unexamined life, it might be said, offers an extraordinary profit margin.

Steve Almond

If I'm having a day where I don't feel I can write the instructions on a Nurofen packet I won't sit there staring. I'll read and I'll be alone. I think that reading, being alone, waiting, is a huge part of it all.

Martin Amis

The only education a writer gets is in reading other people's writing. You should read not through your opinion of whether or not you like something, but to see how the writer does it, why it's effective. Of course, sometimes it's awfully hard to tell golden drops from shit.

Isaac Asimov

Some books are to be tasted, others to be swallowed, and some few to be chewed and digested: that is, some books are to be read only in parts; others to be read but not curiously; and some few to be read wholly, and with diligence and attention.

Francis Bacon

I think it is a useful thing for young people who are learning to write (like me) to spend a lot of time with the old tales. The element of *story* — just sheer extraordinary, marvelous story — is not what we value Joyce for, for example, or Hemingway or Faulkner, as a rule. I love those men very much, but it is refreshing, it seems to me, for writers to become interested in yarns — elaborate lies. *The Arabian Nights* may be a better mentor for many than, say, J.D. Salinger.

John Barth

Reading remains a private, uniquely qualitative nook of our life. As readers, then, we are refugees from the flood of contemporaneous mathematicized homogeneity. With a book, we are at home with ourselves.

Daniel J. Boorstin

If you stuff yourself full of poems, essays, plays, stories, novels, films, comic strips, magazines, music, you automatically explode every morning like Old Faithful. I have never had a dry spell in my life, mainly because I feed myself well, to the point of bursting. I wake early and hear my morning voices leaping around in my head like jumping beans. I get out of bed quickly, to trap them before they escape.

Ray Bradbury

My life has been greatly influenced by many books which I have never read.

Ashleigh Brilliant

I have often wondered how anyone who does not read, by which I mean daily, having some book going all the time, can make it through life. Indeed if I were required to make a sharp division in the very nature of people, I would be tempted to make it there: readers and nonreaders of books … It is astonishing how the presence or absence of this habit so consistently characterizes an individual in other respects; it is as though it were a kind of barometer of temperament, of personality, even of character. Aside from that, for me it constituted something like sanity insurance.

William Brinkley

Read solid books, history, biography and travel — and above all take notes on what you read. Reading without note taking is as senseless as eating without digesting. It is easy to condense into a single page all that you really want to remember out of a big book, and there you have it for reference for years.

Arthur Conan Doyle, who had at least 60 scrapbooks of papers, letters, and clippings.

I have a passion for teaching kids to become readers, to become comfortable with a book, not daunted. Books shouldn't be daunting, they should be funny, exciting and wonderful; and learning to be a reader gives a terrific advantage.

Roald Dahl

And much though each new book keeps lit my light,
Defrauding me of sleep by dubious sleight,
I often wonder what the authors read
One half so rotten as the stuff they write.

Robertson Davies

There was something in my mind — even as I was entranced wondering what was going to happen next — that could appreciate the art of those narratives that I found so riveting. I don't know if that occurs to all young people as they read, but certainly for writers-to-be, there's

”

Opal felt vindicated and, more important, at peace. She had spent her own life reading and last year at this time she'd felt that perhaps hers was a pathetic and wasted life. She hadn't "done" enough. But her adventure in New York had renewed her faith in reading. It wasn't an alternative to experience, or an escape from it. Not if you did it right. Reading was the only way we could transcend our own experience and deeply engage in that of another. Opal had never written a book, but she knew now that the reader was as important as the writer.

Olivia Goldsmith, The Bestseller

”

I don't want to sound like an ad, a public service ad on TV, but the fact is if you can read, you can walk into a job later on. If you don't, then you've got the Army, Iraq, I don't know, something like that. It's, it's not as bright. So, that's my little commercial for that.

Stephen King

It was like looking at my 50 friends. A book was like stepping through a mirror. I could go somewhere else. Each one was a door to a whole kingdom.

Susan Sontag, recalling as a child looking at her small bookcase

that additional line of inquiry in the brain that goes along with the reading: How is this done? Could I do this?

E.L. Doctorow

I don't believe one reads to escape reality. A person reads to confirm a reality he knows is there, but which he has not experienced.

Lawrence Durrell

Drinking strange wine pours strength into the imagination. The dinosaurs had no strange wine. They had no imagination. They lived 130,000,000 years and vanished. Why? Because they had no imagination. Unlike human beings who have it and use it and build their future rather than merely passing through their lives as if they were spectators. Spectators watching television, one might say. The saurians had no strange wine, no imagination, and they became extinct. And you don't look so terrific yourself.

Harlan Ellison

'Tis the good reader that makes the good book; in every book he finds passages which seem confidences or asides hidden from all else and unmistakenly meant for his ear; the profit of books is according to the sensibility of the reader; the profoundest thought or passion sleeps as in a mine, until it is discovered by an equal mind and heart.

Ralph Waldo Emerson

Reading is everything. Reading makes me feel like I've accomplished something, learned something, become a better person. Reading makes me smarter. Reading gives me something to talk about later on. Reading is the unbelievably healthy way my attention deficit disorder medicates itself. Reading is escape, and the opposite of escape; it's a way to make contact with reality after a day of making things up, and it's a way of making contact with someone else's imagination after a day that's all too real. Reading is grist. Reading is bliss.

Nora Ephron

But I don't do a lot of reading anymore. I find it difficult to read when I'm writing and I'm always writing. … I can't go to bed thinking about someone else's story because then I wake up thinking about someone else's story and not mine.

Janet Evanovich

It is to your benefit to read a thousand books in your lifetime, and to get there you need to always be reading. Imagination is a greedy little pig that needs to be hand-fed. Several times a day. Fatten the pig.

Hampton Fancher, screenwriter

Read, read, read. Read everything — trash, classics, good and bad, and see how they do it. Just like a carpenter who works as an apprentice and studies the master. Read! You'll absorb it. Then write. If it is good, you'll find out. If it's not, throw it out the window.

William Faulkner

One way of tolerating existence is to lose oneself in literature as in a perpetual orgy

Gustave Flaubert

So much of reading is sustained in this country, I think, by the fact that women read while men are off golfing or watching football on TV or playing with their flight simulator or whatever. I worry —

I'm sorry that it's, uh – I had some hope of actually reaching a male audience and I've heard more than one reader in signing lines now at bookstores say "If I hadn't heard you, I would have been put off by the fact that it is an Oprah pick. I figure those books are for women. I would never touch it." Those are male readers speaking.

Jonathan Franzen

When you start reading in a certain way, that's already the beginning of your writing. You are learning what you admire, and you're learning to love other writers. The love of other writers is an important first step.

Tess Gallagher

When you're caught up in the experience of reading, you're not stuck inside your own head; someone else's thoughts, shaped by experiences and reflections that aren't yours, unfold themselves before your mind's eye, and you get to taste their structure and flavor, the unique way of looking at the world another mind has developed.

John Michael Greer

In a very real sense, people who have read good literature have lived more than people who cannot or will not read. … It is not true that we have only one life to live; if we can read, we can live as many more lives and as many kinds of lives as we wish.

S.I. Hayakawa, politician

One day Mother Plutarch was reading a romance novel in one corner of the room. She read aloud, as she understood better that way. In reading aloud you assume authority for what you are reading. There are people who read very loudly, and who appear to be giving their word of honor for what they are reading.

Victor Hugo

It was in reading Salman Rushdie's *Shame* that I had my breakthrough. I didn't know you could just throw phantasmagorical stuff into a book like that. I didn't know you could write a book as if there were no rules.

Marlon James

I believe that we ought to read only the kind of books that wound and stab us. If the book we're reading doesn't wake us up with a blow on the head, then why read it? We need the books that affect us like a disaster, that grieve us deeply, like the death of someone we loved more than ourselves, like being banished into forests far from everyone, like a suicide. A book must be the axe for the frozen sea inside us.

Franz Kafka

Book reading is a solitary and sedentary pursuit, and those who do are cautioned that a book should be used as an integral part of a well-rounded life, including a daily regimen of rigorous physical exercise, rewarding personal relationships, and a sensible low-fat diet. *A book should not be used as a substitute or an excuse.*

Garrison Keillor

Read! Read! Read! And then read some more. When you find something that thrills you, take it apart paragraph by paragraph, line by line, word by word, to see what made it so wonderful. Then use those tricks the next time you write.

W.P. Kinsella

I never did read very much [science fiction] except for a four-month period when I read several hundred

”

Good sullen reading is rare in a house, unless one is blessed with an impregnable and soundproof room of one's own: interruptions, restless unnecessary movements, doors opening and closing, apologies, even whisperings, God forbid, and meal-times. For the right deep swimming in a book, give me the sea: I read Josephus through between Freetown and the Fastnet Rock last voyage: the howling of the mariners, the motion of the sea and the elements (except perhaps in their utmost extrem-ity) are nothing, compared with domestic incursions. Since then, mere newspapers, gazett-es, periodical public-ations, all light frothy fare apart from the Proceedings, have imperceptibly drunk the whole of my time and energy.

Patrick O'Brian,
The Yellow Admiral

”

Writers read differently to other people. For a writer, all literature is contemporary. If the language endures, the thought endures. Writers eavesdrop on each other across time. This is a two-way process, because what has been written is continually changed by what is being written. To put it better, as Auden did: "The words of a dead man are modified in the guts of the living."

Jeanette Winterson

of what were supposed to be the best science fiction books ever. This was when I first decided to major in science fiction, as it was selling for me and other things weren't.

R.A. Lafferty

I just cannot read people like Leon Uris and James Michener. When you've covered one line, you can guess the next one. I like people who know the nuances of words, who know how to stick the right one in the right place. Sometimes you can laugh out loud at an exceptionally good phrase. I find it harder and harder to find fiction to read, because I either read it with dismay at how good it is or disgust at how bad it is. I do like the guys like John Cheever that have a sense of story, because, goddammit, you want to know what happens to somebody. You don't want a lot of self-conscious little logjams thrown in your way.

John D. MacDonald

Some people read for instruction, which is praiseworthy, and some for pleasure, which is innocent, but not a few read from habit, and I suppose that is neither innocent nor praiseworthy. Of that lamentable company am I. … Of course to read in this way is as reprehensible as doping, and I never cease to wonder at the impertinence of great readers who, because they are such, look down on the illiterate. From the standpoint of what eternity is it better to have read a thousand books than to have ploughed a million furrows?

W. Somerset Maugham

I know of no sentence that can induce such immediate and brazen lying as the one that begins: "Have you read ..."

Wilson Mizner

If you only read the books that everyone else is reading, you can only think what everyone else is thinking.

Haruki Murakami

I don't want to be corrupted by what I read. I don't wish to react. I wish just to keep on doing my work.

V.S. Naipaul, on why he doesn't read contemporary fiction, reviews, or books about him and his work.

You should write because you love the shape of stories and sentences and the creation of different words on a page. Writing comes from reading, and reading is the finest teacher of how to write.

Annie Proulx

To read a novel requires a certain kind of concentration, focus, devotion to the reading. If you read a novel in more than two weeks, you don't read the novel really. So I think that that kind of concentration, and focus, and attentiveness, is hard to come by. It's hard to find huge numbers of people, or large numbers of people or significant numbers of people who have those qualities.

Philip Roth

There are two motives for reading a book: one, that you enjoy it; the other, that you can boast about it.

Bertrand Russell

Literacy gives us access to the greatest and most influential minds in history: Socrates, say, or Newton have had audiences vastly larger than the total number of people either met in his whole lifetime.

Carl Sagan

Buying books would be a good thing if one could also buy the time to read them in: but as a rule the purchase of books is mistaken for the appropriation of their contents.

Arthur Schopenhauer

Samuel rode lightly on top of a book and he balanced happily among ideas the way a man rides white rapids in a canoe. But Tom got into a book, crawled and groveled between the covers, tunneled like a mole among the thoughts, and came up with the book all over his face and hands.

John Steinbeck, East of Eden

How many a man has dated a new era in his life from the reading of a book? The book exists for us perchance which will explain our miracles and reveal new ones. The at present unutterable things we may find somewhere uttered. These same questions that disturb and puzzle and confound us have in their turn occurred to all the wise men; not one has been omitted; and each has answered them, according to his ability, by his words and his life.

Henry David Thoreau

If I could give young people one piece of advice, it would be, read, read, read! In reading, you will open up new worlds, real and imagined. Read for information, read for pleasure. Our libraries are filled with knowledge and joy, and it's all there free for the taking. The person who DOES NOT read is no better off than the person who CANNOT read.

Abigail Van Buren

[Reading] is the most profound and effective form of meditation practiced on this planet, and far surpasses any dream experienced by a Hindu on a mountaintop. Why? Because [readers], by reading well, can think the thoughts of the wisest and most interesting human minds throughout all history. When [readers] meditate, even if they themselves have only mediocre intellects, they do it with the thoughts of angels. What could be more sacred than that?

Kurt Vonnegut

There is nothing like a good book to put you to sleep with the illusion that life is rich and meaningful.

Robert Penn Warren

Reading is the work of the alert mind, is demanding, and under ideal conditions produces finally a sort of ecstasy. As in the sexual experience, there are never more than two persons present in the act of reading — the writer who is the impregnator, and the reader who is the respondent.

E.B. White

Realism

One ought to know a lot about reality before one writes realistic novels. Since I don't know much about Reality, it will have to be abolished. What the hell, reality is a nice place to visit but you wouldn't want to live there, and literature never did, very long.

John Barth

Novelists have always tried to give their work authority by means of whatever strategy seems appropriate to their times. Defoe did this by denying his own authorship and claiming to be only the editor of *Robinson Crusoe*. … One of the devices used in *World's Fair* to persuade the reader of its authority is the interposition of passages in which members of the family speak in their own voices, as apparently

”

Some of the editors wrote rejection slips that were more creative than anything I had written. On my 10th submission to "Redbook," the printed rejection slip included a handwritten sentence: "Mrs. Clark your stories are light, slight, and trite." My first novella was returned with the succinct note: "We found the heroine as boring as her husband had."

Mary Higgins Clark

It does help, to be a writer, to have the sort of crazed ego that doesn't allow for failure. The best reaction to a rejection slip is a sort of wild-eyed madness, an evil grin, and sitting yourself in front of the keyboard muttering "Okay, you bastards. Try rejecting this!" and then writing something so unbelievably brilliant that all other writers will disembowel themselves with their pens upon reading it, because there's nothing left to write.

Neil Gaiman

transcribed on tape. This was my acknowledgment of the power I had recognized, around that time, in the collections of oral histories that were being published – how impressive I found the testimonies of supposedly ordinary people reporting on their lives.

E.L. Doctorow

Literary realism demands that everybody agree on what real life is – and it is really a very specific subset of American or European life. I love reading the fantasy of middle-class life in Connecticut because I've never lived that before. Do you all really cheat this much? That to me is like, *Wow!*

Victor LaValle

No weird story can truly produce terror unless it is devised with all the care and verisimilitude of an actual hoax.

H.P. Lovecraft

In Japan, I think that other world is very close to our real life, and if we decide to go to the other side it's not so difficult. I get the impression that in the Western world it isn't so easy to go to the other side; you have to go through some trials to get to the other world. But, in Japan, if you want to go there, you go there.

Haruki Murakami

It is often necessary for a writer to distort the particulars of experience in order to see them better.

Wallace Stegner

Contentment and fulfillment don't make for very good fiction.

Anthony Trollope

Writers can't back off from realism, just as an ambitious engineer cannot back off from electricity.

Tom Wolfe

In the course of your daily life this week ... You have overheard scraps of talk that filled you with amazement. You have gone to bed at night bewildered by the complexity of your feelings. In one day thousands of ideas have coursed through your brains; thousands of emotions have met, collided, and disappeared in astonishing disorder.

Virginia Woolf

Rejection

I am only one, only one, only one. Only one being, one at the same time. Not two, not three, only one. Only one life to live, only sixty minutes in one hour. Only one pair of eyes. Only one brain. Only one being. Being only one, having only one pair of eyes, having only one time, having only one life, I cannot read your M.S. three or four times. Not even one time. Only one look, only one look is enough. Hardly one copy would sell here. Hardly one. Hardly one. Many thanks. I am returning the M.S. by registered post. Only one M.S. by one post.

Arthur C. Fifield, publisher, rejecting Gertrude Stein's Sacred Emily

When boiled down to its basics, all any rejection slip ever says is, "We don't feel we could sell enough copies of this to earn our investment back."

Stephen Goldin

I guess I was in my second year in high school when the teacher gave me the bad news. I'd never make it as a writer. To begin with, I didn't know up from down about the English language and, secondly, I was too much of a dreamer...It seemed to me that the teacher had taken that hope away from me, the only real hope I'd ever had since I can remember.

Orrie Hitt

Thanks, but I don't read such trash.

Alfred Knopf, about Harold Robbins' manuscript for The Carpetbaggers. *Knopf had published Robbins' debut,* A Stone for Danny Fisher.

Every time I got a rejection, I would force myself to read another chapter in *The Power of Positive Thinking* by Norman Vincent Peale. There were days it felt like there weren't enough chocolate chip cookies in the world to get through another rejection, you know.

Debbie Macomber

I'm sick and tired of these kinds of women's novels that are just one long whiny complaint.

N.Y. Publisher, about Joanna Russ' The Female Man *(1975)*

No No No No No No No No No No No No No No No No No No No O'Neill.

Eugene O'Neill, replying to the limit of a free 20-word telegram to Howard Hughes' offer of $100,000 for a screenplay.

It is not too much to say that how well a writer copes with rejection determines whether he has a genuine literary vocation or just a literary flair. Rejection along with uncertainty are as much a part of the writer's life as snow and cold are of an Eskimo's: they are conditions one has not only to learn to live with but also learn to make use of. ... The gifted young writer has to learn that his main task is to persist.

Ted Solotaroff

There is humor in Dod Grile, but for every laugh that is in his book there are five blushes, ten shudders and a vomit. The laugh is too expensive.

Mark Twain, rejecting a publisher's request for a blurb for Nuggets & Dust *by Dod Grile – the penname of his acquaintance Ambrose Bierce.*

Reputation

A writer's reputation is twofold. What we think of his work, and what we think of him. What's more, we expect the two halves to relate: if they don't, then one or other of our opinions alters until they do.

Philip Larkin

Reputations are built on very little and are lost on even less.

Betsy Lerner

The one thing one seems able to depend upon in American life is that the pendulum will operate. I must say that I've always been particularly sensitive to the pendulum, since I always seem to be swinging in the opposite direction from it.

Norman Mailer

My past is like this uncontrollable girlfriend that always lets you down in the wrong places.

Robert Plant, rock musician

Research

I don't do any hands-on research. I mean, I'm not a journalist. If anything, I under-research. I hang around a lot and I listen to people, but I don't do police procedurals. I'm not writing anything that's that fact-driven. And while I want to get details correct, it's much more important to create an impression, and that doesn't come from facts.

Lawrence Block

”

Sometimes I spent 12 hours a day in surgical scrubs, assisting forensic pathologists as they performed autopsies in a Richmond, Va., morgue. I will never forget the first time I placed my gloved hands in a chest cavity and was startled to find that the blood was cold.

Patricia Cornwell

I believe that we respond most and best to work in any art form ... if we are pluralistic, flexible, relative in our judgments, if we are eclectic. Eclecticism is not the same as lack of scruple; eclecticism is the selection of the best standards and principles from various systems. It requires more care, more orderliness to be a pluralist than to apply a single theory.

Pauline Kael

It's a mistake to know too much, because then you feel you have to justify it by putting it all in.

Harlan Coben

What I love to do is give early versions of the story to experts in the field I am writing about. They correct me and make suggestions and then I rewrite.

Michael Connelly

Find a way to make a contact. Nothing beats the real thing. You can read lots of good novels and nonfiction accounts and you will learn a lot from these writers — I certainly did — but there is nothing like seeing it with your own eyes. Not only will you get the telling details of the job and character that you will bring to your work but you will get inspired and excited when you observe how it is really done. You will know that you have something original to bring to your story.

Michael Connelly, on getting information from police officers

When I'm in the heat of the writing, I'll make crap up, because I want to keep going. But that's never good enough, and I'm always bothered by that, so in the coming days or weeks, I'll retro-research it, and then if I have to revise or add things, I can do it.

Robert Crais

I undertake an enormous amount of research that I never use; in fact I use as *little* of my historical research as possible. … All I want to be able to do is convey my historical world with the confidence of somebody who happens to know what kind of calendar might be hanging on the wall. What kind of boots that old man sitting in the corner might be wearing, and how much he paid for them.

G. Masterton

I do a great deal of research. I don't want anyone to say, "That could not have happened." It may be fiction, but it has to be true.

Jacquelyn Mitchard

I have a strong work ethic yet I'm incredibly lazy as well. The problem with being a writer is that everything you do can be called research. Sitting in the pub is research. Reading the newspaper can be research. I will put off the evil hour when I start writing for as long as I possibly can.

Ian Rankin, who had published 46 books over 30 years

I want to get into my subject and I did. Getting head from an N.Y.U. student is not going to threaten a marriage of fourteen years.

Gay Talese, on researching his sex book Thy Neighbor's Wife. *(His wife's response: "It was disturbing")*

Revenge

Fiction is always autobiographical. I wanted to break the legs of certain people at Granada.

Lee Child, after he had been fired by the British media company for union activities

That's the best revenge of all: happiness. Nothing drives people crazier than seeing someone have a good fucking life.

Chuck Palahniuk

Reviews & Reviewers

(See **Critics**)

In the art of reviewing I would lay down as a fundamental position, which you must never lose sight of, and which must be the mainspring of all your criticisms — write what will sell.

Edward Copleston (1776-1849), college provost and Anglican bishop, from his satirical essay, "Advice to a Young Reviewer"

My poor brain is a sort of incinerator, which seizes upon huge amounts of literary garbage, quickly reduces it to ashes, and spits them out, retaining only a disgusting slime upon its walls.

Robertson Davies

I've never learned anything from a review. I'm sensitive enough to reviews that I don't read them. The good ones don't make me any happier, and the bad ones, so many of them, they haven't paid attention, or they get things wrong. It's irritating.

Pete Dexter

I do not remember having ever tried to influence a press notice, even when I knew the men who wrote them. I never ask favour, because I think a pressman has quite enough on his hands without being bothered from outside … I care nothing for club life, consequently I do not meet many men who are well known in the London press world.

Nat Gould

What I feel about the authors of pretentious and misleading books is well expressed by the fact that Dante put the fraudulent below adulterers, gluttons, bad-tempered gits, suicides, sodomites, hypocrites, heretics and other riffraff in his sketch of hell. But really I am of a sunny disposition and much prefer to write and talk about books I admire. I spend my working life doing so. Reviewing is what happens when criticism goes on holiday.

Eric Griffiths, book reviewer

I can sit here and complain about mean customer reviews on Amazon.com, but the fact is that I've had advantages most young writers don't get. So I shouldn't even flinch. The publicity doesn't make me who I am. I know who I am — I'm not a sound bite, I'm not my novel.

Molly Jong-Fast

When I was writing my first book, my editor advised me to put everything I wanted the review-reading public to know in the first and last chapters, because those are the only chapters that most reviewers read. In the years since then, I have discovered that indeed most of the quotes pulled by reviewers from my books have come from the first and last sections.

Michael Lind

The prolonged, indiscriminate reviewing of books is a quite exceptionally thankless, irritating and exhausting job. It not only involves praising trash…but constantly INVENTING reactions towards books about which one has no spontaneous feelings whatever. The reviewer, jaded though he may be, is professionally interested in books, and out of the thousands that appear annually, there are probably fifty or a hundred that he would enjoy writing about. If he is a top-notcher in his profession he may get hold of ten or twenty of them: more probably he gets hold of two or three. The rest of his work, however conscientious he may be in praising or damning, is in essence humbug. He is pouring his

"

All those early reviewers who used to say: She's one long cliché ... Of course I am! We all live a cliché. When you are sexually betrayed for the first time in your life, it is the end of the universe as you know it. Nothing is a cliché when it happens to you for the first time. The pain is unbearable.

Joanna Trollope

How a human being could have attempted such a book as the present without committing suicide before he had finished a dozen chapters, is a mystery. It is a compound of vulgar depravity and unnatural horrors.

Graham's Lady Magazine, *review of* Wuthering Heights, *1848*

immortal spirit down the drain, half a pint at a time.

George Orwell

Commercial books don't even get covered. The reason why so many book reviews go out of business is because they cover a lot of stuff that nobody cares about. Imagine if the movie pages covered none of the big movies and all they covered were movies that you couldn't even find in the theater?

James Patterson

It is very easy to be scathing; but if even a morose-natured man could be aware of the torture he inflicts — how with that easy wheel of his "he sets sharp racks at work to pinch and peel" — he would mingle a little of the milk of human kindness with his gall: even if he be not conscious of having ever possessed literary merit himself, he has at least been young and can remember the sensitiveness of youth. Let him spoil the rod on the author of well-seasoned skin (on me, if he likes, and welcome), but spare the child.

James Payn

[Reviewers] are a bunch of pussies. They are backscratchers, afraid for their own careers — novelists reviewing their friends' works. It is very dishonest.

Dale Peck

I simply hate it when reviewers call my work "wacky" or "zany." Those people are going to be hunted down by the Mafia!

Terry Pratchett

No degree of dullness can safeguard a work against the determination of critics to find it fascinating.

Harold Rosenberg

The ideal reviewer writes no books at all, lives outside New York but doesn't resent New York, has no credentials — because every credential is a trap. He simply — well, how to put it? — has an interest in books.

Wilfrid Sheed, critic

I never read a book before reviewing it; it prejudices a man so.

Sydney Smith (1771-1845)

Unless a reviewer has the courage to give you unqualified praise, I say ignore the bastard.

John Steinbeck

Writers are the only people who are reviewed by people of their own kind. And their own kind can often be reasonably generous — *if* you stay in your category. I don't. I do many different things rather better than most people do one thing. And envy is the central fact of writing life.

Gore Vidal

I have lost count of the number of dull books I have hailed as masterpieces, rather than trouble myself to finish.

A.N. Wilson

The reader more or less expects the book reviewer to tell him what the book is like — that is to say, how it is written, what sort of temperament the author has, and what sort of effect he produces.

Edmund Wilson

Reviews, Bad

To my surprise and without Kael- or [John] Simon-like exaggeration, not simply, jarringly, piece by piece, line by line, and without interruption, worthless.

Renata Adler, reviewing Pauline Kael's When the Lights Go Down

(*From a series of messages on Twitter*)
Back from west coast swing of tour. Seattle and Portland great book towns. Really good showing at bookstores. Dallas can go fuck itself hard.

•

Based on book tour, if Dallas slid into sinkhole, nation's IQ would rise by 50 points.

•

Could not get any local publicity in Dallas. Plus pretty vindictive review by a dickasaurus douchejuciest jealous prick. Dumb-assed nonsense.

•

Qualifications of *Dallas Morning* reviewer Alex Lemon. Teaches writing at Texas Christian University. I once again rest my fucking case.

•

A reviewer can say anything he wants. I say anything I want back. If for some godforsaken reason I am at TCU, I will find Alex Lemon.

Buzz Bissinger, reacting to Alex Lemon's negative review of Father's Day

Cliterature

Christopher Buckley, review of Sally Quinn's Regrets Only *(1986). In retaliation, Quinn disinvited Buckley's editor at* Vanity Fair, *Tina Brown, from a birthday party for her husband,* Washington Post *editor Ben Bradlee.*

'Tis strange the mind, that very fiery particle,
Should let itself be snuffed out by an Article.

Lord Byron, disagreeing that Keats died from a negative review

This story gives me a pain in the neck. ... It's pretty near the last word in childishness, and the plot has whiskers like unto Spanish moss on an old oak. I foresaw the end from the beginning.

Phil Cody, Black Mask *circulation manager, editorial memo about Erle Stanley Gardner's story. The memo was accidentally included with the rejection. Gardner accepted the criticism, rewrote the story, and sent it back. It was accepted.*

A tissue of horrible and disgusting absurdity.... Our taste and our judgment alike revolt at this kind of writing.

John Wilson Croker

They are forgotten in a week, but your book will live!

Charles Dickens, to Hans Christian Andersen

Reviews hurt far less than they should; and in a way it seems healthier, in a sick culture, to be rejected than approved. All the pleasure is in the writing.

John Fowles

How well or how badly something is received never really affects me. Because there are things that people have hated that I loved, and vice versa.

Neil Gaiman

It is impossible to imagine how any man's fancy could have conceived such a mass of stupid filth, unless he were possessed of the soul of a sentimental donkey that had died of disappointed love.

Rufus Griswold, reprinted in Walt Whitman's Blades of Grass.

It is utterly incompetent to the primary functions of a book ... We do not open his books with the expectation of being thrilled, or convinced, or deeply moved in any way, and, accordingly, when we find one to be as flat as a Dutch landscape, we remind ourselves that we have wittingly travelled into Holland, and that we have no right to abuse the scenery for being

”

We went for a long walk in the afternoon, and [Hugh Walpole] told me that when somebody wrote a stinker about some book of his, he cried for hours. Can you imagine getting all worked up about a bad notice? I always feel about the critics that there are bound to be quite a number of them who don't like one's stuff and one just has to accept it. They don't get a sob out of me.

P.G. Wodehouse

”

If you've been a journalist, the one thing you know is that everything can be fixed. I spent a year on the rewrite desk in San Antonio. Sometimes you'd get a story, and it was like deboning a fish. It's messy work, but nothing fatal — you just had to think about it.

Laura Lippman

in character.

Henry James, on Trollope's The Belton Estate

To make the Bible readable in the modern sense means to flatten out, tone down, and convert into tepid expository prose what in [the King James Version] is wild, full of awe, poetic, and passionate. It means stepping down the voltage of the K.J.V. so that it won't blow any fuses. Babes and sucklings (or infants) can play with the R.S.V. without the slightest danger of electrocution.

Dwight Macdonald, on the Revised Standard Version of the Bible

As a good German, I should, I suppose, wallow happily in Faust; I can only report that, when I read it, it is patriotically, not voluptuously. Dostoevsky, for some reason that I don't know, simply stumps me; I have never been able to get through any of his novels. George Eliot I started to read too young, and got thereby a taste against her that is unsound but incurable. Against Cooper and Browning I was prejudiced by schoolmasters who admired them. [Eden] Phillpotts seems to me the worst novelist now in practice in England. As for Lawrence and Miss Stein, what makes them hard reading for me is simply the ineradicable conviction that beneath all their pompous manner there is nothing but tosh. The two Scandinavians [Selma Lagerlöf and Bjørnstjerne Bjørnson, both Nobel laureates] I need not explain.

H.L. Mencken, explaining his list of the 10 dullest authors for Vanity Fair *magazine, 1923*

A bad review is even less important than whether it is raining in Patagonia.

Iris Murdoch

The Great Gatsby is purely ephemeral phenomenon...so delicate, so sharp ... a literary lemon meringue.

The New York Herald Tribune

This not a novel to be tossed aside lightly. It should be thrown with great force.

Dorothy Parker, of Benito Mussolini's The Cardinal's Mistress

It seems as if the author wrote under the influence of opium, or attempted to describe the fantastic terrors which afflict a sufferer from *delirium tremens*. A sound mind is incapable of such vagaries, and finds it very difficult to sympathize with them.

The Southern Quarterly Review, *of Edgar Allan Poe's "The Raven"*

The arguments are selected from the customary communistic sources and arguments...Consistency is not, and any informed reader knows that it cannot be, a quality either of the Communistic mind or Communist propaganda.

A.D. Spearman, San Francisco Examiner, *of* The Grapes of Wrath *(1939)*

Revision

I do edit the first draft and make changes that usually amount to not more than 5 percent of the total, and then I send it off.

Isaac Asimov

Revise a lot. You can usually make it funnier.

Dave Barry

You never have to change anything you got up in the middle of the night to write.

Saul Bellow

I get the most effective final copy when I'm not too objective about the first draft. I get words down so the idea is there, and the correct mood and tension. Revision is largely a matter of cutting to speed the pace and eliminate wordage that might be more important to the author than to the reader. Being too objective and critical, too analytical on the first draft sometimes freezes a writer. The writing doesn't come naturally, but is stiff and awkward—self-conscious.

Ray Bradbury

Cheat your landlord if you can and must, but do not try to shortchange the Muse. It cannot be done. You can't fake quality any more than you can fake a good meal.

William S. Burroughs

My own experience is that once a story has been written, one has to cross out the beginning and the end. It is there that we authors do most of our lying.

Anton Chekhov

When I turn in a manuscript, I know it is the story I wanted to tell and it isn't within my power to tell it a better way. If it is praised, I am grateful. If it is roundly criticized, I console myself by saying I did the best I could do.

Mary Higgins Clark

I revise extensively. The heavy work is done, but I like revising. As for editing, though I try to be stringent, you will recall that I resist your editor-like zeal for total clarity — all the lights blazing and not a dark corner to be found. I am a writer much given to light and shade, and I firmly believe that to know all is to despise all.

Robertson Davies

The reason to perfect a piece of prose as it progresses — to secure each sentence before building on it — is that original writing fashions a form. It unrolls out into nothingness. It grows cell to cell, bole to bough to twig to leaf; any careful word may suggest a route, may begin a strand of metaphor or event out of which much, or all, will develop. Perfecting the work inch by inch, writing from the first word toward the last, displays the courage and fear this method induces. ... The reason not to perfect a work as it progresses is that, concomitantly, original work fashions a form the true shape of which it discovers only as it proceeds, so the early strokes are useless, however fine their sheen. Only when a paragraph's role in the context of the whole work is clear can the envisioning writer direct its complexity of detail to strengthen the work's ends.

Annie Dillard

You're finished when anything you do makes it worse instead of better.

Deborah Eisenberg, paraphrasing advice from Mavis Gallant

I do not rewrite unless I am absolutely sure that I can express the material better if I do rewrite it.

William Faulkner

Prose is like hair; it shines with combing.

Gustave Flaubert

Easy reading is damned hard writing.

Thomas Hood

”

I'm a tremendous rewriter; I never think anything is good enough. I'm always rephrasing jokes, changing lines, and then I hate everything. "The Girl Most Likely To" (1973 TV movie) was rewritten seven times, and the first time I saw it I literally went out and threw up! How's that for liking yourself?

Joan Rivers

”

Never use the word "very." It is the weakest word in the English language; doesn't mean anything. If you feel the urge of "very" coming on, just write the word, "damn," in the place of "very." The editor will strike out the word, "damn," and you will have a good sentence.

William Allen White, usually credited to Mark Twain

Half my life is an act of revision; more than half the act is performed with small changes. Being a writer is a strenuous marriage between careful observation and just as carefully imagining the truths you haven't had the opportunity to see. The rest is the necessary, strict toiling with the language; for me this means writing and rewriting the sentences until they sound as spontaneous as good conversation.

John Irving

I revise and revise and revise. I'm so picky. *Yonder* took me seven years to write. That book meant a lot to me. I wanted it to be perfect.

Tony Johnston

Suggesting that a writer delete his words is excruciating for some, and the excision must be made with delicacy. Sometimes this means the use of lightly penciled queries in the margins: *awk? right word? believable? trans? rep?* Of course, what the editor means is: *totally awkward, terrible word, completely unbelievable, how the hell do you expect the reader to make a transition when you haven't,* and *this is so damn repetitive I feel like killing myself.*

Betsy Lerner

The point of a novel revision is to *finish the book.* I guarantee you that as long as you're willing to keep piddling around with the same manuscript, you'll find ways to make it different. You don't want it to be different. You just want to make it as good as it can possibly be, and then get it out the door. Why? Because the definition of a writing career is: Write a book. Write another book. Write another book. Nowhere in that description is included: Take one story and make it a monument to every idea you ever had or ever will.

Holly Lisle

I'm not a very good writer, but I'm an excellent rewriter.

James A. Michener

[I spend months] looking at the manuscript and saying, "This is wrong — but what's wrong?" I ask myself, "If this book were a dream, it would be a dream of what?" But when I'm asking this I'm also trying to believe in what I've written, to forget that it's writing and to say, "This has taken place," even if it hasn't. The idea is to perceive your invention as a reality that can be understood as a dream. The idea is to turn flesh and blood into literary characters and literary characters into flesh and blood.

Philip Roth

I edit maniacally. The Amsterdam story ("The Garden of Eden") literally took me three years to fix. I wrote it, rewrote it, fixed it, pulled it apart — I feel like a mechanic. It's too bad stories aren't like leaky tires, where you can just submerge them and then see where the holes are.

Elissa Schappell

Writing a first draft is like groping one's way into a dark room, or overhearing a faint conversation, or telling a joke whose punchline you've forgotten. As someone said, one writes mainly to rewrite, for rewriting and revising are how one's mind comes to inhabit the material fully.

Ted Solotaroff

I almost always write everything the way it comes out, except I tend much more to take things out rather than put things in. It's out of a desire to really show what's going on at all times, how things smell and look, as well as from the knowledge that I don't want to push things too quickly through to climax; if I do, it won't mean anything. Everything has to be earned, and it takes a lot of work to earn.

Peter Straub

I find that I can criticize my composition best when I stand at a little distance from it — when I do not see it, for instance.

Henry David Thoreau

Well, my wife took a look at the first version of something I was doing not long ago and said: "Goddammit, Thurber, that's high-school stuff." I had to tell her to wait until the seventh draft, it'll work out all right.

James Thurber

What is easy to read has been difficult to write. The labour of writing and rewriting, correcting and recorrecting, is the due exacted by every good book from its author, even if he knows from the beginning exactly what he wants to say. A limpid style is invariably the result of hard labour, and the easily flowing connection of sentence with sentence and paragraph with paragraph has always been won by the sweat of the brow.

G.M. Trevelyan

This is what I find most encouraging about the writing trades: They allow mediocre people who are patient and industrious to revise their stupidity, to edit themselves into something like intelligence. They also allow lunatics to seem saner than sane.

Kurt Vonnegut

If you work hard on something, and think about it very deeply, new ideas sort of bubble to the surface. I find that while rewriting — even just retyping a page — new things come in that I hadn't thought about before. Rewriting is important. I don't think you are finished after only one or two drafts. Rewriting is not only polishing sentences; it is also a process of searching for new things to improve your story.

Bernard Waber

I have had a stream of letters cursing the end of *Leave It to Psmith*, and I shall have to rewrite it. But what a sweat it is altering a story that has gone cold!

P.G. Wodehouse

I write two pages of arrant nonsense after straining; I write variations of every sentence; compromises; bad shots; possibilities; till my writing book is like a lunatic's dream. Then I trust to some inspiration on re-reading; & pencil them into some sense.

Virginia Woolf

Rewriting is the essence of writing well: it's where the game is won or lost. The idea is hard to accept. We all have emotional equity in our first draft; we can't believe that it wasn't born perfect. But the odds are close to 100 percent that it wasn't.

William Zinsser

Rituals & Routines

If I'm at a dull party I'll invent some kind of game for myself and then pick someone to play it with so that I am, in effect, writing a scene. I'm supplying my half of the dialogue and hoping the other half comes up to standards. If it doesn't, I try to direct it that way.

Evan Hunter

Should you fail to achieve success,

”

I always get up and make a cup of coffee while it is still dark — it must be dark — and then I drink the coffee and watch the light come. Writers all devise ways to approach that place where they expect to make the contact, where they become the conduit, or where they engage in this mysterious process. For me, light is the signal in the transaction. It's not being in the light, it's being there before it arrives. It enables me, in some sense.

Toni Morrison

”

Satire is a sort of glass, wherein beholders do generally discover everybody's face but their own.

Jonathan Swift

Satire picks a one-sided fight, and the more its intended target reacts, the more the practitioner gains the advantage.

Garry Trudeau, cartoonist

all these behaviors look only like excuses or sick behavior.

Betsy Lerner

When I'm not writing, I'm a very ordinary person. I respect the daily routine. I get up early in the morning. I go to bed around nine o'clock, unless the baseball game is still going. And I run or I swim. I'm an ordinary guy.

Haruki Murakami

One must be pitiless about this matter of "mood." In a sense, the writing will create the mood. If art is ... a genuinely transcendental function — a means by which we rise out of limited, parochial states of mind — then it should not matter very much what states of mind we are in.

Joyce Carol Oates

When I really do not know what I am saying, or how to say it, I'll open these Pentels, these colored Japanese pens, on yellow lined paper, and I'll start off with very tentative colors, very light colors: orange, yellow or tan. … When my thoughts are more formulated, and I have a sharper sense of trying to say it, I'll go into heavier colors: blues, greens and eventually into black. When I am writing in black, which is the final version, I have written that sentence maybe 12 or 15 or 18 times.

Gay Talese

Roman à clef

[Friends] draw off into coldness and enmity who'd have kinder feelings toward me if I were a photographer of dogs or a fish expert.

Saul Bellow, after friends learn he used them in his books

Turning up in a novel signed by my wife as a somewhat anemic portrait painter with a few ideas lifted from Clive Bell, Leger, etc. puts me in an absurd & Zelda in a ridiculous position. The mixture of fact & fiction is calculated to ruin us both, or what is left of us.

F. Scott Fitzgerald, about his portrayal in Zelda Fitzgerald's Save Me the Waltz *(1932)*

To damn people properly you must have the dope on them.

Ernest Hemingway

If you caricature friends in your first novel they will be upset, but if you don't they will feel betrayed.

Mordecai Richler

Romance

The critics can make fun of Barbara Cartland. I was quite amused by the critic who once called me "an animated meringue." But they can't get away from the fact that I know what women want — and that's to be flung across a man's saddle, or into the long grass by a loving husband.

Barbara Cartland

One of the most interesting things about the [romance] genre is that its most vocal critics are people who declare that they've never read it, but still feel willing to generalize about it.

Michele Jaffe

I insist on pace, and that's much harder with romance. It's hard to do romances where you can't stop turning the pages.

James Patterson, on why he won't write romances

Rules

It's not wise to violate the rules until you know how to observe them.

T.S Eliot

The idea isn't to follow every rule of Gordon's [List] and Tom's and mine, not forever. But it's better to start with some rules. Learn some compulsory skills. After that you can free-style, and if you're lucky and if you're successful a new generation of aspiring writers will copy your style and drive your hard-won, well-crafted voice right into the ground.

Chuck Palahniuk

Russian Literature

I am Wholly Allergic to Russian Literature, drama, & art. For one thing, they all have such Stephen Leacock names, like Ivan Ivanovitch; & for another, I loathe & despise their silly Fatalism.

Georgette Heyer

Sanity

Anyone who spends the most meaningful hours of the day in the exclusive company of other people who do not exist, and who are indeed the product of his or her own imagination, is apt to be a little weird.

Lawrence Block

One has to be just a little crazy to write a great novel.

John Gardner

Satire

The satirist who really loves people loves them so well the way they are that he sees no need to disguise their characteristics — he loves the whole, without retouching. Yet the word used for this unqualifying affection is "cynicism."

Dawn Powell

I don't think a satirist has any greater obligation to society than a bricklayer or anybody else.

Shel Silverstein

Schools

Slotkin's [an instructor Vonnegut knew in college] notion of the importance of the school stuck with me … What Slotkin said was this: no man who achieved greatness in the arts operated by himself; he was top man in a group of like-minded individuals. This works out fine for the cubists, and Slotkin had plenty of good evidence for its applying to Goethe, Thoreau, Hemingway, and just about anybody you care to name. If this isn't 100% true, it's true enough to be interesting — and maybe helpful.

Kurt Vonnegut

Science Fiction

Spending time on background takes time away from your characters. You don't have characterization as it's usually understood by most people. If you consider your background society as a character, that society has all kinds of "characterization," but that's not usually considered so by critics. On the other hand, now that writers are trying to remove the cerebral quality and to add to the emotional, to work with characterization in the older sense, they do it at the cost of the background. In many modern SF stories, you have people very sharply delineated, but you see a society only by flashes of lightning. There is no such thing as a free lunch: if you gain something here, you lose something there.

Isaac Asimov

In science fiction, the characters are not always human beings. They can be alien creatures, robots,

”

I was attracted to science fiction because it was so wide open. I was able to do anything and there were no walls to hem you in and there was no human condition that you were stopped from examining.

Octavia E. Butler

You want to know what "out there" [Hollywood] means to me? Once I was coming down a street in Beverly Hills and I saw a Cadillac about a block long, and out of the side window was a wonderfully slinky mink, and an arm, and at the end of the arm a hand in a white suede glove wrinkled around the wrist, and in the hand was a bagel with a bite out of it.

Dorothy Parker

computers, or even intelligent dolphins. But they must behave like humans, or they will either bore or baffle the reader.

Ben Bova

Science fiction writers, I am sorry to say, really do not know anything. We can't talk about science, because our knowledge of it is limited and unofficial, and usually our fiction is dreadful.

Philip K. Dick

Grownups are reluctant to take science fiction seriously, and with good reason: sci-fi is a hormonal activity, not a literary one. Its traditional concerns are all pubescent. Secondary sexual characteristics are everywhere, disguised. Aliens have dicks. Telepathy allows you to have sex without the nasty inconvenience of touching, no matter how good it feels. Womb-like spaceships provide balanced meals. No one ever has to grow old – body parts are replaceable, like Job's daughters, and if you're lucky you can become a robot. As for the adult world, it's simply not there; political systems tend to be naively authoritarian (there are more lords in science fiction than on public television) and are often ruled by young boys on quests. The most popular sci-fi book in recent years, Frank Herbert's *Dune* sold millions of copies by combining all these themes: it ends with its adolescent hero conquering the universe while straddling a giant worm.

Arnold Klein

All science fiction is comic. Five percent of it is consciously comic and ninety-five percent of it is unconsciously comic. But to laugh at the often very funny ninety-five percent of it is to be put into mortal peril. The "True Believers" would kill us if they could, and perhaps they can.

R.A. Lafferty

A good science fiction story is a story with a human problem and a human solution which would not have happened at all without its science content.

Theodore Sturgeon

You won't get anywhere trying to explain that you subscribe to the Miss Marple theory of literature, which maintains that you don't have to go farther than your front yard to understand the universe. … I've sung in church choirs, had Mary Kay facials, put on garage sales. I've been to the mall and the orthodontist and the second-grade Valentine's party. I've even been to Tupperware parties – only slightly stranger than Venusian eyestalk-bonding ceremonies – at which you participate in arcane contests ("How many words can you make out of 'Tupperware'?" "Warp, put, upper, rue …" I always win. It's the only thing majoring in English is good for) and eat ritual preparations of Cool Whip and graham-cracker crumbs and purchase plastic boxes that burp. Science fiction? Piece of cake.

Connie Willis, on why you don't need to know science to write science fiction

Scottish Literature

If the Nobel Prize came from Scotland they would give it to [Ian Rankin] a writer of fucking detective fiction, or else some kind of child writer, or something that was not even new when Enid Blyton was writing *The Faraway Tree*, because she [J.K. Rowling] was writing about some upper middle-class young magician or some fucking crap.

James Kelman,
Booker-winning Scots novelist

We all hate the commercialisation of literature, but Ian Rankin writes very competently and the Harry Potter books are very entertaining. I don't know if we should feel they are in any way degrading to the high culture we find ourselves participating in and advocating.

Michael Schmidt,
poet, publisher and professor

Screenwriting

Oftentimes, with his books, people misunderstand where the gold lies. … [They] keep the plot and jettison all the textural things — the characters, the dialogue — all that goes. And the plot — even he'll tell you it's insignificant. You have to start with those characters and that may mean reinventing some of the plot.

Scott Frank, screenwriter,
on adapting Elmore Leonard's novels

[N]ormally with movies where they like outlines, I have the whole thing planned out before I start, in every detail. Normally when I do this I am gloomy through the writing period, feeling like a kid with a Colour-By-Numbers painting book, where you're just filling in the colour and trying to stay inside the lines. I figure, if I can't surprise myself, how can I surprise my readers?

Neil Gaiman

I write stories but I have no grace for fucking them up for other mediums. It was hard enough for me to learn to write to be read by the human eye. I do not know how, nor do I care to know how to write to be read by parrots, monkeys, apes, baboons, nor actors.

Ernest Hemingway, on screenwriting

Screenwriting encourages that speed — dialogue is the stuff of movies. People say that writing for the screen is all visual; what they mean by that is that whatever characters are thinking and feeling has to be translated into the visual. … You use simple brushstrokes in a screenplay for things over which you would take much greater pains in a novel.

Richard Russo

The difference between novels and screenplays [is] like the difference between fine painting and a paint-by-the-numbers kit you'd buy at Woolworth's.

Stirling Silliphant

Secrets

I write a lot of stuff so I can keep my secrets. It's all about hiding the truth. It's hiding by not hiding! Like I'm distracting them by saying, "Hey, look at all this perverted shit over here!"

Jonathan Ames

I don't reveal skeletons that would hurt anyone. They may hurt the dead, but the dead belong to me.

Anne Sexton

Self-Censorship

It's important when writing to feel free, answerable to no one. The minute you feel you are answerable, you're throttled. You can't do it.

Edna O'Brien

Self-Confidence

A prolific writer has to have self-assurance. He can't sit around

”

You wouldn't be an artist if you didn't feel somewhere in your heart that you're better than everybody else and you're going to blow them away. ... It takes a fanaticism and a dedication and a single-mindedness.

T. Coraghessian Boyle

I leave this rule for others when I'm dead,
Be always sure you're right —
then go ahead.

Davy Crockett

”

Shyness is common. ... Self-consciousness it was always called when I was young, and that is what it is. To imagine that it shows a sense of modesty is absurd. Modesty. Why, I have never known a truly modest person to be the least bit shy.

Elizabeth Taylor, British novelist, not the actress

I do think I'm one of the best writers around, and I want to be recognized for that.

Dale Peck

doubting the quality of his writing. Rather, he has to love his own writing. I do. I can pick up any one of my books, start reading it anywhere, and immediately be lost in it and keep on reading until I am shaken out of the spell by some external event. Janet [Asimov's second wife] finds this amusing, but I think it's natural. If I didn't enjoy my writing so much, how on earth could I stand all the writing I do?

Isaac Asimov

The fact that there is a lot out there, doesn't make you less. It might put you in a bigger pool to swim with the bigger fish, but someone else's more or much doesn't depreciate the value of "mine."

Don Aslett, business owner

You can't ask "how can I tell if my comic is good," because you can't think about it like that. You HAVE to know that your comic is good, that it has the potential to be good if it isn't now, that it has good qualities, that you are not just throwing ideas onto paper and wondering if people will like it because you have no idea. You have to know what's good about it, or you won't know when it's bad, and you'll never know how to make it better. You don't want to be one of those people who doesn't have the skills to know whether what they make is good or not. Self-editing is simply something people learn over time as they strive to make their comics better, people with the skill to know the difference. You need that skill, so don't be shy about it, look at your comic and think to yourself about what you like and don't like, and be honest about it. Then, like everything else, just keep working.

Kate Beaton, cartoonist

This is my life. I write bestselling novels. My novels go onto the bestseller lists on or shortly after publication. … Each of my novels does this. **So be it! I will find the way to do this. See to it.**

Octavia E. Butler, writing motivational statements on the back of a notebook

A writer like me must have an utter confidence, an utter faith in his star. It's an almost mystical feeling, a feeling of nothing can-happen-to-me, nothing-can-harm-me, nothing-can-touch-me.

F. Scott Fitzgerald

The main rule of writing is that if you do it with enough assurance and confidence, you're allowed to do whatever you like. (That may be a rule for life as well as for writing. But it's definitely true for writing.) So write your story as it needs to be written. Write it honestly, and tell it as best you can. I'm not sure that there are any other rules. Not ones that matter.

Neil Gaiman

If you think you can win, you can win. Faith is necessary to victory.

William Hazlitt

The writer learns to write, in the last resort, only by writing. He must get words onto paper even if he is dissatisfied with them. A young writer must cross many psychological barriers to acquire confidence in his capacity to produce good work, especially his first full-length book, and he cannot do this by staring at a piece of blank paper, searching for the perfect sentence.

Paul Johnson

You need that pride in yourself, as well as a sense, when you are sitting on Page 297 of a book, that the book is going to be read, that somebody is going to care. You can't ever be sure about that, but you need the sense that it's important, that it's not typing; it's writing.

Roger Kahn

I think we can all agree that it would cheat this collection of its true interest to present myself as more modest than I am.

Norman Mailer, from Advertisements for Myself

I think like a genius, I write like a distinguished author, and I speak like a child.

Vladimir Nabokov

An absolutely necessary part of the writer's equipment, almost as necessary as talent, is the ability to stand up under punishment, both the punishment the world hands out and the punishment he inflicts upon himself.

Irwin Shaw

The writer must believe that what he is doing is the most important thing in the world. And he must hold to this illusion even when he knows it is not true.

John Steinbeck

I've always had complete confidence in myself. When I was nothing, I had complete confidence. There were 10 guys in my writing class at Williams College who could write better than I. They didn't have what I have, which is guts. I was dedicated to writing, and nothing could stop me.

John Toland

As for conceit, what man will do any good who is not conceited? Nobody holds a good opinion of a man who has a low opinion of himself.

Anthony Trollope

No one can amount to a damn in the arts if he becomes sweetly reasonable, seeing all sides of a picture, forgiving all sins.

Kurt Vonnegut

If I ever felt inclined to be timid as I was going into a room full of people, I would say to myself, "you're the cleverest member of one of the cleverest families in the cleverest class of the cleverest nation in the world, why should you be frightened?"

Beatrice Webb

Arrogance functions on the oxygen of its own modesty. The self-confidence that is part of being young is sensibly flexible.

Jerome Weidman

Self-Deception

On no subject more so than their own writing are writers more likely to be self-deceiving or, in conversation, more boring.

Michael Korda

Self-Doubt

I've had this saying I've used forever as a self-motivator, a little sign in my office that says, "Trust the talent." What that means to me is, when you're at your darkest moments and you think you're writing the worst thing that's ever been written, and it's going to be a failure, you just want to give up and go to Madrid, the best thing you can do is simply give yourself over to your instincts.

Robert Crais

I experience a lot of doubts when I am working; I never feel confident.

The writer who loses his self-doubt, who gives way as he grows old to a sudden euphoria, to prolixity, should stop writing immediately: the time has come for him to lay aside his pen.

Colette

Some say you just need to believe in yourself. Well, you don't. You just need to get it done. Really, that's all it takes. Just get it done. Trust me on this. If you find yourself doubting, just put it out of your mind and concentrate on getting the job done, however long it takes. Once it's done, the belief will follow.

Gerald M. Kilby

”

I thought kids would like ["A Series of Unfortunate Events"] but I thought they'd never get in the hands of kids. I thought teachers would be revolted and librarians would be offended and all the guardians of children's culture would be horrified. I didn't think these books would sell any. I thought these books would be miserable failures.

Lemony Snicket

About two hundred pages in, I decide the book's no good, and it was a mistake ever to begin it. And I think there is no way to fix it, and I am generally miserable...If I tell my friends about these concerns, they just say, "Oh, I'm sure you'll work it out."

Michael Crichton

You never really know about your own ego. I suppose I've got a fairly heavily developed one. But still, when I write a book and send it to my publisher, I worry and fuss terribly till I hear from him that he likes it and he's going to publish it. I always have the feeling he's going to finally come around saying, "You know, it just won't do. We can't have it."

Robertson Davies

Above all, be the heroine of your life, not the victim.

Nora Ephron

Years later I was still telling myself that I wasn't really a writer, but a trickster – and a very lucky trickster at that. I had written a first novel and it had achieved phenomenal success. I had stumbled upon the secret path and uncovered the rules and had been rewarded with much praise. Unfortunately, all of this was proving to be of very little use to me in the writing of the next novel. How could I have forgotten everything so quickly?

Judith Guest, about Ordinary People

I could weep when I realize how much time I waste, my anxiety, my useless shadow-boxing with the imaginary censure and rejection by others.

Alfred Kazin

The young man or woman who aspires [to be an author] will fail unless he or she has what I've come to think of as divine arrogance, an I-can-do-it conviction; that despite all the negatives, it can be done. ... I mean that assurance I've had even when a manuscript was not going well and doubt assailed me (and with the amount of work I've done I've had those doubts more than most), but as I've risen from bed and gone back to the typewriter I've taken comfort in the thought "Well, there's nobody on this block better qualified to lick this problem than me." I'm not sure I believe it, but I'm willing to act on that faith in myself.

James A. Michener

I was absorbed when I read you had "the sense of having lived one's life so narrowly – with eyes and senses turned inward. An actual sense of the breadth of life does not exist in me. I am narrowly concerned with me. ... All I will ever express will be the little I have gleaned of life for my own purposes." But isn't that what every fine artist-writer ever expressed? If your expression is now more an impressionist one that doesn't make it any less important, or profound... . Yes, you did live "with eyes and senses turned inward" but you had to. Socrates said "Know thyself." And now you do know yourself better than you did, and your work is getting richer and deeper, and it has such an exciting, emotional quality.

Ursula Nordstrom, publisher of juvenile books at Harper & Row, to Maurice Sendak

Again facing hopeless years of good work never properly presented so that the best years seem a riotous waste.

Dawn Powell. A week later, she wrote, "Did a great deal of work on a novel with a feeling of confidence and pleasure in it that I hope sustains itself"

It's rather discouraging to go on writing with so little hope of publication but I try not to think about that. By the way, the letter I wrote to *The Author* about not getting published was never published, which seems to be the final accolade of failure.

Barbara Pym, letter to Philip Larkin

There was a time when I shrugged off my writing in embarrassment.

Carol Shields, Pulitzer Prize winner

Everything isn't riding on one book. It's one book in a long career.

Emma Smith-Stevens

I am profoundly uncertain about how to write. I know what I love or what I like, because it's a direct, passionate response. But when I write I'm very uncertain whether it's good enough. That is, of course, the writer's agony.

Susan Sontag

Maybe what's behind the inequity isn't just a lack of opportunity, but a lack of confidence, an inability among women, or just me, to step up and say *my work matters*, and to really, truly believe it. Maybe I'm not the only one struggling. What did I miss, spending 15 years in a defensive crouch? What is the world missing, when so many of us are reluctant to submit our work, to try for the big job?

Jennifer Weiner

(Because no man has ever admitted to a lack of self-confidence, like P.G. Wodehouse, below.)

I sometimes wonder if I really am a writer. When I look at the sixty-odd books in the shelf with my name on them, and reflect that ten million of them have been sold, it amazes me that I can have done it. I don't know anything and I seem incapable of learning … I feel I've been fooling the public for fifty years.

P.G. Wodehouse

Self-Image

I would recommend the cultivation of extreme indifference to both praise and blame because praise will lead you to vanity, and blame will lead you to self-pity, and both are bad for writers.

John Berryman

The version of ourselves we present to the world bears no resemblance to the truth. If we knew the truth about each other, we could take no one seriously. There isn't one of us could afford to get caught. That's all life is. Trying not to be found out.

William Donaldson

It seemed to me in this pitiful day and a half in New York, after all the silent weeks of misery here, that I had learned nothing after all, acquired nothing that would help me back to the needed serenity; that I was as full of anguish about myself, and, oh, let me say it even here, hatred of others … who are "better," more efficient, who do not flatter and love me unceasingly. I am poisoned by it; it takes me violent efforts and ruthless self-urgings to lift myself out of that pit.

Alfred Kazin

I recommend keeping an Awesome Stuff email folder. Any fun news you get, whether it be your book making a great list, a heartfelt email or review from a reader who loved your book, or an invitation to that cool literary festival you've always

”

I knew 99 percent of them wouldn't watch, but my face and name would get in front of them, and it would plant the subliminal message "He works a lot, this guy!" … The whole idea is to put yourself in a position to be recognized for your work so opportunities increase. False humility or even laziness could prevent that.

Bryan Cranston, the Breaking Bad star, who mailed postcards announcing his appearances on shows like Matlock and Murder, She Wrote to casting directors

”

The majority of self-published books are unreadable crap ... People with no discernible writing talent, or even basic writing skills, are rushing to get their atrocious, unpublishable garbage onto the Kindle as fast as they can. The slush pile has gone digital and has unleashed a tsunami of swill onto Amazon and Smashwords.

Lee Goldberg

wanted to attend, put into that Awesome Stuff folder to read whenever you're feeling sad.

Angie Kim

Self-Promotion

The kinds of writers I care about are just temperamentally not very good at [publicity]. Hard to see Kafka tweeting, hard to see Charlotte Brontë self-promoting. If we don't maintain other avenues for establishing a literary reputation and finding some kind of readership — things like traditional publishing and reviewing, where the writer could just be a writer and not have to wear the flak hat, the salesman hat, the editor hat, the publisher hat — if we don't maintain those, then we hand over the literary world to the personality types who are, I would say, less suited for the kind of work I care about.

Jonathan Franzen

The real key to success in the self-publishing field seems to be drive and dedication. If you're the shy, mousy sort you're probably safer sticking with commercial publishing.

Stephen Goldin

The man who does not advertise is a dead one, whether he knows it or not. Life is too short for you to hide yourself away mantled in your own modesty.

Elbert Hubbard

The grossest violation of literary comity and courtesy that ever passed under our notice.

The Christian Examiner *newspaper of Boston, about Walt Whitman reprinting a private letter of praise from Henry Wadsworth Longfellow in the second edition of* Leaves of Grass

Some fascinating photos might be also taken of me, a burly but agile man, stalking a rarity or sweeping it into my net from a flowerhead.

Vladimir Nabokov, butterfly collector, to Life *magazine*

Great success is not possible without a certain degree of shamelessness, and even of out-and-out charlatanism.

Stendhal

It seems pointless to be quoted if one isn't going to be quotable. … It's better to be quotable than to be honest.

Tom Stoppard

In America the race goes to the loud, the solemn, the hustler. If you think you're a great writer, you must say that you are.

Gore Vidal

Self-Publishing

When I realized that I can invest in my own marketing and do exactly what I think needs to be done — well, then it just feels like: *What is the benefit of having a publisher?*

Anna Todd

In old days books were written by men of letters and read by the public. Nowadays books are written by the public and read by nobody.

Oscar Wilde

Self-Revelation

Memo to writers and others: Never make a joke against yourself that some little bastard can turn into a piece of shit and send your way.

Kingsley Amis, about a joke he made at an award ceremony (see Booker Award*)*

Each artist has a tendency to

reproduce or imitate his own likeness. ... And so you will see that if a painter is choleric he will show anger in his works; if phlegmatic, mildness; if devout, religion; if lustful, sensuality.

Vicente Carducho, Spanish painter (1576-1638)

When I work, I'm just translating the world around me in what seems to be straightforward terms. For my readers, this is sometimes a vision that's not familiar. But I'm not trying to manipulate reality. This is just what I see and hear.

Don DeLillo

I wrote of neuroses and fear and I think all my books laid end to end would be one long documentation of anxiety. If I am cured and well and oh glorious alive then my books should be different. Who wants to write about anxiety from a place of safety? Although I suppose I would never be entirely safe since I cannot completely reconstruct my mind. But what conflict is there to write about then?

Shirley Jackson

A person who publishes a book willfully appears before the public with his pants down.

Edna St. Vincent Millay

A work of art is something produced by a person, but is not that person — it is of her, but is not her. It's a reach, really — the artist is trying to inhabit, temporarily, a more compact, distilled, efficient, wittier, more true-seeing, precise version of herself — one that she can't replicate in so-called "real" life, no matter how hard she tries. That's why she writes: to try and briefly be more than she truly is.

George Saunders

Meditating upon the world and what is most familiar is the pre-occupation of writers. Sometimes that includes re-creating our nearest and dearest, and our secrets. ... The best writers are the most fanatical; so the truest portrait of a writer can never be a study in virtue.

Paul Theroux

I'm willing to show good taste, if I can, in somebody else's living room, but our reading life is too short for a writer to be in any way polite. Since his words enter into another's brain in silence and intimacy, he should be as honest and explicit as we are with ourselves.

John Updike

When you yourself put words on paper, remember that the most damning revelation you can make about yourself is that you do not know what is interesting and what is not. Don't you yourself like or dislike writers mainly for what they chose to show you or make you think about? Did you ever admire an empty-headed writer for his or her mastery of style? No. So your own winning literary style must begin with interesting ideas in your own head.

Kurt Vonnegut

The emotions of fiction are autobiographical, but the facts never are.

Richard Yates

Sentences

The hardest thing about writing, in a sense, is not writing. I mean, the sentence is not intended to show you off, you know. It is not supposed to be "Look at me!" "Look, no hands!" It's supposed to be a pipeline between the reader and you. One condition of the sentence is to write so well that no one

"

In "Augie March," I wanted to invent a new sort of American sentence. Something like a fusion of colloquialism and elegance ... I felt that American writing had enslaved itself without sufficient reason to English models.

Saul Bellow

A physical setting should never be built up too elaborately ... For example, nothing is worse than reading a detailed description of a room. Something of the size and style and color and perhaps three telling details are all that is necessary.

Mary Stewart

”

Be honest because human beings are very self-deluding creatures. We lie to ourselves most of the time. We lie to ourselves a lot in the bedroom. We want something out of sex other than ecstasy at times and the only way to write about sex is to write about it as a human interaction where often you are lying to yourself or the other person is lying to himself.

Erica Jong

notices that you're writing.

James Baldwin

You expect far too much of a first sentence. Think of it as analogous to a good country breakfast: what we want is something simple, but nourishing to the imagination. Hold the philosophy, hold the adjectives, just give us a plain subject and verb and perhaps a wholesome, nonfattening adverb or two.

Larry McMurtry

The sentence is my primary element, my tool, goal, bliss. Each new sentence is a heart-in-the-mouth experiment.

Cynthia Ozick

I'm less interested in sentences now and more interested in stories. … I don't believe in showing off. Showing off can get in the way of a good story.

James Patterson, reflecting on his first novel, the Edgar-award winning The Thomas Berryman Number

Solving the problem of the book you're writing always remains hard work, and your progress is snail-like. Even if you write a book in two years, sometimes you get a page a day, sometimes you get no pages … every sentence raises a problem, and essentially what you're doing is connecting one sentence to the next. And you write a sentence and you have to figure out what comes next or what doesn't come next.

Philip Roth

The most attractive sentences are not perhaps the wisest, but the surest and the soundest.

Henry David Thoreau

Setting

Atmosphere is the result of presenting the physical details in such a way as to create emotional reaction.

Peggy Simson Curry

The writer must have a very active sense of place as such, and a conviction of its importance in human affairs. To write such a story artificially, without a mastering sense of the thing which it attempts to convey, would be futile and absurd.

John T. Frederick

To "be there" [in the imagination] is a tremendous help in [telling my story]. It enables me to pare down descriptive passages to the very minimum, because all I have to do is describe the few key features in any particular room or garden or landscape that strikes me the most, just as if I were really there.

G. Masterton

A crowded, bustling street creates torment, perhaps even terror … a moonlit night in balmy weather creates a love-filled heart … a tawdry, run-down rooming house creates suspicion, even paranoia. The point is the physical setting becomes the picture frame within which the emotional reaction blooms.

William Noble

Sex

All a writer has to do to get a woman is to say he's a writer. It's an aphrodisiac.

Saul Bellow

Virginia Woolf said writers must be androgynous. I'll go a step further. You must be bisexual. If you can't carry out the act … That's up to you; you'd better get as close as you can imaginatively. You must create men who love women and women who love men or your books will be lopsided. In the beginning of everyone's work the dice are always loaded toward one's own sex or sex preference. Learning to unload those dice, to throw the bones honestly, is what maturity as an individual and as a writer is all about.

Rita Mae Brown

Pornography is a cheat. It is an attempt to provide sexual by secondhand means. Now sex is a thing which has to be experienced firsthand, if you are really going to understand it, and pornography is rather like trying to find out about a Beethoven symphony by having somebody tell you about it and perhaps hum a few bars. It's not the same thing. Sex is primarily a question of relationships. Pornography is a do-it-yourself kit.

Robertson Davies

If readers are in search of sexual problems, or suchlike nastiness, they will not find them in my writings. I have no desire to wallow in filth.

Nat Gould

Literary realism has this sort of indie-film attitude toward sex. Violence is violent, but sex isn't sexy. It's compulsive, nobody's happy, and they enjoy the cigarette way more than the sex.

Marlon James

You don't want to repeat [sex scenes] yourself for one. You don't want to fall into the clichés for another. And you don't want to be licentious really. You want to be descriptive, if you can be. And you're not setting out to arouse anybody. A friend of mine read the book [*The Humbling*] and told me that he was tremendously aroused by those scenes so I don't want to tell you what I think about him, but I didn't intend for that to be said.

Philip Roth

Sex Scenes

Most of the writers who do [sex scenes] best don't "do" it at all, but simply allow it to happen in a way that can easily be supplied by any reader who happens to have done it.

Diana Athill

She had only a thin Silk Night-Gown on, which flying open as he caught her in his Arms, he found her panting Heart beat Measures of Consent, her heaving Breast swell to be pressd by his, and every Pulse confess a Wish to yield; her Spirits all dissolvd sunk in a Lethargy of Love; her snowy Arms unknowning graspd his Neck .... In fine, there was but a Moment betwixt her and Ruin.

Eliza Haywood, from Love in Excess *(1724)*

Softcore porn is the literary equivalent of those feathery wimp-whips and talcum'd handcuffs you see in the windows of sex toy shops. If you're going to torture your lover, at least break the skin, I say. ... [A]s far as writing goes, the best sex is the most implicit.

Howard Jacobson

As for the F word, Anthony Burgess once criticized the notion that to use it in matter-of-fact prose is to hark back to "a golden age of Anglo-Saxon candour"; the word was taboo from the start, because it stands for brutal or at best impersonal sex. "A man can fuck a whore but, unless his wife is a whore, he cannot fuck his wife ... There is no love in it." A writer like Franzen, who describes two lovers as "fucking," trivializes their

Not only were her thighs perfect columns, but all that lay between them was impressively beautiful, too, with an aesthetic value that I had never found there before. The mount was of a classical femininity: round and smooth and plump; the fleece, if not quite golden, was blond and curly and soft, and the portals were a deep tender rose.

Edmund Wilson, from Memoirs of Hecate County *(1942), banned by the New York Supreme Court. His then-friend Vladimir Nabokov told him, "The reader ... derives no kick from the hero's love-making. I should have as soon tried to open a sardine can with my penis."*

”

The person who writes books must always be enveloped by a separation from others. It is the solitude of the author, of writing.

Marguerite Duras

I never found the companion that was so companionable as solitude.

Henry David Thoreau

relationship accordingly.

B.R. Myers

Could a king, a prince, a duke — nay, even one of those ubiquitous invisibles who, we are led to believe, accompanies us when thinking, speaking, or acting — could even this sinless atom refrain from tainting its spotless gear with the wish of a human heart, as those grey eyes looked in bashful tenderness into the glittering jet revolvers that reflected their sparkling lustre from nave to circumference, casting a deepened brightness over the whole features of an innocent girl, and expressing, in invisible silence, the thoughts, nay, even the wish, of a fleshy triangle whose base had been bitten by order of the Bodiless Thinker.

Amanda McKittrick Ros,
from Irene Iddesleigh *(1897)*

Short Stories

[Writing short fiction] was good for me, because I realized you could actually put a lot of material in 30 pages. And if you're going to write 700 pages, they better be full. You better have an idea which is going to justify that length, justify the audience reading the thing for that long.

Clive Barker

A collection of stories is not a novel — it's different expressions of the same mind within a circumscribed period of time.

Deborah Eisenberg

Stories are best written in either one jump or three, according to the length. The three-jump story should be done in three successive days, then a day or so for revise and off she goes.

F. Scott Fitzgerald

I'll give you the whole secret of short-story writing. Here it is. Rule 1: Write stories that please yourself. There is no Rule 2.

O. Henry

You use almost everything from your life. It's your material. Every story starts with some piece of fact and in anything I've ever written you'll be able to find that fact even if it's just a tiny sliver of a thing.

Garrison Keillor

A short story is a different thing altogether–a short story is like a quick kiss in the dark from a stranger. That is not, of course, the same thing as an affair or a marriage, but kisses can be sweet, and their very brevity forms their own attraction.

Stephen King

A short story as a way of indicating the complexity of life in a few pages, producing the surprise and effect of a profound knowledge in a short time.

Bernard Malamud

A skillful literary artist has constructed a tale. If wise, he has not fashioned his thoughts to accommodate his incidents; but having conceived, with deliberate care, a certain unique or single effect to be wrought out, he then invents such incidents — he then combines such events as may best aid him in establishing this preconceived effect. If his very initial sentence tend not to the outbringing of this effect, then he has failed in his first step. In the whole composition there should be no word written, of which the tendency, direct or indirect, is not to the one pre-established design. And by such means, with such care and skill, a picture is at length painted which leaves in the mind of him who contemplates it with a kindred art, a sense of the fullest satisfaction.

Edgar Allan Poe, misquoted as "A short story must have a single mood and every sentence must build towards it."

Short stories can be rather stark and bare unless you put in the right detail. ... Details make stories human, and the more human a story can be the better.

V.S. Pritchett

You have never seen a short story in your life. The events of life have never fallen into the form of the short story or the form of a poem, or into any other form. Your own consciousness is the only form you need.

William Saroyan

Simile

A simile must be as precise as a slide rule and as natural as the smell of dill.

Isaac Babel

Simplicity

Reality is fairly simple. My critics say my characters are cardboard, but the people I know and write about tell me I get it all right. The mark of a superior person is to take complexity and find the simplicity in it.

Tom Clancy

Slang

All slang is metaphor and all metaphor is poetry.

G.K. Chesterton

Sleep

It is a common experience that a problem difficult at night is resolved in the morning after the committee of sleep has worked on it.

John Steinbeck

Solitude

[When a man must] abstain from nearly everything that his neighbours innocently and pleasurably use, and from the rubs and trials of human society itself into the bargain, we recognise that valetudinarian healthfulness which is more delicate than sickness itself.

Robert Louis Stevenson

I think it would be hard for me on a South Sea island or in the Maine woods. I like company and entertainment, people around. The actual process of writing, though, demands complete, noiseless privacy, without even music; a baby howling two blocks away will drive me nuts.

William Styron

South, The

[Virginia society was] living perpetually in the shadow of the Civil War, a society curiously lacking in the sense of time, but oppressively fanatical when dealing with contemporary problems; obsessed by principle, but living on pluck; dedicated to "culture" and ... suspicious of ideas other than its own.

Alfred Kazin

When I'm asked why Southern writers particularly have a penchant for writing about freaks, I say it's because we're still able to recognize one.

Flannery O'Connor

Why has the South produced so

”

I ran his life like a tidy ship — I took care of the kids, the bookkeeping and bill paying, and got the insurance we needed. I shopped and cooked and saw that he always had clean clothes in his closet and a car full of gas.

Norris Church Mailer, Norman Mailer's wife

I think you must remember that a writer is a simpleminded person to begin with and go on that basis. He's not a great mind, he's not a great thinker, he's not a great philosopher, he's a storyteller.

Erskine Caldwell

Sometimes one can overanalyze, and I try not to do that. To a great degree, much of the structure has got to come naturally out of the writing. I think if you try to preordain, you're going to stifle yourself. You've got a general idea, but the rest has to come naturally out of the writing, the narrative, the character and the situation.

Robert Ludlum

many good writers? Because we got beat.

Walker Percy

Speaking

The true use of speech is not so much to express our wants as to conceal them.

Oliver Goldsmith

Speak when you're angry and you'll make the best speech you'll ever regret.

Groucho Marx

Most writers are not quick-witted when they talk. Novelists, in particular, drag themselves around in society like gut-shot bears.

Kurt Vonnegut

Spouses

The greatest service a wife can render her writer husband is not typing his manuscripts for him, but keeping people away from him. Of course, a husband might do the same, if his wife is the writer.

Patricia Highsmith

She says I'm not her favorite writer. But she always criticizes my work very seriously. She's my first reader, so when I finish writing I pass the manuscript to my wife, and she reads it, and she returns the draft with two hundred Post-its. I hate Post-its very much. She says, "You should rewrite these parts!" ... [I rewrite it] then I hand it back to her, and this time she gives it back with one hundred Post-its. Fewer Post-its – that's good.

Haruki Murakami

Elizabeth [Fowles] is at the centre of the books, as she was of John Fowles's life. There were no publishable novels before her coming. There were none after her going.

Eileen Warburton

Story

History tells how it was. A story – how it might have been.

Alfred Andersch

Every fine story must leave in the mind of the sensitive reader an intangible residuum of pleasure, a cadence, a quality of voice that is exclusively the writer's own, individual, unique.

Willa Cather

Yes – oh dear yes – the novel tells a story.

E.M. Forster

A story is made up of "incidents," just as a play is made up of scenes. An incident consists of a narrative of continuous action, without lapse of time – without, in other words, a gap in the sequence of events. … Most typical short stories are composed of from five to ten incidents (or scenes), which are more or less closely connected in time and place.

John T. Frederick

The story is one of the basic tools invented by the mind ... for the purpose of gaining understanding. There have been great societies that did not use the wheel, but there have been no societies that did not tell stories.

Ursula K. Le Guin

An honest tale speeds best being plainly told.

William Shakespeare

Structure

(See **Plot, Outline**)

I see a story or an article or a book as a pattern and not just as a succession of words. I know exactly how to fit each item in the piece into the pattern, so that it is never necessary for me to work from an outline. Even the most complicated plot, or the most intricate exposition, comes out properly, with everything in the right order.

Isaac Asimov

For a book to really work, form and function must go hand in hand, just like with buildings, as any decent architect will tell you.

Tracy Chevalier

It's all *about*, it's about — it's in the air — it, so to speak, follows me and dogs me.

Henry James, when asked how he formed the design of his new book

All people write what they know, for God's sake. It's the air you breathe. The challenge is finding the structure that shows your stuff off to its best effect.

Betsy Lerner

The road trip at the end of the second act works. Look at *The Great Gatsby*. Almost all of the main characters arbitrarily jump in cars and drive into Manhattan where the emotional showdown occurs. … It's based on Heidegger, sort of, and his idea that escaping from your Dasein or destiny is pointless. The larger world reminds characters of their smallness and mortality, and it prompts them to take disastrous action.

Chuck Palahniuk

What you're trying to do is hook one sentence to the sentence before and the next one to that sentence. And as you do, you're building a house, you know. ... The architect and the contractor, they know what the house is going to look like when it's done — and that's the big difference. I don't have any idea what it will look like when it's done. I don't have any idea whether it will even be done, because you don't know what you're doing when you're at work.

Philip Roth

There are some books that refuse to be written. They stand their ground year after year and will not be persuaded. It isn't because the book is not there and worth being written — it is only because the right form for the story does not present itself. There is only one right form for a story, and if you fail to find that form the story will not tell itself. You may try a dozen wrong forms but in each case you will not get very far before you discover that you have not found the right one — and that the story will always stop and decline to go any further.

Mark Twain

Style

(See **Voice**)

I haven't consciously tried to develop it [style]. The only thing I've consciously tried to do was put myself in a position to hear the people I wanted to hear talk.

Nelson Algren

Style is everything and nothing. It is not that, as is commonly supposed, you get your content and soup it up with style; style is absolutely embedded in the way you perceive.

Martin Amis

”

I have no leisure to think of style or of polish, or to select the best language, the best English — no time to shine as an authoress. I must just think aloud, so as not to keep the public waiting.

Isabel Burton

[Style] is like anal sex. If that's what I want to do to you and you're not into it, then go away, because that's what will keep happening.

A.L. Kennedy

”

Let us guess that whenever we read a sentence & like it, we unconsciously store it away in our model-chamber; & it goes, with the myriad of its fellows, to the building, brick by brick, of the eventual edifice which we call our style.

Mark Twain

I've been called a stylist until I really could tear my hair out. And I simply don't believe in style. The style is you. ... You do not create a style. You work and develop yourself; your style is an emanation from your own being.

Katherine Anne Porter

I don't think that style is consciously arrived at any more than one arrives at the color of one's own eyes. After all, your style *is* you. At the end the personality of a writer has so much to do with the work.

Truman Capote

If the truth were self-evident, eloquence would be unnecessary.

Cicero

An author arrives at a good style when his language performs what is required of it without shyness.

Cyril Connolly

In practice certain obscurities of style, though they may repel many readers, can and do serve the reputation of several authors very well. They make certain that no one is going to see right away how banal the material is, or how childish or second-rate the thinking. And this is not the end. Hardly anyone who has put himself to the long trouble of guessing meanings so hard to get at is going to admit that the findings weren't worth the work — or bluntly, he has let himself be made a fool of. He will in nine cases out of ten save face by being next to the author himself in claiming this work is of Profound Significance.

James Gould Cozzens

What is gained by urging aspiring writers to be simple and direct, choosing the concrete word in preference to the abstract, and avoiding complexities of structure? … What about the kinds of writing to which a simple style is unsuited? What if a simple style does not agree with the author's personality? Does anybody seriously wish that Sir Thomas Browne had written like Bunyan? The perusal of many of these guides to writing persuades me that their authors do not really care about simplicity for its own sake, but despair of teaching their readers anything complex. There are better styles; their secret is that a man must teach them to himself.

Robertson Davies

When I was a student at Pratt in the 1950s, studying illustration, I remember a fellow student asking one of our instructors, "When do we learn about style?"

"We won't learn about style," he replied. "Style happens naturally. If you keep on working, eventually the way you can and want to express yourself will surface. Meanwhile, do the assignments, listen to the critiques, don't miss your drawing classes, painting classes, design classes and by all means look at everything. Go to the galleries and the museums. Your own style will surface."

Tomie dePaola, children's book writer and illustrator

You should really stay true to your own style. When I first started writing, everybody said to me, "Your style just isn't right because you don't use the really flowery language that romances have." My romances — compared to what's out there — are very strange, very odd, very different. And I think that's one of the reasons they're selling.

Jude Deveraux

All the fun is in how you say a thing.

Robert Frost

A book may be amusing with numerous errors, or it may be very dull without a single absurdity.

Oliver Goldsmith

No style is good that is not fit to be spoken or read aloud with effect.

William Hazlitt

If a man writes clearly enough any one can see if he fakes. If he mystifies to avoid a straight statement, which is very different from breaking so-called rules of syntax or grammar to make an effect which can be obtained in no other way, the writer takes a longer time to be known as a fake and other writers who are afflicted by the same necessity will praise him in their own defense. True mysticism should not be confused with incompetence in writing which seeks to mystify where there is no mystery but is really only the necessity to fake to cover lack of knowledge or the inability to state clearly.

Ernest Hemingway

Don't just plan to write — write. It is only by writing, not dreaming about it, that we develop our own style.

P.D. James

What is easy is seldom excellent.

Samuel Johnson

A good stylist should have a narcissistic enjoyment as he works. He must be able to objectivize his work to such an extent that he catches himself feeling envious ... In short, he must display the highest degree of objectivity which the world calls vanity.

Karl Kraus

If you can tell stories, create characters, devise incidents, and have sincerity and passion, it doesn't matter a damn how you write.

W. Somerset Maugham

So many writers write small, shallow things in a complicated, difficult style. I think what I want to do is write serious, complicated, difficult things in a very easy style that is fluid and comfortable to read. In order to write those difficult things, you have to be willing to go down, deeper and deeper. So, in the forty years that I've been writing, I have worked out a technique for that. It's like a physical technique — not an intellectual technique.

Haruki Murakami

To improve one's style means to improve one's thoughts.

Friedrich Nietzsche

If you've nothing to say, say it any way you like. Stylistic innovations, contorted story lines or none, exotic or genderless pronouns, internal inconsistencies, the recipe for preparing your lover as a cannibal banquet: feel free. If what you have to say is important and/or difficult to follow, use the simplest language possible. If the reader doesn't get it then, let it not be your fault.

Larry Niven

The true writer has nothing to say, just a way of saying it.

Alain Robbe-Grillet

I'm very concerned with the rhythm of language. "The sun came up" is an inadequate sentence. Even though it conveys all the necessary information, rhythmically it's lacking. The sun came up. But, if you say, as Laurie Anderson said, "The sun came up like a big bald head," not only have you, perhaps, entertained the fancy of the reader, but you have made a more complete sentence. The sound of a sentence.

Tom Robbins

Proper words in proper places,

”

The most commercial success, it seems to me, goes to people who do the same thing every time; readers know what to expect from such a writer, and are never disappointed. But, you know, screw that. I'm spoiled, and insist on writing what I want to write. Had it been otherwise, I might have made more money over the years. But I doubt I'd have written as many books, or kept at it as long.

Lawrence Block

There are two types of manga artist who succeed in this world ... One is the type of person who draws what they want to draw. To put it in rather negative terms they're the ones who rely on natural instinct ... or in positive terms, they're the "genius" types. And the other is the type of manga artist like you, Takagi, who creates a hit through calculation. And the one who has the potential of creating a smash hit is by far the non-calculating person.

Akira Hattori, **Bakuman**

make the true definition of a style.

Jonathan Swift

Style is what's there when you look at someone's writing and you know that they wrote it and nobody else did.

Fay Weldon

If you're writing for a magazine or a newspaper, then you're a guest. It's as if you're a guest violinist in some great conductor's orchestra. You play to his rhythm, to his audience. You're invited in and he edits you and tells you what he wants. On the other hand, when you're writing a book, the only reason you're writing it is to say it your own way, in your own words, and tell the story the way you see it.

Theodore H. White

I've always felt that my "style" — the careful projection onto paper of who I think I am — was my only marketable asset, the only possession that might set me apart from other writers. Therefore I've never wanted anyone to fiddle with it. ... Editors have told me that I'm the only writer they know who cares what happens to his piece after he gets paid for it. Most writers won't argue with an editor because they don't want to annoy him; they're so grateful to be published that they agree to having their style ... violated in public. But to defend what you've written is a sign that you are alive.

William Zinsser

Suburbs, Revolutionary Road

To read *Revolutionary Road* is to have forced upon us a fresh sense of our critical modern shortcomings: failures of work, education, community, family, marriage ... and plain nerve.

Jeremy Larner, New Republic *reviewer*

Eschewing the pitfalls of obvious caricature or patent moralizing, Mr. Yates chooses the more difficult path of allowing his characters to reveal themselves — which they do with an intensity that excites the reader's compassion as well as his interest.

Martin Levin,
The New York Times *reviewer*

The Wheelers are young, pathetic, trapped, half educated, and without humor — meaningless characters leading meaningless lives. Mr. Yates's attempt to lend drama to their predicament, through an unconvincing introduction of madness and violence in the story, serves only to emphasize the flimsy nature of his work.

The New Yorker, *unsigned review*

No fair-minded reader could finish *Revolutionary Road* without admiration for Mr. Yates's impressive skill; but whether the mentally ill Wheelers deserve the five years of labor Mr. Yates has lavished upon them is another question.

Orville Prescott,
The New York Times *reviewer*

The novel is really about the inadequacy of human beings to their own aspirations, and its target is not America but existence.

F.J. Warnke, Yale Review *reviewer*

The Wheelers may have thought the suburbs were to blame for all their problems, but I meant it to be implicit in the text that it was their delusion, their problem, not mine. ... I meant it more as an indictment of American life in the nineteen-fifties.

Richard Yates

No matter where you go, there you are.

Buckaroo Banzai
(My personal take on the novel)

Success at Writing

(See **Bestsellers**)

Success is outliving your failures.

Erma Bombeck

I take the word successful to mean successful only in terms of the story itself: does it have its own life, does it move, does it have feelings, is it an entirety and a whole? If one can say yes to all these questions, the story is successful. Whether it sells or not is unimportant.

Ray Bradbury

There are so many different kinds of writing and so many ways to work that the only rule is this: Do what works. Almost everything has been tried and found to succeed for somebody. The methods, even the ideas, of successful writers contradict each other in a most heartening way, and the only element I find common to all successful writers is persistence — an overwhelming determination to succeed.

Sophy Burnham

You don't start out writing good stuff. You start out writing crap and thinking it's good stuff, and then gradually you get better at it. That's why I say one of the most valuable traits is persistence.

Octavia E. Butler

I like to say there are three things that are required for success as a writer: talent, luck, discipline. … [Discipline] is the one that you have to focus on controlling, and you just have to hope and trust in the other two.

Michael Chabon

Success is never final and failure is never fatal.

Winston Churchill

What I tell kids when I make commencement speeches at colleges is, "The only person who can kill your dream is yourself." Those aren't just words. They're true. Some people who want to act brilliant would say they're too simple, but the truth is usually simple. You keep hold of your dream, you work hard, and you've always got a chance of getting what you wanted. I believe that. I had to believe that. And it worked for me.

Tom Clancy

There is no secret to success except hard work and getting something indefinable which we call "the breaks." In order for a writer to succeed, I suggest three things — read and write — and wait.

Countee Cullen

For blurb requests, I only give them if you've been a student of mine in the past. For correspondence, I always write back if it's a kid. … I changed my personal email about seven months in [to make it harder to reach him].

Anthony Doerr, on the changes he's had to make with success

The race is not to the swift nor the battle to the strong ... but time and chance happen to them all.

Ecclesiastes

Many of life's failures are experienced by people who did not realize how close they were to success when they gave up.

Thomas Edison

Success is feminine and like a woman; if you cringe before her she

I say the goal is not to be good — it's to be great. The idea is to have the audience leave, and say, "You've got to see this." You have to work backwards from that result.

Steve Martin

Keep away from those who try to belittle your ambitions. Small people always do that, but the really great make you believe that you too can become great.

Mark Twain

”

Nice writing isn't enough. It isn't enough to have smooth and pretty language. You have to surprise the reader frequently, you can't just be nice all the time. Provoke the reader. Astonish the reader. Writing that has no surprises is as bland as oatmeal. Surprise the reader with the unexpected verb or adjective. Use one startling adjective per page.

Anne Bernays

will override you. So the way to treat her is to show her the back of your hand. Then maybe she will do the crawling.

William Faulkner

Premature success gives one an almost mystical conception of destiny as opposed to will power... . The man who arrives young believes that he exercises his will because his star is shining.

F. Scott Fitzgerald

Only two classes of books are of universal appeal. The very best and the very worst.

Ford Madox Ford

The best way to become a successful writer is to read good writing, remember it, and then forget where you remember it from.

Gene Fowler

Follow the accident, fear the fixed plan — that is the rule.

John Fowles

If you want to make money, I should say to the aspirant, you had much better undertake the merchandising of woolen underwear or the repairing of Fords. These vocations are easier to learn and less overcrowded, and the average returns are far higher. Also, I have an old-fashioned notion that you have a better chance of saving your soul.

John T. Frederick

Success in your own lifetime is the kiss of death for immortality.

Kinky Friedman

I'm a control freak, so I need to allow myself to take full advantage of an assistant once I hire one. It's a little overwhelming how much nonwriting work comes with writing success.

Roxane Gay, who has an assistant handling her Facebook page, four publicists at three publishers, and two agents who handle her speaking offers, including travel and hotels

I suspect I have spent just about exactly as much time actually writing as the average person my age has spent watching television, and that, as much as anything, may be the real secret here.

William Gibson

Success makes you ridiculous; you end up wearing nightgowns to dinner.

Natalie Goldberg

Always remember this, if you have a success, you have it for the wrong reasons. If you become popular it is always because of the worst aspects of your work. They always praise you for the worst aspects. It never fails.

Ernest Hemingway

As far as high achievements, that's for other people to decide. I try to keep myself amused. Every day I do that is a good day.

Stephen King

I saw mediocre writers who were brilliant at networking and superb writers who couldn't part with their pages. Some seemed blessed with the confidence of entitlement, others cursed with paralyzing insecurities. I saw their defenses and fears, their hopes and ambitions. Very soon I was able to recognize which writers would hunker down for the long haul, revising their texts over and over, and which felt that simply producing a manuscript should be enough to secure a publishing contract.

Betsy Lerner, editor

Publishing is like flying. You keep finding out that there's another class above you.

Laura Lippman

If you want to get rich from writing, write the sort of thing that's read by persons who move their lips when they're reading to themselves.

Don Marquis

A successful book cannot afford to be more than 10% new.

Marshall McLuhan

Truly reaching your audience and offering them something of value is perhaps as good a definition of successful writing as I've ever heard.

Dinty W. Moore

The man who has made a financial success of writing is in the worst danger of all, and it is hardly a secret that I am one of those who has made money. But I believe, and I suppose I have always believed, that the writer who loafs after he has made a financial success is confessing that the money was all he was after in the first place. That was never my idea. Much as I like owning a Rolls-Royce, for instance, I could do without it. What I could not do without is a typewriter, a supply of yellow second sheets, and the time to put them to good use.

John O'Hara

As is the case in all branches of art, success depends in a very large measure upon individual initiative and exertion, and cannot be achieved except by dint of hard work.

Anna Pavlova, dancer

The secret of popular writing is never to put more on a given page than the common reader can lap off it with no strain WHATSOEVER on his habitually slack attention.

Ezra Pound

As a successful author, the bad news is that having been successful financially previously does not make the books any easier to write. Once you have become a No. 1 bestseller then the pressure is for the next book to be a No. 1 bestseller. Or at least to sell more copies than the previous book.

Ian Rankin

My measure of success is money. I have no interest in artistic triumphs that are financial losers. I would like to have an artistic success that also made money, of course, but if I had to make a choice between the two, I would take the dough.

Damon Runyon

I haven't as good an opinion of my work as you hold of it, but I've always done what I could to secure and enlarge my good opinion of it. I've always said to myself, "Everybody reads it and that's something — it surely isn't pernicious, or the most acceptable people would get pretty tired of it." And when a critic said by implication that it wasn't high and fine, through the remark "High and fine literature is wine" I retorted (confidentially, to myself), "yes, high and fine literature is wine, and mine is only water; but everybody likes water."

Mark Twain

I think what's most disturbing about success is that it's very hazardous to your health, as well as to your daily routine. Not only are

”

As long as I live I shall never forget my sensations when I opened the first of the three letters and learned that I was to appear in print. I can still see the narrow hall, the letterbox out of which I fished the letters, and the flight of stairs up and down which I ran, senselessly and incessantly, in the attempt to give my excitement some muscular outlet.

Edith Wharton

”

Every human being has hundreds of separate people living under his skin. The talent of a writer is his ability to give them their separate names, identities, personalities and have them relate to other characters living with him.

Mel Brooks

What is talent? Talent is nothing more than a pursued interest. In other words, things that you're interested in, you'll spend a lot more time working at, than something you're not interested in. So that's all talent is.

Bob Ross, painter

there intrusions on your time, but there is a kind of corrosion of your own humility and sense of necessary workmanship. You get the idea that anything you do is in some way marvelous.

John Updike

I think I succeeded as a writer because I did not come out of an English department. I used to write in the chemistry department. And I wrote some good stuff. If I had been in the English department, the prof would have looked at my short stories, congratulated me on my talent, and then showed me how Joyce or Hemingway handled the same elements of the short story. The prof would have placed me in competition with the greatest writers of all time, and that would have ended my writing career.

Kurt Vonnegut

I think the success of every novel depends largely on one or two high spots. The thing to do is to say to yourself "which are my big scenes?" And then get every drop of juice out of them.

P.G. Wodehouse

Suffering

Writer are very melodramatic about themselves, frequently, and they like to pretend that they just go down into the depths of hell when they're doing their work and that they suffer in order that you may buy their book and be refreshed and delighted. Baloney. Some of them, I think, suffer, but frequently they suffer for reasons other than because they're writers. It's because they're in trouble of some kind. They're boozers or something of the sort.

Robertson Davies

There are moments and hours when I have nothing in my heart but rage and despair, a blind man's rage and despair.

James Joyce

Not to take one's own suffering seriously, to make light of it or even laugh at it, is considered good manners in our culture. This attitude is even called a virtue, and many people are proud of their lack of sensitivity toward their own fate and, above all, their own childhood.

Alice Miller

I suppose it's a terrible thing for an author to say, but an author likes characters who are screwed up: Angua is screwed up, Granny Weatherwax is screwed up. They are not at ease with themselves, and that makes them fun for the author.

Terry Pratchett

Suffering and I have had a basically glancing, flirtatious acquaintanceship.

John Updike

Suicide

Death is the greatest evil, because it cuts off hope.

William Hazlitt

I spend a hell of a lot of time killing animals and fish, so I won't kill myself.

Ernest Hemingway

John Berryman said that for a writer any ordeal that doesn't kill him is terrific. The fact that his ordeal did finally kill him doesn't make what he was saying wrong.

Philip Roth

Surprise

Here's a compositional secret. It's so

obvious and simple, you'll say to yourself, "This man is bullshitting me." I am not. This is one of the most fundamental things in all theatrical movie composition and yet magicians know nothing of it. Ready? Surprise me. That's it. Place 2 and 2 right in front of my nose, but make me think I'm seeing 5. Then reveal the truth, 4!, and surprise me. Now, don't underestimate me, like the rest of the magicians of the world. Don't fool yourself into thinking that I've never seen a set of linking rings before and I'll be oh-so-stunned because you can "link" them. Bullshit. Here's how surprise works. While holding my attention, you withhold basic plot information. Feed it to me little by little. Make me try and figure out what's going on. Tease me in one direction. Throw in a false ending. Then turn it around and flip me over. I do the old Needle trick. I get a guy up on stage, who examines the needles. I swallow them. He searches my mouth. They're gone. I dismiss him and he leaves the stage. The audience thinks the trick is over. Then I take out the thread. "Ha ha! Floss!" they exclaim. I eat the floss. Then the wise ones start saying, "Not floss, thread. Thread. Needles. Needles and thread. Oh my god he's going to thread the need..." And by that time they're out and sparkling in the sunshine.

Teller, of Penn and Teller

Talent

Talent is like a faucet; while it is open, one must write. Inspiration is a farce that poets have invented to give themselves importance.

Jean Anouilh

Any writer, I suppose, feels that the world into which he was born is nothing less than a conspiracy against the cultivation of his talent — which attitude certainly has a great deal to support it. On the other hand, it is only because the world looks on his talent with such a frightening indifference that the artist is compelled to make his talent important.

James Baldwin

When God hands you a gift, he also hands you a whip.

Truman Capote

The one talent that's indispensable to a writer is persistence. You must write the book, else there is no book. It will not finish itself. Do not try to commit art. Just tell the damn story. If it is entertaining, people will read it, and the objective of writing is to be read.

Tom Clancy

Talent alone cannot make a writer. There must be a man behind the book.

Ralph Waldo Emerson

Everyone has talent. What is rare is the courage to follow the talent to the dark place where it leads.

Erica Jong

I see the notion of talent as quite irrelevant. I see instead perseverance, application, industry, assiduity, will, will, will, desire, desire, desire.

Gordon Lish

Of course you want to be admired. Any poet wants to be admired — to be a great poet. But who is a great poet? Maybe a handful in the world's history. So that's irrelevant. What's really going to come out of

”

If anybody has vision in life, you can do it. You know, I'm actually very, very skilled at drawing and painting. When I was in art school I would always win awards, and win scholarships. But if you have vision in life, you can do anything, using your fingers, using your hands as tools. It's having the vision. So, you know, I don't believe that people are just born with some form of, of talent, that some abstract thing. It's about being able to have vision. And if you have vision, you can exercise [it].

Jeff Koons, artist

When you're stuck, and sure you've written absolute garbage, force yourself to finish and THEN decide to fix or scrap it — or you will never know if you can.

Jodi Picoult

Always carry a notebook. And I mean always. The short-term memory only retains information for three minutes; unless it is committed to paper you can lose an idea for ever.

Will Self

your work is something else. If you have succeeded at all you have become part — however small a part — of the consciousness of your time. Which is enough. No?

Archibald MacLeish

I think you're born with a certain sensitivity and awareness and perception, and I think you have to develop the manual skill. With either one alone, you'll be absolutely nowhere. I've known people with tremendous technical ability that haven't gone very far. I've also known people with tremendous insight that never bothered to learn their craft.

Shel Silverstein

If a man has talent and cannot use it, he has failed. If he has a talent and uses only half of it, he has partly failed. If he has a talent and learns somehow to use the whole of it, he has... won a satisfaction and a triumph few men ever know.

Thomas Wolfe

Talking About Writing

You shouldn't pay very much attention to anything writers say. They don't know why they do what they do. They're like good tennis players or good painters, who are just full of nonsense, pompous and embarrassing, or merely mistaken, when they open their mouths. … If you begin to think about it too much, I guess you might tie yourself in knots, like when you think consciously about tying your necktie or tying your shoes. At least I have never heard much that any writer has said about writing that didn't embarrass me, including the things I say about it.

John Barth

I have a superstition that if I talk about plot, it's like letting sand out of a hole in the bottom of the bag.

Shirley Hazzard

I've never discussed my writing with others much, but I don't believe it can do any harm. I don't think that there's any risk that ideas or materials will evaporate.

Aldous Huxley

I just think that it's bad to talk about one's present work, for it spoils something at the root of the creative act. It discharges the tension.

Norman Mailer

I don't care to talk about a novel I'm doing because if I communicate the magic spell, even in an abbreviated form, it loses its force for me. Once you have talked, the act of communication has been made.

Angus Wilson

Teaching

I had … faced the painful truth every committed young writer must eventually face, that he's on his own. Teachers and editors may give bits of good advice, but they usually do not care as much as does a writer himself about his future, and they are far from infallible; in fact, I am convinced, after years of teaching and editing, and watching others do the same, that a large sample of comments by teachers and editors, myself included, would show these comments to be more often wrong, for the particular writer, than right.

John Gardner

What to do with our girls? Make professional novelists of them, says the editor of *Atalanta*; and she — *dux foemina facti* [Latin: A woman doing the deed], this editor is a lady — has started a School of Fiction to teach the gentle art. It is rather appalling. As if there were not enough novels already, and enough young ladies wasting good ink and foolscap by spoiling them with bad stories, we are to have our young maidens regularly trained to the business, and let loose upon the world, in batches, every year to pursue their devastating calling, as if they were dentists or pharmaceutical chemists. Novelists — even female novelists — are born, not made. Jane Austen and Fanny Burney were the forced growth of no "School of Fiction" whatsoever. If it is "in" a woman to write, she will be able to tell a story well with no other training than a good education and early familiarity with good literature.

The Lounger, a columnist for The Critic, *1892*

My opinion is that they don't stifle enough of them. There's many a bestseller that could have been prevented by a good teacher.

Flannery O'Connor, asked if university writing programs stifle writers

Good writing, writing that works, does contain observable, repeatable phenomena, and the person who has noted them can "impart knowledge or skill; give instruction; provide knowledge of; cause to learn by example or experience." Those are my dictionary's definitions of *teach.*

Gary Provost

Techniques, Writing

Technique alone is never enough. You have to have passion. Technique alone is just an embroidered potholder.

Raymond Chandler

As a writer, you paint strokes and leave suggestions so readers can create their own pictures. That allows you to know someone by a small action and it saves countless pages of explanation.

Mary Higgins Clark

Let the writer take up surgery or bricklaying if he is interested in technique. There is no mechanical way to get the writing done, no shortcut. The young writer would be a fool to follow a theory. Teach yourself by your own mistakes; people learn only by error. The good artist believes that nobody is good enough to give him advice. He has supreme vanity. No matter how much he admires the old writer, he wants to beat him.

William Faulkner

I remember when I was about seven, reading C.S. Lewis' Narnia books and discovering the concept of the parenthetical aside to the reader from the omniscient author. And going, "I want to do that." I thought, "wow, look, you can chat directly to the reader! You're God!"

Neil Gaiman

I think technique is different from craft. Craft is what you can learn from other verse. ... Technique ... involves the discovery of ways to go out of ... normal cognitive bounds and raid the articulate.

Seamus Heaney

The language must be careful and must appear effortless. It must not sweat. It must suggest and be provocative at the same time.

Toni Morrison

Don't base a character on someone you know. But it may be a good

"

Don't say you were a bit confused and sort of tired and a little depressed and somewhat annoyed. Be tired. Be confused. Be depressed. Be annoyed. Don't hedge your prose with little timidities. Good writing is lean and confident.

William Zinsser

Less than fifteen per cent of the people do any original thinking on any subject. The greatest torture in the world for most people is to think.

Luther Burbank, horticulturalist

What is a suspense novel? People in doubt, people mystified, people groping on their way from one situation to another, from childhood to middle-age, from joy to sorrow — these are the figures in a true suspense novel. They are traveling along the road of uncertainty toward an unseen goal.

Daphne du Maurier

idea to base the character on a type of character that you know, because lots of other people will know people like that.

Terry Pratchett

The fact that life just sprawls all over the place is kind of scary, and so human beings look to artists like you and me to organize life, to make sense out of it. … Where there is no unity there is no sense of satisfaction. As a writer, you must aim for unity in everything that you write or you will not satisfy your readers. Don't just write a bunch of words. Write words that have something to do with each other.

Gary Provost

Every believable character has a personal void that affects all of their actions and choices, which drives their steps and haunts their happiness. What does your character a-void?

Damon Suede

Read it aloud. I may be wrong, still it is my conviction that one cannot get out of finely wrought literature all that is in it by reading it mutely.

Mark Twain

Thinking

Don't think. Thinking is the enemy of creativity. It's self-conscious, and anything self-conscious is lousy. You can't try to do things. You simply must do things.

Ray Bradbury

The poet is neither an intellectual nor an emotional being alone; he feels his thoughts and thinks his sensations.

Elizabeth Drew

One of my friends whom I hold in high esteem admitted to me the other day that when he wants to work nowadays … he has to turn on his radio. The droning of the loudspeaker — so he says — puts him in a favorable frame of mind and ideas pour out. I cannot help but thinking that this is not the act of a true musician. For thought has a rhythm of its own, which must either clash with the rhythm from outside and lose energy, or else submit to the outer impulse in restless slavery.

Georges Duhamel

The unconscious mind takes the germ of an idea and develops it, but usually this happens only when a writer has tried hard, and logically, to develop it himself. After he has given it up for a few hours, getting nowhere, a great advancement of the plot will pop into his head. I have been waked up in the night sometimes by a plot advancement or a solution of a problem that I had not even been dreaming about.

Patricia Highsmith

A man is not idle because he is absorbed in thought. There is visible labor and there is invisible labor.

Victor Hugo

Don't think and then write it down. Think on paper.

Harry Kemelman

I never quite know when I'm not writing. Sometimes my wife comes up to me at a party and says, "Dammit, Thurber, stop writing." She usually catches me in the middle of a paragraph.

James Thurber

A man who reads, who thinks, or who calculates, belongs to the species and not to the sex; in his better moments, he even escapes being human.

Marguerite Yourcenar

Thrillers

The thriller is an extension of the fairytale. It is melodrama so embellished as to create the illusion that the story being told, however unlikely, could be true.

Eric Ambler

Straight pillow fantasies of the bang-bang, kiss-kiss variety.

Ian Fleming, describing his books in a letter to Raymond Chandler. Pauline Kael titled her collection of movie reviews, Kiss Kiss Bang Bang, *saying she saw them on an Italian poster and it was "the briefest statement imaginable on the basic appeal of movies."*

I think suspense should be like any other color on a writer's palette. I suppose I'm in the minority but I think it's crazy for "literary fiction" to divorce itself from stories that are suspenseful and assign anything with cops or spies or criminals to some genre ghetto.

Jess Walter

Mogger (my Heaven! what names you give your characters!) whom you have established as a sinister menace, is weakened by that scene where Teame hits him. It is an error, I think, ever to have your villain manhandled by a minor character. Just imagine Moriarty socked by Doctor Watson. A villain ought to be a sort of scarcely human invulnerable figure. The reader ought to be in a constant state of panic, saying to himself: "How the devil is this superman to be foiled?" The only person capable of hurting him should be the hero.

P.G. Wodehouse

Time

How we spend our days is, of course, how we spend our lives. What we do with this hour, and that one, is what we are doing. A schedule defends from chaos and whim. It is a net for catching days. It is a scaffolding on which a worker can stand and labor with both hands at sections of time. A schedule is a mock-up of reason and order – willed, faked, and so bought into being; it is a peace and a haven set into the wreck of time; it is a lifeboat on which you find yourself, decades later, still living. Each day is the same, so you remember the series afterward as a blurred and powerful pattern.

Annie Dillard

It is very dangerous to give an optimal career for everybody, but I feel quite sure that if I'd started by having independent means, if I hadn't had to bother about earning a living and could have given all my time to poetry, it would have had a deadening influence on me. … The danger, as a rule, of having nothing else to do is that one might write too much rather than concentrating and perfecting smaller amounts. That would be my danger.

T.S. Eliot

When I was working 60 to 70 hours a week in my law office, and spending three to four months a year in Jackson in the Legislature, I had no time to write – zero time. But I figured I could *make* time if I could carve out little segments. I knew it would be a slow process, but I didn't care because I was in no hurry. I learned two very valuable lessons in doing that. One, you can't get in a hurry. Two, write every day

”

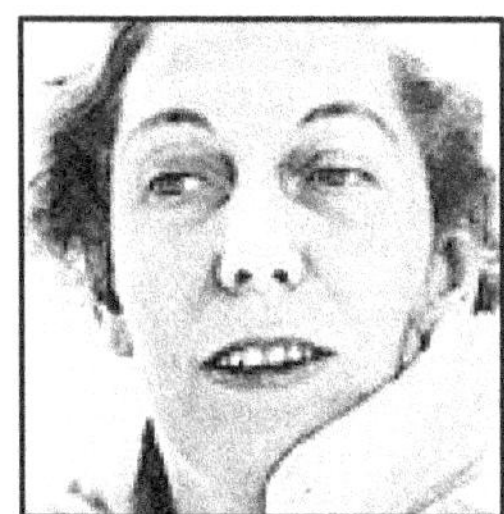

Time can throb like a pulse, tick like a bomb, beat like the waves of a rising tide against the shore; it can be made out as the whisper of attrition, or come to an end with the explosion of a gun. For time is of course subjective, too ("It tolls for thee.")

Eudora Welty

THE TITLE CANNOT BE CHANGED.

Carl Van Vechten, responding to his publisher's request that a 1951 reprint of his 1926 novel bore a new title instead of Nigger Heaven.

It is a terrifying thing to bring your inner life out of the closet and read it aloud to a group... Because I encourage excellence, and each of us has our own excellent, and excellence only comes with not being afraid of who you are. To learn to speak your truth honestly with a clear voice takes lots of practice, and every trick in the book to keep you going down the arduous, cruel, lonely, glorious path of a writer.

Tom Spanbauer

if you want to see your novel completed.

John Grisham

Time is but the shadow of the world upon the background of Eternity.

Jerome K. Jerome

The clock is anything that limits the story's length by forcing it to end at a designated time. In so many books a pregnancy is the clock. … But a clock can come in many forms. In *Bringing Up Baby* the clock is the assembly of a dinosaur skeleton. … Not all clocks act as countdowns. Some merely mark change. Take Scarlett O'Hara's waist, for example. As the book begins it's seventeen inches, the smallest waist in six counties. But as time passes, her waist size grows, becoming the method for measuring time.

Chuck Palahniuk

[T]here is nothing harder to estimate than a writer's time, nothing harder to keep track of. There are moments — moments of sustained creation — when his time is fairly valuable; and there are hours and hours when a writer's time isn't worth the paper he is not writing anything on.

E.B. White

Titles

[J. R. Salamanca's *Lilith*] was a powerful and affecting book, and the character who dominated it, who sparked it, was the character named Lilith, but she didn't turn up at all in the first sixty or eighty pages. I don't remember what the original title was, but I suggested to Jack that he change it to *Lilith*, because that way through all the opening pages of the book when Lilith hadn't yet appeared, the reader would be expecting her. So just by changing the title one created a tension that wouldn't have been there otherwise.

Robert Gottlieb

Tools, Writing

All I needed was a steady table and a typewriter … a marble-topped bedroom washstand table made a good place; the dining room table between meals was also suitable.

Agatha Christie

I am rather particular about my instruments: lined Bristol cards and well-sharpened, not too hard, pencils capped with erasers.

Vladimir Nabokov

Transitions

I learned a lot about transitions from reading Mickey Spillane. In the early Mike Hammer books, he hardly ever explained how Hammer got from one place to another, or wasted time setting up scenes elaborately. There were no slow dissolves in those books. They were all fast cuts, with each scene beginning right on the heels of the one before it. Since the books had enormous appeal to a generally unsophisticated audience, I would assume few readers had trouble following the action line, for all the abruptness of the transition.

Lawrence Block

Transitions are critically important. I want the reader to turn the page without thinking she's turning the page. It must flow seamlessly.

Janet Evanovich

Translations

A linguistic work translated into another language is like someone going across the border without his skin and putting on the local garb on the other side.

Karl Kraus

Truth

Better a cruel truth than a comfortable delusion.

Edward Abbey

"Herr Brecht, what a wonderful story you have just told us! Is it true?" Brecht: "Of course not. If it were true, it would not have been a good story."

Bertolt Brecht

The idea the truth lies on the far side of madness informs not only a considerable spread of Western literature but also, so commonly is it now held, an entire generation's experiment with hallucinogens.

Joan Didion

Truth never turns tail like a disinterested cat: it purrs, it winks its feline eyes, it sees, it envisions; truth is the breath in the air, the breath that someone else somewhere in the world will inhale, and then speak, in the end.

Nuruddin Farah

Frank Norris, who wrote *The Pit*, *McTeague*, and other naturalistic novels that were banned, said: "I don't fear; I don't apologize because I know in my heart that I never lied; I never truckled. I told the truth." And I think the real truth of fiction is that fiction is the truth; moral fiction is the truth inside the lie. And if you lie in your books, you are immoral and have no business writing at all.

Stephen King

He who does not bellow the truth when he knows the truth makes himself the accomplice of liars and forgers.

Charles Pierre Péguy

A lie can run around the world before the truth has got its boots on.

Terry Pratchett, paraphrasing Jonathan Swift's "Falsehood flies, and the Truth comes limping after it"

[People] believe the lies far more than they believe the truth.

Jean Rhys

Someone asked me after a screening of *Paris, Texas:* "Is that a true story?" I said: "It is now."

Wim Wenders, movie director

Everyone realizes that one can believe little of what people say about each other. But it is not so widely realized that even less can one trust what people say about themselves.

Rebecca West

Unpublished Works

An unfinished thing is a thing that might as well be rubbed out. It's better, if there's something good in it that I might make use of elsewhere, to leave it at the back of my mind than on paper in a drawer. If I leave it in a drawer it remains the same thing but if it's in the memory it becomes transformed into something else.

T.S. Eliot

Nothing stinks like a pile of unpublished writing.

Sylvia Plath

Usage

Usage is the only test. I prefer a phrase that is easy and unaffected to a phrase that is grammatical.

W. Somerset Maugham

”

What obsesses a writer starting out on a lifetime's work is the panic-stricken search for a voice of his own.

John Mortimer

Your writing voice is the deepest possible reflection of who you are. The job of your voice is not to seduce or flatter or make well-shaped sentences. In your voice, your readers should be able to hear the contents of your mind, your heart, your soul.

Meg Rosoff

When a Woman appears in the World under any distinguishing Character, she must expect to be the mark [target] of the ill Nature.

Catherine Cockburn, (1679-1749), English poet, playwright, and essayist

Villains

You must not take any risk of humanizing your villains in a story of action. And by humanizing I mean treating them subjectively instead of objectively. Taking Moriarty as the pattern villain, don't you see how much stronger he is by being an inscrutable figure and how much he would have been weakened if Conan Doyle had switched off to a chapter showing his thoughts? A villain ought to be a sort of malevolent force, not an intelligible person at all.

P.G. Wodehouse

Violence

I don't think the violence is mindless. It has causes that are very identifiable; in each case you know why the violence has been perpetrated. Some critics say that those scenes are sickening, and my reaction is, "Good. They're supposed to be." If you care about a character and then see this awful stuff happening to him, it should be sickening.

Colin Harrison

Voice

(See **Style**)

The limitation of the great stylists — Henry James, say, or Hemingway — is that you remember their voices long after you've forgotten the voices of any of the people they wrote about. In one of the Psalms, God says, "Be still and know that I am God." I've always taken that to be good literary advice, too. Be still the way Tolstoy is still, be still the way Anthony Trollope is still, so that your characters can become gods and speak for themselves and come alive in their own way.

Frederick Buechner

I don't want just words. If that's all you have for me, you'd better go.

F. Scott Fitzgerald

To gain your own voice, you have to forget about having it heard. Renounce that and you get your own voice automatically. Try to become a saint of your own province and your own consciousness, and you won't worry about being heard in *The New York Times*.

Allen Ginsberg

Oftentimes an originator of new language forms is called "pretentious" by jealous talents. But it ain't whatcha write, it's the way atcha write it.

Jack Kerouac

You have to follow your own voice. You have to be yourself when you write. In effect, you have to announce, "This is me, this is what I stand for, this is what you get when you read me. I'm doing the best I can — buy me or not — but this is who I am as a writer."

David Morrell

One of the hard things, and this relates certainly to commercial fiction as well as writing for television and movies, is just getting the voice down. Once the voice is there, it's easier.

James Patterson

I myself find that I trust my own writing most, and others seem to trust it most, too, when I sound most like a person from Indianapolis, which is what I am. What alternatives do I have?

Kurt Vonnegut

Voice is not just the result of a single sentence or paragraph or page. It's not even the sum total of a whole story. It's all your work laid out across the table like the bones and fossils of an unidentified carcass.

Chuck Wendig

Wit

There's a hell of a distance between wisecracking and wit. Wit has truth to it; wisecracking is simply calisthenics with words.

Dorothy Parker

True wit should break a wise man's heart. It should strike at the exact point of weakness and it should scar. It should rest on a pillar of truth and not on a gelatin base, and the truth is not so shameful that it cannot be recorded.

Dawn Powell

Women

Women are learning that genius has no sex. How should a woman write? I answer, as men, as all should write to whom the power of expression has been given — honestly and without fear.

Mary E. Bryan (1838-1913)

A sane man of letters can be the lover of a woman who writes books, but he should only be the husband of a woman who sews shirts.

Denis Diderot

A woman's career, particularly if it is successful, is often blamed for the breakup of a marriage, but never a man's.

Eva Figes

There are two ways to be a female novelist: play the game and ply everyone you encounter with sugar, or be a cool, distant ice queen, ideally ensconced for much of the year at some remote liberal arts college, disseminating your opinions only to your rapt students and never to, say, Facebook.

Emily Gould

So few grown women like their lives.

Katherine Graham

Powerful men often succeed through the help of their wives. Powerful women only succeed in spite of their husbands.

Lynda Lee-Potter

Good! Not bad, eh? Imagine your own brother, just turned 18 but lying to every girl that he is 22, drawing that letter from a girl after whom nearly everybody in the English class is rushing! ... Goodbye now, my dearest Kamla, and keep well and don't write letters like the one above, because, you see, I lied to that girl.

V.S. Naipaul, to his sister about a tearful letter from a woman

Writing and motherhood take up the same sort of space in a woman's life — that shrinking, typically non-remunerative space that we reserve for fulfillment, for reinvention, for growth. Both writing and motherhood are sentimentalized and undervalued in the market; both seen as a choice, a lifestyle, something you should feel lucky to do if you get to.

Meaghan O'Connell

Literature cannot be the business of a woman's life, and it ought not to be. The more she is engaged in her proper duties, the less leisure she will have for it, even as an accomplishment and recreation. To those duties you have not yet been called, and when you are, you will

Words are to be taken seriously. I try to take seriously acts of language. Words set things in motion. I've seen them doing it. Words set up atmospheres, electrical fields, charges. I've felt them doing it. Words conjure. I try not to be careless about what I utter, write, sing. I'm careful about what I give voice to.

Toni Cade Bambara

Never use a metaphor, simile, or other figure of speech which you are used to seeing in print. Never use a long word where a short one will do. If it is possible to cut a word out, always cut it out. Never use the passive where you can use the active. Never use a foreign phrase, a scientific word, or a jargon word if you can think of an everyday British equivalent. Break any of these rules sooner than say anything outright barbaric.

George Orwell

be less eager for celebrity.

Robert Southey, answering Charlotte Brontë when she asked if she could be a successful writer

I know this, and the knowledge eats me like an inward animal: there is nothing worse for a woman than to be deprived of her womanliness. For me, there is nothing worse than the knowledge that my life holds nothing for me but being a writer.

Jean Stafford, reflecting on her failed marriage to poet Robert Lowell

Word Processors

The word processor has facilitated not just the mechanics of one's writing but has actually facilitated plot. … You write on a word processor: you open the store in the morning, you do what you do, and then it occurs to you, gee, wasn't there some kind of reference to that earlier on? So you put the machine into the search mode, and you find what the reference was earlier, and you can begin to use these things as tools, or nails, in putting the plot together. … The word processor enables one to concentrate exponentially; you have absolute command of the entire novel all at once.

Stanley Elkin

Words

The price of learning to use words is the development of an acute self-consciousness. Nor is it enough to pay attention to words only when you face the task of writing — that is like playing the violin only on the night of the concert. You must attend to words when you read, when you speak, when others speak. Words must become ever present in your waking life, an incessant concern, like color and design if the graphic arts matter to you, or pitch and rhythm if it is music, or speed and form if it is athletics.

Jacques Barzun

Why shouldn't we quarrel about a word? What is the good of words if they aren't important enough to quarrel over? Why do we choose one word more than another if there isn't any difference between them?

G.K. Chesterton

I like long and unusual words, and anybody who does not share my tastes is not compelled to read me. Policemen and politicians are under some obligation to make themselves comprehensible to the intellectually stunted, but not I. Let my prose be tenebrous and rebarbative; let my pennyworth of thought be muffled in gorgeous habiliments; lovers of Basic English will look to me in vain.

Robertson Davies

[In *Service of the Dead*, Dexter used the word "boustrephon," which means to go to the end of a field and return. His editor wanted him to eliminate it.] Usually I take advice from anybody. But I rather liked the word. I got letters from people saying "What a splendid word. Thank you for introducing me to it."

Colin Dexter

The basic tool for the manipulation of reality is the manipulation of words. If you can control the meaning of words, you can control the people who must use the words.

Philip K. Dick

I discovered what every good writer knows, that getting down one's exact meaning helps one to discover what one means.

John Gardner

We're endlessly reinventing the English language. The problem with jargon is that it's almost a subtractive element of language. Fiction writing has an additive quality. It takes preexisting forms and recombines them, freshens the language and makes you think, "I've never seen it said that way." When you really think about how abstract language truly is, and how immediate it becomes for us emotionally, when we say, "I thought I was the only person who felt that, or sensed that..."

Allan Gurganus

You can get what you need to write (as opposed to what you need to make a big nuisance of yourself at cocktail parties) by shutting yourself in a room by yourself for 20 minutes a day and reading aloud from E.B. White's *Charlotte's Web*, and going on from that to other works of skill, until you begin to see, by hearing, how much the choice and arrangement of the words contribute to the impact of the story, even when no sound is uttered in its reading. And you will begin to see, very quickly — guaranteed.

George V. Higgins

In reading the Reporters [summaries of legal cases], enter in a Common-place book every case of value, condensed into the narrowest compass possible which will admit of presenting distinctly the principles of the case. This operation is doubly useful, inasmuch as it obliges the student to seek out the pith of the case, and habituates him to a condensation of thought, and to an acquisition of the most valuable of all talents, that of never using two words where one will do. It fixes the case, too, more indelibly in the mind.

Thomas Jefferson

I threw the thesaurus out years ago. I found that every time you look up a word, if you want some word and you can think of an approximately close synonym for it and look it up, you only get cliché usages. It's much better to use a big dictionary and look up derivations and definitions of various usages of a different word.

James Jones

Our language contains perhaps a score of words that may be described as absolute words. These are words that properly admit of no comparison or intensification.... My own modest list of words that cannot be qualified by "very" or "rather" or "a little bit" includes unique, imperative, universal, final, fatal, complete, virgin, pregnant, dead, equal, eternal, total, unanimous, essential, and indispensable.

James J. Kilpatrick

Words are, of course, the most powerful drug used by mankind.

Rudyard Kipling

Words have weight, sound and appearance; it is only by considering these that you can write a sentence that is good to look at and good to listen to.

W. Somerset Maugham

Although the narrator of *Freedom* tells us on the first page, "There had always been something not quite right about the Berglunds," one need read only that the local school "sucked" and that Patty was "very into" her teenage son, who in turn was "fucking" the girl next door, to know that whatever is wrong with these people does not matter. The language a writer uses to create a world is that world, and Franzen's strenuously contemporary and

Never use an abstract term if a concrete one will serve. Appeal directly to your reader's emotions rather than indirectly through the intermediary of the intellectualizing process. Tell him that the man "gave a dollar to the tramp" rather than that he "indulged in an act of generosity."

David Lambuth

I was at a panel recently on the topic of how writers make a living and it quickly became clear to me that everyone was younger than me by at least ten years and did not know any writers who made a living at writing. Everyone was speaking of side jobs and having them for their whole lives, invoking famous writers who had worked at other jobs their whole lives as if this was virtuous and not the result of an at least decades-long scam on fees for writers.

Alexander Chee

therefore juvenile language is a world in which nothing important can happen. Madame Bovary's marriage sucked, Heathcliff was into Catherine: these words fail the context not just because they are of our own time. There is no import in things that "suck," no drama in someone's being "into" someone else.

B.R. Myers

A word is not the same with one writer as with another. One tears it from his guts. The other pulls it out of his overcoat pocket.

Charles Pierre Péguy

Words are the small change of thought.

Jules Renard

It's sad about words that meant quite a lot. I mean a word like splendid. Nobody says a thing is splendid. You never say a thing is splendid, or a person is splendid. Do you? Splendor's gone. Magnificent is gone.

Jean Rhys

Sitting at my desk trying to invent a word yesterday brought back memories of the last time I did so. I had tried for days and days to hit upon the right name for "the receptacle in which a Dark wizard has hidden a fragment of his soul for the purposes of attaining immortality." Finally, after much transposition of syllables, I scribbled "Horcrux" on a piece of paper and knew it was The One. But what if somebody had already used it? With some trepidation I typed "Horcrux" into Google and, to my delight, saw what I was looking for: "Your search — 'Horcrux' — did not match any documents." So anyway, yesterday I Googled "Horcrux" again. 401,000 results. As you might imagine, this gave me something of a lift as I went back to scribbling nonsense words on the back of a takeaway menu.

J.K. Rowling

Always look up words in a good dictionary, even when you know what they mean.

Paul Scott

Try to imagine the concrete, lived reality that words point to. Words like, for example, "war."

Susan Sontag

A written word is the choicest of relics. It is something at once more intimate with us and more universal than any other work of art. It is the work of art nearest to life itself. It may be translated into every language, and not only be read but actually breathed from all human lips; not be represented on canvas or in marble only, but be carved out of the breath of life itself. The symbol of an ancient man's thought becomes a modern man's speech.

Henry David Thoreau

The difference between the *almost right* word and the *right* word is really a large matter — 'tis the difference between the lightning-bug and the lightning.

Mark Twain

Writers take words seriously — perhaps the last professional class that does — and they struggle to steer their own through the crosswinds of meddling editors and careless typesetters and obtuse and malevolent reviewers into the lap of the ideal reader.

John Updike

Words have basic inalienable meanings, departure from which is either conscious metaphor or inexcusable vulgarity.

Evelyn Waugh

Work

There's isn't a week that goes by that I don't think about getting a proper day job again.

Austin Kleon

Beneath the surface of art is a life largely spent doing other work: basement shifts, rent gigs, and adjunct positions whose earnings shore up our literary work. Day jobs are a mechanism beneath the business of literature.

Manjula Martin

Literary is a work very hard to do.

Julia A. Moore, a universally derided poet known as the "Sweet Singer of Michigan"

The best work in literature is always done by those who do not depend on it for their daily bread and the highest form of literature, Poetry, brings no wealth to the singer.

Oscar Wilde

Work Habits

I am a completely horizontal author. I can't think unless I'm lying down, either in bed or stretched on a couch and with a cigarette and coffee handy. I've got to be puffing and sipping. As the afternoon wears on, I shift from coffee to mint tea to sherry to martinis.

Truman Capote

I need an hour alone before dinner, with a drink, to go over what I've done that day. I can't do it late in the afternoon because I'm too close to it. Also, the drink helps. It removes me from the pages.

Joan Didion

No texting, no email, no Facebook, no Instagram. Whatever it is you're doing, it needs to stop while you write.

Nathan Englander

A man may write at any time, if he will set himself doggedly to it.

Samuel Johnson

After I get up it takes me an hour and a half of fiddling around before I can get up the courage and nerve to go to work. I smoke half a pack of cigarettes, drink six or seven cups of coffee, read over what I wrote the day before. Finally there's no further excuse. I go to the typewriter. Four to six hours of it. Then I quit and we go out. Or stay home and read.

James Jones

I prefer to get up very early in the morning and work. I don't want to speak to anybody or see anybody. Perfect silence. I work until the vein is out.

Katherine Anne Porter

My usual method … is to spend the mornings turning over the text in my mind. Then in the afternoon, between two and five, I call in a secretary and dictate to her. I can do about 2,000 words. It took me about 10 years to learn.

James Thurber

I found it expedient to bind myself by certain self-imposed practices. When I have commenced a new book, I have always prepared a diary, divided into weeks, and carried for the period which I have allowed myself for the completion of the work. In this I have entered, day by day, the number of pages I have written, so that if at any time I have slipped into idleness for a day or two, the record of that idleness has been there, staring me in the face, and

”

There comes a moment in the day, when you have written your pages in the morning, attended to your correspondence in the afternoon, and have nothing further to do. Then comes the hour when you are bored; that's the time for sex.

H.G. Wells

Thinking is the activity I love best, and writing to me is simply thinking through my fingers. I can write up to 18 hours a day. Typing 90 words a minute, I've done better than 50 pages a day. Nothing interferes with my concentration. You could put on an orgy in my office and I wouldn't look up — well, maybe once.

Isaac Asimov

demanding of me increased labour, so the deficiency might be supplied.

Anthony Trollope

When I stop, the rest of the day is posthumous. I'm only really alive when I'm working.

Tennessee Williams

Worldbuilding

A good science-fiction story usually deals with a society distinctly different from the one we are familiar with; a society that does not exist and has never existed; that is completely imaginary. That imaginary society has to be built up in detail without internal contradiction even while the plot is unfolding. The society can't be skimped; it should (at its best) be as interesting as the plot and catch just as strongly at the reader's attention.

Isaac Asimov

Write, How I

I keep a hotel room in my hometown and pay for it by the month. I go around 6:30 in the morning. I have a bedroom, with a bed, a table, and a bath. I have Roget's Thesaurus, a dictionary, and the Bible. Usually a deck of cards and some crossword puzzles. … I'm usually out of there by 2. And then I go home and I read what I've written that morning, and I try to edit then.

Maya Angelou

My way of working is to get a general idea for a story (whether short story or novel), figure out a satisfactory ending, pick out a beginning, and then take off like a bullet, racing ahead and making it up as I go along. I don't plan out anything. (Even my nonfiction is written without preliminary outlines and according to some plan that works itself out only as I write.)

Isaac Asimov

I need noise in interruptions and irritation: irritation and discomfort are a great starter. The loneliness of doing it any other way would kill me.

Anita Brookner

I write my first version in longhand, then I do a complete revision, also in longhand. ... Then I type a third draft on yellow paper, a very special certain kind of yellow paper.

Truman Capote

I always know the beginning, and know most of the ending, and what lies between is the stuff I have to make up as I go. But I always bear in mind that everything has a cost, and that in life there is no reset button.

Harlan Coben

My methods of work are not made out to any particular plan. I write when the mood is on me. I never dictate a single work, but write the entire story with my pen. I write slowly and very seldom make any corrections afterward. Often when I have done so I have found the result so unsatisfactory that I have restored what I had originally written. If I do make an alteration it usually entails reconstruction of part of the story. First impressions always seem to me the best.

Arthur Conan Doyle

If I find a subject that interests me, then I try to decide how best to write about it. Some things seem better suited for nonfiction, and others seem to be fiction in content or nature. A friend of mine once asked me how I could switch from one to another. I don't regard it as switching; it's just whatever subject happens to interest me, and then I decide how I can best tell the story.

Evan S. Connell

The detail of a thing has to filter through my blood, and then it comes out like a native product, but it takes forever.

Stephen Crane, on his slow method of composition

I'm always keeping random notes on scraps of paper. I always carry a pencil and a notebook. Coming on the train today I had an idea for a story I'm writing and jotted it down – on just a little scrap of paper. Then I clip these together. I'll look at them in, say, three weeks' time, and see what I've got.

Don DeLillo

I have often "written" with the mechanical aid of a twenty-foot conference table. You lay your pages along the table's edge and pace out the work. … After a couple of hours, you have taken an exceedingly dull nine-mile hike.

Annie Dillard

I start by sitting down and just seeing what my hand does, really, on a piece of paper. One's need to tell a certain thing, to communicate a certain thing, surface despite one's inhibitions against it. So the best thing – well for me – the best way to proceed is not to think about controlling what I intend to do, but just to do and then see where it is I'm going.

Deborah Eisenberg

There are no rules. Do whatever you have to do to get the end of the thing you're writing.

Neil Gaiman, asked if writers should edit as they write

So long as a story is true to human nature all you need do is change the local color to make it fit any town. North, East, South or West. If you have the right kind of an eye – the kind that can disregard high hats, cutaway coats and trolley cars – you can see all the characters in the "Arabian Nights" parading up and down Broadway at midday.

O. Henry

All I do is write. I usually start at seven in the morning, take 20 minutes for lunch and continue until about four in the afternoon.

Orrie Hitt, who wrote about 150 books, nobody knows for sure

I wrote the book by working my way forward in the research chronologically, writing as I went along, while my memories of the material were still fresh, and also my own reactions were very fresh. Which I think imparts a certain air of discovery to the text. And almost as if I were writing a novel, I found myself living within Jack's story. It was on my mind constantly. I would wake up in the morning with new insights. A lot of writing, you know, is this unconscious process, but I was just sort of living within his story very, very intensely.

Joyce Johnson, Jack Kerouac's lover

Using any scraps of paper [Knut Hamsun] could find ... he would scribble down ideas as soon as they seized hold of him. He would arrange these notes in little piles of paper slips spread out over his table, like a game of patience. It was Hamsun's task to see which slips would slot together, making a greater whole or blending with each other, to come to life.

Ingar Kolloen, biographer

”

My sister used occasionally to say to me, "You really look like an idiot walking along the street talking to yourself." But when you first start to think out a book, the nicest thing to do is to go for a long walk somewhere. "The Mysterious Affair at Styles" I wrote going along and talking as I went ... You can't do anything until you have thought of the characters and you can feel they are real to you. Not necessarily to anyone else but to you. And you can go walking about the garden with them.

Agatha Christie

”

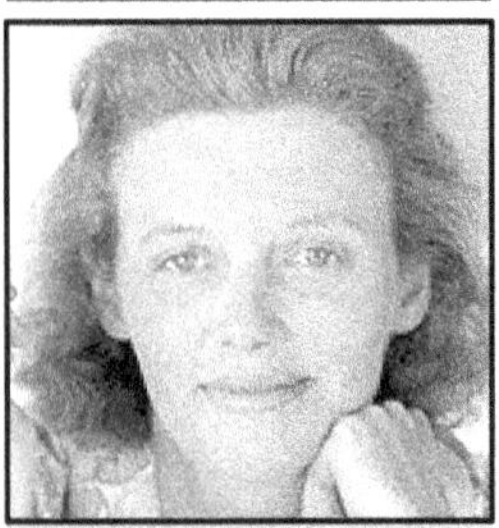

I will read anything rather than work. For this reason, and because I have four boys, I do about half of my "work" in the family car, parked alongside a sign that says "Littering is Punishable by a $50 Fine" ... Out in the car, where I freeze to death or roast to death depending on the season, all is serene. The few things there are to read in the front-seat area (Chevrolet, E-gasoline-F, 100-temp-200) I have long since committed to memory. So there is nothing to do but write, after I have the glove compartment tidied up.

Jean Kerr

Jackie [Susanne] wrote on pink paper, and she had apparently not yet discovered the "Shift" key on her typewriter (a pink IBM Selectric): she wrote everything in capital letters, like a long telegram, and added revisions in a large, forceful circular hand, with what looked like a blunt eyebrow pencil.

Michael Korda

I write in a very confessional way, because to me it's so exciting and fun. There's nothing funnier on earth than our humanness and our monkeyness. There's nothing more touching, and it's what I love to come upon when I'm reading; someone who's gotten really down and dirty, and they're taking the dross of life and doing alchemy, turning it into magic, tenderness and compassion and hilarity. So I tell my students that if they really love something, pay attention to it. Try to write something that they would love to come upon.

Anne Lamott

If I come up with an idea, I gauge it against these words: First is *provocative*. I want my reader to think. And relevant: I know my reader … It's important that whatever idea I have is relevant to their lives. I have to tell the story in the most creative way I can think to tell it, and that often means: Where do I start the story, and whose point of view do I choose? It has to be entertaining. I'm not here to preach, I'm not here to teach … And it has to be realistic.

Debbie Macomber

I like a room with a view, preferably a long view. I dislike looking out on gardens. I prefer looking at the sea, or ships, or anything which has a vista to it.

Norman Mailer

I knew that I should never write as well as I could wish, but I thought with pains I could arrive at writing as well as my natural defects allowed. On taking thought it seemed to me that I must aim at lucidity, simplicity, and euphony. I have put these three qualities in the order of the importance I assigned to them.

W. Somerset Maugham, who was attributed after his death with the more familiar "There are three rules for writing a novel. Unfortunately, no one knows what they are."

When I'm writing a novel, I wake up around four in the morning and go to my desk and start working. That happens in a realistic world. I drink real coffee. But, once I start writing, I go somewhere else. I open the door, enter that place, and see what's happening there. I don't know — or I don't care — if it's a realistic world or an unrealistic one. I go deeper and deeper, as I concentrate on writing, into a kind of underground. While I'm there, I encounter strange things. But while I'm seeing them, to my eyes, they look natural. ... So I look around that world and I describe what I see, and then I come back. Coming back is important. If you cannot come back, it's scary. But I'm a professional, so I can come back.

Haruki Murakami

I write and write and write, and rewrite, and even if I retain only a single page from a full day's work, it *is* a single page, and those pages add up. As a result I have acquired the reputation over the years of being prolix when in fact I am measured against people who simply don't work as hard or as long.

Joyce Carol Oates

I imagine a meter mounted in my forehead, with "P" on this side ("Positive") and "N" on this side ("Negative"). I try to read what I've written uninflectedly, the way a first-time reader might ("without hope and without despair"). Where's the needle? Accept the result without whining. Then edit, so as to move the needle into the "P" zone. Enact a repetitive, obsessive, iterative application of preference: watch the needle, adjust the prose, watch the needle, adjust the prose (rinse, lather, repeat), through (sometimes) hundreds of drafts. Like a cruise ship slowly turning, the story will start to alter course via those thousands of incremental adjustments. The artist, in this model, is like the optometrist, always asking: Is it better like this? Or like this?

George Saunders

I have an opening scene in my head, a closing scene (usually) and a couple of significant moments from the middle of the story. Everything else is up for grabs. I like writing this way because it allows me to be as surprised as anyone else by what I write, but it's definitely a "working without a net" sort of proposition.

John Scalzi

I do it compulsively. I write with a pad and a pen. I like a big, yellow legal pad. And once I get that pad open, I can't stop. It's kind of like free-diving, you know. You have a certain amount of air and then you just have to come up. I'm good for an hour or two and then I collapse on the couch and sleep.

Jerry Seinfeld, comedian

I'm paralysed as a writer unless I write according to this queer dictatorial sense I have.

Muriel Spark

I have written a great many stories and I still don't know how to go about it except to write it and take my chances.

John Steinbeck

There are two kinds of confidence which a reader may have in his author … There is a confidence in facts and a confidence in vision. The one man tells you accurately what has been. The other suggests to you what may, or perhaps what must have been, or what ought to have been. The former require simple faith. The latter calls upon you to judge for yourself, and form your own conclusions. … Research is the weapon used by the former; observation by the latter. Either may be false, — wilfully false; as also may either be steadfastly true. As to that, the reader must judge for himself. But the man who writes *currente calamo* [Latin: without hesitation], who works with a rapidity which will not admit of accuracy, may be as true, and in one sense as trustworthy, as he who bases every word upon a rock of facts. I have written very much as I have, travelled about; and though I have been very inaccurate, I have always written the exact truth as I saw it ; — and I have, I think, drawn my pictures correctly.

Anthony Trollope

First coffee, then a bowel movement. Then the muse joins me.

Gore Vidal

A lot of critics think I'm stupid because my sentences are so simple and my method is so direct: they think these are defects. No. The point is to write as much as you know as quickly as possible.

Kurt Vonnegut

”

I begin with the motive. Why would a person feel that this particular course of action was the only way out for them? Next I have to build the story of the person. Their life, personality, likes, dislikes, emotions, their line of work, family and so forth. They have to seem real, alive, that if you were to go to that time, they would actually be living there. I will then look at the crime and how it happened, the means and the opportunity.

Anne Perry

The lyf so short, the craft so long to lerne.

Geoffrey Chaucer

”

A writer needs three things, experience, observation and imagination, any two of which, at times any one of which, can supply the lack of the others.

William Faulkner

It's not enough for writers of color to learn craft; we need to navigate the impossible waters of an unwelcoming industry.

Daniel Jose Older

Write, How Much To

I wrote each of those soft-core books in about ten working days, which mean doing twenty pages a day, which is not an impossible figure. There were times when I would buckle down and do the book in one week instead of two, which meant doing forty pages a day, and that was pretty tiring, but do-able. I'd just sit there with a typewriter all day.

Lawrence Block

When I am keen on a book I am prepared to work all day, with an hour or two of walk or siesta in the afternoon.

Arthur Conan Doyle

If you write a half hour a day it makes a lot of writing year by year. To be sure all day and every day you are waiting around to write that half hour a day.

Gertrude Stein

Three hours a day will produce as much as a man ought to write.

Anthony Trollope

I believe over-longness is the worst fault in writing. I had such a good farcical plot in this one that I got all hopped up and felt that it wasn't possible to give them too much of the superb stuff, so every scene I wrote was elaborated till it lost its grip. To give you some idea, I now reach on page 45 a situation which in the original I got to on page 100! That's 15,000 words out first start. I expect to cut 30,000.

P.G. Wodehouse, on rewriting The Luck of the Bodkins *for* The Saturday Evening Post

Write, Learning To

Writing can be learned but it can't be taught. And talent can't even be learned. It can be developed, but only if it's there. And the absence of talent is never visible.

Lawrence Block

When a writer thinks of his readers, common sense will tell him that a few of them will certainly not be his intellectual equals, but that the majority will be so, and that there will be some who are greatly his superiors; he should comport himself like a gentleman toward all of them. It is in this matter that I fall foul of so many American writers on writing; they seem to think that writing is a confidence game by means of which the author cajoles a restless, dull-witted, shallow audience into hearing his point of view. Such an attitude is base, and can only begat base prose.

Robertson Davies

[I owe painting] ... for revealing the nature of reality to me. I have always had difficulty seeing how a landscape looked, if I had not first got the key to it from a great painter.... Constable, Gainsborough and Turner showed me England.

Isak Dinesen

When I started writing, I knew a lot more theoretically than I do now. Now I just do it and accept the gift of it. The mysterious gift. And I think that's probably the experience of people who have the calling, as they work year after year.

E.L. Doctorow

This and nothing else is the desperately sought and tragically fragile writer's process: in his imagination, he sees made-up people doing things — sees them clearly — and in the act of wondering what they will do next he sees what they will do next, and all this he writes down in the best, most accurate words he can find, understanding even as he writes that he may have to find better words later, and that a change in the words may mean a sharpening or deepening of the vision, the fictive dream or vision becoming more and more lucid, until reality, by comparison, seems cold, tedious, and dead. This is the process he must learn to set off at will and to guard against hostile mental forces.

John Gardner

I love to write. But it has never gotten any easier to do and you can't expect it to if you keep trying for something better than you can do.

Ernest Hemingway

Vita brevis, / ars longa, / occasio praeceps, / experimentum periculosum, / iudicium difficile.
(Life is short, / and art long, / opportunity fleeting, / experimentations perilous, / and judgment difficult.)

Hippocrates

You learn to write by writing.

Samuel Johnson

The longer I live the more I become convinced that the only thing that matters in literature is that (more or less irrational) *shamantsvo* of a book, i.e., That the good writer is first of all an enchanter.

Vladimir Nabokov

To be a writer, you must read a lot. And write a lot, whatever you are able to write at this point in your career.

Robert B. Parker

True ease in writing comes from art, not chance, as those move easiest who have learned to dance.

Alexander Pope

If there is a magic in story writing, and I am convinced there is, no one has ever been able to reduce it to a recipe that can be passed from one person to another. The formula seems to lie solely in the aching urge of the writer to convey something he feels important to the reader. If the writer has that urge, he may sometimes, but by no means always, find the way to do it. You must perceive the excellence that makes a good story good or the errors that makes a bad story. For a bad story is only an ineffective story.

John Steinbeck

Let their work be to them as is his common work to the common laborer. No gigantic efforts will then be necessary. He need tie no wet towels round his brow, nor sit for thirty hours at his desk without moving, — as men have sat, or said that they have sat.

Anthony Trollope, about his method for writing 49 novels in 35 years. The advice in his posthumous memoirs "extinguished its author's good name for a quarter of a century," wrote literary historian Michael Sadleir.

A man who is not born with the novel-writing gift has a troublesome time of it when he tries to build a novel. I know this from experience. He has no clear idea of his story; in fact he has no story. He merely has some people in his mind, and an incident or two, also a locality, and he trusts he can plunge those people into those incidents with interesting results.

Mark Twain

Write, What To

The writer has a grudge against society, which he documents with accounts of unsatisfying sex, unrealized ambition, unmitigated

”

[Writing routine] is not a pattern, it's not a discipline, it's a madness. Every morning I wake up at seven o'clock and my subconscious says, "Well, I'll tell you what you're going to do today, Ray. You're not in charge, I am." That part of me that's the writer dictates the day. I have no control over it. Every day is wonderful. It may be a poem one morning, it may be a short story, it could be part of a novel, a one-act play. Whatever IT wants, not what I want. It's fun. I can hardly wait to see what I'm going to do next.

Ray Bradbury

”

Every man has a woman in him, just as every woman has a man in her. Every black has many things in common with every white, just as every white has many things in common with every Oriental. These similarities are good, they're connections, they can help us live peacefully with one another. But the differences are more important than the similarities because the differences give life its fizz, its brew. Everything that makes life really challenging and interesting emerges out of these differences.

Tom Robbins

loneliness, and a sense of local and global distress.

Renata Adler

Most fictions, including short stories, have their origin in the subconscious. Very often you can feel them arrive. It is an exquisite sensation. Nabokov called it "a throb," Updike "a shiver:" the sense of pregnant arrest. The subconscious is putting you on notice: you have been brooding about something without knowing it. Fiction comes from there – from silent anxiety. And now it has given you a novel to write.

Martin Amis

Whatever we say, we're always talking about ourselves.

Alison Bechdel

The book is the boss.

Alfred Bester

It was a literary experiment where I was choosing a subject not because of a great attraction to the subject, because that was not true, but because it suited my purposes literally speaking.

Truman Capote, of In Cold Blood, *which would take six years to research and write.*

Most of the basic material a writer works with is acquired before the age of fifteen.

Willa Cather

One of the best clues about what to write is what one likes to read. Even as a kid I read the *Sunday News* section called "Justice." I'd study all the clues and keep my hand over the answer trying to solve it myself.

Mary Higgins Clark

The most important thing is you can't write what you wouldn't read for pleasure. It's a mistake to analyze the market thinking you can write whatever is hot. You can't say you're going to write romance when you don't even like it. You need to write what you would read if you expect anybody else to read it.

Michael Crichton

Writing is turning one's worst moments into money.

J.P. Donleavy

The implicit task is always: "What does it feel like to be a human being?" Whoever the character is, how far out can I crawl into the mental processes of that character? It's very rare that one says to oneself, "This is what's happening, this is what this moment is. It means blah-blah..." That's just not the experience of being alive, the experience of a moment.

Deborah Eisenberg

I cannot have a temperament other than my own. Nor an aesthetic other than the one which is the consequence of my temperament.

Gustave Flaubert

The rules on what is possible and what is impossible in the arts were made by people who had not tested the bounds of the possible by going beyond them, and you can. If you don't know it's impossible, it's easier to do.... If you have an idea of what you want to make, what you were put here to do, then just *go and do* that.

Neil Gaiman

Write what disturbs you, what you fear, what you have not been willing to speak about. Be willing to be split open.

Natalie Goldberg

I had spent a long time screwing up as a screenwriter in Hollywood and had finally come to the conclusion I wasn't suited to writing as part of a team. I wanted to be more in control of everything my characters did, so I decided to write detective fiction because that's what my father had done. It was an act of imitation, if not homage, which I acknowledged by dedicating *A is for Alibi* to him. I wanted to surprise him with the first finished copy, so he died without knowing. From that moment, I decided that if I ever had another good idea, I was going to do it right away.

Sue Grafton

I think most writers … write about episodes meaningful to them in terms of their own imaginations. Now that would include a great deal of what they experience, but I'm not sure there's an autobiographical intention. … I believe I'm telling the truth when I say that, when I wrote *Catch-22*, I was not particularly interested in war; I was mainly interested in writing a novel, and that was a subject for it. That's been true of all my books. Now what goes into these books does reflect a great deal of my more morbid nature — the fear of dying, a great deal of social awareness and social protest, which is part of my personality. None of that is the objective of writing. Take five writers who have experienced the same thing, and they will be completely different as people, and they'd be completely different in what they do write, what they're able to write.

Joseph Heller

What a writer has to do is write what hasn't been written before or beat dead men at what they have done.

Ernest Hemingway

In general…there's no point in writing hopeless novels. We all know we're going to die; what's important is the kind of men and women we are in the face of this.

Anne Lamott

Start writing, no matter what. The water does not flow until the faucet is turned on.

Louis L'Amour

If you feel you need to seek advice as to what you should be writing, you are probably not ready to write. And this is my advice to you: Stop altogether and see how long you can go without writing.

Betsy Lerner, editor

I think we've developed a fascination with the dysfunctional whereas reality for most people is mundane and well-meaning. Most people lead lives that are not full of necrophiliacs. I confront the weighty issues but I put a different slant on the response to them. Of course writers must bear witness, but there is a role for novels that say something about human nature and ambition in the small compass.

Alexander McCall Smith

What I want in my reading and writing is a realised world that I can judge by some kind of recognition. And character, too, that great and wonderful 19th-century invention!

Ian McEwan

To produce a mighty book, you must choose a mighty theme. No great and enduring volume can ever be written on the flea, though many there be who have tried it.

Herman Melville

If there's a book you really want to read, but it hasn't been written yet,

”

Religion and immorality are the only things that sell books nowadays. I am going to start a middle course and give them crime and blood and three murders to a chapter; such is the insanity of the age that I do not doubt the success of the venture.

Edgar Wallace, before publishing his first thriller

Find your best time of the day for writing and write. Don't let anything else interfere. Afterwards it won't matter to you that the kitchen is a mess.

Esther Freud

"

The conclusion to be drawn is that I am happiest writing in small rooms. They make me feel comfortable and secure. And it took me years to figure out that I need to write in a corner. Like a small animal burrowing into its hole, I shift furniture around, and back myself into a cozy corner, with my back to the wall ... and then I can write.

Danielle Steel

then you must write it.

Toni Morrison

Looking back through my work, I see that it is invariably where I lacked a political purpose that I wrote lifeless books and was betrayed into purple passages, sentences without meaning, decorative adjectives and humbug generally.

George Orwell

The only way you *can* write is by the light of the bridges burning behind you.

Richard Peck

Your nature, the nature of your particular talent, is rarely as balanced as your intentions, and I realised some time ago that I belong at the vulgar end of the literary spectrum.

Philip Pullman

Fundamentally, all writing is about the same thing: it's about dying, about the brief flicker of time we have here, and the frustrations that it creates.

Mordecai Richler

You begin every book as an amateur and as a dummy. And in the writing, you discover the book. Of course, you're in charge. But gradually by writing sentence after sentence, the book, as it were, reveals itself through your language.

Philip Roth

In truth, I never consider the audience for whom I'm writing. I just write what I want to write.

J.K. Rowling

We cannot be all the writers all the time. We can only be who we are. Which leads me to my second point: writers do not write what they want, they write what they can.

Zadie Smith

Find a subject you care about which you in your heart feel others should care about. It is this genuine caring, and your games with language, which will be the most compelling and seductive element in your style. I am not urging you to write a novel, by the way — although I would not be sorry if you wrote one, provided you genuinely cared about something.

Kurt Vonnegut

Once you start illustrating virtue as such you had better stop writing fiction. Do something else, like Y[MCA]-work. Or join a committee. Your business as a writer is not to illustrate virtue, but to show how a fella may move towards it — or away from it.

Robert Penn Warren

Advice to young writers who want to get ahead without any annoying delays: don't write about Man, write about *a* man.

E.B. White

Write, When To

Only the "Hitlers of the World" work at night; no honest artist does.

W.H. Auden

A typical day for me would be that I would get up around four, four-thirty. And I write some. Make coffee sometimes, or not. I write for maybe an hour and a half. *But then I get really sleepy.* So I go back to sleep and then I wake up at around eight-thirty [and work some more].

Nicholson Baker

I really think people's bodies are on different clocks. I even feel now like I just woke up and I've been awake for three or four hours. And I'll feel this way until seven o'clock tonight when I'll start to pick up and then by nine it will be O.K. to start writing. My favorite hours are from 12:00 to 3:00 a.m. for writing.

Ann Beattie

I write when the spirit moves me, and the spirit moves me every day.

William Faulkner

I like to write when I feel spiteful: It's like having a good sneeze.

D.H. Lawrence

I wish I had a routine for writing. I get up in the morning and I go out to my studio and I write. And then I tear it up! That's the routine, really. Then, occasionally, something sticks. And then I follow that. The only image I can think of is a man walking around with an iron rod in his hand during a lightning storm.

Arthur Miller

Be ruthless about protecting writing days, i.e., do not cave in to endless requests to have "essential" and "long overdue" meetings on those days. The funny thing is that, although writing has been my actual job for several years now, I still seem to have to fight for time in which to do it. Some people do not seem to grasp that I still have to sit down in peace and write the books, apparently believing that they pop up like mushrooms without my connivance.

J.K. Rowling

My most important discovery has been that I have optimum hours for writing. These are between 10 a.m. and 2 p.m. For a lifetime I've told myself that I was a nighttime writer — it seemed romantic. But actually I'm tired at night, and that's when I prefer to read and research. Whatever your optimum hours are, don't cheat yourself of them. This is a daily battle. If you spend them answering the phone, attending to correspondence, etc., you'll find yourself empty-handed and out of sorts during your low tide.

Amy Wallace

Write, Where To

I try to keep my space very, very contained, because I feel that inspiration and the spirits and the story and the characters live there for as long as I'm writing.

Isabel Allende

What the writer needs is an empty day ahead. A big round quiet space of empty hours to, as it were, tumble about in. Hours that must be filled, hours that force one to think, to get the words on paper. Oh, let the writer do his living between books!

Catherine Drinker Bowen

Appealing workplaces are to be avoided. One wants a room with no view, so imagination can meet memory in the dark.

Annie Dillard

The ideal view for daily writing, hour on hour, is the blank brick wall of a cold-storage warehouse. Failing this, a stretch of sky will do, cloudless if possible.

Edna Ferber

I need an office so I can have a place where I don't write.

Jonathan Safran Foer

Homes are bad places. Either they are so comfortable ... yet psychic and family connections are such that you

”

I certainly couldn't care less if I ever performed again, and don't care much if I ever direct another film, but I would not like to be in a position not to write.

Woody Allen

I can't understand why a person will take a year to write a novel when he can easily buy one for a few dollars.

Fred Allen, comedian

”

My work as a writer has from the beginning aimed at tracing the lightning flashes of the mental circuits that capture and link points distant from each other in time and space.

Italo Calvino

Well, my book is written — let it go, but if it were only to write over again there wouldn't be so many things left out. They burn in me; they keep multiplying and multiplying, but now they can't ever be said; and besides they would require a library — and a pen warmed up in hell.

Mark Twain, about A Connecticut Yankee in King Arthur's Court

can never enjoy those comforts... . Or else you have no comfortable place to work in your home and in spite of privacy or other ideal personal relations are unable to enjoy it. Yet in both cases there is a hold that interferes with your life work that bitches you, ruins you, sends you to the madhouse or the grave.

Dawn Powell

It is no secret that the best place to write, in my opinion, is a cafe; you don't have to make your own coffee, you don't feel that you are in solitary confinement while you work and when inspiration fails, you can take a walk to the next cafe while your batteries re-charge. In my opinion, the best writing cafe is just crowded enough so that you blend in, but not so crowded that you end up sharing a table with somebody who tries to read chapter twenty upside down, has staff who don't glower at you if you sit there too long (though these days I can afford to keep ordering coffees even if I don't drink them, so that's less of a problem) and doesn't play very loud music, which is the only noise that disturbs me when I'm writing.

J.K. Rowling

She prefers to write outdoors ... Miss Stein likes to look at rocks and cows in the intervals of her writing. The two ladies drive around in their Ford till they come to a good spot. Then Miss Stein gets out and sits on a campstool with pencil and pad, and Miss Toklas fearlessly switches a cow into her line of vision. If the cow doesn't seem to fit in with Miss Stein's mood, the ladies get into the car and drive on to another cow.

The New Yorker

Write, Why

But the insidious weakness of literary workmen lies chiefly in their inability to realize that quiet work like theirs, which calls for no physical effort, may be a stimulant more exhausting than alcohol, and as morbid as morphine. The fascination of the silent midnight, the veiled lamp, the smoldering fire, the white paper asking to be covered with elusive words; the thoughts grouping themselves into architectural forms, and slowly rising into dreamy structures, constantly changing, shifting, beautifying their outlines — this is the subtlest of solitary temptations, and the loftiest of the intoxications of genius.

Henry Adams

Why had I become a writer in the first place? Because I wasn't fit for society; I didn't fit into the system.

Brian Aldiss

You write out of — well, I wouldn't call it indignation, but a kind of irritability that these people on top should be so contented, so absolutely unaware of these other people, and so sure that their values are the right ones. I mean, there's a certain satisfaction in recording the people underneath, whose values are as sound as theirs, and a lot funnier, and a lot truer in a way. There's a certain overall satisfaction in kind of scooping up a shovelful of these people and dumping them in somebody's parlor.

Nelson Algren

If you can't annoy somebody with what you write, I think there's little point in writing.

Kingsley Amis

When you're writing, you're trying to find out something which you don't know.

James Baldwin

God wasn't too bad a novelist, except he was a Realist. Some of the things he did are right nice: the idea that ontogeny recapitulates phylogeny is a masterstroke; if you thought that up you'd be proud of yourself. But a certain kind of sensibility can be made very uncomfortable by the recognition of the *arbitrariness* of physical facts and the inability to accept their *finality*. Take France, for example: France is shaped like a tea pot, and Italy is shaped like a boot. Well, okay. But the idea that that's the only way it's ever going to be, that they'll never be shaped like anything else — that can get to you after a while. … And it seems to me that this emotion, which is a kind of metaphysical emotion, goes almost to the heart of what art is, at least some kinds of art, and this impulse to imagine alternatives to the world can become a driving impulse for writers. I confess that it is for me.

John Barth

I did not want to write, but I had to resign myself to it in the end.

Samuel Beckett

Producing stories and poems may not be a good way to make a living, but it's a wonderful way to make a life.

Doris Betts

I write to discover what I think. After all, the bars aren't open that early.

Daniel J. Boorstin, on why he wrote early in the morning

Start writing more. It'll get rid of all those moods you're having.

Ray Bradbury

They asked me if I were on a desert island and knew nobody would ever see what I wrote, would I go on writing. My answer is most emphatically yes, I would go on writing for company. Because I'm creating an imaginary — it's always imaginary — world in which I would like to live.

William S. Burroughs

The only obligation any artist can have is to himself. His work means nothing, otherwise. It has no meaning.

Truman Capote

I choose to create because writing is a labor of love and also an act of defiance, a way to light a candle in a gale wind.

Alice Childress

A common question asked of writers is "When did you decide to become a writer?" The answer, of course, is that we didn't decide anything. It was decided for us. I firmly believe that mythical godmothers make appearances at our cradles, and bestow their gifts. The godmother who might have blessed me with a singing voice did not show up; the goddess of dance was nowhere in sight; the chef-to-the-angels was otherwise engaged. Only one made the journey to my cradle, and she whispered, "You will be a storyteller."

Mary Higgins Clark

There are three reasons for becoming a writer. The first is that you need the money; the second, that you have something to say that you think the world should know; and the third is that you can't think what to do with the long winter evenings.

Quentin Crisp

I think insecurity goes hand in hand

”

There are but few contented and happy men here below; grief and care prevail everywhere; perhaps your labors may one day be the source from which the weary and worn, or the man burdened with affairs, may derive a few moments' rest and refreshment.

Joseph Haydn, composer

”

We want to be famous as a writer, as a poet, as a painter, as a politician, as a singer, or what you will. Why? Because we really don't love what we are doing. If you loved to sing, or to paint, or to write poems — if you really loved it you would not be concerned with whether you are famous or not.

Jiddu Krishnamurti

with the thing that makes you write books in the first place. The process of exploring a book might come from spending your life figuring yourself out and not being sure of where you stand.

Pete Dexter

I write entirely to find out what I'm thinking, what I'm looking at, what I see and what it means. What I want and what I fear.

Joan Didion

I had a wonderful conference yesterday with a graduate student who told me, among other things, that writers write for emotional reasons, and I said, "No, writers do not write for emotional reasons — they write because they want to make something." I asked her if she knew the Stephen Sondheim musical with the number about making a hat — "a hat, a hat, I made a hat where there never was a hat." That's so moving to me I choke up when I tell you about it, and I said that's what writing is about, that's what all art is about: you've made a hat where there never was a hat! That's why people write.

Stanley Elkin

I know that I have to do it and it's such a compulsion. I know that I have to do it to feel good about myself. I know that my need to impress people and improve myself hasn't abated with age. Nine books in, you'd think that it might. It gets worse.

James Ellroy

The aim of every artist is to arrest motion, which is life, by artificial means and hold it fixed so that 100 years later, when a stranger looks at it, it moves again since it is life.

William Faulkner

To practice art in order to earn money, flatter to the public, spin facetious or dismal yarns for reputation or cash — that is the most ignoble of professions.

Gustave Flaubert

As a writer, I am trying to express those things that are most scary to me, because I am alone with them. Why do I write? It's not that I want people to think I am smart, or even that I am a good writer. I write because I want to end my loneliness. Books make people less alone. That, before and after everything else, is what books do. They show us that conversations are possible across distances.

Jonathan Safran Foer

I am slightly mercenary. I write for money. I feel no compulsion to write. If someone said, "You are not going to write another word of fiction," it wouldn't matter a damn.

Frederick Forsyth

There are many reasons why novelist write, but they all have one thing in common — a need to create an alternative world.

John Fowles

You write with ease to show your breeding
But easy writing is cursed hard reading.

Benjamin Franklin

One wants to tell a story, like Scheherazade, in order not to die. It's one of the oldest urges of mankind. It's a way of stalling death.

Carlos Fuentes

The world always seems brighter when you've just made something that wasn't there before.

Neil Gaiman

It had never occurred to him until then to think that literature was the best plaything that had ever been invented to make fun of people.

Gabriel Garcia Marquez

I write because I hate. A lot. Hard. And if someone asks me the inevitable next dumb question, "Why do you write the way you do?" I must answer that I wish to make my hatred acceptable because my hatred is much of me, if not the best part. Writing is a way of making the writer acceptable to the world — every cheap dumb nasty thought, every despicable desire, every noble sentiment, every expensive taste. There isn't very much satisfaction in getting the world to accept and praise you for things that the world is prepared to praise. The world is prepared to praise only shit. One wants to make sure that the complete self, with all its qualities, is not just accepted but approved … not just approved — whoopeed.

William Gass

The writer needs casual connection with his society, some sense that his work does something to make everyone's privacy a privilege rather than a burden.

Herbert Gold

Writing is a form of therapy; sometimes I wonder how all those who do not write, compose or paint can manage to escape the madness, melancholia, the panic and fear which is inherent in a human situation.

Graham Greene

The most that a writer can do — and this is only rarely achieved — is to write in such a way that the reader finds himself in a place where the unwordable happens off the page. Most of the time it doesn't happen but trying for it is part of being the hunting-and-finding animal one is. This process is what I care about.

Russell Hoban

It's the thing that makes me get up in the morning. Otherwise, there's not really an awful lot of point to my life any more — except very nice friends and things.

Elizabeth Jane Howard, on writing daily at 90

Readers are what it's all about, aren't they? If not, why am I writing?

Evan Hunter

Writers write to influence their readers, their preachers, their auditors, but always, at bottom, to be more themselves.

Aldous Huxley

I do think that the quality which makes a man want to write and be read is essentially a desire for self exposure and is masochistic. Like one of those guys who has a compulsion to take his thing out and show it on the street.

James Jones

I knew when I became a writer that you didn't go into it for money, and you didn't go into it for glory. You went into it because there was nothing else you could do.

Molly Jong-Fast

I lead a fairly boring life except when I write. And when I write, man, I have wonderful adventures.

Stephen King

The only reason anyone writes stories is so they can understand the past and get ready for some future

”

There's very little invention in my books. What came first with most of them was the wish to get rid of this awful sadness that weighed me down. I found when I was a child that if I could put the hurt into words, it would go. It leaves a sort of melancholy behind and then it goes.

Jean Rhys

”

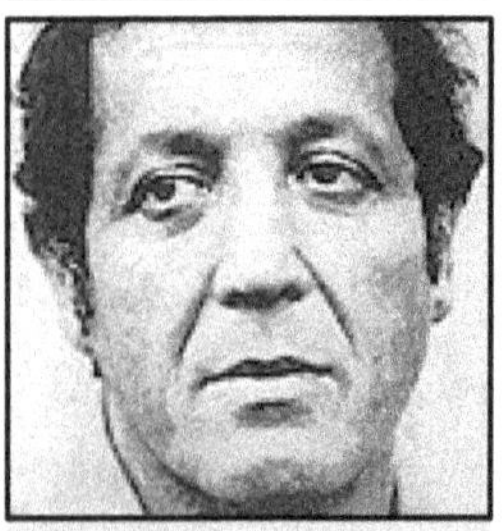

Writing itself, if not misunderstood and abused, becomes a way of empowering the writing self. It converts anger and disappointment into deliberate and durable aggression, the writer's main source of energy. It converts sorrow and self-pity into empathy, the writer's main means of relating to otherness. Similarly, his wounded innocence turns into irony, his silliness into wit, his guilt into judgment, his oddness into originality, his perverseness into his stinger.

Ted Solotaroff, editor and literary critic

mortality; that's why all the verbs in stories have -ed endings ... even the ones that sell millions of paperbacks. The only two useful art forms are religion and stories.

Stephen King

I try to reflect the world as I see it. The world contains lesbian people, black people, gay people and straight people and they do all kinds of dirty stuff together that sometimes you put in a movie.

Hanif Kureishi

Work is when you're bored to death by what you're doing.

Karl Lagerfeld, fashion designer

We tell ourselves stories to make sense of life. Narrative is reassuring. There are days when life is so absurd, it's crippling – nothing makes sense, but stories bring order to the absurdity.

Norman Mailer

[Writers write out of a sense of deprivation.] Attention, love, approval. The attention they feel they missed when they were young. This usually means attention from parents. It may not appear to be a serious matter to anyone looking in on the family from the outside, but to the child involved, who may be a particularly sensitive child by nature, it is serious.

William Maxwell

To put something in the world that wasn't there before.

Mary McCarthy

I was up at six this morning, and I was writing a story. I don't know what it's for. I have no idea. It's just some stuff that was running through my head, and I started writing. It just comes. Talking about it is always useless. It isn't until you sit there with the pen and the paper that anything happens. Nothing happens till you make it happen, so I sit down with a notebook, and it starts coming. If I don't, it doesn't, and I get frustrated.

Frank McCourt

I started writing for cash at the age of 13, and "Bitch gotta make rent" is the cure for any existential wobbles about how to express yourself. If you're turning over a minimum of 10,000 words a week – this week, working on my new novel, I did 10,000 words IN TWO DAYS – then your conscious mind generally gets out of the way, and you plug straight into your unconscious, instead.

Caitlin Moran

I write for my pleasure but publish for money.

Vladimir Nabokov

Writing is like breathing. I could not live without breathing and I could not live without writing.

Pablo Neruda

All writers are vain, selfish, and lazy, and at the very bottom of their motives there lies a mystery. Writing a book is a horrible, exhausting struggle, like a long bout of some painful illness. One would never undertake such a thing if one were not driven on by some demon whom one can neither resist nor understand. For all one knows that demon is simply the same instinct that makes a baby squall for attention. And yet it is also true that one can write nothing readable unless one constantly struggles to efface one's own personality. Good prose is like a window pane.

George Orwell

Do not write to be liked. Write to be remembered.

Chuck Palahniuk

I can think of no more urgent reason to write books today than out of an overwhelming sense of despair at the state of the world.

Dale Peck

It seems as if I was fated to write ... which is horrible. But I can only do one thing. I'm rather useless, but perhaps not as useless as everyone thinks.

Jean Rhys

Wealth

Harold Robbins, after Hemingway asked him about his literary ambitions.

I started writing and making up characters in the first place because nothing or not much away from the typewriter was reaching my heart at all.

J.D. Salinger

A question that all my conferees must ask themselves one day or another, whether they are writers, painters, musicians, sculptors feeling all the same fury to express themselves. Why? People will speak of a gift. Why not a malediction?

Georges Simenon

I write fiction because it's a way of making statements I can disown, and I write plays because dialogue is the most respectable way of contradicting myself.

Tom Stoppard

Freud somewhere claims that a child's first gifts, to its parents, are its feces, whose presentation (in the appropriate receptacle) is roundly praised. And, as in this primal benefaction, the writer extrudes his daily product while sitting down, on a healthy basis of regularity and avoidance of strain. The artist who works in words and anecdotes, images and facts wants to share with us nothing less than his digested life.

John Updike

You'll never make a living at being a writer. Hell, you may even die trying. But that doesn't mean you shouldn't write. You should write for the same reasons you should take dancing lessons. For the same reason you should learn what fork to use at a fancy dinner. For the same reason you need to see the world. It's about grace. The primary benefit of practicing any art, whether well or badly, is that it enables one's soul to grow.

Kurt Vonnegut

Writing saved me from the sin and inconvenience of violence.

Alice Walker

Writing is also, financially, a crapshoot. Always has been. Sometimes, good writers starve. Sometimes, dreadful writers succeed. John Grisham's sentences thud and crepitate all over the page, and he has become a literary tycoon. Edgar Allan Poe nearly starved. Mostly, you become a writer not because you want to get rich or famous, but because you have to write; because there is something inside that must come out. When a baby is to be born, she is born.

Gene Weingarten

Indeed, great fiction shows us not how to conduct our behavior but how to feel. Eventually, it may show us how to face our feelings and face our actions and to have new inklings about what they mean. A good novel of any year can initiate

”

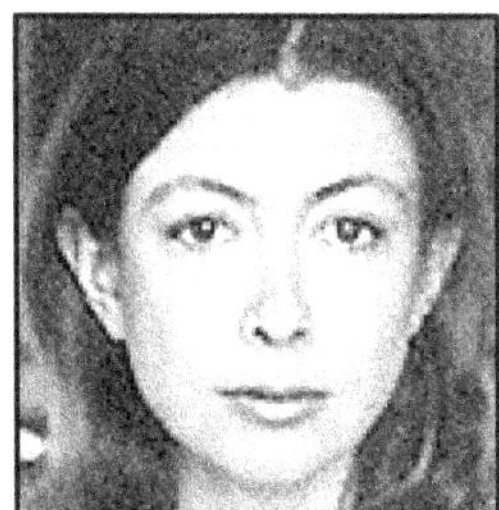

I wrote stories from the time I was a little girl, but I didn't want to be a writer. I wanted to be an actress. I didn't realize then that it's the same impulse. It's make-believe. It's performance.

Joan Didion

A cop told me, a long time ago, that there's no substitute for knowing what you're doing. Most of us scribblers do not. The ones that are any good are aware of this. The rest write silly stuff. The trouble is this: the readers know it.

George V. Higgins

”

I felt trapped within my home and trapped in school, and it was through the pages of books that I was released into other worlds. I literally read my way from the A's to the Z's in the children's section of the library. ... From the age of twelve I made the vital connection between inarticulate feeling and the written word.

Gloria Naylor

us into our own new experience.

Eudora Welty

All that I ever hope to say in my books is that I love the world.

E.B. White

Q: Mr. Wilder, why do you write?
I think I write in order to discover on my shelf a new book which I would enjoy reading, or to see a new play that would engross me.

Q: Do your books and plays fulfill this expectation?

No.

Thornton Wilder

If you ask me what I came to do in this world, I, an artist, I will answer you: I am here to live out loud.

Emile Zola

Writer, Evolution of a

Against the disease of writing one must take special precautions, for it is a dangerous and a contagious disease.

Peter Abelard (1079-1142)

The minor artist, who can be idiosyncratic, keeps to one thing, does it well, and keeps on doing it... The minor writer never risks failure. When he discovers his particular style and vision, his artistic history is over. The major writer, on the other hand, is of two kinds. One is the kind who spends most of his life preparing to produce a masterpiece, like Dante or Proust. Such writers have a long history in developing their writing, and they risk dying before it bears fruit. The other kind of major artist is engaged in perpetual endeavors. The moment such an artist learns to do something, he stops and tries to do something else, something new — like Shakespeare, or Wagner, or Picasso. How do the two different types of major writers create their work, and what is important to them? The first type is interested in finding out what the masterpiece will be, the second is more interested in discovering how to tackle a new problem and is not concerned about whether the work will succeed.

W.H. Auden

Studied piano for six years, decided [I] couldn't squeak by owing to immensely talented right hand and nowhere left. Joined Army before graduating high school, left Army sadder, wiser. Took up art, illustrated magazines, did cartoons, decided I was great faker but lousy artist, gave it up. Tried acting, star ascended like lead dirigible. Quit acting. Got married. Attempted short story, sold it, did another, got it rejected, did another finally found what I had been looking for. Have been writing [ever since], no intention of quitting.

Charles Beaumont

I was walking along the road, kicking stones, and I realized that I wanted to be a writer, an artist. How did it happen? That's what I ask myself. My relatives were nothin', dirt-poor farmers. I don't believe in possession, but something took over inside me, some little demon that made me a writer.

Truman Capote

The teacher would promise that I would tell a story [for completing a math assignment]. I told serials. This was very shrewd of me, because I knew if I didn't finish the story by the end of the period, which was an hour, then everyone would ask to hear the end during the next period.

John Cheever

What is demanding and fulfilling is writing a single word, trying to write *le mot juste*, as Flaubert said; writing several of them, which become a sentence. When a writer does that, day after day, working alone with little encouragement, often with discouragement flowing in the writer's own blood, and with an occasional rush of excitement that empties oneself, so that the self is for minutes longer in harmony with eternal astonishments and visions of truth, right there on the page on the desk. And when a writer does this work steadily enough to complete a manuscript long enough to be a book, the treasure is on the desk. If the manuscript itself, mailed out to the world, where other truths prevail, is never published, the writer will suffer bitterness, sorrow, anger, and, more dangerously, despair, convinced that the work is not worthy, so not worth those days at the desk. But the writer who endures and keeps working will finally know that writing the book was something hard and glorious, for at the desk a writer must try to be free of prejudice, meanness of spirit, pettiness, and hatred; strive to be a better human being than the writer normally is, and to do this through concentration on a single word, and then another, and another. This is splendid work, as worthy and demanding as any, and the will and resilience to do it are good for the writer's soul. If the work is not published, or is published for little money and less public attention, it remains a spiritual, mental, and physical achievement.

Andre Dubus

The last night of 1857 – My life has deepened unspeakably during the last year: I feel a greater capacity for moral and intellectual enjoyment, a more acute sense of my deficiencies in the past, a more solemn desire to be faithful to coming duties, than I remember at any former period of my life. And my happiness has deepened too: the blessedness of a perfect love and union grows daily. I have some severe suffering this year from anxiety about my sister [who had tuberculosis] and what will probably be a final separation from her – there has been no other real trouble. Few women, I fear have had such reason to think the long sad years of youth were worth living for the sake of middle age – so goodbye, dear 1857! May I be able to look back on 1858 with an equal consciousness of advancement in work and heart.

George Eliot, journal entry. She was 38, living with married writer George Henry Lewes, and beginning to publish her fiction

I wrote always in secret, but I wrote ceaselessly in dim corners, under beds, or, in the blessed summer days, under the deep shrubbery and beneath low-hanging boughs. Until my first book was finished no one, except my mother, who suspected but did not speak of it, was aware that, below the animated surface, I was already immersed in some dark stream of identity, stronger and deeper and more relentless than the external movement of living. It was not that I had so early found my vocation. At the age of seven my vocation had found me. The one permanent interest, the single core of unity at the center of my nature, was beginning to shape itself, and to harden. I was born a novelist, though I formed myself into an artist. Looking back on my life I can see that a solitary pattern has run through it, from earliest childhood. Always I have had to learn for

”

Perhaps it would be better not to be a writer, but if you must, then write. If all feels hopeless, if that famous "inspiration" will not come, write. If you are a genius, you'll make your own rules, but if not — and the odds are against it — go to your desk no matter what your mood, face the icy challenge of the paper — write.

J.B. Priestly

”

I suppose there must be idiots who dream of signing deals with publishers while fully intending to drink martinis in cool bars or ride around on skateboards. But the actual writers I know are experts in neurotic self-torture. Every page of writing is the result of a thousand tiny decisions and desperate acts of will.

Helen Garner

myself, from within. Always I have persevered in the face of an immense disadvantage — in the face of illness, of partial deafness, which came later, of the necessity to blaze my own trail through the wilderness that was ignorance. To teach one's self is to be forced to learn twice. Yet, no doubt it is true, as my friends assure me, that when one hews out from rock a philosophy or an understanding, it stays fast in the mind. Only a hunger and thirst for knowledge can bring perseverance.

Ellen Glasgow

I didn't realize I was a writer until somewhere after I published my second book and somebody asked me what would I be doing if I wasn't writing. I couldn't answer the question.

Marlon James

It's wise to plan early on where you'd like to go, do serious self-analysis to determine what you want from a writing career. … When I began, I thought I'd be comfortable as a straight genre writer. I just kept switching genres as my interests grew. I've since been fortunate that — with a great deal of effort — I've been able to break the chains of genre labeling, and do larger and more complex books. But it's difficult, and few people who develop straight genre reputations ever escape them.

Dean Koontz

I would advise anyone who aspires to a writing career that before developing his talent he would be wise to develop a thick hide.

Harper Lee

At eight or nine I was writing little stories in school and feeling the glow. To any one of my friends who'd listen I'd recapitulate at tedious length the story of the last movie I'd seen. ... As a writer I learned from Charlie Chaplin.

Bernard Malamud

Ask any writer or filmmaker or painter just how much of a given project truly represents what he/she envisioned it to be. You'll hear twenty percent … ten … five … few will claim more than thirty. The mastery of one's medium is the degree to which that percentage can be increased, the degree to which the artist's ideas survive the journey — or, for some artists, the degree to which the inevitable detours are made useful by the artist.

Scott McCloud

From a very early age, perhaps the age of five or six, I knew that when I grew up I should be a writer ... I had the lonely child's habit of making up stories and holding conversations with imaginary persons, and I think from the very start my literary ambitions were mixed up with the feeling of being isolated and undervalued. I knew that I had a facility with words and a power of facing unpleasant facts, and I felt that this created a sort of private world in which I could get my own back for my failure in everyday life.

George Orwell

When I started to get more serious about [songwriting], that this is really going to be a career for me, I really want this, round about '76 or '77, I threw away the previous 400- and 500-odd songs, because they were just shit, and it was like, "OK, I got to get better now," and the rest is hysterectomy [laughs]. I had to get good and so it was to find out how the masters do it, copy the masters until you can emulate and then kill them and then stand a bit higher on a pile of their corpses. That's always the same no matter what you're going to be — a painter, a cyclist, a wrestler or whatever it is — you've got to ape the masters until you're as good as them and then, hopefully, you feel that you're somehow better than them in some way and can get yourself to a higher place.

Andy Partridge, songwriter

And you have to be driven. You have to have the three D's: drive, discipline and desire. If you're missing any one of those three, you can have all the talent in the world, but it's going to be really hard to get anything done.

Nora Roberts

Until I was twenty-eight I had a kind of buried self who didn't know she could do anything but make white sauce and diaper babies. I didn't know I had any creative depths. I was a victim of the American Dream, the bourgeois, middle-class dream. All I wanted was a little piece of life, to be married, to have children... . But one can't build little white picket fences to keep nightmares out. The surface cracked when I was about twenty-eight. I had a psychotic break and tried to kill myself.

Anne Sexton

The writer's duty is to keep on writing.

William Styron

I never wanted to be a writer. I mean, that was the last thing I wanted; I expected to be a politician. Unfortunately — or fortunately, as the case may be — I was a writer. I simply could *not* write. A writer is someone who writes, that's all. You can't stop it; you can't make yourself do anything else but that.

Gore Vidal

Everybody should write to find out who they are and where they are....I think that creative writers are in the process of becoming. They are humanity becoming. I think they draw on telepathic sources and so forth. But when you teach people who are not wanting to become hacks, that are really trying to get something out of their system, it's like reaching into the mouth of the student and taking hold of a piece of a tape, in the back of the student's mouth without getting bitten, and seeing what the hell's written on it, and then just keep pulling it out and the person doesn't know what the hell it is. I think it becomes an exhausting thing to do. That's about it. A lot of people decline to do it anymore. It becomes too unpleasant.

Kurt Vonnegut

Writer, Image of a

Writing is one of the glamour jobs that about a thousand people want to do for every one who manages to do it. I mean the world is *absolutely* overflowing with wannabes. It seems, sometimes, that there are more people who want to be writers than there are who read. So it's perceived as glamorous. But I've come to realize that nothing is glamorous, that glamour is wholly in the eyes of the beholder, and the farther one is from what's going on, the more glamorous it all looks. Because the reality of it is that writing involves sitting at a desk somewhere typing — and that's what one's work is.

Lawrence Block

I love being a writer. It means you can work wherever you want. You

”

I am a writer and I've always been a writer. I'm a writer like a dog's a dog. It may not be a good dog. It may not be a pretty dog. It may not be a fashionable dog. But it is a dog from the tip of its tail to the tip of its nose and that's the way I'm a writer.

Katherine Dunn

I think of myself as a conduit. I am the disposable thing trying to identify the eternal thing. Experience enters and product exits.

Chuck Palahniuk

A novelist is a tradesman who supplies books to the public. Writing books is not a hobby; it is a job, a trade like any other.

Dorothy L. Sayers

Constant work, constant writing and constant revision. The real writer learns nothing from life. He is more like an oyster or a sponge. What he takes in he takes in normally the way any person takes in experience. But it is what is done with it in his mind, if he is a real writer, that makes his art.

Gore Vidal

don't have to go to meetings. I rarely have to wear jacket and tie. You have no bosses except the public, perhaps.

Peter Mayle

Writer, What Is a

Any proper writer ought to be able to write anything from an Easter Day sermon to a sheep-dip handout.

Kingsley Amis

Writers write. That may be an obvious thing to say but [it's true]. There's no such thing as a potential writer, there's only somebody who is *doing the thing*. It's like saying you're a potential boat builder. No, you're a boat builder when you're building a boat.

Clive Barker

The writer is that person who, embarking upon her task, does not know what to do.

Donald Barthelme

A writer is not someone who expresses his thoughts, his passion or his imagination in sentences but someone who thinks sentences. A Sentence-Thinker.

Roland Barthes

You are the prism gathering all the white light of experience and in turn throwing your spectrum onto the page.

Ray Bradbury

It is a lonely and ungrateful profession and personally I'd much rather have been a barrister, or even an actor.

Raymond Chandler

Many people hear voices when no one is there. Some of them are called mad and are shut up in rooms where they stare at the walls all day. Others are called writers and they do pretty much the same thing.

Meg Chittenden

I have always looked upon writing as a trade. I simply apprenticed myself to it.

Catherine Cookson

Although it is not necessary for a writer to be a prick, neither does it hurt. A writer is an eternal outsider, his nose pressed against whatever window on the other side of which he sees is material. Resentment sharpens his eye, hostility hones his killer instinct.

John Gregory Dunne

The writer, like the priest, must be exempted from secular labor. His work needs a frolic health; he must be at the top of his condition.

Ralph Waldo Emerson

A good shoemaker makes good shoes, and a good writer writes good stories if he's a storyteller, and I'm a storyteller.

Howard Fast

The writer's only responsibility is to his art. He will be completely ruthless if he is a good one. He has a dream. It anguishes him so much he must get rid of it. He has no peace until then. Everything goes by the board: honor, pride, decency, security, happiness, all, to get the book written. If a writer has to rob his mother, he will not hesitate; "The Ode on a Grecian Urn" is worth any number of old ladies.

William Faulkner

Writers aren't people exactly. Or, if they're any good, they're a whole lot of people trying so hard to be one person. It's like actors, who try so pathetically not to look in mirrors. Who lean backward trying — only to see their faces in the reflecting chandeliers.

F. Scott Fitzgerald

It's not a god-given calling. There's nothing holy or magic about it. It's a craft that mostly involves a lot of work, most of it spent sitting making stuff up and writing it down, and trying to make what you have made up and written down somehow better.

Neil Gaiman

All good books are alike in that they are truer than if they had really happened and after you are finished reading one you will feel that all that happened to you and afterwards it all belongs to you: the good and the bad, the ecstasy, the remorse and sorrow, the people and the places and how the weather was. If you can get so that you can give that to people, then you are a writer.

Ernest Hemingway

To be a writer is to sit down at one's desk in the chill portion of every day, and to write; not waiting for the little jet of the blue flame of genius to start from the breastbone — just plain going at it, in pain and delight. To be a writer is to throw away a great deal, not to be satisfied, to type again, and then again, and once more, and over and over...

John Hersey

Write as if you were dying. At the same time, assume you write for an audience consisting solely of terminal patients. That is, after all, the case. What would you begin writing if you knew you would die soon? What could you say to a dying person that would not enrage by its triviality?

Christopher Hitchens

The way you define yourself as a writer is that you write every time you have a free minute. If you didn't behave that way you would never do anything.

John Irving

If we didn't read people who were bastards, we'd never read anything. Even the best of us are at least part-time bastards.

Mary Karr

Sitting down at the typewriter or picking up a pencil is a physical act; the spiritual analogue is looking out of an almost forgotten window, a window which offers a common view from an entirely different angle ... an angle which renders the common extraordinary. The writer's job is to gaze through that window and report on what he sees.

Stephen King

Being a writer is an awful lot like having a lot of homework every single day of your life.

Marko Kloos

I'm an artist, and if you give me a tuba, I'll bring you something out of it.

John Lennon

Writers have no real area of expertise. They are merely generalists with a highly inflamed sense of punctuation.

Lorrie Moore

Good writers are monotonous, like good composers. Their truth is self-repeating ... They keep trying to perfect their understanding of the one problem they were born to understand.

Alberto Moravia

If you want to know the difference between a real writer and all those

”

[The writer] has to be the kind of man who turns the world upside down and says, "Lookit, it looks different, doesn't it?"

Morris West

I have been successful probably because I have always realized that I knew nothing about writing and have merely tried to tell an interesting story entertainingly.

Edgar Rice Burroughs

”

I don't think getting older is good for the creative process. Writing is so hard. It's the only time in your life when you have to think.

Elizabeth Hardwick

When your Daemon is in charge, do not try to think consciously. Drift, wait, and obey.

Rudyard Kipling

wannabes who punish us with their memoirs and literary novels, it's this: the real writer is incapable of seeing the world through anything but the prism of metaphor and narrative, which renders that world as falsely as chronology renders the progress of time. The real writer suspects that character is just a by-product of these two forces — that what we think of as ourselves is nothing more than an assortment of chemicals acted upon by internal and external stimuli — and in some ways it is his urgent need to disprove this hypothesis, to assert at least the possibility of an existence independent of fate, that drives him to write fiction. It's true, it's true, what you have always suspected is true: it's ourselves we blame, ourselves we're trying to save. Not you.

Dale Peck

The things you remember have no form. When you write about them, you have to give them a beginning, a middle, and an end. To give life shape — that is what a writer does. That is what is so difficult.

Jean Rhys

I am not a teacher; only a fellow traveller of whom you asked the way. I pointed ahead — ahead of myself as well as of you.

George Bernard Shaw

A man does not write one novel at a time or one play at a time or even one quatrain at a time. He is engaged in the long process of putting his whole life on paper. He is on a journey and he is reporting in: "This is where I think I am and this is what this place looks like today."

Irwin Shaw

You can't want to be a writer, you have to *be* one.

Paul Theroux

To be a writer or maybe any sort of artist, I think you have to feel slightly off balance, something isn't quite right. You know you're not central to your society. … Writing is an expression of discomfort in a way. You want to fix something.

Kurt Vonnegut

Context is all. And a relatively pure heart. *Relatively* pure — for if you had a pure heart you wouldn't be in the book-writing business in the first place.

Robert Penn Warren

Writer, What Is a Good

With a novelist, like a surgeon, you have to get a feeling that you've fallen into good hands — someone from whom you can accept the anesthetic with confidence.

Saul Bellow

I do my best work when I feel least like its source and most like its channel.

Lawrence Block

They certainly aren't thinkers. They're not idea men or spreaders of knowledge. Not primarily, at least. The fiction writer is, first, an emotionalist. Whether he admits it or not. A story is not successful through logic, or beautiful thinking, or by its appeal to the intellect, though these elements must be present. It succeeds in its appeal to the readers' emotions. Many of the best loved stories are weak in plot and idea, implausible in conception. They are great because they get under the reader's skin, causing him to react sympathetically with the characters.

Ray Bradbury

I am not a genius. I am a craftsman who writes books at the cost of long and painful labour.

Graham Greene

There are no dull subjects. There are only dull writers.

Richard Le Gallienne

Storytelling is like sex. We all do it naturally. Some of us are better at it than others.

David Mamet

What are the hallmarks of a competent writer of fiction? The first, it seems to me, is that he should be immensely interested in human beings, and have an eye sharp enough to see into them, and a hand clever enough to draw them as they are. The second is that he should be able to set them in imaginary situations which display the contents of their psyches effectively, and so carry his reader swiftly and pleasantly from point to point of what is called a good story.

H.L. Mencken

What I like in a good author is not what he says, but what he whispers.

Logan Pearsall Smith

Writer's Block

Sit in sun. Sun goes behind cloud. Look at watch. Notice that second hand does not always point directly at little marks on dial. Sometimes it does, though. Why? Feel panic at how quickly life slips by. Get to work.

Nicholson Baker

A lot of people suffer from writer's block. It's because they read the same damn thing every day! After awhile you can't even see it anymore — you come to a dead halt. So, in any art form, stay away from it. Get the work done, and hide it. Your subconscious will give you the gift of your art. … It's all got to be instinctive, joyful and fun. You've got to play at it, don't take anything too serious. You must never imagine that you're Norman Mailer — that's dangerous.

Ray Bradbury

I don't get writing blocks except from the stationer… . I can't understand the American literary block — as in [Ralph] Ellison or Salinger — unless it means that the blocked man isn't forced economically to write (as the English writer, lacking campuses and grants, usually is) and hence can afford the luxury of fearing the critics' pounce on a new work not as good as the last.

Anthony Burgess

When in doubt have a man come through the door with a gun in his hand.

Raymond Chandler

Write even when you don't want to, don't much like what you are writing, and aren't writing particularly well.

Agatha Christie

You bid me rouse myself. Go, bid a man paralytic in both arms rub them briskly together, and that will cure him. Alas! (he would reply) that I cannot move my arms is my complaint.

Samuel Taylor Coleridge, answering a friend who asked why he didn't write, 1804

The only thing that infuriates me is that I have more unwritten stories in me than I can conceivably write in a lifetime.

Howard Fast

Get it down. Take chances. It may be bad, but it's the only way you can do anything really good.

William Faulkner

"

My prescription for writer's block: write badly. Bad writing is easier. And it must be popular, there so much of it.

P.J. O'Rourke

I can fix a bad page, but I can't fix a blank one.

Nora Roberts

I am not at all in a humor for writing; I must write on until I am.

Jane Austen

”

The public reaction to Endless Love immediately put me into competition with myself — "I sure hope the next one meets with that kind of success." And with that bald-faced utterance, I ripped the pen from my fingers, broke it in half, and basically didn't work for about a year.

Scott Spencer

The procrastinator thinks, "If I never finish, I can never be judged."

Joseph Ferrari, psychologist

Sometimes you can lick an especially hard problem by facing it always the very first thing in the morning with the very freshest part of your mind. This has so often worked with me that I have an uncanny faith in it.

F. Scott Fitzgerald

A blocked writer has the discipline to stay at the desk but cannot write. A procrastinator, on the other hand, cannot bring himself to sit down at the desk; yet if something forces him to sit down he may write quite fluently.

Alice Flaherty, neurologist

Being a writer is a very peculiar sort of job: It's always you versus a blank sheet of paper (or a blank screen) and quite often the blank piece of paper wins.

Neil Gaiman

I think writing that book [*The Kiss*] freed her up to write the next book that she needed to write. If you don't write the book you must write, not only is that book blocked, but all the books after that are blocked.

Colin Harrison, about his wife, Kathryn Harrison

When one of those spells comes on, I quit trying to work and go out and see something of life. You can't write a story that's got any life in it by sitting at a writing table and thinking. You've got to get out into the streets, into the crowds, talk with people and feel the rush and throb of real life — that's the stimulant for a story writer.

O. Henry

The progress of any writer is marked by those moments when he manages to outwit his own inner police system.

Ted Hughes

Over the years, I've found one rule … It's a simple rule. If you tell yourself you are going to be at your desk tomorrow, you are … asking your unconscious to prepare the material … If you wake up in the morning with a hangover … your unconscious, after a few such failures to appear, will withdraw.

Norman Mailer

When I sit down in order to write, sometimes it's there; sometimes it's not. But that doesn't bother me anymore. I tell my students there is such a thing as "writer's block," and they should respect it. You shouldn't write through it. It's blocked because it ought to be blocked, because you haven't got it right now.

Toni Morrison

I haven't experienced any writer's block. Once I sit at my desk, I naturally know what's going to happen next. If I don't, or if I don't want to write something, I don't write. ... I write when I want to write, what I want to write, the way I like to write.

Haruki Murakami

I don't think that writer's block exists really. I think that when you're trying to do something prematurely, it just won't come. Certain subjects just need time. … You've got to wait before you write about them.

Joyce Carol Oates

This is instead of telephoning because I can't look you in the voice. I simply cannot get that thing done yet never have done such hard night and day work never have so wanted anything to be good and all I have is a pile of paper covered with wrong words. Can only keep at it and hope to heaven to get it done. Don't know why it is so terribly difficult or I so terribly incompetent.

Dorothy Parker, telegram to her editor

I'm a professional — professionals can't afford to wait for inspiration.

Robert B. Parker

If I'm stuck, and I often am stuck, I walk out the door and I'm in the woods. I walk around for 10 minutes, and I come back and try again.

Philip Roth

The best thing is to write anything, anything at all that comes into your head, until gradually there is a calm and creative day.

Stephen Spender

Abandon the idea that you are ever going to finish. Lose track of the pages and write just one page for each day, it helps. Then when it gets finished, you are always surprised.

John Steinbeck

When I was in practice, I was only consulted by creative people when their creativity was blocked in some way. I think the organization required by producing creative work is protective against mental illness... Many would be mentally ill if they didn't create.

Anthony Storr, psychiatrist and nonfiction author

Writer's block doesn't come from the psychology [of the writer]. It comes from the structure of the story. It comes from the fact that a writer writes themselves into a corner and they can't get out, and so, what do they do, they give it up. And so what they've done is essentially thrown away a fantastic story idea because they couldn't execute and the main reason they couldn't execute it, they came up with the wrong desire line, or they came up with a goal that's accomplished too easily, or accomplished halfway through the story.

John Truby

When I hear about writer's block, this one and that one! Fuck off! Stop writing, for Christ's sake: You're not meant to be doing this. Plenty more where you came from.

Gore Vidal

If you are in difficulties with the book, try the element of surprise: attack it at an hour when it isn't expecting it.

H.G. Wells

Writers Conferences

I do have the feeling that other writers can't help you with writing. I've gone to writers' conferences and writers' sessions and writers' clinics, and the more I see of them, the more I'm sure it's the wrong direction. It isn't the place where you learn to write. I've always felt strongly that a writer shouldn't be engaged with other writers, or with people who make books, or even with people who read them. I think the farther away you get from the literary traffic, the closer you are to sources. I mean, a writer doesn't really *live*, he observes.

Nelson Algren

Writers, Women

Men like women who write, even though they don't say so. A writer is a foreign country.

Marguerite Duras

For women, writing is a medium which they place between themselves and the world of men.

Christa Wolf

Writers kid themselves — about themselves and other people. Take the talk about writing methods. Writing is just work — there's no secret. If you dictate or use a pen or type or write with your toes — it is still just work.

Sinclair Lewis

"

When you depict sad or unlucky people, and want to touch the reader's heart, try to be colder — it gives their grief, as it were, a background, against which it stands out in greater relief. As it is, your heroes weep and you sigh. Yes, you must be cold.

Anton Chekhov

Seize the moment. Remember all those women on the Titanic who waved off the dessert cart.

Erma Bombeck

This is what's known in the woman's movement as sisterhood, and it is good politics, I suppose, but it is not good criticism. Or honesty. Or the truth. Furthermore, it is every bit as condescending as the sort of criticism men apply to books about women these days — that unconsciously patronizing tone that treats books by and about women as some sort of sub-genre of literature, outside the mainstream, not quite relevant, interesting really, how-these-women-do-go-on-and-we-must-try-to-understand-what-they-are-getting-at-whatever-it-is.

Nora Ephron

Writers like Jane Smiley and Amy Tan today seem conscious and confident of an attentive audience. Whereas all the male novelists I know, including myself, are clueless as to who could possibly be buying our books.

Jonathan Franzen

Writers, and particularly female writers, have to fight for the conditions they need to work.

Doris Lessing

As artists [Faith Baldwin, Edna Ferber, and Kathleen Norris] are rot, but as providers they're oil wells; they gush. … I'm a feminist, and God knows I'm loyal to my sex, and you must remember that from my very early days, when this city was scarcely safe from buffaloes, I was in the struggle for equal rights for women. But when we paraded through the catcalls of men and when we chained ourselves to lamp posts to try to get our equality — dear child, we didn't foresee *those* female writers. Or Clare Booth Luce, or Perle Mesta, or Oveta Culp Hobby.

Dorothy Parker

(Equality comes when the mediocre rise to the top regardless of race, creed, color national origin, sex, or age.)

Every word a woman writes changes the story of the world, revises the official version.

Carolyn See

If one is a woman writer there are certain things one must do — first, not be too good; second, die young, what an edge Katherine Mansfield has on all of us; third, commit suicide like Virginia Woolf. To go on writing and writing well just can't be forgiven.

Rebecca West

I would venture to guess that anonymous, who wrote so many poems without signing them, was often a woman.

Virginia Woolf

Writing

Writing, like just about everything else, is a holistic pursuit. You don't do it just with your fingertips. You use your entire body and mind and spirit. And you don't just do it when you're putting words on paper. You do it every minute of every hour. If you are a writer, you are literally writing whenever you are being yourself. And, of course, the more completely you are being yourself, the more effectively you are writing.

Lawrence Block

Writing always means hiding something in such a way that it is then discovered.

Italo Calvino

Writing, when properly managed (as you may be sure I think mine is), is but a different name for conversation.

Laurence Sterne

We walk through volumes of the unexpressed and, like snails, leave behind a faint thread excreted out of ourselves.

John Updike

Writing Advice

A writer friend advised, when I was starting out on my first book: "Write like you talk." I took that to mean that good writing must have a conversational quality, should not be arch or pretentious. And as you are aware when speaking to others when their attention lapses, so when writing you must think: How do I hold the reader's attention?

Ken Aluetta

Falsely straining yourself to put something into a book where it doesn't really belong, it's not doing anybody any favors. And the reader can tell.

Margaret Atwood

You've got to just go out and do whatever makes sense to your imagination. You've got to have the strength of your vision, you've got to have the truth of your vision. Otherwise it'll be hack work.

Clive Barker

Writing a story is like going down a path in the woods. You follow the path. You don't worry about getting lost. You just go.

Jan Brett

You can lose a reader, completely and forever, in fifteen seconds. Never leave him even a fifteen-second interval without a hook to jerk him back.

Terry Carr, editor

It's no good starting out by thinking one is a heaven-born genius — some people are, but very few. No, one is a tradesman — a tradesman in a good honest trade. You much learn the technical skills, and then, within that trade, you can apply your own creative ideas; but you must submit to the discipline of form.

Agatha Christie

We all tell a story a different way. I've always felt that footsteps on the stairs when you're alone in the house, and then the handle of the door turning can be scarier than the actual confrontation. So, as a result, I'm on the reading list from age 13 to 90.

Mary Higgins Clark

You keep moving to stay ahead of whatever is behind you. You write like a shark. You keep moving, with the thought that if you slow down, you might drown.

Michael Connelly

One of the important things about writing is to boil it down and not bore the hell out of everybody with stuff which could be much more conveniently said.

Robertson Davies

Writing is an exploration. You start from nothing and learn as you go. ... Writing is like driving at night in the fog. You can only see as far as your headlights, but you can make the whole trip that way. ... Writing is a socially acceptable form of schizophrenia.

E.L. Doctorow

Learn to write well, or not to write at all.

John Dryden

All the talent, all the gifts in the

”

I believe it was the late Rosalind Russell who gave this wisdom to a young actor: "Do you know what makes a movie work? Moments. Give the audience half a dozen moments they can remember, and they'll leave the theater happy." I think she was right, and if you're lucky enough to write a movie with half a dozen moments, make damn sure they belong to the star.

William Goldman, screenwriter

”

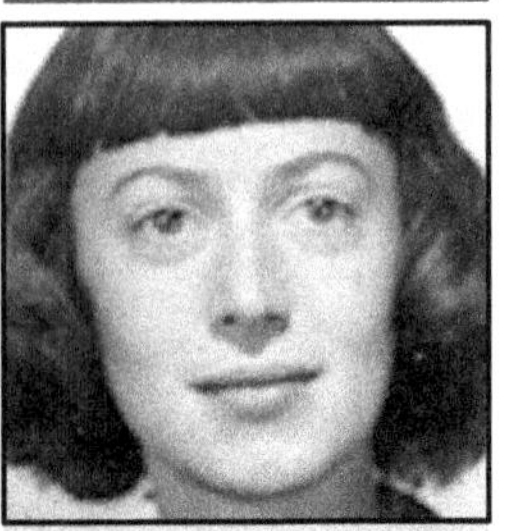

As for "Write what you know," I was regularly told this as a beginner. I think it's a very good rule and have always obeyed it. I write about imaginary countries, alien societies on other planets, dragons, wizards, the Napa Valley in 22002. I know these things. I know them better than anybody else possibly could, so it's my duty to testify about them.

Ursula K. Le Guin

Don't get it right, just get it written.

James Thurber

world can't put words on the page for you. What puts it down on the page is just the simple, raw guts to sit down and do it.

Katherine Dunn

By memorizing great writing — the lines, the speeches, the dialogues of the poets and dramatists — you'll be keeping inside you the best company, the highest teaching. It will restore your heart, reward your mind, and provide immediate inspiration. Through recitation you can prime your faculties to write dramas wherever — on the subway, in the car, on the street, in the dentist's chair.

Hampton Fancher, screenwriter

Listen closely. There's a remote possibility that you might learn something: First, I don't give a damn if my work is commercial or not…I'm the writer. If what I write is good, then people will read it. That's why literature exists. An author puts his heart and guts on the page. For your information, a good novel can change the world. Keep that in mind before you attempt to sit down at a typewriter. Never waste time on something you don't believe in yourself.

John Fante

You don't write because you want to say something, you write because you've got something to say.

F. Scott Fitzgerald

Writing is easy. All you do is stare at a blank sheet of paper until drops of blood form on your forehead.

Gene Fowler

The comment which calls the reader's attention to the fact that clear blue eyes suggest honesty, or that a certain speech reveals the broadmindedness of the speaker, should never be resorted to. If the detail is not strong enough to convey its own significance, it should be either strengthened or discarded. If it is strong enough, the interpretative comment is worse than superfluous.

John T. Frederick

The ear does it. The ear is the only true writer and the only true reader.

Robert Frost

You must learn to overcome your very natural and appropriate revulsion for your own work.

William Gibson, on the secret of writing

As writers we live life twice, like a cow that eats its food once and then regurgitates it to chew and digest it again. We have a second chance at biting into our experience and examining it. … This is our life and it's not going to last forever. There isn't time to talk about someday writing that short story or poem or novel. Slow down now, touch what is around you, and out of care and compassion for each moment and detail, put pen to paper and begin to write.

Natalie Goldberg

The object of writing a novel is to tell a story that will hold the reader from start to finish — a story that grips him so that he will not put the book down until he has read the last page.

Nat Gould

The secret is to write just anything, to dare to write just anything, because when you write just anything, you begin to say what is important.

Julien Green

1. You must *write*.
2. You must finish what you *write*.
3. You must refrain from rewriting except to editorial order.
4. You must put it on the market.
5. You must keep it in on the market until it is sold.

Robert Heinlein

The most essential gift for a good writer is a built-in, shockproof bullshit detector. This is the writer's radar and all good writers have it.

Ernest Hemingway

There is no rule on how to write. Sometimes it comes easily and perfectly: sometimes it's like drilling rock and then blasting it out with charges.

Ernest Hemingway

Write. Rewrite. When not writing or rewriting, read. I know of no shortcuts.

Larry L. King

Making people believe the unbelievable is no trick; it's work. … Belief and reader absorption come in the details: An overturned tricycle in the gutter of an abandoned neighborhood can stand for everything.

Stephen King

Writing is not hard. Just get paper and pencil, sit down, and write as it occurs to you. The writing is easy — it's the occurring that's hard.

Stephen Leacock

The idea is to get the pencil moving quickly. Once you've got some words looking back at you, you can take two or three — or throw them away and look for others.

Bernard Malamud

In creative writing classes in college, the professors will say, "Write what you know." And that's often misinterpreted to mean you should write a thinly veiled autobiography. [Like] a graduate student in English Literature at University, writing a story in which the hero is a graduate student in English Literature at University. It would seem to, on the surface, disallow science fiction and fantasy and so forth, since none of us are actually barbarians or knights or lords or even peasants.

But I think you have to interpret "Write what you know" much more broadly than that. We're talking about emotional truth here. We're talking about reaching inside here to make your characters real. If you're going to write about a character witnessing a loved one die, you have to dig into yourself, and say, "Did you ever remember losing a loved one?" Even if it's only a dog that you loved as a child or something. Tap that vein of emotional energy.

In some ways, it's not terribly different from what method actors do…. We observe other people from the outside. The only person we ever really know inside and out is ourselves, and we have to reach into ourselves to find the power that makes great fiction real.

George R.R. Martin

I sat down with six girls who were working with me. They were very dissimilar types, and not especially avid readers. Yet, they were all mad about Erich Segal's *Love Story*. They enjoyed books that made them cry. If you didn't cry, the book wasn't worth reading. So, I said, "That's it, mate. No matter what else you do in a book, don't forget the buckets of tears."

Colleen McCullough

Write out of the reader's imagi-

”

The most solid advice for a writer is this, I think: Try to learn to breathe deeply, really to taste food when you eat, and when you sleep really to sleep. Try as much as possible to be wholly alive with all your might, and when you laugh, laugh like hell. And when you get angry, get good and angry. Try to be alive. You will be dead soon enough.

William Saroyan

The main rule of a writer is never pity your manuscript. If you see something is no good, throw it away and begin again. A lot of writers have failed because they have too much pity. They have already worked so much, they cannot just throw it away. But I say that the wastepaper basket is the writer's best friend. My wastepaper basket is on a steady diet.

Isaac Bashevis Singer

nation as well as your own. Supply the significant details and let the reader's imagination do the rest. Make the reader a coauthor of the story.

Patrick F. McManus

You have to be a little patient if you're an artist: People don't always get you the first time.

Kate Millett

Any writer overwhelmingly honest about pleasing himself is almost sure to please others.

Marianne Moore

I always conceived my function to be to entertain the reader. They could find the score elsewhere. Basically, I find, most people hate to be informed ... People need to be amused, shocked, titillated or angered. But if you can amuse or shock or make them indignant enough, you can slip lots of information into your message. ... Satire is the best weapon in the writer's arsenal to attack injustice. Frothing at the mouth turns the reader off. Angry voices are always assaulting us from all sides. The humorless we always have with us. And they always have their soapbox. The din of indignation gets deafening.

Jim Murray, sportswriter

You can't use abstracts, no adverbs, you can't use Latinates, because they're just fancy language that makes you look smart ... everything has to be unpacked. Always try not to use any form of "to be" or "to have." It's a lesser form of any active verb. Some people in the workshop are writing incredibly commercial chick lit and we can still say "this is a moment where you need to go on the body," where you describe the physical sensations of the character at that moment or you really describe the visceral as a way of cutting. We like ways of demonstrating things that are more filmic.

Chuck Palahniuk, quoting the lessons he learned from Tom Spanbauer's "Dangerous Writing" workshop

I can't think of any writing advice I ever paid any attention to, good or bad, so I don't know why anyone should listen to me.

Robert B. Parker

Make 'em laugh; make 'em cry; make 'em wait.

Charles Reade

Someone asked me once, in a Q&A what three pieces of advice I had for other writers. Here they are:

Stop making excuses and write.
Stop whining and write.
Stop fucking around and write.
I take my own advice.

Nora Roberts

One skill that every writer needs is the ability to sit still in the deeply uneventful business.

Philip Roth

There are simple maxims … Which I think might be commended to writers of expository prose. First: Never use a long word if a short one will do. Second: If you want to make a statement with a great many qualifications, put some of the qualifications in separate sentences. Third: Do not let the beginning of your sentence lead the reader to an expectation which is contradicted by the end.

Bertrand Russell

If you never permit your style to flag, if you never lower your standards for the parts of speech, you might even endure the worst of patches.

Wilfrid Sheed

A writer with good ideas is going to do better than a writer who is only good with words.

Stirling Silliphant

You want people to read to the next question.

Misty Simon

If you want to be a writer, don't worry so much about writing. Read as much as you can. Read as many different writers as you can. Soak up the styles. You can learn all kinds of ways to say things.

R.L. Stine

Simply piling on a bunch of accidents and attacks doesn't make a book "exciting" unless they cause significant internal growth and reflection.

Damon Suede

The "best advice" I think is in reading good writers, not seeking advice from them, for we learn the best by emulating the best.

Gay Talese

I have found that a story leaves a deeper impression when it is impossible to tell which side the author is on.

Leo Tolstoy

Writing means working in solitude, sitting still day after day. Occasionally I say to myself, "This is a damn insult to life."

Kurt Vonnegut

Advice? I don't have advice. Stop aspiring and start writing. If you're writing, you're a writer. Write like you're a goddamn death row inmate and the governor is out of the country and there's no chance for a pardon. Write like you're clinging to the edge of a cliff, white knuckles, on your last breath, and you've got just one last thing to say, like you're a bird flying over us and you can see everything, and please, for God's sake, tell us something that will save us from ourselves. Take a deep breath and tell us your deepest, darkest secret, so we can wipe our brow and know that we're not alone. Write like you have a message from the king. Or don't. Who knows, maybe you're one of the lucky ones who doesn't have to.

Alan Watts

Drop 30% of your Latinisms ... Mow down every old cliché, uproot all the dragging circumlocutions, compress, diversify, clarify, vilify, & you'll make a book that will be read and talked of.

Edith Wharton

Learn from good technicians. You can't learn from genius. You can only imitate.

Angus Wilson

Writing Advice, Humorous

To write a story in just five minutes you need – as well as the customary pen and blank paper, of course – a small hourglass which will provide accurate information both on the passing of time and on the vanity and worthlessness of the things of this life.

Bernardo Atxaga

Particularly disliking forewords, I seldom read them; yet it seems that I scarcely ever write a story that I do not inflict a foreword on my long-

"

Writing is the expression of thought. There is no abstract writing. All literature implies moral standards and criticisms — the less explicit the better.

Evelyn Waugh

The only people who can be excused for letting a bad book loose on the world are the poor devils who have to write for a living!

Molière

"

The test of whether or not a writer has divined the natural shape of his story is just this: after reading it, can you imagine it differently, or does it silence your imagination and seem to you absolute and final?

Truman Capote

The first requisite is to be intelligible. The second is to be interesting. The third is to be clever.

Arthur Conan Doyle

suffering readers. Occasionally I also have to inject a little weather and scenery in my deathless classics, two further examples of literary racketeering that I especially deplore in the writings of others. Yet there is something to be said in extenuation of weather and scenery, which, together with adjectives, do much to lighten the burdens of authors and run up their word count.

Edgar Rice Burroughs, foreword to Skeleton Men of Jupiter

The only advice I have to give a young novelist is to fuck a really good agent.

John Cheever

My advice to the would-be writer is that he start slowly, writing short undemanding things, things such as telegrams, flipbooks, crank letters, signature scarves, spot quizzes, capsule summaries, fortune cookies and errata. Then, when he feels he's ready, move up to the more challenging items such as mandates, objective correlatives, passion plays, pointless diatribes, minor classics, manifestos, mezzotints, oxymora, exposes, broadsides and papal bulls. And above all, never forget that the pen is mightier than the plowshare. By this I mean that writing, all in all, is a hell of a lot more fun than farming. For one thing, writers seldom, if ever, have to get up at five o'clock in the morning and shovel manure. As far as I'm concerned, that gives them the edge right there.

Michael O'Donoghue, quoting Willa Cather's "advice" on writing

Writing, Bad

It is a sobering experience for any poet to read the last page of the Book Section of the *Sunday Times* where correspondents seek to identify poems which have meant much to them. He is forced to realize that it is not his work, not even the work of Dante or Shakespeare, that most people treasure as magic talismans in times of trouble, but grotesquely bad verses written by maiden ladies in local newspapers; that millions in their bereavements, heartbreaks, agonies, depressions, have been comforted and perhaps saved from despair by appalling trash while poetry stood helplessly and incompetently by.

W.H. Auden

Shakespeare and Dickens resemble Dumas, not only in the fact that their bad parts are very bad, but in the fact that their bad parts are very long. When they began talking nonsense they went at it steadily, and there was no doubt about it. You could compile the worst book in the world entirely out of selected passages from the best writers in the world.

G.K. Chesterton

The man who writes only for the eye generally writes badly; the man who writes to be heard will write with some eloquence, some regard for the music of words, and will reach nearer to his reader's heart and mind. Of course, fools and clods will write like fools and clods, whatever means they use.

Robertson Davies

And bad literature of the sort called amusing is spiritual gin.

George Eliot

Each chapter ought to be interesting; there ought to be no flagging. And how can this be continued through to five or six hundred closely printed pages? There must be some padding, some reference to the appearance of rooms, which any furniture catalogue will supply; some description of wearing apparel, probably culled from a West-End fashion-book; some airing of grievances on political topics, which read better in a newspaper; or some sermonising which would be considered dull in a ten-minutes' discourse from the pulpit.

Nat Gould

Writing, Good

The best thing I can do when I'm working is just get words on paper every day, and turn off the critical sense that tells me that what I'm writing is no good. Because writing that I feel good about and that comes easily and is a joy, and writing that I feel terrible about and doesn't come easily and is agony, often wind up being qualitatively indistinguishable.

Lawrence Block

A good story, a good play, a good film does the following things: that we build a tension toward laughter, and at a given point in a good play, or a good film, or a good story, we give permission to laugh, and people laugh and release that tension. In a tragedy, we build a tension all during the drama, or the film, or the story toward crying, and we then give permission to cry, and people may cry and release that tension. When it comes to love, if we see a beautiful thing, if we see a beautiful woman, if we're telling a love story let's say, and we have a tension build then for the fruition of this love, we give permission to love. We give permission for the pursuit and the conquering, and this tension is relieved.

Ray Bradbury

A good novel tells us the truth about its hero, but a bad novel tells us the truth about its author.

G.K. Chesterton

Inevitably, you react to your own work — you like it, you don't like it, you think it's interesting or boring — and it is difficult to accept that those reactions may be unreliable. In my experience, they are. I mistrust either wild enthusiasm or deep depression. I have had the best success with material that I was sort of neutral about.

Michael Crichton

The key to writing fiction is remembering just how closely linked fiction and reality are. Fiction is just like reality, except it's more elegant. It also makes more sense, unless it's written badly, in which case you've got bad fiction. I like stories that make sense; maybe I'm old-fashioned that way.

Peter David

Good writing is supposed to evoke sensation in the reader — not the fact that it is raining, but the feel of being rained upon.

E.L. Doctorow

Good writing is like a bomb: it explodes in the face of the reader.

Nuruddin Farah

If we write and speak clearly, we are likelier to think clearly and to remain comparatively free.

E.M. Forster

Read the first five pages. Count clichés. If you find one, the buzzer goes off: It's not a serious novel. A serious novelist notices clichés and eliminates them. The serious novelist doesn't write "quiet as a mouse" or paint the world in

”

It has to have that lovely, logical, just gutting inevitability. That's where you want to get to in fiction, whether popular fiction or high literary fiction or whatever — you want to get to the point where everything feels inevitable, where what you're getting is a true, and I use this word in the "Sandman" sense: a true account of what happened. True, in the sense that it's much more real and important than facts.

Neil Gaiman

Anyone can have ideas — the difficulty is to express them without squandering a quire of paper [25 sheets] on an idea that ought to be reduced to one glittering paragraph.

Mark Twain

I would never sit down and write for pleasure because it's too much like hard work. Ninety percent of the work gets done in the last 10 percent of the time.

Douglas Adams

clichéd moral terms.

Jonathan Franzen

One can derive all the principles of effective fiction from the idea that the writer must make his dream vivid and continuous. The dream is not vivid, of course, if too many words are abstract, not concrete, if too many verbs are passive, too many metaphors familiar or dull, and so on; and the dream is not continuous if some element in the writing distracts the reader from the story to thoughts about the stupidity of the writer — his inability to use proper grammar, his excessive loquacity, his deviation into sentimentality, mannerism, or frigidity, and so on.

John Gardner

There are a hundred faults in this thing, and a hundred things might be said to prove them beauties; but it is needless. A book may be amusing with numerous errors, or it may be very dull without a single absurdity.

Oliver Goldsmith, his ad copy for The Vicar of Wakefield *(1766)*

An appealing character strives against great odds to attain a worthwhile goal. That's pretty much the formula for all fiction.

Dan Greenburg

Deliberately puzzling or confusing a reader may keep him reading for a while, but at too great an expense. Even just an "aura" of mystery in a story is usually just a lot of baloney. Who are these people? What are they up to? Provoking such questions from a reader can be a writer's way of deferring exposition until he feels the reader is ready for the explanation of it all. But more likely it's just fogging things up. A lot of beginning writer's fiction is like a lot of beginner's poetry: deliberately unintelligible so as to make the shallow seem deep.

Rust Hills

One of my agents used to say to me, "Mack, you shouldn't submit anything anywhere unless you [would] read it aloud to them."

MacKinlay Kantor

The first secret of good writing: we must look intently, and hear intently, and taste intently.

James J. Kilpatrick

The way to write is well, and how is your own business. Nothing else on the subject makes sense.

A.J. Liebling

The point of good writing is knowing when to stop.

L.M. Montgomery

Any writer is inevitably going to work with his own anxieties and desires. If the book is any good it has got to have in it the fire of a personal unconscious mind.

Iris Murdoch

If you're going to write, don't pretend to write down. It's going to be the best you can do, and it's the fact that it's the best you can do that kills you.

Dorothy Parker

There are a lot of ways to write good books. You can have *The Corrections*, which is very complicated sociology, or James Joyce, where the allusions and the writing are stunning. But my work is just pure storytelling.

James Patterson

Whenever you feel an impulse to

perpetrate a piece of exceptionally fine writing, obey it — wholeheartedly — and delete it before sending your manuscript to the press. *Murder your darlings.*

Arthur Quiller-Couch

Honest writing always makes people nervous, and they'll think of all kinds of ways to make your life hell.

J.D. Salinger

Vigorous writing is concise.

William Strunk Jr.

You have reached the felicity in writing marked by the fact that your pieces sound like you, creating by the printed word the illusion that you are actually present and saying your say. This is all a writer can ask. He is not entitled to ask for more than this.

Alexander Woollcott

Writing, How Often

Don't be a slug. Write it down, because you will not remember it in the morning. I get up at 3 a.m. to write. I force myself to write. The muse only comes to you when you're sitting ... in front of the computer.

Richard Ford

When the writing is going well, I can work all day. When it's not, I spend a lot of time gardening and standing in front of the refrigerator.

Francine Prose

When I was excited about life, I didn't want to write at all. I've never written when I was happy. I didn't want to. But I've never had a long period of being happy. Do you think anyone has?

Jean Rhys

I can't explain the fact that there have been a series of books coming rather regularly out of me. I work most days and if you work most days and you get at least a page done a day, then at the end of the year you have 365.

Philip Roth

The fact is he writes too fast. An average six or eight months is too short a time for the gestation and production of a first-class novel.

The Spectator,
on Anthony Trollope's production

My novels, whether good or bad, have been as good as I could make them. Had I taken three months of idleness between each they would have been no better.

Anthony Trollope

I try to write a certain amount each day, five days a week. A rule sometimes broken is better than no rule.

Herman Wouk

Writing, Pleasures of

The only people who like to write terribly are those that do.

Franklin Pierce Adams, newspaper columnist, about an author who was "terribly eager" to write every day

I have never written a book that didn't teach me far more than it taught any reader.

Isaac Asimov

Part of the pleasure of writing is taking risks. Part of the pleasure of it is doing something which makes you think: "Boy, am I going to pull this one off?" The fact is, you never know.

Clive Barker

I sat at the typewriter for the first time and fell in love with the words that emerged like drops, one by one, and remained on the white sheet of paper ... every drop became something that if spoken would have flown away, but on the sheets as words, became solidified, whether they were good or bad.

Oriana Fallaci, journalist

"You better love your work and the doing. Because what comes after, there's no guarantees. Sometimes, you get the frosting on the cake. Sometime, you don't. But if you love the doing and you believe in what you do, it's OK."

David Lynch, director

You're all alone when you're a writer. Sometimes you just feel you need a humanity bath. Even a ride on the subway will do that. But it's much more interesting to talk about books. After all, that's what life used to be for writers: they talk books, politics, history, America. Nothing has replaced that.

Saul Bellow

I never take a vacation because what would it be from? I became a novelist many years ago so that I might live in a continuum of make-believe in which there are no weekends and, more importantly, no Monday mornings.

Thomas Berger

I am totally happy when I am plunged into the midst of adventures with my characters. I never interfere with my people. I let them live and in living write the story for me. So that means that in a single day of running with my characters I can write a complete first draft story. I believe first drafts, like life and living, must be immediate, quick, passionate. By writing a draft in a day I have a story with a skin around it.

Ray Bradbury

Writing is like being in love. You never get better at it or learn more about it. The day you think you do is the day you lose it. Robert Frost called his work a lover's quarrel with the world. It's ongoing. It has neither a beginning nor an end. You don't have to worry about learning things. The fire of one's art burns all the impurities from the vessel that contains it.

James Lee Burke

Writing is not terrible, it's wonderful. I keep my own hours, do what I please. When I want to travel, I can. But mainly I'm doing what I most wanted to do all my life. I'm not into the agonies of creation.

Raymond Carver

What is great about being a writer is you work hard, but at least you can get decent coffee and sit somewhere comfortable most of the time.

John Cleese

It was only after two years' work, that it occurred to me that I was a writer. … It was only when I found myself writing things I didn't realise I knew that I said, "I'm a writer now." The novel had become an incentive to deeper thinking. That's really what writing is – an intense form of thought.

Don DeLillo

Putting a book together is interesting and exhilarating. It is sufficiently difficult and complex that it engages all your intelligence. It is life at its most free. Your freedom as a writer is not freedom of expression in the sense of wild blurting; you may not let rip. It is life at its most free, if you are fortunate enough to be able to try it, because you select your materials, invent your task, and pace yourself. … The obverse of this freedom, of course, is that your work is so meaningless, so fully for yourself alone, and so worthless to the world, that no one except you cares whether you do it well, or ever.

Annie Dillard

When writing a novel, that's pretty much entirely what life turns into: "House burned down. Car stolen. Cat exploded. Did 1,500 easy words, so all in all it was a pretty good day."

Neil Gaiman

Enjoyment is *not* a goal, it is a feeling that accompanies important ongoing activity.

Paul Goodman

I don't know if I could *ever* take pleasure in writing. I've never been able to enjoy the process. Everything about being a writer is fun, except the actual work of it. When I'm at the computer, I'm sweating. And writing is lonely. Nobody can help you. I remember being so tired during the writing of the first two books.

John Grisham

Writing is not necessarily something to be ashamed of, but do it in private and wash your hands afterward.

Robert Heinlein

[I] suffer like a bastard when [I] don't write, or just before, and feel empty and fucked out afterwards. But [I] never feel as good as while writing.

Ernest Hemingway

I think that the joy of writing a novel is the self-exploration that emerges and also that wonderful feeling of playing God with the characters. When I sit down at my writing desk, time seems to vanish. … I think the most important thing for a writer is to be locked in a study.

Erica Jong

I did it for the buzz. I did it for the pure joy of the thing. And if you can do it for joy, you can do it forever.

Stephen King

Sometimes people ask, does writing make you happy? But I think that's beside the point. It makes you agitated, and continually in a state where you're off balance. You seldom feel serene or settled. You're like the person in the fairy tale *The Red Shoes*: you've just got to dance and dance, you're never in equilibrium.

Hilary Mantel

Writing is one of the most easy, pain-free, and happy ways to pass the time in all the arts. For example, right now I am sitting in my rose garden and typing on my new computer. Each rose represents a story, so I'm never at a loss for what to write. I just look deep into the heart of the rose and read its story and write it down through typing, which I enjoy anyway. I could be typing "kjfiu joewmv jiw" and would enjoy it as much as typing words that actually make sense. I simply relish the movement of my fingers on the keys. Sometimes, it is true, agony visits the head of a writer. At these moments, I stop writing and relax with a coffee at my favorite restaurant, knowing that words can be changed, rethought, fiddled with, and, of course, ultimately denied. Painters don't have that luxury. If they go to a coffee shop, their paint dries into a hard mass.

Steve Martin

I had expected to be thrilled when I received my first copy of my first book, but when I opened the package and held the first copy in my hands, I found that I just felt sort of flat ... I learned then and have relearned many times since, that the best part of a writer's life is actually *doing* it, making up characters, filling the blank page, creating scenes that

”

There are few feelings more joyous than reading back over the week's work and thinking "that's not bad at all," as opposed to the all-too-frequent, "it's rubbish, I've wasted a week and I'll have to re-write the lot." And if you think that's an exaggeration or false modesty, you are very, very wrong. It's perfectly possible to put in eight-hour days and have nothing to show for them but a single idea that, if reworked completely, might be passable.

J.K. Rowling

[Fiction writing] is extremely embarrassing not only because one reveals to oneself one's deep interests, which might not be the deep interests one would most like to present to the world or to oneself, but also because one does it so badly at first. And it really takes time to make something good.

Deborah Eisenberg

readers in distant places might connect to.

Larry McMurtry

(This was also my experience with Writers Gone Wild.*)*

The vanity of man is quite illimitable. In every act of his life, however trivial, and particularly in every act which pertains to his profession, he takes all the pride of a baby learning to walk. It may seem incredible but it is nevertheless a fact that I myself get great delight out of writing such banal paragraphs as this one. The physical business of writing is extremely unpleasant to me, as it is to most other human beings, but the psychic satisfaction of discharging bad ideas in worse English is enough to make me forget it entirely.

H.L. Mencken

I'm a writer, and I'm writing, but at the same time I feel as though I were reading some exciting, interesting book. So I enjoy the writing.

Haruki Murakami

I am not conscious of working especially hard, or of "working" at all. Writing and teaching have always been, for me, so richly rewarding that I don't think of them as work in the usual sense of the word.

Joyce Carol Oates

Writing became such a process of discovery that I couldn't wait to get to work in the morning: I wanted to know what I was going to say.

Sharon O'Brien

While writing, the very toil gives pleasure and itself is lessened, and the glowing work glows along with the writer's heart.

Ovid

It's "did I have fun doing it?" Because before I ever got paid, before I sold anything, I was thinking, "Am I having fun doing this, and if not can I do it in a different way so I am having fun?"

Chuck Palahniuk, on what he values most in writing

Freedom. I can do what I want when I want to. I don't punch a clock. I don't go to work. I used to work, and I never liked it.

Robert B. Parker

I really do love to write. The curious thing is that during the last month or six weeks of a book, when I am editing, rewriting, refining and polishing my work, I say to myself: "If you're a good boy and finish this before the deadline, you're going to be allowed to write another book!" Because during the first month or two when you're working on a book (when a lot of options are still open) you don't have to be too disciplined. You're writing a lot, going down a lot of blind alleys, you're finding out how the plot is going to work etc. That is a fun period, and I look forward to it.

Terry Pratchett

Writing can also be very exciting. If you're really in the mood to write, you write without apparently wanting to. But it doesn't always happen that way. It's a struggle, and it's very tiring.

Jean Rhys

It's all the art of impersonation, isn't it? That's the fundamental novelistic gift... . There has to be some pleasure in this job, and that's it. To go around in disguise. To act a character. To pass oneself off as what one is not. To pretend. The sly and cunning masquerade... . You don't necessarily, as a writer, have to abandon your biography completely to engage in an act of impersonation. It may be more intriguing when you don't. You distort it, caricature it, parody it, you torture and subvert it, you exploit it — all to give the biography that dimension that will excite your verbal life.

Philip Roth

Writing is very difficult and gives me a great deal of pleasure, partly because it is so difficult.

Maurice Sendak

I want to be thoroughly used up when I die, for the harder I work the more I live.

George Bernard Shaw

Writing is a beautiful act. It is making something that will give pleasure to others later.

Susan Sontag

Writing is the only thing that, when I do it, I don't feel I should be doing something else.

Gloria Steinem

When I'm writing I find it's the only time that I feel completely self-possessed, even when the writing itself is not going too well. It's fine therapy for people who are perpetually scared of nameless threats as I am most of the time — for jittery people. Besides, I've discovered that when I'm not writing I'm prone to developing certain nervous tics, and hypochondria.

William Styron

Nothing is more satisfying than to write a good sentence. It is no fun to write lumpishly, dully, in prose the reader must plod through like wet sand. But it is a pleasure to achieve, if one can, a clear running prose that is simple yet full of surprises. This does not just happen. It requires skill, hard work, a good ear, and continued practice.

Barbara Tuchman

Writing, Stresses From

Writing isn't easy for me, and hasn't been easy for years now. I don't think it will ever be easy so long as I try to make everything I write as good as it can possibly be.

Lawrence Block

The anxiety involved is intolerable. And ... the financial rewards just don't make up for the expenditure of energy, the damage to health caused by stimulants and narcotics, the fear that one's work isn't good enough. I think, if I had enough money, I'd give up writing tomorrow.

Anthony Burgess

Writing a book is an adventure. To begin with it is a toy, then an amusement. Then it becomes a mistress, and then it becomes a master, and then it becomes a tyrant and, in the last stage, just as you are about to be reconciled to your servitude, you kill the monster and fling him to the public.

Winston Churchill

The professional writers who dread writing, as many do, are usually those whose critical sense is not only strong but unsleeping, so that it won't allow them to do even a first draft at top speed. They are in most cases the "bleeders" who write one sentence at a time and can't write it until the sentence before has been revised.

Malcolm Cowley, literary critic

”

Beginning a novel is always hard. It feels like going nowhere. I always have to write at least 100 pages that go into the trashcan before it finally begins to work. It's discouraging, but necessary to write those pages. I try to consider them pages -100 to zero of the novel.

Barbara Kingsolver

That's the biggest problem for writers — the constant, grumbling pain in your arse. You are hunched over your keyboard for upwards of seven hours a day, compacting your lower spine, and essentially murdering your arse with a chair. Were I not a writer, I'd like to think I'd have the peachy, zingy buttocks of Gigi Hadid.

Caitlin Moran

You'll find a writer who is honest and he'll probably tell you that he writes because he'd rather do that than anything else in the world. And this business about the suffering ... all second-rate artists like you to think that they suffer horribly.

Robertson Davies

It would concern the reader little, perhaps, to know how sorrowfully the pen is laid down at the close of a two-years' imaginative task; or how an Author feels as if he were dismissing some portion of himself into the shadowy world, when a crowd of the creatures of his brain are going from him for ever.

Charles Dickens

Sometimes I don't understand why my arms don't drop from my body with fatigue, why my brain doesn't melt away. I am leading an austere life, stripped of all external pleasure, and am sustained only by a kind of permanent frenzy, which sometimes makes me weep tears of impotence but never abates. I love my work with a love that is frantic and perverted, as an ascetic loves the hair shirt that scratches his belly. Sometimes, when I am empty, when words don't come, when I find I haven't written a single sentence after scribbling whole pages, I collapse on my couch and lie there dazed, bogged down in a swamp of despair, hating myself and blaming myself for this demented pride that makes me pant after a chimera. A quarter of an hour later, everything has changed; my heart is pounding with joy.

Gustave Flaubert

I was in such a harmful pattern. In a way, it would begin on a Friday, when I would realize what I'd been working on all week was bad. I would polish it all day to bring up the gloss, until by 4 in the afternoon I'd have to admit it was bad. Between 5 and 6, I'd get drunk on vodka shot glasses. Then have dinner, much too late, consumed with a sick sense of failure.

Jonathan Franzen, about a bad patch he endured writing The Corrections

The broken marriages, the ruinous addiction, the living in penury, the lower back pain — all these you feed back into your work. Take yourself too seriously and you're lost. You'll wind up teaching creative writing somewhere.

Neil Gaiman

A famous writer who wants to continue writing has to be constantly defending himself against fame.

Gabriel Garcia Marquez

I often get very tense working, so I often have to get up and wander around the house. It's very bad on my stomach.

William Gass

Don't be a writer. Nobody asked you to be a writer. This is what it costs. This is what you have to do. If you can't take it, don't do it.

Dashiell Hammett, to his lover, Lillian Hellman, during the writing of her first play, The Children's Hour

I know no one but you who can be fully sensible of the turmoil and anxiety, the sacrifice of all what is called comfort, the readiness to measure time by what is done and to die in six hours could plans be brought to conclusions — the looking upon the sun, the moon, the stars, the earth and its contents, as materials to form greater things — that is to say ethereal things.

John Keats

Contrary to what many of you might imagine, a career in letters is not without its drawbacks — chief among them the unpleasant fact that one is frequently called upon to actually sit down and write. This demand is peculiar to the profession and, as such, galling, for it is a constant reminder to the writer that he is not now, nor will he ever really be, like other men.

Fran Lebowitz

Writers always love distraction: I'm always happy for a day I don't have to write. But if I go long enough without it, it's like going without exercise. I miss it and after a while I get restless.

Robert B. Parker

I loathe writing. On the other hand, I'm a great believer in money.

S.J. Perelman

It almost seems as though a writer's works, like the water in an artesian well, mount to a height which is in proportion to the depth to which suffering has penetrated his heart.

Marcel Proust

Writing isn't hard work, it's a nightmare. Coal mining is hard work. This is a nightmare... . There's a tremendous uncertainty that's built into the profession, a sustained level of doubt that supports you in some way. A good doctor isn't in a battle with his work. In most professions there's a beginning, a middle, and an end. With writing, it's always beginning again.

Philip Roth

One holds so much of a novel in one's head during the years of work that when it's done and the thing in your head evaporates it's a little like having your brain removed. I felt lobotomized.

Salman Rushdie

Writing is not a profession but a vocation of unhappiness.

Georges Simenon

I am so sick of ... feeling that nothing I can possibly ever say can convey what it's like to be inside this particular skull.

Jean Stafford

Must remember the trouble I had in *Mice & Men*. Thought I'd never get it done or make it work. I don't know. Every book seems the struggle of a whole life. And then, when it is done — pouf. Never happened. Best thing is to get the words down every day. And it is time to start now.

John Steinbeck, from his writing diary

I get a fine feels when I'm doing well, but that pleasure is pretty much negated by the pain of getting started each day. Let's face it, writing is hell.

William Styron

The good writing of any age has always been the product of someone's neurosis, and we'd have a mighty dull literature if all the writers that came along were a bunch of happy chuckleheads.

William Styron

I'm always full of a nameless apprehension. I have written nine contemporary novels, but I send them off with my heart in my mouth and then I pace round chewing my cuticles until somebody rings to say it's all right. I try not to tell other people how I'm feeling because whingeing is so unattractive. But I do worry. I do need the seal of approval from outside.

Joanna Trollope

I think my fiction is better than it was, but writing is also less *Fun*

”

I always think about people that write books. What a horrible feeling it must be to have poured your soul into a book over a number of years and somebody comes up to you and goes, "I loved your book," and they walk away, and you have no idea what worked and what didn't. That to me is hell.

Jerry Seinfeld

”

I try to write a thousand words every day. I've actually put up my daily word counts online for my last several novels. I do this to keep myself honest, saying exactly when I wrote what part of the book. Certainly the comment I most often get is, "That's not really a lot of words," but it goes to show that just steadily working will get you a book. I try to make a thousand words a day, but that isn't always the reality.

Holly Black

than it was. I have a lot of dread and terror and inadequacy-shit, now, when I'm trying to write. I didn't used to. Maybe the terror is part of the necessary reverence, and maybe it's an inescapable part of the growing-up-as-a-writer-or-whatever process; but it can't — *cannot* — be the goal and terminus of that process. In other words there must be some way to turn terror into Respect and dread into a kind of stolidly productive humility.

David Foster Wallace

As long as I'm working I feel all right, but in between stories it's rotten.

P.G. Wodehouse

Old-pro novelists harbour a crusty collegiality borne of the awareness of the attrition involved in pushing that cannon up the hill, enduring false starts, racking fatigue, spent livers, sunken eyeballs, crises of faith, year-round seasonal affective disorder and carpal tunnel syndrome, only to stagger into publication day and have Michiko Kakutani of *The New York Times* nail them in the neck with a poison blow dart.

James Wolcott, about writers like Mailer, Styron, Roth, and Vidal

Writing Speed

All through my career I've written 1,000 words a day — even if I've got a hangover. You've got to discipline yourself if you're professional. There's no other way.

J.G. Ballard

One thing that helps is to give myself permission to write badly. I tell myself that I'm going to do my five or 10 pages no matter what, and that I can always tear them up the following morning if I want. I'll have lost nothing — writing and tearing up five pages would leave me no further behind than if I took the day off.

Lawrence Block

I wish I were faster, and more fluent, that I knew much sooner what I was going for. I wish I were more efficient in every way. I'm just not, and I can't seem to do anything about it. It just takes many months of scrabbling around in swampy territory to figure out what it is that I want. There's always a point at which I think I have a final draft, then I read it and ask myself, "Why have I written this?" Then I go back and write it again and that's the final draft.

Deborah Eisenberg

I write slowly, because I write badly. I have to rewrite everything many many times just to achieve mediocrity.

William Gass

You know that I write slowly. This is chiefly because I am never satisfied until I have said as much as possible in a few words, and writing briefly takes far more time than writing at length.

Carl Gauss

Writing, When To Stop

I don't believe in draining the reservoir, do you see? I believe in getting up from the typewriter, away from it, while I still have things to say.

Henry Miller

You go with what's alive. Two thousand pages of narrative and six lines of dialogue may be just the ticket for one writer, and two thousand pages of dialogue and six lines of narrative the solution for another.

Philip Roth

Keep going. Writing is finally play, and there's no reason why you should get paid for playing. If you're a real writer, you write no matter what. No writer need feel sorry for himself if he writes and enjoys the writing, even if he doesn't get paid for it.

Irwin Shaw

Beware of creating tedium! I know no guard against this so likely to be effective as the feeling of the writer himself. When once the sense that the thing is becoming long and has grown upon him, he may be sure that it will grow upon his readers.

Anthony Trollope

Write without pay until someone offers pay. If nobody offers within three years, the candidate may look upon this as a sign that sawing wood is what he was intended for.

Mark Twain

Young Adult

As a child, I read because books — violent and not, blasphemous and not, terrifying and not — were the most loving and trustworthy things in my life. I read widely, and loved plenty of the classics so, yes, I recognized the domestic terrors faced by Louisa May Alcott's March sisters. But I became the kid chased by werewolves, vampires, and evil clowns in Stephen King's books. I read books about monsters and monstrous things, often written with monstrous language, because they taught me how to battle the real monsters in my life.

And now I write books for teenagers because I vividly remember what it felt like to be a teen facing everyday and epic dangers. I don't write to protect them. It's far too late for that. I write to give them weapons — in the form of words and ideas — that will help them fight their monsters. I write in blood because I remember what it felt like to bleed.

Sherman Alexie

Kids will read up but not down; they will pick up a book about a kid a few years older than they are but not the other way around.

Nora Raleigh Baskin

There has been a sanitization. The YA of my era — of the '70s and '80s — was able to be explicit, because no one was looking at it. Readers hunger for anything they actually experience.

Lizzie Skurnick

Children have a deep desire to live inside the books they read. Create a world they can't wait to go back to and you've developed a captive audience that's difficult to replicate among adults.

R.L. Stine

The content that they're pushing on young people is not what they want to read. There's so much anxiety coming from social media with teenagers that we have to give them characters that are real and that are not always happy; and that have bad parents and not great, supportive parents; and that are not going on these journeys to save the world with a bow.

Anna Todd

Afterword

Finis to all the manuscripts I've
penned,
And to life's fitful fever here an end,
An end to lime-white women
golden-tressed,
And in God's hand at Judgment be
the rest.

Anonymous, 16th century

Let me sum it up for you.
• Information is not knowledge.
• Knowledge is not wisdom.
• Wisdom is not truth.
• Truth is not beauty.
• Beauty is not love.
• Love is not music.
• Music is the best.

Frank Zappa

Illustration Credits

Every attempt was made to secure photos only from the public domain, Creative Commons licensed, or other permissible sources.

11: Chester Himes by Carl Van Vechten, Library of Congress, Prints & Photographs Division, Carl Van Vechten Collection, [reproduction number, e.g., LC-USZ62-54231]
12: Eric Simonoff courtesy of Henrypenn1, Wikipedia
15: Leslie Fiedler, Jac. de Nijs / Anefo (Wikipedia)
20: Debbie Macomber, Deborah Feingold, https://www.prhspeakers.com/speaker/debbie-macomber
27: Clive Barker, courtesy of Steven Friedrich, Wikipedia
41: Christopher Myers, courtesy of the author
62: Thomas Pynchon, Simpsons screen grab
68: Edmund White, David Shankbone, Wikipedia
97: Sophie Hannah, courtesy of Edwardx, Wikipedia
98: Nora Ephron, courtesy of Penguin Random House, Ilona Lieberman
100: Alice Hoffman, courtesy of Deborah Feingold, https://www.hadassahmagazine.org/2008/06/02/profile-alice-hoffman/
102: Nuruddin Farah, courtesy of Nuruddin Farah, Wikipedia
104: Barbara Kingsolver, courtesy of Steven L. Hopp, official website
105: Chinua Achebe, courtesy of Stuart C. Shapiro, Wikipedia
106: John Edgar Wideman, courtesy of Geoffrey A. Landis, Wikipedia
107: Bill Roorbach, courtesy of Mellllll582, Wikipedia
117: Sylvia Plath, Giovanni Giovannetti/Grazia Neri, Wikipedia
121: Gilbert Seldes, courtesy of Carl Van Vechten
126: Norman Mailer, courtesy Grlucas from Wikipedia, https://commons.wikimedia.org/wiki/File:Norman_Mailer,_2006.jpg
127: Terry Pratchett, Rob Wilkins/Courtesy of Doubleday
128: Wilkie Collins, Illustrated Caricature of Wilkie Collins (https://commons.wikimedia.org/wiki/Main_Page) by Frederick Waddy
129: Mary McCarthy, Dick DeMarsico, World Telegram staff photographer - Library of Congress. New York World-Telegram & Sun Collection. http://hdl.loc.gov/loc.pnp/cph.3c14725
136: Hampton Fancher, Flickr, courtesy of Gage Skidmore
137: Helen Prejean, Penguin Random House Speakers Bureau
138: Gabor Szekely, courtesy of Gjshisha, Wikipedia
142: Edna O'Brien, courtesy of Andrew Lih, Wikipedia
143: Lionel Shriver, courtesy of Tony Sarowitz, Wikipedia
144: Tom Wolfe, courtesy of MoSchle, Wikipedia
154: Porochista Khakpour, author photo, https://porochistakhakpour.com/bio/
156: Sean Connery, courtesy of Stuart Crawford at https://www.flickr.com/photos/potatojunkie/
158: Susan Sontag, courtesy of Lynn Gilbert, Wikipedia
162: Neil Gaiman, courtesy of Kyle Cassidy
175: T. Coraghessian Boyle, author website
176: Dale Peck, Penguin Random House
177: Colette, courtesy of Henri Manuel, Wikipedia
177: Gerald M. Kilby, author website
180: Lee Goldberg, author photo
182: Erica Jong, author photo
195: Jeff Koons, courtesy of Bengt Oberger, Wikipedia
199: Carl Van Vechten, Wikipedia
206: Alexander Chee, © 2018 Larry D. Moore, Wikipedia
213: Ray Bradbury, courtesy of Alan Light, Wikipedia
216: Danielle Steel, author photo
217: Fred Allen, publicity photo, Wikipedia
220: Krishmamurti, author photo
227: Chuck Palahniuk, Twitter profile
231: Nora Roberts, author photo
232: Scott Spencer courtesy of Robert Birnbaum
236: James Thurber, Wikicommons
237: William Saroyan, courtesy of Tzolag Hovsepian, Wikicommons
238: Isaac Bashevis Singer, Israel Press and Photo Agency (I.P.P.A.) / Dan Hadani collection, National Library of Israel, Wikipedia
245: J.K. Rowling, Twitter profile
250: Holly Black, courtesy of the author
251: Frank Zappa, album cover

Index

A **bold** page number means the person's photo or book cover the quote is from is on that page.
Page numbers with (2) or (3) after them means there are that many quotes by that person on the page.

Abbey, Edward (1927-1989): 201
Abbott, Rachel (b. 1952): **30**
Abdel-Magied, Yassmin (b. 1991): 143
Abelard, Peter (c. 1979-1142): 224
Achebe, Chinua (1930-2013): **105**
Ackerman, Diane (b. 1948): 59, **66**
Adams, Cara Blue: 115
Adams, Douglas (1952-2001): 55, 131, **242**
Adams, Franklin Pierce (1881-1960): 243
Adams, Henry (1838-1918): 218
Adams, Scott (b. 1957): **45**, 88
Addison, Joseph (1672-1719): 44, 50
Adler, Renata (b. 1937): **21**, 166, 213
Aiken, Conrad (1889-1973): 61
Aiken, Howard (1900-1973): 132
Alain (E.A. Chartier) (1868-1951): 71
Alcott, Louisa May (1832-1888): **74**, 116
Aldiss, Brian (1925-2017): 76, 218
Aldrich, Thomas Bailey (1836-1907): 73
Aldridge, John W. (1922-2007): 115
Alexander, Lloyd (1924-2007): 76
Alexie, Sherman (b. 1966): 251
Algren, Nelson (1909-1981): 14, 50, 69, 118, 136, 153, 187, 218, 233
Allen, Fred (1894-1956): 217
Allen, Woody (b. 1935): 217
Allende, Isabel (b. 1942): 111, 217
Almond, Steve (b. 1966): 16, 105, 156
Altacruise, Chris: 115, 142
Aluetta, Ken (b. 1942): 235
Ambler, Eric (1909-1998): 199
Ames, Jonathan (b. 1964): 175
Amis, Kingsley (1922-1995): 26, 33, 180, 218, 228
Amis, Martin (b. 1949): 59, 69, **97**, 130, 153, 156, 187, 214
Andersch, Alfred (1914-1980): 186
Angelou, Maya (1928-2014): 79, 208
Anonymous reader: 74
Anonymous: 21, 134, 251
Anouilh, Jean (1910-1987): 195
Anson, Jay (1921-1980): **152**
Aquinas, Thomas (1225-1274): 44
Aragi, Nicole (b. 1962): 30
Arendt, Hannah (1906-1975): 95, 110
Aristotle (384-322 B.C.): **16**
Arnold, Matthew (1822-1888): 48, 78
Asimov, Isaac (1920-1992): **63**, 119, 156, 168, 173, 175, 187, **208** (3), 243
Aslett, Don (b. 1935): 176
Athill, Diana (1917-2019): 183
Atlas, James (1949-2019): 16
Atuchity, Kenneth (b. 1944): 66
Atwood, Margaret (b. 1939): 16, 62, 74, **152**, 235
Atxaga, Bernardo (b. 1951): **134**, 239
Auden, W.H. (1907-1973): 14, 16, 19, 43, 62, 101, 121, 132, 133, 139, 140, 216, 224, 240
Austen, Jane (1775-1817): 15, **231**
Babel, Isaac (1894-1940): 150, 185
Bacchylides (c.518-c.451 B.C.): 132
Bach, Richard (b. 1936): 145
Bacon, Francis (1561-1626): 156
Baekeland, Brooks: 131
Bailey, Paul (b. 1937): 26
Baker, Nicholson (b. 1957): 216, 231
Baker, Russell (1925-2019): **149**
Baldwin, James (1924-1987): 143, 181, 195, 218
Ballard, J.G. (1930-2009): 250
Balzac, Honoré de (1799-1850): 146
Bambara, Toni Cade (1939-1995): **203**
Banville, John (b. 1945): 47
Banzai, Buckaroo: 191
Baring, Maurice (1874-1945): 26
Barker, Clive (b. 1952): **27**, 33, 59, 69, 90, 184, 228, 235, 243
Barnes, Julian (b. 1946): 105
Barry, Dave (b. 1947): **29**, 168
Barth, John (b. 1930): 91, 127, 132, 156, 161, 196, 219
Barthelme, Donald (1931-1989): 228
Barthes, Roland (1915-1980): 100, 228
Barzun, Jacques (1907-2012): 204
Baskin, Nora Raleigh (b. 1961): 251
Bates, Arlo (1850-1918): 44
Baxter, Charles (b. 1947): 21
Beaton, Kate (b. 1983): 176
Beattie, Ann (b. 1947): 217
Beaumont, Charles (1929-1967): 76 (2), 224
Bechdel, Alison (b. 1960): 214
Beckett, Samuel (1906-1989): 92, 103, 118, 219
Beecher, Henry Ward (1813-1887): 30, 88
Beerbohm, Max (1872-1956): 50
Behan, Brendan (1923-1964): 51, 146
Belle, Jennifer (b. 1968): 21
Belloc, Hilaire (1870-1953): 48
Bellow, Saul (1915-2005): 48, 71, 123, 125, 128, 131, 168, 172, **181**, 182, 230, 244
Benchley, Robert (1889-1945): 134, 150
Bendis, Brian Michael (b. 1967): 65
Bennett, Arnold (1867-1931): 125
Benson, A.C. (1862-1925): 111
Berenstain, Stan (1923-2005) and Jan (1923-2012): 51
Berger, Thomas (1924-2014): 244
Bergk, Johann Adam (1769-1834): **155**
Berkmann, Marcus (b. 1960): 150
Bernays, Anne (b. 1930): **192**
Bernhard, Thomas (1931-1989): 24
Berryman, John (1914-1972): 179
Besant, Walter (1836-1901): 148
Bester, Alfred (1913-1987): 214
Betts, Doris (1932-2012): 219
Bierce, Ambrose (1842-c. 1914): 77, 128
Binstead, Arthur (1861-1914): 102
Bird, Brad (b. 1957): 19
Birrell, Augustine (1850-1933): 26
Bissinger, Buzz (b. 1954): 167
Black Anti-Defamation Association: 152
Black, Holly (b. 1971): **250**
Blake, Richard (b. 1960): 77, 86 (2)
Blake, William (1757-1827): 134
Block, Lawrence (b. 1938): 21, 34, 59, 141, 142, 150, 163, 173, **189**, 200, 212 (2), 227, 230, 234, 241, 247, 250
Bloom, Harold (1930-2019): 24
Bogan, Louise (1897-1970): 139
Bombeck, Erma (1927-1996): 191, **234**
Boorstin, Daniel J. (1914-2004): 21, 157, 219
Borges, Jorge Luis (1899-1986): 34, 102
Bova, Ben (1932-2020): 173
Bowen, Catherine Drinker (1897-1973): 103, 119, 217
Bowen, Elizabeth (1899-1973): 56, 62
Boyd, Brian (b. 1952): 34, 66
Boyle, T. Coraghessian (b. 1948): **175**
Bracken, Peg (1918-2007): **89**
Brackett, Leigh (1915-1978): **34**
Bradbury, Ray (1920-2012): 31, 42, 62, 89, 92, 98, 101, 108, 132, 137, 157, 169, 191, 198, **213**, 219, 228, 230, 231, 241, 244
Bradford, Barbara Taylor (b. 1933): 115
Bradley, Marion Zimmer (1930-1999): 128
Brecht, Bertolt (1898-1956): 201
Brenan, Gerald (1894-1987): 85
Brett, Jan (b. 1949): 235
Brett, Simon (b. 1945): 56, **120**, 127
Brilliant, Ashleigh (b. 1933): 103, 157
Brinkley, William (1917-1993): 157
Brontë, Charlotte (1816-1855): 131
Brookner, Anita (1928-2016): 208
Brooks, Mel (b. 1926): **194**
Brooks, Terry (b. 1944): 76
Broun, Heywood (1888-1939): **20**
Brown, Dr. Michael S. (b. 1941): 123
Brown, George Mackay (1921-1996): 90
Brown, Rita Mae (b. 1944): **13**, 16, 29, 82, 103, 182
Broyard, Anatole (1920-1990): 15
Bryan, Mary E. (1846-1913): 203
Bryant, Dorothy (1930-2017): 152
Buchan, John (1875-1940): 78
Buck, Pearl S. (1892-1973): 92
Buckley, Christopher (b. 1952): 167
Buechner, Frederick (b. 1926): 202
Bukowski, Charles (1920-1994): 31, **125**
Bulwer-Lytton, Edward (1803-1873): 80
Burbank, Luther (1849-1926): **197**
Burgess, Anthony (1917-1993): 34, 44, 71, 105, 116, 130, 231, 247

Burgess, Gelett (1866-1951): 23, 62
Burke, James Lee (b. 1936): 244
Burnham, Sophy (b. 1936): 191
Burroughs, Edgar Rice (1875-1950): 229, 239
Burroughs, William S. (1914-1997): 61, 92, 169, **219**
Burton, Isabel (1831-1896): **187**
Burton, Robert (1577-1640): 134
Bushnell, Candace (b. 1958): 108
Butler, Octavia E. (1947-2006): **173**, 176, 191
Butler, Samuel (1835-1902): 26
Byatt, A.S. (b. 1936): 40
Byrne, David (b. 1952): 104
Byron, Lord (1788-1824): 99, 167
Calder, Liz (b. 1938): 101
Caldwell, Erskine (1903-1987): **185**
Calvino, Italo (1923-1985): 113, **218**, 234
Campbell, Hayley (b. 1986): **73**
Camus, Albert (1913-1960): 26, **125**
Capote, Truman (1924-1984): 34, 51, 65 (2), 82, 116, 150, 188, 195, 207, 208, 214, 219, 224, **240**
Card, Orson Scott (b. 1951): 62
Carducho, Vicente (1576-1638): 180
Carlyle, Thomas (1795-1881): **59**
Carnegie, Dale (1888-1955): 34
Carr, Terry (1937-1987): 235
Cartland, Barbara (1901-2000): 66, 172
Carver, Judy (b. 1945): 73
Carver, Raymond (1938-1988): 244
Cather, Willa (1873-1947): 16, 186, 214
Catullus (c.84-c.54 B.C.): 140
Cecil, David (1902-1986): 10
Cervantes (1547-1616): 141
Chabon, Michael (b. 1963): 191
Chamfort, Nicolas-Sebastien (1741-1794): 150
Chandler, Raymond (1888-1959): 34, 48, **82**, 114, 121, 197, 228, 231
Chaon, Dan (b. 1964): 123
Chaplin, Charlie (1889-1977): 43
Char, Rene (1907-1988): 101
Charles, Elizabeth (1828-1896): 41
Chateaubriand, François-René de (1768-1848): **131**
Chaucer, Geoffrey (c. 1340s-1400): **211**
Chee, Alexander (b. 1967): **206**
Cheever, John (1912-1982): 13 (2), 34, 64, 224, 240
Cheever, Susan (b. 1943): 16
Chekhov, Anton (1860-1904): 51, 59, 99, 169, **234**
Chesterfield, Lord (1694-1773): 42
Chesterton, G.K. (1874-1936): 86, 95, 139, 153, 185, 204, 240, 241
Cheuse, Alan (1940-2015): 25
Chevalier, Tracy (b. 1962): 187
Chicago Sun-Times critic: **146**
Child, Lee (b. 1954): 164
Childress, Alice (1916-1994): 219
Chiles, Nick (b. 1965): **11**
Chinese proverb: 34
Chittenden, Meg (1935-2016): 228
Christie, Agatha (1890-1976): 40, 121, **135**, 200, **209**, 231, 235
Churchill, Winston (1874-1965): 191, 247
Ciardi, John (1916-1986): 115, 138
Cicero (106-43 B.C.): **95**, 188
Clancy, Tom (1947-2013): 31, 130, 185, 191, 195
Clark, Mary Higgins (1927-2020): 29, 34, 89, 121, **161**, 169, 197, 214, 219, 235
Clark, Roy Peter (b. 1948): 109
Clarke, Arthur C. (1917-2008): 104, **108**, 130, 145
Clear, James (b. 1986): 85
Cleese, John (b. 1939): 46, 244
Clemens, Olivia (1845-1904): **35**
Close, Chuck (b. 1940): 58, 92
Coady, Lynn (b. 1970): 25
Coben, Harlan (b. 1962): 164, 208
Cochran, Masie: **96**
Cockburn, Catherine (1679-1749): **202**
Cocteau, Jean (1889-1963): 48
Cody, Phil: 167
Coe, Jonathan (b. 1961): 26
Coghlan, Sarah: 92
Coleman, Ashley (b. 1981): 11, 116
Coleman, Elliott: 35
Coleman, JaQuavis: 92
Coleridge, Samuel Taylor (1772-1834): **50**, 68, 90, 134, 139, 153, 231
Colette (1873-1954): 105, **177**
Collins, Jackie (1937-2015): **35**
Collins, Wilkie (1824-1889): **128**
Colton, Charles Caleb (1777-1832): 153
Conan Doyle, Arthur (1859-1930): 105, 119, **120**, 157, 208, 212, **240**
Condon, Richard (1915-1996): 35, 65
Congreve, William (1818-1899): 141
Conkling, Roscoe (1829-1888): 82
Connell, Evan S. (1924-2013): 208
Connelly, Michael (b. 1956): 11, 48, 137, 164 (2), 235
Connery, Sean (1930-2020): **156**
Connolly, Cyril (1903-1974): 67, 80, 105, 154, 188
Conrad, Barnaby (1922-2013): 35, 154
Conrad, Jessie (1873-1936): 35
Conrad, Peter (b. 1948): 146
Conroy, Frank (1936-2005): 71
Cook, Thomas (1947): 35
Cookson, Catherine (1906-1998): 228
Coonts, Stephen (b. 1946): 35
Cooperative Children's Book Center: 40
Copleston, Edward (1776-1849): 164
Coren, Giles (b. 1969): 62
Cornwell, Patricia (b. 1956): 31, 35, 76, 87, 131, **163**
Correia, Larry (b. 1977): 25
Cotterell, Geoffrey (1919-2010): 73
Coward, Noël (1899-1973): **19**, 65
Cowley, Malcolm (1898-1989): 114, 247
Cozzens, James Gould (1903-1978): 188
Crais, Robert (b. 1953): 35, 133, 164, 177
Crane, Stephen (1871-1900): 209
Cranston, Bryan (b. 1956): **179**
Crawford, Michael (b. 1942): **113**
Creeley, Robert (1926-2005): 139
Crichton, Michael (1942-2008): 178, 214, 241
Crisp, Quentin (1908-1999): **80**, 111, 219
Crockett, Davy (1734-1820): **175**
Croker, John Wilson (1780-1857): 167
Cron, Lisa: **36**
Cullen, Countee (1903-1946): 191
Cummings, E.E. (1894-1962): 139, 141
Cunningham, Michael (b. 1952): **60**, 77
Curry, Peggy Simson (1911-1987): 182
Cussler, Clive (1931-2020): 22, 137
Dahl, Roald (1916-1990): 41, 90, 154, 157
Dalrymple, Theodore (b. 1949): 144
Danziger, Paula (1944-2004): **71**
Davenport, Guy (1927-2005): 16, 77
David, Peter (b. 1956): 241
Davies, Robertson (1913-1995): foreword, 20, 22, 42, 43, 51, 63, 87, 88, 93, 111, 116, 131, 132, 146, 150, 154, 157, 165, 169, 178, 183, 188, 194, 204, 212, 235, 240, 248
Day-Lewis, Cecil (1904-1972): 141
De Botton, Alain (b. 1969): **42**, 150
De Vries, Peter (1910-1993): 88
DeLillo, Don (b. 1936): 36, 103, 181, 209, 244
dePaola, Tomie (1934-2020): 188
Deveraux, Jude (b. 1947): 188
Dewey, John (1859-1952): 90
Dexter, Colin (1930-2017): 137, 204
Dexter, Pete (b. 1943): 165, 219
Dick, Philip K. (1928-1982): 174, 204
Dickens, Charles (1812-1870): 21, 63, 85, 167, 248
Dickens, William (b. 1953): 11
Dickey, Colin (b. 1977): 91
Dickey, James (1923-1997): 139
Dickinson, Emily (1830-1886): 148
Diderot, Denis (1713-1784): 203
Didion, Joan (b. 1934): 57, **83**, 123, 201, 207, 220, **223**
Dillard, Annie (b. 1945): 17, **69**, 77, 111, 169, 199, 209, 217, 244
Dinesen, Isak (1885-1962): 212
Dirda, Michael (b. 1948): 110, **118**
Disraeli, Benjamin (1804-1881): 27
Dix, Dorothy (1861-1951): **76**
Doctorow, E.L. (1931-2015): 69, 71, 86, 93, 97, 127, 142, 144, 154, 157, 161, 212, 235, 241
Doerr, Anthony (b. 1973): 191
Dominguez, Adriana: 148

Donaldson, William (1935-2005): 179
Donleavy, J.P. (1926-2017): 214
Dorrance, Gordon (1890-1957): 63
Downey Jr., Robert (b. 1965): 72
Drabble, Margaret (b. 1939): **150**
Drew, Elizabeth (b. 1935): 198
Dryden, John (1631-1700): 235
Du Bois, W.E.B. (1868-1963): **102**
du Maurier, Daphne (1907-1989): **198**
Duberman, Martin (b. 1930): 152
Dubus, Andre (1936-1999): 150, 225
Duhamel, Georges (1884-1966): 103, 131, 198
Duncan, Lois (1934-2016): **36**
Dunn, Katherine (1945-2016): 93, **227**, 235
Dunne, John Gregory (1932-2003): 228
Duras, Marguerite (1914-1996): **184**, 233
Durie, Tristan: **15**
Durrell, Lawrence (1912-1990): **118**, 158
Dyer, Geoff (b. 1958): 72
Dylan, Bob (b. 1941): 46, 141, 145
Ecclesiastes: 191
Eco, Umberto (1932-2016): 85, **92**, 105
Edel, Leon (1907-1997): 22
Edison, Thomas (1847-1931): 191
Editorial, *The Times*: 31
Egan, Jennifer (b. 1962): 79
Eisenberg, Deborah (b. 1945): 67, 72, 169, 184, 209, 214, **246**, 250
Eliot, George (1819-1880): 36, **87**, 225, 240
Eliot, T.S. (1888-1965): 11, 46, 51, 55, 64, 93, 111, 134, 136, 145 (2), 148, 172, 199, 201
Elkin, Stanley (1930-1995): 36, 115, 121, 204, 220
Ellis, Warren (b. 1968): 60
Ellison, Harlan (1934-2018): 45, 60, 65, 158
Ellison, Ralph (1913-1994): **14**
Ellroy, James (b. 1948): 36, 151, 220
Emerson, Ralph Waldo (1803-1882): 17, 36, 57, 67, 87, 103, 105, 114, 131, 151, 158, 195, 228
Englander, Nathan (b. 1970): 207
Ephron, Nora (1941-2012): 93, **98**, 124, 154, 158, 178, 234
Epstein, Joseph (b. 1937): 27, 30, 51, 82, **147**
Erasmus (1469-1536): **28**
Evanovich, Janet (b. 1943): 158, 200
Evans, Harold (1928-2020): 134
Fadiman, Clifton (1904-1999): 42
Fallaci, Oriana (1929-2006): **21**, **243**
Fancher, Hampton (b. 1938): 36, 56, 119, **136**, 158, 236
Fante, John (1909-1983): 236
Farah, Nuruddin (b. 1945): **102**, 201, 241
Fast, Howard (1914-2003): 78, 228, 231
Faulkner, William (1897-1962): 98, 99, 119, 127, 158, 169, 191, 197, **212**, 217, 220, 228, 231
Feirstein, Bruce (b. 1956): 64
Ferber, Edna (1885-1968): 74, 217
Ferrari, Joseph: 232
Fforde, Jasper (b. 1961): **85**
Fiedler, Leslie (1917-2003): **15**, 24, 48, 51, 115, 128
Fifield, Arthur C.: 162
Figes, Eva (1932-2012): 203
Fischer, Tibor (b. 1959): 24
Fitzgerald, F. Scott (1896-1940): 69, **78**, 82, 172, 176, 184, 192, 202, 228, 232, 236
Fitz-Gibbon, Bernice (1894-1982): 46
Flaherty, Alice (b. 1957): 232
Flanagan, Caitlin (b. 1961): 96
Flaubert, Gustave (1821-1880): 17, 27, 66, 103, 147, 158, 169, 214, 220, 248
Fleming, Ian (1908-1964): 199
Flutter, Jane Murray (b. 1935): 74
Foer, Jonathan Safran (b. 1977): 43, 217, 220
Foote, Tim (1926-2016): 64
Ford, Ford Madox (1873-1939): 55, 192
Ford, Richard (b. 1944): 104, 243
Foreman, Jonathan (b. 1965): 143
Forster, E.M. (1879-1970): 31, 68, 186, 241
Forsyth, Frederick (b. 1938): 220
Fowler, Gene (1890-1960): **64**, 192, 236
Fowler, Henry W. (1858-1933): 151
Fowles, John (1926-2005): 48, 58, 74, 167, 192, 220
France, Anatole (1844-1924): 134
Francis, Dick (1920-2010): 22
Frank, Anne (1929-1945): **57**
Frank, Scott (b. 1960): 175
Franklin, Benjamin (1706-1790): 82, 103, 220
Franzen, Jonathan (b. 1959): 22, 48, 57, 110, 116, 119, 125, 129, 143, 145 (2), 147, 158, 180, 234, 241, 248
Frederick, John T. (1893-1975): 10, 21, 36, 83, 90, 105, 142, 182, 186, 192, 236
Freud, Esther (b. 1963): **215**
Friedman, Jane: 116, 147
Friedman, Kinky (b. 1944): 108, 148, 154, 192
Friedman, Ron (b. 1932): **145**
Frost, Robert (1874-1963): 46, 83, 141, 188, 236
Fry, Christopher (1907-2005): 43
Frye, Northrop (1912-1991): 48
Fuentes, Carlos (1928-2012): 220
Fussell, Paul (1924-2012): 60
Gaddis, William (1922-1998): 66, 75
Gaiman, Neil (b. 1960): 60, 68, 115, 116, 126, **162**, 167, 175, 176, 197, 209, 214, 220, 229, 232, **241**, 244, 248
Galbraith, John Kenneth (1908-2006): **150**
Gallagher, Tess (b. 1943): 159
Garcia Marquez, Gabriel (1927-2014): 20, 71, 105, 111, 127, 221, 248
Gardner, John (1933-1982): 17, 72, 78, 137, 173, 196, 204, 212, 242
Garner, Dwight (b. 1965): 11, 44
Garner, Helen (b. 1942): **226**
Gass, William (1924-2017): **78**, 105, 221, 248, 250
Gauss, Carl (1777-1855): 250
Gay, Roxane (b. 1974): 192
Genovese, Eugene D. (1930-2012): 152
George, Elizabeth (b. 1949): **37**, 121, 127
Gibbon, Edward (1737-1794): 93
Gibbs, Wolcott (1902-1958): 48, 63
Gibson, William (b. 1948): 108, 192, 236
Gide, Andre (1869-1951): 36
Giff, Patricia Reilly (b. 1935): **37**
Ginsberg, Allen (1926-1997): 202
Giovanni, Nikki (b. 1943): 69, 119
Giraudoux, Jean (1882-1944): **133**
Gissing, George (1857-1903): 117
Glasgow, Ellen (1873-1945): 225
Glasser, Milton (1929-2020): 45
Godden, Rumer (1907-1998): 67
Goethe, Johann (1749-1832): 17, 103, 139, 154
Gold, Herbert (b. 1924): 221
Goldberg, Lee (b. 1962): **180**
Goldberg, Natalie (b. 1948): **66**, 192, 214, 236
Golden, Marita (b. 1950): **140**
Goldin, Stephen (b. 1947): 26, 162, 180
Goldman, William (1931-2018): **235**
Goldsmith, Oliver (1728-1774): 80, 145, 186, 188, 242
Goldsmith, Olivia (1954-2004): **157**
Gómez de la Serna, Ramón (1888-1963): 124
Goncourt Brothers: 15
Goncourt, Edmond (1822-1896): 91, 111
Goodman, Paul (1911-1972): 17, 245
Gordimer, Nadine (1923-2014): 87
Gordon, William J.J. (1919-2003): 46
Gorey, Edward (1925-2000): **16**, 127
Gornick, Vivian (b. 1935): 111
Gottlieb, Robert (b. 1931): 64, 122, 200
Gould, Emily (b. 1981): 203
Gould, Nat (1857-1919): 117, 144, 165, 183, 236, 240
Gradinger, Rebecca: 29
Grafton, Sue (1940-2017): 36, **47**, 121, 215
Graham, Katherine (1917-2001): 203
Graham, Martha (1894-1991): **59**
Graham's Lady Magazine: **166**
Grant, D.I. Alan: 80
Grant, Ulysses S. (1822-1885): 83
Grass, Günter (1927-2015): 87
Graves, Robert (1895-1985): 19, 139, 141
Greeley, Andrew (1928-2013): 154
Green, John (b. 1977): 79
Green, Julien (1900-1998): 236
Greenburg, Dan (b. 1936): 242
Greene, Bob (b. 1947): 10, 48, **110**
Greene, Graham (1904-1991): 20, **56**, 73, 148, 221, 230

Greer, John Michael (b. 1962): 159
Griffiths, Eric (1953-2018): 165
Grigson, Geoffrey (1905-1985): 10
Grisham, John (b. 1955): 51, 60, 75, 81, 132, 199, 245
Griswold, Rufus (1815-1857): **50**, 167
Guedalla, Philip (1889-1944): 23, 87
Guest, Judith (b. 1936): 178
Gurganus, Allan (b. 1947): 46, 105, 205
Hailey, Arthur (1920-2004): 70
Hale, Constance (b. 1958): 83
Hall, Donald (1928-2018): 111
Halliwell, Leslie (1929-1989): **136**
Hamill, Pete (1935-2020): 114
Hammett, Dashiell (1894-1961): 248
Hampton, Christopher (b. 1946): 51
Hanff, Helene (1916-1997): **55**
Hannah, Sophie (b. 1971): **97**
Hansberry, Lorraine (1930-1965): **135**
Hardwick, Elizabeth (1916-2007): 82, **230**
Hardy, Thomas (1840-1928): 118
Harmon, Dan (b. 1973): 46
Harrison, Colin (b. 1960): 70, 202, 232
Hart-Davis, Rupert (1907-1999): 122
Haskell, Molly (b. 1939): 100
Hattori, Akira: **190**
Hawthorne, Nathaniel (1804-1864): 82, 87, 106, 119
Hayakawa, S.I. (1906-1992): 159
Haycraft, Colin (1905-1985): 12
Haydn, Joseph (1732-1809): **219**
Hays, Will (1879-1954): 10
Haywood, Eliza (c. 1693-1756): 183
Hazlitt, William (1778-1830): 95, 176, 189, 194
Hazzard, Shirley (1931-2016): 196
Heaney, Seamus (1939-2013): 197
Hebbel, Friedrich (1813-1863): 136
Hecht, Ben (1894-1964): **48**
Heine, Heinrich (1797-1856): **32**, 134, 138
Heinemann, William (1863-1920): 12
Heinlein, Robert (1907-1988): 32, **63**, 154, 236, 245
Heller, Joseph (1923-1999): 215
Hemingway, Ernest (1899-1961): 36, 68, 79, 84, 123, 172, 175, 189, 192, 194, 213, 215, 229, 237 (2), 245
Hemingway, Gregory (1931-2001): 74
Henahan, Donal (1921-2012): 112
Hendra, Tony (b. 1941): 133
Henry, O. (1862-1910): 103, 184, 209, 232
Hensher, Philip (b. 1965): 37
Hepburn, Katharine (1907-2003): 66
Herbert, Frank (1920-1986): 85
Herbert, Zbigniew (1924-1988): 10
Hersey, John (1914-1993): 229
Hesse, Herman (1877-1962): 100
Heyer, Georgette (1902-1974): **62**, 147, 173
Higgins, George V. (1939-1999): 37, 57, 71, 154, 205, **223**
Highsmith, Patricia (1921-1995): 48, 103, 186, 198
Hills, Rust (1924-2008): 37, 137, 242
Hilton, James (1900-1954): 37
Himes, Chester (1909-1984): **11**
Hippocrates (c.460-c.370 B.C.): 213
Hitchcock, Alfred (1899-1980): 107, **137**
Hitchens, Christopher (1949-2011): 60, 112, 229
Hitt, Orrie (1916-1975): 162, 209
Hoban, Russell (1925-2011): 41, 221
Hoffman, Alice (b. 1952): **100**
Holmes, Oliver Wendell (1841-1935): 67, 132
Hood, Thomas (1799-1845): 169
Hoover, Michelle: 29
Hopper, William DeWolf (1858-1935): 72
Hornby, Nick (b. 1957): 17, 117
Housman, A.E. (1859-1936): 139
Howard, Elizabeth Jane (1923-2014): **130**, 221
Howells, William Dean (1837-1920): 44
Hubbard, Elbert (1856-1915): 64, 131, 180
Hughes, Langston (1901-1967): 12, **88**
Hughes, Ted (1930-1998): 232
Hugo, Victor (1802-1885): 90, 159, 198
Hunter, Evan (1926-2005): 79, 148, 171, 221
Hurston, Zora Neale (1891-1960): 54
Huxley, Aldous (1894-1963): 27, 69, 70, 196, 221
Ibn Gabirol, Solomon (1021/1022-1070?): 49
Ihimaera, Witi (b. 1944): **54**, 151
Inge, William (1913-1973): 17
Ingham, Bernard (b. 1932): 82
Innes, Hammond (1913-1998): 27
Irving, John (b. 1942): 13, 32, 127, 170, 229
Irving, Washington (1783-1859): 49, 87
Isherwood, Christopher (1904-1986): 95
Jackson, Shirley (1916-1965): **124**, 181
Jacobson, Howard (b. 1942): 183
Jaffe, Michele (b. 1970): 172
James, Clive (1939-2019): 17
James, Henry (1843-1916): 17, 37, 51, 117, 125, 136, 167, 187
James, Marlon (b. 1970): **44**, 85, 159, 183, 226
James, P.D. (1920-2014): 26, **99**, 122, 128, 148, 189
James, William (1842-1910): 58
Jamison, Kay Redfield (b. 1946): **114**
Jamison, Leslie (b. 1983): 115
Jarrell, Randall (1914-1965): 154
Jefferson, Thomas (1743-1826): 32, 125, 205
Jennings, Elizabeth (1926-2001): 52
Jerome, Jerome K. (1859-1927): 200
Jillette, Penn (b. 1955): 125
Jobs, Steve (1955-2011): 17, 103
Johnson, Diane (b. 1934): **23**
Johnson, Joyce (1935): 97, 209
Johnson, Paul (b. 1928): 176
Johnson, Rebecca (b. 1966): 24
Johnson, Samuel (1709-1784): 10, 14, 16, 21, 24, 27, 49, 52 (2), 63, 73, 75, 76, 85, 101, 103 (2), 189, 207, 213
Johnston, Tony (b. 1970): 170
Jones, James (1921-1977): 14, 205, 207, 221
Jong, Erica (b. 1942): **182**, 195, 245
Jong-Fast, Molly (b. 1978): 165, 221
Jordan, Hillary (b. 1963): **32**
Joseph, Michael (1897-1958): 21
Joyce, Nora (1884-1951): 37
Joyce, James (1882-1941): **75**, 91, 194
Jung, Carl (1875-1961): 17
Juster, Norton (b. 1929): 41
Kael, Pauline (1919-2001): 95, **164**
Kafka, Franz (1883-1924): 57, 159
Kahn, Roger (1927-2020): 176
Kaiser, Ernest: 152
Kantor, MacKinlay (1904-1977): 242
Kaplan, Harold (1927-1998): 96
Karr, Mary (b. 1955): 229
Kaufman, Margo (1954-2000): **88**
Kavanagh, Patrick (b. 1946): 141
Kazin, Alfred (1915-1998): **43**, 178, 179, 185
Keats, John (1795-1821): 17, 60, 68, 101, 248
Keillor, Garrison (b. 1942): 13, 159, 184
Kelman, James (b. 1946): 32, 174
Kemelman, Harry (1908-1996): 198
Kenko, Yoshida (1283-1350): **103**
Kennedy, A.L. (b. 1965): 97, **187**
Kerouac, Jack (1922-1969): 49, 202
Kerr, Jean (1922-2003): **210**
Kesey, Ken (1935-2001): 73, **93**
Kettering, Charles (1876-1958): **72**
Khakheperreseneb: 132
Khakpour, Porochista: **154**
Kidd, Chip (b. 1964): **25**, 101, 104, 109
Kilby, Gerald M.: **177**
Killens, John Oliver (1916-1987): 122
Kilpatrick, James J. (1920-2010): 205, 242
Kim, Angie (b. 1969): 179
Kim, Suki (b. 1970): 143
King, Florence (1936-2016): 58
King, Larry L. (1929-2012): 237
King, Stephen (b. 1947): 25, 32, 47, 68, 75, 76, 78, 79, 83, 87, 93, 97, 106, 129, **158**, 184, 192, 201, 221 (2), 229, 237, 245
Kingsolver, Barbara (b. 1955): 104, **130**, **247**
Kinsella, W.P. (1935-2016): 159
Kipling, Rudyard (1865-1936): 135, 151, 205, **230**
Klein, Arnold: 174
Kleon, Austin (b. 1983): 47, 109, 133, 207
Kloos, Marko (b. 1971): 229

Klosterman, Chuck (b. 1972): **51**
Knausgaard, Karl Ove (b. 1968): 112
Knopf, Alfred (1892-1984): 163
Kolloen, Ingar (b. 1951): 209
Koons, Jeff (b. 1955): **195**
Koontz, Dean (b. 1945): 12, 88, 94, 226
Korda, Michael (b. 1933): 177, 210
Kosinski, Jerzy (1933-1991): 54, 78
Kraus, Karl (1874-1936): 98, 106, 189, 200
Krishnamurti, Jiddu (1895-1986): 68, **220**
Krishna: **10**
Kumin, Maxine (1925-2014): 138
Kureishi, Hanif (b. 1954): 222
Kwok, Jean (b. 1968): 96
Lafferty, R.A. (1914-2002): 24, 101, 159, 174
Lagerfeld, Karl (1933-2020): **65**, 222
Lambuth, David (1879-1948): **205**
Lamott, Anne (b. 1954): **56**, 134, 210, 215
L'Amour, Louis (1908-1988): 113, 215
Locker-Lampson, Frederick (1821-1895): 145
Landis, Max (b. 1985): 49
Landor, Walter Savage (1775-1864): 41, 42
Lane, Anthony (b. 1962): 80
Lang, Andrew (1844-1912): 154
Larkin, Philip (1922-1985): 139, 163
Larner, Jeremy (b. 1937): 190
LaValle, Victor (b. 1972): 81, 162
Lawrence, D.H. (1885-1930): 52, 131, 148, 217
Lawrence, Jerome (1915-2004): 88
Leacock, Stephen (1869-1944): 42, 108, 237
Leather, Stephen (b. 1956): 109
Lebowitz, Fran (b. 1950): 27, **60**, 148, 249
Le Carré, John (1931-2020): 120, 137
Lederer, Richard (b. 1938): 83
Lee, Gypsy Rose (1911-1970): 117
Lee, Harper (1926-2016): **31**, 226
Lee-Potter, Lynda (1935-2004): 203
Lees-Milne, James (1908-1997): 61
Le Gallienne, Richard (1866-1947): 231
Le Guin, Ursula K. (1929-2018): 13, 131, **153**, 186, **236**
L'Engle, Madeleine (1918-2007): 37, 41, 109, 154
Lennon, John (1940-1980): 229
Leonard, Elmore (1925-2013): 37, 57, 83, 120
Leopardi, Giacomo (1798-1837): 25
Lerner, Betsy: **51**, 73, 77, 117, 119, 123, 163, 170, 171, 187, 192, 215
Lescroart, John (b. 1948): 133
Lessing, Doris (1919-2013): **92**, 234
Levin, Martin (1919-2008): 190
Levine, Philip (1928-2015): 91
Lewis, C.S. (1898-1963): 61, 83
Lewis, Gwyneth (b. 1959): 56
Lewis, Michael (b. 1960): 49, 52, 98, 124
Lewis, Sinclair (1885-1951): 10, 52, 123, **233**
Li, Yiyun (b. 1972): 14
Lichtenberg, Georg Christoph (1742-1799): 27, 148, **153**
Liebling, A.J. (1904-1963): 242
Lileks, James (b. 1958): 61
Lind, Michael (b. 1962): 165
Lippman, Laura (b. 1959): 112, **168**, 193
Lipsyte, Robert (b. 1938): 150
Lish, Gordon (b. 1934): **76**, 195
Lisle, Holly (b. 1960): 170
Lo, Malinda (b. 1974): 117
Lodge, David (b. 1935): 24, 106
Loewy, Raymond (1893-1986): **25**
Lombardi, Vince (1913-1970): 14
London, Jack (1876-1916): 15, 94
Longfellow, Henry Wadsworth (1807-1882): 47
Lopez, Barry (b. 1945): 104
Lorde, Audre (1934-1992): 77
Lounger, The: 196
Lovecraft, H.P. (1890-1937): **109**, 162
Lowell, A. Lawrence (1856-1943): 117
Lowell, Amy (1874-1925): 66
Lowell, James Russell (1819-1891): 135
Lowell, Robert (1917-1977): 114
Luce, Kelly: 64
Ludlum, Robert (1927-2001): **186**
Lukas, J. Anthony (1933-1997): **83**
Luther, Martin (1483-1546): 27
Lutwack, Leonard (1917-2008): 99
Lynch, David (b. 1946): **244**
Lynch, Scott (b. 1978): 75
Macaulay, Thomas Babington (1800-1859): 41, 83
Macdonald, Dwight (1906-1982): 168
MacDonald, John D. (1916-1986): 122, 148, 160
Machado, Antonio (1875-1939): 145
MacLeish, Archibald (1892-1982): 195
Macomber, Debbie (b. 1948): **20**, 94, 163, 210
Mailer, Norman (1923-2007): 32, 52, 54, 99, 101, **126**, 137, 163, 177, 196, 210, 222, 232
Mailer, Norris Church (1949-2010): **185**
Malamud, Bernard (1914-1986): **43**, 52, 63, 184, 226, 237
Malik, Nesrine: 143
Mamet, David (b. 1947): 37, 231
Mandela, Nelson (1918-2013): 45
Mansfield, Katherine (1888-1923): 101
Mantel, Hilary (b. 1952): **24**, 110, 245
Marchbanks, Samuel: 53, 89
Marquis, Don (1878-1937): 132, 138, 193
Marshall, Colin: 66
Martial, Marcus Valerius (38/41-102/104): **101**
Martin, George R.R. (b. 1948): **89**, 237
Martin, Manjula: 207
Martin, Steve (b. 1945): **191**, 245
Marx, Groucho (1890-1977): **91**, 186
Masterton, G.: 37, 164, 182
Mattoo, Priyanka: 120
Maugham, W. Somerset (1874-1965): 13, 37, 71, 89, 102, 110, 112, 145, 147, 160, 189, 201, 205, 210
Mauriac, Francois (1885-1970): 155
Maurois, Andre (1885-1967): 42
Maxwell, William (1908-2000): 222
Mayle, Peter (1939-2018): 227
Maynard, Joyce (b. 1953): 112, 114
McCall Smith, Alexander (b. 1948): 23, 37, 215
McCarthy, Cormac (b. 1933): 14, **129**
McCarthy, Mary (1912-1989): 129, 222
McCloud, Scott (b. 1960): 44, **70**, 226
McCourt, Frank (1930-2009): 113, 117, 222
McCullough, Colleen (1937-2015): 237
McEwan, Ian (b. 1948): 116, 129, 215
McFarlane, Leslie (1902-1977): 133
McGrath, Charles: 64
McGrath, Patrick (b. 1950): 14
McKillop, Alan: 126
McLuhan, Marshall (1911-1980): 193
McManus, Patrick F. (1933-2018): 237
McMillan, Terry (b. 1951): 65, **77**, 137
McMurtry, Larry (b. 1936): 38, 182, 245
McNeil, Steve (b. 1979): 12
Melville, Herman (1819-1891): 147, 215
Menaker, Daniel (1941-2020): 63
Mencken, H.L. (1880-1956): **18**, 32, 49, 108, 151, 168, 231, 246
Michaels, Lorne (b. 1944): 138
Michener, James A. (1907-1997): 119, 170, 178
Millay, Edna St. Vincent (1892-1950): 181
Miller, Alice (1923-2010): 194
Miller, Arthur (1915-2005): 49, 136, 217
Miller, Henry (1891-1980): 58, 132, 250
Millett, Kate (1934-2017): 238
Milne, A.A. (1882-1956): 117
Milton, John (1608-1674): **27**, 32, 135
Mitchard, Jacquelyn (b. 1956): 164
Mitchel, John (1815-1875): 27
Mizner, Wilson (1876-1933): 53, 135, 141, 160
Molière (1622-1673): **239**
Montaigne, Michel de (1533-1592): title page, 10, 73, 135
Montesquieu, Charles de (1689-1755): 21
Montgomery, L.M. (1874-1942): **14**, 242
Montherlant, Henri de (1895-1972): 27
Moore, Alan (b. 1953): **116**
Moore, Dinty W. (b. 1955): 193
Moore, Julia A. (1847-1920): 20, 207
Moore, Lorrie (b. 1957): 229
Moore, Marianne (1887-1972): 238
Moore, Susanna (b. 1945): **121**
Moore, Thomas (1779-1852): 114

Moore, Wayétu (b. 1985): 114
Moran, Caitlin (b. 1975): 222, **248**
Moravia, Alberto (1907-1990): **93**, 229
Morgan, J.P. (1837-1913): 119
Morrell, David (b. 1943): 202
Morrison, Blake (b. 1950): 102
Morrison, Toni (1931-2019): 20, 38, 53, 64, 81, 94, 100, 106, 128, 144, **171**, 197, 215, 232
Mortimer, John (1923-2009): 122, **201**
Moshfegh, Ottessa (b. 1981): **64**
Mowat, Farley (1921-2014): 71
Muir, Frank (1920-1998): 22
Mukherjee, Bharati (b. 1940-2017): 38
Müller, Max (1823-1900): 100
Murakami, Haruki (b. 1949): 38, 75, **95**, 120, 133, 155, 160, 162, 172, 186, 189, 210, 232, 246
Murdoch, Iris (1919-1999): 90, **106**, 128, 168, 242
Murray, Donald M. (1925-2007): 79, 124
Murray, Jim (1919-1998): 238
Myers, B.R. (b. 1963): 15, 183, 205
Myers, Christopher (b. 1975): **41**
Myers, Walter Dean (1937-2014): 148, **151**
Myhrvold, Nathan (b. 1959): 55
N.Y. Publisher: 163
Nabokov, Vladimir (1899-1977): 38, 63, 64, 81, 91, 112, 177, 180, 200, 213, 222
Naipaul, V.S. (1932-2018): 106, 160, 203
Nash, Richard: 30, 149
Naylor, Gloria (1950-2016): **224**
Neruda, Pablo (1904-1973): **53**, 122, 141, 222
New York Herald Tribune, The: 168
New Yorker, The: 190, 218
Nichols, Beverly (1898-1983): 112
Nicoll, James (b. 1961): 100
Nietzsche, Friedrich (1844-1900): 18, 189
Nin, Anaïs (1903-1977): **58**, 61, 126
Nishikawa, Kinohi (b. 1979): 12
Niven, Larry (b. 1938): 38, 189
Nobel Prize judge: 124
Noble, William: 182
Nock, Albert Jay (1870-1945): 116
Nordstrom, Ursula (1910-1988): 178
Norris, Mary (b. 1952): 83
Oates, Joyce Carol (b. 1938): 38, **79**, 92, 172, 210, 232, 246
Oatley, Keith (b. 1939): 66, 78
O'Brian, Patrick (1914-2000): 86, 129, **159**
O'Brien, Edna (b. 1930): **142**, 175
O'Brien, Sharon: 246
O'Connell, Meaghan: 203
O'Connor, Flannery (1925-1964): 38, **114**, 129, 155, 185, 197
O'Donoghue, Michael (1940-1994): 240
O'Hara, John (1905-1970): 193
O'Nan, Stewart (b. 1961): **94**
O'Neill, Eugene (1888-1953): 53, 163
O'Rourke, P.J. (b. 1947): 89, **231**
Okri, Ben (b. 1959): 129
Older, Daniel Jose (b. 1980): 149, **212**
Oliver, Ariadne: 146
Orlean, Susan (b. 1955): 30, 97, 117, **123**
Orwell, George (1903-1950): 28, 30, 32, 41, 69, 96, 119, 165, **204**, 216, 222, 226
Ostman, Cami: **72**
Ovid (43 B.C.-17/18 A.D.): 246
Ozick, Cynthia (b. 1928): 65, **81**, 126, 182
P. Morgan, Edward (1910-1993): 27
Paglia, Camille (b. 1947): 65
Palahniuk, Chuck (b. 1962): 10, 15, 18, 29, 38, 44, 68, 75, 94, 106, 124, 142, 152, 164, 173, 187, 200, 223, **227**, 238, 246
Paleotti, Gabriele (1522-1597): 42
Pamuk, Orhan (b. 1952): 25, 28
Pareto, Vilfredo (1848-1923): 96
Parini, Jay (b. 1948): 113
Parker, Dorothy (1893-1967): 84, 118, 151, 168, **174**, 203, 232, 234, 242
Parker, Joan (1932-2013): 118
Parker, Nate (b. 1979): 152
Parker, Robert B. (1932-2010): 10, 12, 38, 85, 91, **132**, 213, 233, 238, 246, 249
Parr, Jack (1918-2004): 53
Partridge, Andy (b. 1953): 226
Pascal, Blaise (1623-1662): 102
Patchett, Ann (b. 1963): 29, 128
Patten, Brian (b. 1946): 140
Patterson, James (b. 1947): 53, 78, 102, 155, 166, 172, 182, 202, 242
Patterson, Richard North (b. 1947): 38
Patton, Gen. George (1885-1945): **45**
Pavlova, Anna (1881-1931): 193
Payn, James (1830-1898): 166
Peacock, Thomas Love (1785-1866): 151
Pearce, Joseph Chilton (1926-2016): **47**
Pearson, Hesketh (1887-1964): 151
Peck, Dale (b. 1967): 49, 54, 106, 112, 129, 134, 166, **176**, 223, 229
Peck, Richard (1934-2018): 216
Péguy, Charles Pierre (1873-1914): 201, 206
Percy, Walker (1916-1990): 185
Perkins, Max (1884-1947): 53, 65, 67, **132**, 149
Perelman, S.J. (1904-1979): 249
Pérez Galdós, Benito (1843-1920): 18
Perry, Anne (b. 1938): **211**
Peschel, Bill (b. 1960): 102, 112
Peschel, Teresa (b. 1960): 118
Pétain, Henri Philippe (1856-1951): 112
Picasso, Pablo (1881-1973): **17**, 47
Picoult, Jodi (b. 1966): **196**
Plant, Robert (b. 1948): 163
Plath, Sylvia (1932-1963): **117**, 140, 201
Plimpton, George (1927-2003): 22
Poe, Edgar Allan (1809-1849): 22, 62, 184
Pope, Alexander (1688-1744): **134**, 213
Porter, Cole (1891-1964): 42
Porter, Katherine Anne (1890-1980): 65, 82, 128, **188**, 207
Pound, Ezra (1885-1972): 18, 106, 193
Powell, Dawn (1896-1965): 39, **80**, 88, 173, 178, 203, 218
Powell, Padgett (b. 1952): 72
Powers, Richard (b. 1957): 120
Pratchett, Terry (1948-2015): 28, 30, 39, 43, 62, 79, 89, **127**, 138, 166, 194, 197, 201, 246
Pravda: 124
Prejean, Helen (b. 1939): **137**
Prescott, Orville (1906-1996): 190
Price, Leah (b. 1970): 23
Priestly, J.B. (1894-1984): **225**
Pritchett, V.S. (1900-1997): 18, 113, **122**, 185
Pronzini, Bill (b. 1943): 57
Prose, Francine (b. 1947): 143, 243
Proulx, Annie (b. 1935): 90, 100, 122, 160
Proust, Marcel (1871-1922): 18, 53, 110, 249
Provost, Gary (1944-1995): 83, 197, 198
Prynne, William (1600-1669): 136
Pullman, Philip (b. 1946): 20, 33, **90**, 216
Purdy, James (1914-2009): 72
Puzo, Mario (1920-1999): **38**
Pym, Barbara (1913-1980): 179
Pynchon, Thomas (b. 1937): **62**
Quasimodo, Salvatore (1901-1968): 140
Quiller-Couch, Arthur (1863-1944): 242
Ramón Gómez de la Serna (1888-1963): 124
Rankin, Ian (b. 1960): 164, 193
Raven, Simon (1927-2001): 20
Reade, Charles (1814-1884): 238
Reed, Ishmael (b. 1938): 129
Reinhardt, Gottfried (1913-1994): 118
Renard, Jules (1864-1910): 72, 106, 118, 131, 206
Reston, James (1909-1995): 124
Rexroth, Kenneth (1905-1982): 140
Rhodes, Richard (b. 1937): **86**, 133
Rhys, Jean (1890-1979): 55, 201, 206, **221**, 223, 230, 243, 246
Ribblesdale, Lord (1854-1925): 151
Richardson, Mike (b. 1950): 74
Richler, Mordecai (1931-2001): 172, 216
Rickenbacker, Eddie (1890-1973): 45
Rilke, Rainer Maria (1875-1926): **52**
Rinehart, Mary Roberts (1876-1958): **122**
Rivers, Joan (1933-2014): **169**
Robbe-Grillet, Alain (1922-2008): 18, 189
Robbins, Harold (1916-1997): **65**, 155, 223
Robbins, Tom (b. 1932): 189, **214**
Roberts, Nora (b. 1950): 59, 82, 227, **231**, 238
Robinson, Edwin Arlington (1869-1935): 67
Rodriguez, Richard (b. 1944): **107**, 123
Rooney, Andy (1919-2011): 90
Roorbach, Bill (b. 1953): **107**
Ros, Amanda McKittrick (1860-1939): 184

Rosenberg, Harold (1906-1978): 166
Rosoff, Meg (b. 1956): **201**
Ross, Bob (1942-1995): **194**
Roth, Philip (1933-2018): 33, 61, 63, 70, 81, 86, 94, 108, 136, 142, 146, 160, 170, 182, 183, 187, 194, 216, 233, 238, 243, 246, 249, 250
Rowling, J.K. (b. 1965): **33**, 90, 206, 216, 217, 218, **245**
Rule, Ann (1931-2015): **85**
Runyon, Damon (1880-1946): 193
Rushdie, Salman (b. 1947): 70, 249
Ruskin, John (1819-1900): 110
Russell, Bertrand (1872-1970): 10, 73, 160, 238
Russo, Richard (b. 1949): 39, 43, 175
Sackville-West, Vita (1892-1962): 104, 128
Safire, William (1929-2009): 84
Sagan, Carl (1929-2009): 160
Sainte-Beuve, Charles Augustin (1804-1869): 53
Saintsbury, George (1845-1933): 50
Salinger, J.D. (1919-2010): 21, 149, 223, 243
Salter, James (1925-2015): 65
Samoun, Abigail: 41, **148**
Sand, George (1804-1876): **154**
Santayana, George (1863-1952): 53
Saroyan, William (1908-1981): 136, 185, **237**
Sarraute, Nathalie (1900-1999): **139**
Sartre, Jean-Paul (1905-1980): 124
Saunders, George (b. 1958): 181, 210
Sayrafiezadeh, Saïd (b. 1968): 59
Sayers, Dorothy L. (1893-1957): 53, 75, 151, **228**
Scalzi, John (b. 1969): 211
Schappell, Elissa: 170
Schmidt, Michael (b. 1983): 175
Schopenhauer, Arthur (1788-1860): 54, 80, 160
Schulz, Charles M. (1922-2000): 89
Schwartz, Lynne Sharon (b. 1939): 67
Scott, Paul (1920-1978): 206
Scott, Walter (1771-1832): 15
Sedaris, David (b. 1956): **58**
Sedgwick, Anne Douglas (1873-1935): **22**
See, Carolyn (1934-2016): 234
Seinfeld, Jerry (b. 1954): 211, **249**
Seldes, Gilbert (1893-1970): **121**
Self, Will (b. 1961): 20, **196**
Sendak, Maurice (1928-2012): 47, **74**, 77, 247
Seneca the Younger (4 B.C.-65 A.D.): 68
Settle, Mary Lee (1918-2005): 149
Sexton, Anne (1928-1974): **39**, 45, 61, 76, 120, 128, 139, 140, 145, 175, 227
Shaffer, Peter (1926-2016): 136
Shakespeare, William (1564-1616): 13, 186
Shapiro, Dani (b. 1962): 113
Sharpe, Tom (1928-2013): 42
Shaw, George Bernard (1856-1950): 50, 89, 118, 149, 151, 230, 247
Shaw, Irwin (1913-1984): 177, 230
Sheed, Wilfrid (1930-2011): 78, 166, 238
Shelley, Mary (1797-1851): 14
Shelley, Percy Bysshe (1792-1822): 140, 141
Shenk, Joshua Wolf: 79
Sheridan, Richard Brinsley (1751-1816): 135
Shields, Carol (1935-2003): 179
Shirky, Clay (b. 1964): **46**
Shostakovich, Dmitri (1906-1975): 18
Shriver, Lionel (b. 1957): **143** (2), 145
Sibelius, Jean (1865-1957): 54
Sicha, Choire (b. 1971): **117**
Silliphant, Stirling (1918-1996): **49**, 175, 239
Silverstein, Shel (1930-1999): 173, 196
Simenon, Georges (1903-1989): 44, 91, 223, 249
Simic, Charles (b. 1938): 140
Simmons, S.H.: 147
Simon, Misty: 239
Simonoff, Eric (b. 1967): **12**
Simpson, Helen (b. 1957): 59
Sinclair, Upton (1878-1968): 33
Singer, Isaac Bashevis (1903-1991): 39, 70, 108, **238**
Skurnick, Lizzie (b. 1973): 251
Sloane, William (1906-1974): 39, 84
Smiles, Samuel (1812-1904): 72
Smith, Liz (1923-2017): 82
Smith, Logan Pearsall (1865-1946): 22, 66, 231
Smith-Stevens, Emma: 179
Smith, Sydney (1771-1845): 28, **49**, 63, 82, 166
Smith, Zadie (b. 1975): 216
Snicket, Lemony (b. 1970): 31, **40**, 142, **178**
Snyder, Maria V. (b. 1973): **10**
Socrates (c.470-c.399 B.C.): 109, **141**
Solotaroff, Ted (1928-2008): 163, 170, **222**
Solzhenitsyn, Aleksandr (1918-2008): 69
Sontag, Susan (1933-2004): 50, 58, 96, 99, 104, 120, 126, 135, 155, **158**, 179, 206, 247
Sophocles (497/6-406/5 B.C.): 39
Southern Quarterly Review, The: 168
Southey, Robert (1774-1843): 73, 203
Spanbauer, Tom (b. 1946): **200**
Spark, Muriel (1918-2006): 211
Sparks, Nicholas (b. 1965): 22
Spearman, A.D. (1899-1977): 168
Spectator, The: 243
Spencer, Scott (b. 1945): **232**
Spender, Stephen (1909-1995): 233
Spillane, Mickey (1918-2006): 66, **75**, 94, 109
Stafford, Jean (1915-1979): 204, 249
Stahl, Levi: 119
Steel, Danielle (b. 1947): 216
Stegner, Wallace (1909-1993): 162
Steichen, Edward (1879-1973): 47
Stein, Gertrude (1874-1946): 212
Steinbeck, John (1902-1968): 11, 24, 28, 54, 64, 88, 107, 113, **119**, 149, 161, 166, 177, 185, 211, 213, 233, 249
Steinem, Gloria (b. 1934): 80, 247
Stendhal (1783-1842): **42**, 126, 180
Stephens, J.F. (1880-1950): **131**
Stern, Gerald (b. 1925): 68
Sternberg, Josef von (1894-1969): 68
Sterne, Laurence (1713-1768): 135, 234
Stevens, Wallace (1879-1955): 91, 140
Stevenson, Robert Louis (1850-1894): 28, **108**, 185
Stewart, Mary (1916-2014): 86, **181**
Stillman, Peter: 113
Stine, R.L. (b. 1943): 41, 239, 251
Stone, I.F. (1907-1989): 102
Stone, Robert (1937-2015): 14, 130
Stoppard, Tom (b. 1937): 180, 223
Storey, William Kelleher (b. 1955): 124
Storr, Anthony (1920-2001): 233
Strachey, Lytton (1880-1932): 106
Straub, Peter (b. 1943): 170
Straus, Peter: 118
Strayed, Cheryl (b. 1968): **26**, 118
Strindberg, August (1849-1912): 18
Strunk Jr., William (1869-1946): 84, 243
Sturgeon, Theodore (1918-1985): 174
Styron, William (1925-2006): 102, 110, 152, 153 (2), 185, 227, 247, 249 (2)
Suede, Damon: 11, 39, 104, 198, 239
Sumner, Bernard (b. 1956): 47
Susann, Jacqueline (1918-1974): **67**, 147
Swain, Dwight (1915-1992): 66
Swift, Jonathan (1667-1745): 64, 80, 141, **172**, 189
Szekely, Gabor J. (b. 1947): **138**
Talese, Gay (b. 1932): 164, 172, 239
Tan, Amy (b. 1952): 155
Tarkovsky, Andrei (1932-1986): 18
Taylor, Charles: 45
Taylor, Elizabeth (1912-1975): **176**
Taylor, Theodore (1921-2006): 138
Teachout, Terry (b. 1956): **18**
Teller (b. 1948): 67, 92, 98, 194
Tencarre, Kristi: **46**
Tennyson, Alfred Lord (1809-1892): 54
Terence (c.195/185-c. 159? B.C.): 132
Terry, Ellen (1847-1928): 58, 91
Tey, Josephine (1896-1952): **119**
Thackary, William Makepeace (1811-1863): 89
The Christian Examiner: 180
Thelwell, Mike (b. 1939): 153
Theroux, Paul (b. 1941): **70**, 113, 114, 181, 230
Thomas à Kempis (c. 1380-1471): 28

Thomas, Dylan (1914-1953): **139**
Thompson, Jim (1906-1977): 138
Thoreau, Henry David (1817-1862): 31, 43, 45, 70, 84, 161, 171, 182, **184**, 206
Thurber, James (1894-1961): 81, 84, 89, 171, 198, 207, **236**
Todd, Anna (b. 1989): **19**, 77, 81, 180, 251
Toland, John (1670-1722): 177
Tolentino, Jia (b. 1988): 144
Tolkien, J.R.R. (1892-1973): 62, 138
Tolstoy, Leo (1828-1910): 18, 108, 124, 239
Treuer, David (b. 1970): 100
Trevelyan, G.M. (1876-1962): 171
Trillin, Calvin (b. 1935): 74, 149
Trilling, Diana (1905-1996): 96
Trilling, Lionel (1905-1975): 73
Trollope, Anthony (1815-1882): 94, 162, 177, 207, 211, 212, 213, 243, 251
Trollope, Frances (1779-1863): **39**
Trollope, Joanna (b. 1943): **165**, 249
Truby, John (b. 1952): 233
Trudeau, Garry (b. 1948): **172**
Trump, Donald (b. 1946): 102, 147
Tuchman, Barbara (1912-1989): **26**, 104, 124, 247
Tufte, Virginia (1918-2020): 84
Tupper, Martin Farquhar (1810-1889): 28
Twain, Mark (1835-1910): 23, 28, 33, 43, 45, 47, 64, 70, **71**, 76, 78, **84** (2), **87**, 97, **98**, 107, **111**, 125, 132, **133**, 135, 146, 149, 163, 187, **188**, **191**, 193, 198, 206, 213, **218**, **242**, 251
Tyler, Anne (b. 1941): **79**
Tynan, Kenneth (1927-1980): 15, 54, 107, 136
Ugresic, Dubravka (b. 1949): 22, 25, 55, 132
Unamuno, Miguel de (1864-1936): 155
Underhill, Evelyn (1875-1941): 146
Unwin, Stanley (1884-1968): 13
Updike, John (1932-2009): **12**, 19, 39, 50, 97, **103**, 114, 140, 143, 181, 193, 194, 206, 223, 235
Uris, Leon (1924-2003): 131
Valéry, Paul (1871-1945): 139
Van Buren, Abigail (1918-2013): 161
Van Vechten, Carl (1880-1964): 30, **199**
Vargas Llosa, Mario (b. 1936): **77**, 130
Vidal, Gore (1925-2012): 45, 114, 126, 166, 180, 211, 227, **228**, 233
Vizinczey, Stephen (b. 1933): 61
Voltaire (1694-1778): 132
Vonnegut, Kurt (1922-2007): 28, 33, 40, 95, 96, 107 (2), 150, 161, 171, 173, 177, 181, 186, 194, 202, 211, 216, 223, 227, 239
Voss, Christopher: 123
Waber, Bernard (1921-2013): 171
Walker, Alice (b. 1944): 12, **40**, 104, 118, 152, 223
Wallace, Amy (1955-2013): 217
Wallace, David Foster (1962-2008): 25, 47, 155, 249
Wallace, Edgar (1875-1932): 96, **215**
Wallace, Irving (1916-1990): 33
Wallas, Graham (1858-1932): **141**
Walter, Jess (b. 1965): 199
Warburton, Eileen (b. 1924): 186
Warhol, Andy (1928-1987): 140
Warner, Marina (b. 1946): 24
Warnke, F.J.: 190
Warren, Patricia Nell (1936-2019): 87
Warren, Robert Penn (1905-1989): 161, 216, 230
Watts, Alan (1915-1973): 239
Waugh, Evelyn (1903-1966): 21, 42, 151, 206, **239**
Wayne, John (1907-1979): 45
WDVA Radio Ad: 109
Webb, Beatrice (1858-1943): 13, 177
Webster, John (c. 1580-c. 1632): 40
Weidman, Jerome (1913-1998): 177
Weiner, Jennifer (b. 1970): 29, 95, 179
Weingarten, Gene (b. 1951): 77, 223
Weldon, Fay (b. 1931): **30**, 120, 190
Wells, H.G. (1866-1946): 140, **207**, 233
Welty, Eudora (1909-2001): 57, 130, **199**, 223
Wenders, Wim (b. 1945): 201
Wendig, Chuck (b. 1976): 202
West, Mae (1893-1980): 134
West, Morris (1916-1999): **229**
West, Rebecca (1892-1983): 10, 19, 23, 33, 201, 234
Westlake, Donald E. (1933-2008): 149
Wexler, Jerry (1917-2008): 20
Wharton, Edith (1862-1937): 40, 50, 114, 127, **193**, 239
White, E.B. (1899-1985): 14, 20, 33, 69, 72, 155, 161, 200, 216, 224
White, Edmund (b. 1940): 19, 23, **68**
White, Theodore H. (1915-1986): 190
White, William Allen (1868-1944): **170**
Whitehead, Alfred North (1861-1947): 19
Whitman, Walt (1819-1892): 11, 102, **146**
Wideman, John Edgar (b. 1941): **106**
Wiesel, Elie (1928-2016): 28
Wilde, Oscar (1854-1900): 19, 23, 29, 78, 90, 99, 180, 207
Wilder, Billy (1906-2002): 155
Wilder, Thornton (1897-1975): 54, **81**, 99, 100, 107, 136, 136 (2), 224
Williams, T. Harry (1909-1979): 110
Williams, Tennessee (1911-1983): 50, 109, 208
Williams, William Carlos (1883-1963): 110
Willis, Connie (b. 1945): 174
Wilson, A.N. (b. 1950): 166
Wilson, Angus (1913-1991): 78, 196, 239
Wilson, August (1945-2005): 40, 125, 136, 156
Wilson, Edmund (1895-1972): 54, 80, 107, 122, 166, **183**
Winchell, Walter (1897-1972): 50
Winkler, Paul: 72
Winterson, Jeanette (b. 1959): 50, 65, **160**
Wodehouse, P.G. (1881-1975): 40 (2), 56, 81, 90, 109, 138, 140, **167**, 171, 179, 194, 199, 202, 212, 250
Wolcott, James (b. 1952): 250
Wolf, Christa (1929-2011): **233**
Wolfe, Gene (1931-2019): 127, 156
Wolfe, Thomas (1900-1938): 56, 196
Wolfe, Tom (1930-2018): 55, 133, **144**, 150, 162
Wood, James (b. 1965): **24**, 26
Woolf, Leonard (1880-1969): 104
Woolf, Virginia (1882-1941): 50, 61, 67, 162, 171, 234
Woollcott, Alexander (1887-1943): 61, 84, 243
Wordsworth, William (1770-1850): 107, 140
Wouk, Herman (1915-2019): **112**, 243
Wright, Steven (b. 1955): 98
Yates, Richard (1926-1992): 181, 190
Yeats, W.B. (1865-1939): 19, 66, 124
Yolen, Jane (b. 1939): 100
Yorke, Thom (b. 1968): 47
Yourcenar, Marguerite (1903-1987): 198
Zappa, Frank (1940-1993): 97, 102, **251**
Zehme, Bill: 43
Zimmerman, Robert (b. 1941): 72
Zinsser, William (1922-2015): 67, 125, 150, 171, 190, **197**
Zola, Emile (1840-1902): 224
Zusak, Markus (b. 1975): **90**

About the Author

Bill Peschel is a former journalist who shares a Pulitzer Prize with the staff of *The Patriot-News* in Harrisburg, Pa. He also is a mystery fan who runs the Wimsey Annotations. The author of *Writers Gone Wild* (Penguin), he publishes through Peschel Press the 223B Casebook Series of Sherlockian parodies and pastiches; a collection of Sherlock Holmes stories featuring Mark Twain; reprints of Victorian true crime books; and annotated editions of mysteries by Dorothy L. Sayers and Agatha Christie. Peschel lives with his family in Hershey, where the air really does smell like chocolate.

About Peschel Press

Peschel Press was founded in 2010 by Bill and Teresa Peschel in Hershey, Pa. As longtime readers, we're dedicated to publishing "the history behind the mystery." Whether it's fiction or nonfiction, we'll tell the whole story and provide a deeper, richer reading experience. We appear at bookstores in the Hershey area, and at shows in the mid-Atlantic region.

To keep up with our appearance schedule and new books, **visit www.peschelpress.com and sign up for our monthly newsletter**.

Other Peschel Press Books

The Bride from Dairapaska
Science fiction romance series on a terraformed Mars

A Dictionary of Flowers and Gems
Discover the language of flowers and powers of gems!

Sew Cloth Grocery Bags
Easy to make with our instructions; no pattern required

The Complete, Annotated Mysterious Affair at Styles
Poirot's debut

The Casebook of Twain & Holmes
Mark Twain in Sherlock Holmes' world

Career Indie Author

Tell Your Stories and Build a Business That Will Last a Lifetime

As a storyteller, you know a lot about developing your plot, creating characters, and editing your work. But do you know how to protect your copyright, record your income and expenses, the risks and rewards between "going wide" and sticking with Kindle Unlimited, and how to market your work? Have you thought about what tasks you should outsource and what you can do in-house?

Running your own business successfully means understanding the business mindset, where cash flow is the life blood and decisions you make at the start of your career will affect everything that follows.

Career Indie Author charts the landscape of indie publishing in the 21st century, where you set the rules and choose your path to publishing.

Career Indie Author will show you:

• With our one-page business plan, develop what you want to write, what help you need, how much money you'll spend, and your timetable for success.

• The factors that go into a successful book.

• Why pen names are vital to your marketing and branding.

• How to track income, expenses, and book sales.

• What you must have (a web site, an Amazon Author Page) and what is optional (social media) and what to avoid (Hollywood services).

• The basics of marketing your books, using advertising, price discounting, mailing lists, and newsletters, including sample campaigns by indie and traditional authors.

• The basics of launching a newsletter / readers' group and mailing list services.

• The basics of sharing your message on social media.

• Where to learn more about improving your writing and marketing your books.

• The risks of working too hard, neglecting your health, and giving in to distractions.

Developed from the lessons learned over the decade Bill and Teresa Peschel have operated Peschel Press, *Career Indie Author* can help you decide these important questions before you spend your first dollar.

Truth Is Stranger Than Fiction

If you've imagined famous writers to be desk-bound drudges, think again. *Writers Gone Wild* rips back the (book) covers and reveals the seamy underside of the writing life.

Insightful, intriguing, and irresistibly addictive, *Writers Gone Wild* contains 200 stories drawn from the lives of classic writers, such as:

- The night Dashiell Hammett hired a Chinese prostitute to break up S. J. Perelman's marriage (and ran off with his wife).
- Why Sylvia Plath bit Ted Hughes on the cheek.
- Why Ernest Hemingway fought a book critic, a modernist poet, and his war correspondent/wife Martha Gellhorn (but not at the same time).
- The near-fatal trip Katherine Anne Porter took while high on marijuana in Mexico.
- Why women's breasts sent Percy Bysshe Shelley screaming from the room.
- How William Faulkner's career was revived thanks to a publisher's bribe to a popular radio broadcaster.
- The day Virginia Woolf snuck onto a Royal Navy ship disguised as an Abyssinian prince.

Pull up a chair, turn on a good reading light, pour yourself your favorite libation, and discover what your favorite writers were up to while away from their desks.

Writers Gone Wild is published by Penguin, and we sell signed copies at our public appearances.

Writers Gone Wild
The Feuds, Frolics, and Follies of Literature's Great Adventurers, Drunkards, Lovers, Iconoclasts, and Misanthropes
BILL PESCHEL

Excerpt: Poe's Poison Pen (1835)

Although known for his stories and poems of the macabre, Edgar Allan Poe earned his living writing articles and notes for magazines such as the "Southern Literary Messenger." Many of them are ephemeral pieces of gossip, but when he reviewed books, his pen could sting.

One such opportunity came when Laughton Osborn's two-volume "Confessions of a Poet," crossed his desk. In an unsigned review, Poe pointed out that the most remarkable feature of this novel about the life and loves of Julian Farquharson, "is the bad paper on which it is printed, and the typographical ingenuity with which matter barely enough for one volume has been spread over the pages of two."

At the end, Poe noted that the fictional Farquharson intended to commit suicide after finishing his "Confessions," and advised him to check the priming of his pistol or else "there would be no answering for the consequences. We might even have a second series of the Confessions."

A decade after Poe roasted his novel, Osborn met Poe in New York City, where he was working for another literary magazine. Osborn sent a note asking about the review. Didn't Poe work for them at the time? Did he write it?

Not at all, Poe wrote back. He denied even being an editor for the journal, despite being identified as such on the masthead. "Your 'Confessions of a Poet' I read many years ago," Poe wrote, "with a very profound sentiment of admiration for its author . . . I have written warmly in its defence--."

It was an outright lie, but as an admirer of Poe's writings, Osborn forgave him.

www.ingramcontent.com/pod-product-compliance
Lightning Source LLC
Chambersburg PA
CBHW080847190726
48292CB00010B/2908

9781950347278